Dying, Death, and Bereavement

Books of Related Interest

The Cancer Book
Geoffrey M. Cooper

Carpe Diem: Enjoying Every Day with a Terminal Illness
Ed Madden

Human Aging and Chronic Disease
Cary S. Kart/Eileen K. Metress/Seamus P. Metress

Life and Death: Grappling with the Moral Dilemmas of Our Time
Louis P. Pojman

Life and Death: A Reader in Moral Problems
Louis P. Pojman

Perspectives on Death and Dying
Eileen K. Metress/Gere Fulton

Dying, Death, and Bereavement
Theoretical Perspectives
and Other Ways of Knowing

Edited by

Inge B. Corless, R.N., Ph.D., F.A.A.N.
MGH Institute of Health Professions
Massachusetts General Hospital
Boston

Barbara B. Germino, Ph.D., R.N., F.A.A.N.
The University of North Carolina, Chapel Hill

Mary Pittman, Dr.P.H.
President, Hospital Research and Education Trust
American Hospital Association
Chicago

JONES AND BARTLETT PUBLISHERS
BOSTON   LONDON

Editorial, Sales, and Customer Service Offices

Jones and Bartlett Publishers
One Exeter Plaza
Boston, MA 02116
1–800–832–0034
1–617–859–3900

Jones and Bartlett Publishers International
P.O. Box 1498
London W6 7RS
England

Library of Congress Cataloging-in-Publication-Data
Dying, death, and bereavement : theoretical perspectives and other ways of
  knowing / edited by Inge B. Corless, Barbara B. Germino, Mary Pittman.
      p.   cm.
    Includes bibliographical references and index.
    ISBN 0-86720-631-4
    1. Death.   2. Bereavement.   I. Corless, Inge B.   II. Germino,
  Barbara B.   III. Pittman, Mary.
  BD444.D3748   1994
  155.9'37--dc20   94-8604
                                                                        CIP

Editor: Joseph E. Burns
Project Coordinator: Joan M. Flaherty
Production service: TKM Productions
Designer: Suzanne Pescatore, TKM Productions
Cover designer: Hannus Design Associates

Printed in the United States of America
98 97 96 95 94   10 9 8 7 6 5 4 3 2 1

To all our teachers,
including those
we have cared for,
loved, and lost

Contents

Part Two

Concepts Central to the Study and Practice of Thanatology   107

Foreword

Dame Cicely Saunders

Trained as a nurse during the war and being invalided out, Dame Cicely Saunders obtained a war degree at Oxford and became a medical social worker. Concern for the pain control of dying patients and the distress of their families moved her to study medicine, and in 1958, she began work among the patients of St. Joseph's Hospice. The experience there was one of the roots of St. Christopher's Hospice, which she founded, together with a small group, and which opened in 1967. From the start, it was planned as a teaching center and a focus of research in the control of pain and other distress in terminal illness. This work has been recognized world wide and was the catalyst for the hospice movement.

Dame Cicely has received a number of honorary degrees, including Honorary Doctorate of Science from Yale in 1969, Lambeth Doctorate of Medicine from the Archbishop of Canterbury in 1977, Doctorate from the Open University in 1978, and Honorary Doctorate of Law, Columbia University, New York, in 1979. She has been a member of the Attendance Allowance Board since it started, and from 1973 to 1978 was a member of the Medical Research Council. Dame Cicely was awarded the Templeton Prize for Progress in Religion in 1981. Other honorary degrees have followed, including honorary doctorates in law and civil law from Oxford and Cambridge Universities in 1986.

She is an Honorary Fellow of the Royal College of Physicians, the Royal College of Surgeons, and the Royal College of Nurses. She was awarded the British Medical Association's Gold Medal for Distinguished Merit in July 1987 and was made a Freeman of the London Borough of Bromley in October 1987. In 1988, she was made an Honorary Fellow of the Royal College of Psychiatrists. In 1989, Dame Cicely was awarded the Order of Merit by Her Majesty the Queen.

Over 40 years ago, I had the opportunity and privilege of accompanying an isolated man who talked through his thoughts and feelings with me during the last two months of his life. A Jew from Warsaw, he had lost his family and believed that he had made no impact on the world during his short life of 40 years. The first ideas of hospice developed during our conversations and for me they are summed up in two of his phrases. The first referred to the fact that he would leave me a small legacy—a founding gift for a then nameless place. He said, "I'll be a window in your home." The second was a response to my offer to read him something from the Old Testament, as he was quietly returning to the faith of his fathers. His response was, "No, thank you. I only want what is in your mind and in your heart." At the time, it was a specific challenge to which I tried to respond but later I came to see it as a demand on us all for everything we could bring of thought, experience, and skill to the care of people facing death, to be offered together with personal concern. Setting these two demands together with the idea of a window challenged the beginnings of hospice to be open to many adventures and developments, focused always on close attention to individual people, their needs, and their potentials.

The story since February 1948 when David Tasma died "at peace," as he told me, has been one of surprising growth. This book brings together much of the experience of many workers during these years, all facing the demands on mind and heart in a spirit of openness. The original vision seems to have the capacity to keep us recognizably addressing the same concerns in our diverse cultures and settings. It appears that those of us who work in the whole field of death, dying, and bereavement have all tried to listen to those people who are facing their individual journey through this part of life. It is from them that we all continue to learn and find inspiration, whether we are concerned with researching and developing ever-improving symptom control, more understanding of psychosocial tensions and possibilities, or better ways of sharing in what surely has to be the work and support of an interdisciplinary team.

Seven years as an R.N. volunteer in one of the early Protestant Homes (St. Luke's Hospital, originally Home for the Dying Poor, opened in 1893) followed by another seven years as a physician in St. Joseph's Hospice (opened 1905) gave me opportunities to meet and listen to innumerable patients, to observe the regular giving of oral opiates at St. Luke's, and to introduce this method of giving analgesics to St. Joseph's Hospice. It enabled me to monitor our improving clinical practice and development with a retrieval system and to lay the medical foundations of St. Christopher's, opened in 1967 as the first home care and teaching hospice. A Christian as well as a medical foundation, its aim was "to express the love of God to all who come, in every possible way, in skilled nursing and medical care, in the use of every scientific means of relieving suffering and distress, in understanding personal sympathy, with respect for the dignity of each person as a human being, precious to God and man" (Aim & Basis, 1965). Emphasis was laid on the fact that all those working in the hospice would give their own contribution in their own way, in a spirit of freedom, while patients would seek *their* own way to peace without any pressure. It was emphasized, too, that it would be group work, open to further development.

It was not long before such a religious foundation was challenged by those wishing to enter this field without any such commitment. Certain of our own calling but concerned to open doors as well as windows, we refused to be dogmatic, concerned only that anyone in this field must expect his or her own philosophy to be challenged and to be faced with the difficult questions that may arise from people who are calling on their own resources in crisis. That the spiritual element of the "total pain" complex included far more than any form of personal religion became obvious as its physical, emotional, and social elements were also addressed with developing experience.

From the beginning, hospice learning and attitudes have formed bridges. First, the bridges between people as staff and volunteers have enabled these people to listen to their patients and families. The way forward must surely come in the same fashion. Patients are the true founders of the hospice movement and the field of related studies and development. Our moves into the future will be safeguarded if we go on listening, aware that the words of one individual or family may open up a whole new scene.

It has also been important to build a bridge to the researchers and in due course to enter this field ourselves. Early meetings with such pioneers as Beecher, Eddy, and Houde were followed by productive contact with Melzack and Wall. In an editiorial in the influential journal, *Pain*, Wall (1986) wrote, "The immediate origins of pain and suffering need immediate attention while the long-term search for basic care proceeds. The old methods of care and caring have to be rediscovered and the best of modern medicine has to be turned to the task of new study and therapy specifically directed at pain." The challenge to continue to look at all aspects of suffering still faces us, and we have to back up our demonstrations of effective relief with research studies that are widely published. Our teaching must be objectively based and we should be offering our patients continually improving understanding and therapy.

Workers in the field addressed in this comprehensive book also have a responsibility to build bridges into the community, both professional and general. That so many dying people all over the world are ineptly treated faces us with an almost overwhelming challenge, as does the isolation enforced on them and their bereaved families by the disregard of the public. Hospice is about living until the end, still as part of the community.

As we learned to demonstrate something of what could be done by what has come to be termed *palliative medicine*, we could begin to build effective bridges with the acute services. We have had to discover when and how to draw in other specialties and learn from them as well as educate from our standpoint. In no way are we to take the high moral ground, but we need to meet effectively as we come from our different professional backgrounds and across the disciplines.

We will often have appropriate treatment to offer between the two extremes of all life-prolonging intervention possible and the threat of legalized active shortening of life with all its social dangers. We have to earn the attention and respect that will draw us in for the right patients at the right time. The hospital support or palliative care team can have a central role in this area and is charting an important way forward.

Our whole field has not only been about need but, above all, about achievement. We are concerned that a person should live this part of life, whether in dying or in bereavement, to their maximum potential, not only in physical ease or activity but also in family relationships and in addressing their most important inner values. A time of crisis can be a time of growth, often at surprising speed, of resolving long-standing problems and of reconciliation, both with oneself and with those around. Hospice workers find that the freedom from distress they aim to give by their treatment and hospitality opens up new space for personal development. Bridges are built among the conflicted families who are more and more often referred to us in recognition of what we try to offer.

Good communication can facilitate unexpected sharing and responses and develop the growth through loss we see so often. Here, I believe we reach the central and most positive area of our concerns. We have all been inspired by those we have seen bringing unexpected gains out of loss, whether it be of health, life, or bereavement. It may come out of distress that is very painful to share as we try to maintain the bridge between us. The rewards come from the resolutions that happen surprisingly frequently—but not always. At times, we can only stay beside unresolved problems or, at best, trust that what we have offered is the best we can, hoping it is good enough. A lifetime's difficulties may remain unchanged and it would be unrealistic to expect anything else.

It is the individual's inner values that matter when there is only a limited time left or when the most important person has died. The spiritual dimension encompasses searches for meaning in many varied ways. We have never been concerned that the people we serve should see things our way; rather, they should discover or reinforce their own way, asking for help if they wish, in freedom from any pressure or obligation. We have found that not only is our own search for meaning continually stimulated by the often desperate situations we face but also that this constant challenge helps develop a climate of shared discovery and hope.

Reference

Wall, P. D. (1986). Editorial: "25 Volumes of Pain." *Pain*, 25, 1–4.

Photo credit: page ix, Grace Goldin

Introduction

The fields of death, dying, and bereavement were given credence through the work of pioneers who examined the situation then current and asked how it might be other. The mega-death machine created and perpetrated by Adolf Hitler and the Nazis, as well as that developed in Los Alamos (New Mexico) by the Americans, confronted the world with death on a scale unlike that witnessed in recent memory.

The writings of scholarly survivors depicted the horrors created by human beings. Survivor guilt and the curiosity of astute observers probed those horrific experiences to uncover how individuals withstood the onslaught on physical, psychological, social, and spiritual well-being, including the anguish of watching the deaths of the beloved and countless others.

After a period of silence in which dying and death were hidden by a world rebuilding and eager to forget the excesses of the past, the press of increasing numbers of elderly individuals produced a new confrontation with dying. Haunted by the specter of the Holocaust and the preceding elimination of undesirables (i.e., the elderly and mentally retarded, by a German leadership dedicated to sanitizing its population), health care professionals were in a quandary as to how to be of help to their suffering elderly clients without replicating or seeming to replicate the practices of Nazi Germany. While some terminally ill individuals, in the tradition of Seneca, sought to choose the time and method of their deaths, others who were health care providers sought to find another approach.

Perhaps as a counterbalance to humans' cataclysmic inhumanity to ourselves, researchers and clinicians worked to remove that sting of death created by humankind. It was not that death lost its sting; rather, scholars through dint of scientific inquiry and their clinician colleagues diminished that pain exacerbated by humans.

The approach taken in *Dying, Death, and Bereavement: Theoretical Perspectives and Other Ways of Knowing* reflects the multidimensionality of this area of knowledge. As scholars from various disciplines have attempted to understand, study, teach, and apply their knowledge, they have learned the importance of the different ways of knowing and understanding, some of which are exemplified by the chapters in this book. The chapters included in theoretical perspectives provide an "outside-in" map of the landscape of dying, death, and bereavement. The chapters that capture personal experiences offer an "inside-out" picture of this terrain. Both are valuable in achieving depth and breadth of understanding.

Understanding also entails knowledge of how the practices pertaining to dying, death, and bereavement are emblematic of the culture's values. This book is one attempt at contributing to such knowledge. Its purpose is to serve as a text for courses on death and dying as well as a resource for others interested in accessing a theoretical approach to the field. Whether used as a core text or anthology of readings, *Dying, Death, and Bereavement* provides access to primary sources rather than the interpretation of the field by any one scholar. Students in nursing, medicine, teacher education, sociology, philosophy, psychology, public health, religion, mortuary science, as well as those seeking a liberal arts education, will find this book of value. Health care professionals in hospitals, hospice programs, nursing homes, and extended care facilities as well as those engaged public health will find this text useful as they develop an increasing sophistication and depth of understanding of the ramifications of dying, death, and bereavement.

Dying, Death, and Bereavement incorporates the current thinking of some of the most renowned scholars in the field. They are individuals from various disciplines long known and much loved for the ways in which they have enlightened and enriched us. Other contributors include some of the rising stars of our intellectual firmament. Our contributors provide other works that add to our knowledge.

Robert Kastenbaum and Beatrice Kastenbaum have edited a very readable *Encyclopedia of Death* (1989, Oryx Press), which begins with "Acquired Immune Deficiency Syndrome (AIDS)" and ends with "zombie" and discusses 129 other topics including Ars Moriendi, cryonic suspension, Jonestown, Kaddish, and the survival beliefs and practices of various creeds. Kastenbaum's fourth revision of his classic in the field, *Death, Society and Human Experience*, also highly readable, contains new chapters on AIDS, ethics, and decision making, and a new section on murder and terrorism. Readers may also want to peruse Kastenbaum's *The Psychology of Death* (Springer), a currently revised version of an earlier work, which contains chapters with such intriguing titles as "How Do We Construct Death?" "Death Anxiety in the Midst of Life," "A Will to Live and an Instinct to Die?" and "Getting on with Life," to name a few.

Another text the reader may want to consider is *Suicide Across the Life Span—Premature Exits* (Hemisphere) by Stillion, McDowell, and May. The authors begin their book with a very interesting history of suicide in Western culture. Their examination of the psychoanalytic, psychosocial, behavioral, humanistic, cognitive, sociological, and biological perspectives on the nature and causes of suicide reminds us that the framework applied both enlarges and limits what is perceived.

The subtitle to *Suicide Across the Life Span* is *Premature Exits*—a thought-provoking phrase. The question of premature exits, the rights of the individual, and the obligations of society, particularly through its health care system, bring us full circle to some of the themes considered in *Dying, Death, and Bereavement.* There are a number of other excellent new (and older) books by the contributors to this and the reference volume (Bertman, Bluebond-Langner, Feifel, Fulton, Martinson, Rando, Silverman, Strauss, and Vachon) for the individual who wishes to learn more about this field. The contributors to this volume have been encouraged to cite their previous works so as to provide a guide to this intellectual landscape.

This book captures the thoughts and words of some of the trailblazers of the field. We are privileged to have had the opportunity to work with these individuals. They have the benefit of foresight, hindsight, and insight. Their efforts provide a compass to the fields of dying, death, and bereavement. With this guide, the reader, whether novice or expert in the field, will be well served.

Acknowledgments

We acknowledge all of those who have contributed to this book directly and indirectly. We are grateful for the ongoing support of our families— Inge's daughters Theresa and Patricia; Barbara's husband Vic, daughter Laurie, son Mark, and granddaughter Talia; Mary's husband David and sons Mark and Scott. Our editor, Joe Burns, graciously gave us the space to develop this project and the ongoing support to complete it. Joan Flaherty, with her other ways of knowing, and Lynda Griffiths of TKM Productions took our collective product and transformed it into a book. We're grateful to them. The cover design by Dick Hannus incorporates a butterfly created by a hospice patient, Adam Jamilkowski, and his daughter C. J., who kindly gave us permission to share it more widely. Our thanks to them.

Contributors

Sally Bailey, MPF
Director of Arts
Connecticut Hospice
Branford, Connecticut

Jeanne Quint Benoliel, PhD
Professor Emeritus
University of Washington
Seattle, Washington

Sandra Bertman, PhD
Professor of Humanities in
  Medicine
University of Massachusetts
  Medical School
Worcester, Massachusetts

Myra Bluebond-Langner, PhD
Professor of Anthropology
Rutgers University
Camden, New Jersey

Stephen Connor, PhD
Executive Director
Hospice of Central Kentucky
Elizabethtown, Kentucky

Laurel Archer Copp, PhD
Professor
University of North Carolina
Chapel Hill, North Carolina

Alice S. Demi, PhD
Professor of
  Psychiatric Mental Health
School of Nursing
Georgia State University,
Atlanta, Georgia

Herman Feifel, PhD
Author, Consultant
Clinical Professor Emeritus
Psychiatry and the Behavioral
  Sciences
University of Southern California
Los Angeles, California

Patricia Z. Fischer, PhD
School of Public Health
University of North Carolina
Chapel Hill, North Carolina

Robert Fulton, PhD
Professor of Psychology
Center for Death Education
University of Minnesota,
Minneapolis, Minnesota

JoAnn E. Glittenberg, PhD
Professor and Chair
School of Nursing
University of Arizona
Tucson, Arizona

Ruth E. Harvey
Author, Volunteer
St. Peter's Hospice
Schenectady, New York

David Head, MA
Chaplain
Trinity Hospice
London, England

Robert Kastenbaum, PhD
Professor of Communications
Arizona State University
Tempe, Arizona

Ida Martinson, RN, PhD
Professor
Health Care Nursing
University of California
San Francisco, California

Margaret Shandor Miles, PhD
Professor and Chair
School of Nursing
University of North Carolina
Chapel Hill, North Carolina

Barbara Mims, MSW
Coordinator
Homemakers Program for Family
   and Child Services
Beaverton, Oregon

Virginia Neelon, RN, PhD
Associate Professor of Nursing
University of North Carolina
Chapel Hill, North Carolina

Therese A. Rando, PhD
Clinical Psychologist
Therese A. Rando Associates, Ltd.
Warwick, Rhode Island

Dame Cicely Saunders, MD, OBE
Founder of St. Christopher's
   Hospice
Sydenham, England

Diane Scott-Dorsett, PhD
Associate Professor
School of Nursing
University of California
San Francisco, California

Phyllis Silverman, PhD
Professor
Institute of Health Professions
Massachusetts General Hospital
Boston, Massachusetts

Judith Stillion, PhD
Professor of Psychology
Western Carolina University
Cullowhee, North Carolina

Anselm Strauss, PhD
Professor Emeritus of Psychology
School of Nursing
University of California
San Francisco, California

Mary L. S. Vachon, PhD
Associate Professor
Departments of Psychiatry and
   Behavioural Science
University of Toronto
North York, Ontario, Canada

Florence Wald, MN, MS, FAAN
Former Dean
   Yale School of Nursing
Author, Resources Consultant
Connecticut Hospice
Branford, Connecticut

Part One

Death and Dying as a Field of Inquiry

One

Death and Dying as a Field of Inquiry

Jeanne Quint Benoliel

Jeanne Quint Benoliel's interest in death and dying resulted from a complex interplay of personal and professional life circumstances. Like others of her generation, Benoliel's views on life were influenced greatly by some critical cohort experiences that included her teenage years during the Great Depression and her early adulthood as an Army nurse in the South Pacific in World War II.

Benoliel's research interests derived directly from clinical observations as a nurse and from questions about how people adapted to living with life-threatening diseases and disfiguring surgeries. Her entry into research followed a somewhat atypical career pattern. Being one of the pioneers in death research was a wonderful experience and a great opportunity to meet and work with a great many talented people. Benoliel was fortunate to have had the opportunity to work with Anselm Strauss from whom a great deal was learned. Benoliel's best piece of research writing was the article, "Institutionalized Practices of Information Control," based on mastectomy study findings. Her clinical interests continue to center on the establishment of community-based services for long-term care so that people who are dying can live and die at home, if they choose.

Death and dying have long held a fascination for human beings. Across historical time, this fascination has been manifest in song, poetry, drama, literature, sculpture, and dance. Life and death are the foundational themes of origin stories across cultures; the meanings attributed to them provide the basic belief systems of religious and societal traditions. Over the centuries, human groups have used a variety of social rituals and ceremonies to give meaning to their individual and collective experiences with loss, illness, dying, and death.

Systematic inquiry into the nature of death and dying as human experiences is a phenomenon of the twentieth century. Undoubtedly, this shift in orientation can be tied to the importance attached to science and scientific thinking as ways of viewing the world. Further, the impact of science and applied technology on practically every facet of human existence led to new situations in which death and dying became "social problems." The development of the field can be understood as a response to the changed nature of living and dying in the current century, resulting from the impact of rapid social and technological changes (Benoliel, 1978).

Historical Origins

The appearance of systematic research on death and dying appeared in the aftermath of the World War II. Prior to 1940, studies of death had been mainly anthropological investigations of death customs in primitive societies and psychoanalytic perspectives on death as proposed by Freud (Benoliel, 1983a). The need for a social psychology of bereavement was identified by Eliot (1933), and Worcester (1935) wrote about some philosophic and pragmatic issues affecting care of the dying.

Opening the Field, 1940–1960

In the aftermath of war, interest in death and dying as subjects for scientific investigation was stimulated by a number of factors: the rapid expansion of organized sciences and societally funded research; the appearance of the mental health movement with a central focus on suicide prevention; a depersonalization of many aspects of human existence associated with new technologies; and a powerful death anxiety that has been attributed to the use of atomic weapons at Hiroshima and Nagasaki (Benoliel, 1978).

The War itself provided experiences that stimulated a number of pioneer inquiries, including Anthony's (1940) classic investigation concerning children's awareness of death and Lindemann's (1944) empirical study of acute grief processes in the survivors of persons killed in a catastrophic nightclub fire. After 1950, the major contributions were of two kinds: essays focusing on critical issues concerning death and dying, and empirical studies of identified areas of interest. Among the former were Gorer's (1956) argument that death had replaced sex as the major topic of avoidance in modern society and Volkart and Michael's (1957) proposal that bereavement practices were related directly to variations in cultural values and kinship structures. Among the latter were Habenstein and Lamers's (1960) cross-cultural study of burial and funeral customs across the world and Marris's (1958) investigation of the bereavement reactions of widows in London. In psychology, Feifel began his pioneer studies on attitudes toward death and edited a book (1959) that demonstrated the value of multidisciplinary inquiry into the meaning of death and gave legitimacy to empirical research in the field.

Informal Networks, 1960–1970

The decade from 1960 to 1970 might be described best as the period of pioneer endeavors in which essentially isolated individuals contributed to knowledge about the personal, interpersonal, and social meanings of death and dying. Among the contributors to this growth in knowledge were Fulton (1965), Glaser and Strauss (1965, 1968), Hinton (1967), Sudnow (1967), Weisman and Hackett (1961), Blauner (1966), and Lifton (1968). In the realm of philosophical inquiry, Choron (1963) traced the development of Western ideas about death and Koestenbaum (1964) argued for the different meanings of death of the self and death of another. Other pioneers wrote about their efforts to improve services to dying people—for example, through hospice services (Saunders, 1969) or counseling services in hospitals (Kubler-Ross, 1969).

During this period, individuals engaged in inquiry on death and dying began to meet informally, and efforts were started to create communication networks among them. In 1966, Richard Kalish and Robert Kastenbaum initiated a newsletter that in 1970 became *Omega: The Journal on Death and Dying,* currently a leading journal in the field. In New York, the Foundation of Thanatology was created by Austin Kutscher as a center for bringing together people from many disciplines with a shared interest in death issues and concerns.

Through informal networks, opportunities came about for multidisciplinary investigations involving academicians and practitioners in shared research endeavors. My entry into the field began with research (1961–1963) on women's adaptations during the year following a mastectomy. The findings showed how the cultural meanings of cancer (associations with deterioration of the body, painful death, and abandonment by others) affected these women's lives in two ways. Underlying fears about cancer recurrence contributed to a sense of having an uncertain future (Quint, 1963, 1964). Physicians and nurses provided the women with little information about the extent of the disease and possible outcomes of treatment—findings illustrating how institutionalized practices of information control blocked access to important information and contributed to a form of social isolation (Quint, 1965). These findings showed how inquiry could lead to different understandings of the meaning of death: (1) as a personal experience associated with having a life-threatening disease and (2) as a subject matter inhibiting social transactions between providers and recipients of caregiving services.

This research experience brought me into contact with Anselm Strauss, which led to my joining a team to study the influence of structural and historical conditions on the interactional experiences of dying patients and their providers. These findings emphasized the influence of cultural values and social context characteristics on (1) what dying patients were or were not told about their situation (Glaser & Strauss, 1965), (2) different social patterns of dying associated with different diseases (Glaser & Strauss, 1968), and (3) the education of student nurses for work involving death and dying patients (Quint, 1967).

My entry into inquiry about death came about through a combination of personal and professional experiences, the details of which have been given elsewhere (Benoliel, 1989; Schorr & Zimmerman, 1988). The experiences on the dying patient study provided a socialization into the world of social science and fostered an appreciation for the powerful influence of sociocultural context on human choices and behaviors. From that experience came publications about the influence of work environments on nurses' behaviors with dying patients (Quint, 1966), student nurses' experiences with death and dying (Quint & Strauss, 1964), and some thoughts about preparing nurses to care for the fatally ill (Quint, 1968).

My primary research interest was in understanding how identities are defined, shaped, and altered when individuals undergo major loss experiences or must adapt to a status that is negatively valued in the culture. Such statuses include being a dying patient or having a stigmatizing illness. My understanding of this phenomenon was enhanced by investigating the impact of chronic illness—specifically, diabetes mellitus—on the identity development of young people entering adolescence (Benoliel, 1983b). These findings pointed to the importance of the family as a key influence on attitudes and behaviors developed by these young people in relation to the status of being diabetic.

Formalization of Networks, 1970–1980

After 1970, efforts were initiated to formalize the networks of "death people." A gathering of interested persons in Columbia, Maryland, in 1974 led to the formation of the International Work Group on Death, Dying, and Bereavement. Soon thereafter came the Forum on Death Education and Counseling (later the Association), and in 1978, the National Hospice Organization was formed. These organizations were manifest expressions of a growing public and professional interest in the practice implications of knowledge about death through education, counseling, and hospice/palliative care services.

My interest continued to center on understanding how individuals and families lived with life-threatening diseases. A useful framework for inquiry was Parkes's (1971) concept of psychosocial transition. From clinical observations, McCorkle and Benoliel began to develop instruments to measure symptom distress (McCorkle & Young, 1978) and enforced social dependency (Benoliel, McCorkle, & Young, 1978) for longitudinal studies of cancer patients and their families. The measures were projected for use in understanding how cancer patients and their families adapted to the changes imposed by advanced disease and altered their goals in the face of forthcoming death.

Early in the decade, I initiated a descriptive study of recorded patterns of dying in teaching hospitals, using the concept of dying trajectory as a framework. These findings showed the influence of biomedical technology on death characteristics in hospitals between 1961 and 1970, specifically increases in death and dying on critical care wards (Benoliel, 1977a, 1977b). Analysis of data from the dying patient studies resulted in guidelines for assessment of loss and grief (Benoliel, 1971), description of grief experiences of physicians and nurses in response to death-related events (Benoliel, 1974a), some effects of life-threatening illness and sudden death on family dynamics (Benoliel, 1974b), and methodological issues to be considered in investigations of death-related social situations (Benoliel, 1975).

The decade included growing numbers of conferences and workshops focused on the use of death knowledge in practice; research findings into thoughts about practice, such as the psychosocial complexities of nursing care for the terminal patient (Benoliel, 1972); challenges faced by providers in choices between care goals and cure goals (Benoliel, 1976); the variety of circumstances under which nurses are in contact with dying patients (Benoliel, 1977c); the impact of death and dying on families (Benoliel, 1979); and issues for nurses in providing holistic care to families living with terminal illness (Benoliel & McCorkle, 1978). Some ideas on the intricacies of empirical studies on death and dying were translated into consultation with new investigators. Among these were Lesley Degner, who initiated a six-year study of life-prolonging health care practices in Canada. These findings on the intricate nature of life-death decision making in health care and the social negotiations involved were published by Degner and Beaton in 1987.

Expansion of Ideas, 1980–1990

In the 1980s, the formalization efforts of the previous decade expanded, and multidisciplinary interests extended to include legal and ethical concerns as well as death education activities for the public and for professionals (Benoliel, 1982; Pine, 1986). Standards for death education and counseling and certification procedures were developed by the Association for Death Education and Counseling as efforts to upgrade the services offered to the general public (Pridonoff, 1990). The journals, *Omega* and *Death Studies*, flourished. Periodically, entire issues were devoted to topics of great public and professional concern, such as cultural and religious perspectives on death (*Death Studies*, 12 (2), 1988), AIDS (*Death Studies*, 12 (5–6), 1988), and long-term effects of death education and counseling (*Death Studies*, 13 (2), 1989).

In nursing, inquiry into the nature of a patient's experience of terminal illness became important. Research included efforts to understand the effects of uncertainty on the meanings attributed to different diseases (Mishel & Braden, 1988) and the influence of time on death perspectives of terminally ill adults (Reed, 1986). McCorkle and Benoliel initiated a comparative study of the responses of patients with heart disease and patients with cancer to symptom distress, mood disturbance, and other psychosocial variables. The results showed similar patterns of response over time, with the cancer patients consistently indicating more distress, more concerns, and more social dependency than those with heart disease (Donaldson, McCorkle, Georgiadou, & Benoliel, 1986; McCorkle & Benoliel, 1983).

In an effort to evaluate the effects of nursing care activities on the well-being of cancer patients at home, McCorkle and Benoliel completed a longitudinal study of the process and the influences of three community-based home care programs and found evidence that specialized nursing services provided help in symptom control, were associated with fewer hospitalizations (McCorkle, Benoliel, & Georgiadou, 1989), and helped patients to forego enforced social dependency for longer periods of time than those not receiving such services (McCorkle & Benoliel, 1990).

During the same decade, Benoliel and McCorkle conducted a program to prepare nurses for leadership in the delivery of community-based services to advanced cancer patients and their families (Benoliel, 1982; Tornberg, McGrath, & Benoliel, 1984). The principles underlying the program came from knowledge gained through clinical practice and empirical research about the effect of dying on peoples' lives. Some of the principles were shared in publications—for example, care of terminally ill children (Benoliel, 1986a) and the cancer patient's right to have information and to decide his or her future (Benoliel 1986b).

An extension of my early inquiry in the 1960s on the socialization of student nurses to work with death and dying was performed by Degner and Gow in Canada in the 1980s. These investigators used a longitudinal quasi-experiment to evaluate the effectiveness of a planned course on palliative care compared to a four-year integrated instructional approach on the death anxiety of student nurses and their attitudes toward care of the dying (Degner & Gow, 1988). The findings provided positive support for the influence of a planned instructional program on attitudes toward working with the dying as well as a theoretical model to guide future death education in nursing.

In the 1980s, it became increasingly clear that despite the good efforts of many people, inquiry about death and dying was not very influential against the power of U.S. culture with its emphasis on saving lives at all costs (Benoliel, 1988a). In earlier research, Germaine (1979) and Martocchio (1982) showed how the social structure and culture of the hospital controlled much of what happened to patients, families, and providers in the system. In contemplating the pervasive influence of institutionalized values on the organizational institutions in which dying patients received care and in which health care students were educated, it seemed important to raise questions about some of the problems to be faced in offering personalized care in large complex settings and about the difficulties of educating new providers for the nature of the work (Benoliel, 1987–88, 1988b).

Future Death Inquiry

Ironically, the influence of science and technology on human experiences with death and dying has led to two dehumanizing outcomes: (1) machines and techniques of warfare capable of mass destruction of human beings and the environments in which they live and (2) machines and techniques of medicine capable of maintaining individual survival almost beyond the bounds of human decency. In the United States in the 1980s, one might say that death became a political issue, given the high proportion of societal resources allocated to research and development for either defense or biomedicine and the concomitant cutback in resources for social and educational programs. Perhaps it is not surprising that in the early 1990s, legal and ethical inquiry concerning the effects of technology on death and dying has increased, and violence as a way of solving human problems has become a common occurrence on urban streets.

Since the advent of science as the predominant world view affecting human societies, the meaning of death has been governed increasingly by the metaphors of conquest and control. Thus, cancer can be defeated in much the same way as enemy soldiers, and in both situations the modes of attack are weapons of destruction. Coming out of a patriarchal tradition, the predominant ethical orientation in the Western world has centered on autonomy and independence of the individual, abstract critical thinking, and a morality of rights and justice. Such a perspective permits individuals to make principled and "morally correct" decisions without personal involvement in the human needs and concerns of the persons involved (Noddings, 1989).

Feminist perspectives on death, dying, and caregiving may become increasingly important as the world becomes more crowded, the environment becomes more tainted, the gaps between the haves and the have-nots widen, and the number of vulnerable people in need of caregiving services increases. Noddings (1989) has proposed the need for a shift in ethical orientation away from the current emphasis on the individual toward an emphasis on relationships between individuals. A relational ethic does not derive from abstract ideas but is learned out of experiences of caring and being cared for. It incorporates a commitment to respond to other people with an attitude of caring.

Relational ethics are built on the assumption that the evils of the world—pain, separation, and helplessness—are experiences that cannot be conquered and destroyed. Like death, they are part and parcel of the human condition, and humans have the choice of living through these experiences with others or of withdrawing from involvement in such relationships. Inquiry in death and dying in the twenty-first century can ill afford to ignore the need for new metaphors, such as relational ethics, in searching for ways to understand the meaning of these experiences for human beings.

References

Anthony, S. (1940). *The child's discovery of death.* New York: Harcourt.

Benoliel, J. Q. (1971). Assessments of loss and grief. *Journal of Thanatology, 1,* 182–194.

Benoliel, J. Q. (1972). Nursing care for the terminal patient: A psychosocial approach. In B. Schoenberg, A. C. Carr, D. Peretz, & A. H. Kutscher (Eds.), *Psychosocial aspects of terminal care* (pp. 145–161). New York: Columbia University Press.

Benoliel, J. Q. (1974a). Anticipatory grief in physicians and nurses. In B. Schoenberg, A. C. Carr, A. H. Kutscher, D. Peretz, & I. K. Goldberg (Eds.), *Anticipatory grief* (pp. 218–228). New York: Columbia University Press.

Benoliel, J. Q. (1974b). The dying patient and the family. In S. B. Troup & W. A. Green (Eds.), *The patient, death. and the family* (pp. 111–123). New York: Charles Scribner's Sons.

Benoliel, J. Q. (1975). Research related to death and the dying patient. In P. J. Verhonick (Ed.), *Nursing research I* (pp. 189–227). Boston: Little, Brown.

Benoliel, J. Q. (1976). Overview: Care, cure and the challenge of choice. In A. Earle, N. I. Argondizzo, & A. H. Kutscher (Eds.), *The nurse as caregiver for the terminal patient and his family* (pp. 9–30). New York: Columbia University Press.

Benoliel, J. Q. (1977a). Social characteristics of death as a recorded hospital event. *Communicating nursing research* (Vol. 8) (pp. 245–267). Boulder, CO: Western Interstate Commission for Higher Education.

Benoliel, J. Q. (1977b). A comparison of technological influences on dying characteristics in one teaching hospital during 1966 and 1971. *Communicating nursing research* (Vol. 10) (pp. 315–331). Boulder, CO: Western Interstate Commission for Higher Education.

Benoliel, J. Q. (1977c). Nurses and the human experience of dying. In H. Feifel (Ed.), *New meanings of death* (pp. 123–142). New York: McGraw-Hill.

Benoliel, J. Q. (1978). The changing social context for life and death decisions. *Essence, 2* (2), 5–14.

Benoliel, J. Q. (1979). Dying is a family affair. In E. R. Prichard, J. Collard, J. Starr, J. A, Lockwood, A. H. Kutscher, & I. B. Seeland (Eds.), *Home care—Living with dying* (pp. 17–34). New York: Columbia University Press.

Benoliel, J. Q. (Ed.). (1982). *Death education for the health professional*. New York: Hemisphere Publishing.

Benoliel, J. Q. (1983a). Nursing research on death, dying, and terminal illness: Development, present state, prospects. *Annual Review of Nursing Research, 1*, 101–130.

Benoliel, J. Q. (1983b). Grounded theory and qualitative data: The socializing influence of life-threatening disease on identity development. In P. J. Wooldridge, M. H. Schmitt, J. K. Skipper, & R. C. Leonard (Eds.), *Behavioral science & nursing theory* (pp. 141–187). St. Louis: Mosby.

Benoliel, J. Q. (1986a). Terminal illness. In G. Scipien, M. Barnard, M. Chard, J. Howe, & P. Phillips (Eds.), *Comprehensive pediatric nursing* (3rd ed.) (pp. 725–751). New York: McGraw-Hill.

Benoliel, J. Q. (1986b). The cancer patient's right to know and decide: An ethical perspective. In R. McCorkle & G. Hongladarom (Eds.), *Issues and topics in cancer nursing* (pp. 5–17). Norwalk, CT: Appleton-Century-Crofts.

Benoliel, J. Q. (1987–88). Health care providers and dying patients: Critical issues in terminal care. *Omega 18*, 341–363.

Benoliel, J. Q. (1988a). Institutional dying: A convergence of cultural values, technology, and social organization. In H. Wass, F. M. Berardo, & R. A. Neimeyer (Eds.), *Dying: Facing the facts* (2nd ed.) (pp. 159–184). New York: Hemisphere Publishing.

Benoliel, J. Q. (1988b). Health care delivery: Not conducive to teaching palliative care. *Journal of Palliative Care, 4* (1&2), 41–42.

Benoliel, J. Q. (1989). From research to scholarship: Challenges, choices, and transitions. *Communicating nursing research* (Vol. 22) (pp. 17–35). Boulder, CO: Western Institute of Nursing.

Benoliel, J. Q., & McCorkle, R. (1978). A holistic approach to terminal illness. *Cancer Nursing, 2*, 43–49.

Benoliel, J. Q., McCorkle, R., & Young, K. (1978). Development of a social dependency scale. *Research in Nursing & Health, 3*, 3–10.

Blauner, R. (1966). Death and social structure. *Psychiatry, 29*, 378–394.

Choron, J. (1963). *Death and western thought*. New York: Collier-Macmillan.

Degner, L. F., & Beaton, J. I. (1987). *Life-death decisions in health care*. New York: Hemisphere Publishing.

Degner, L. F., & Gow, C. M. (1988). Preparing nurses to care for the dying: A longitudinal study. *Cancer Nursing, 11*, 160–169.

Donaldson, G., McCorkle, R., Georgiadou, F., & Benoliel, J. Q. (1986). Distress, dependency, and threat in newly diagnosed cancer and heart disease patients. *Multivariate Behavioral Research, 21*, 267–298.

Eliot, R. D. (1933). A step toward the social psychology of bereavement. *Journal of Abnormal and Social Psychology 27*, 114–115.

Feifel, H. (1959). *The meaning of death*. New York: McGraw-Hill.

Fulton, R. (Ed.). (1965). *Death and identity*. New York: Wiley.

Germain, C. P. H. (1979). *The cancer ward: An ethnography*. Wakefield, MA: Nursing Resources, Inc.

Glaser, B. G., & Strauss, A. L. (1965). *Awareness of dying*. Chicago: Aldine.

Glaser, B. G., & Strauss, A. L. (1968). *Time for dying*. Chicago: Aldine.

Gorer, G. (1956). The pornography of death. In W. Phillips & P. Rahv (Eds.), *Modern writing* (pp. 56–62). New York: Berkeley.

Habenstein, R. W., & Lamers, W. M. (1960). *Funeral customs the world over*. Milwaukee: Bulfin.

Hinton, J. M. (1967). *Dying*. Baltimore: Penguin.

Koestenbaum, P. (1964). The vitality of death. *Journal of Existentialism, 18*, 139–166.

Kubler-Ross, E. (1969). *On death and dying*. New York: Macmillan.

Lifton, R. (1968). *Death in life: Survivors of Hiroshima*. New York: Random House.

Lindemann, E. (1944). Symptomatology and management of acute grief. *American Journal of Psychiatry, 101*, 141–148.

Marris, P. (1958). *Widows and their families*. London: Routledge & Kegan Paul.

Martocchio, B. O. (1982). *Living while dying*. Bowie, MD: Brady.

McCorkle, R., & Benoliel, J. Q. (1983). Symptom distress, current concerns and mood disturbance after life-threatening disease. *Social Science & Medicine, 17*, 431–438.

McCorkle, R., & Benoliel, J. Q. (1990). The effects of home care on patients' functional status. In S. G. Funk, S. M. Tornquist, M. T. Champagne, L. A. Copp, & R. A. Wiese (Eds.), *Key aspects of recovery* (pp. 315–326). New York: Springer.

McCorkle, R., Benoliel, J. Q., & Georgiadou, F. (1989). The effects of home care on patients' symptoms, hospitalizations, and complications. In S. F. Funk, E. M. Tornquist, M. T. Champagne, L. A. Copp, & R. A. Wiese (Eds.), *Key aspects of comfort* (pp. 303–312). New York: Springer.

McCorkle, R., & Young, K. (1978). The development of a symptom distress scale. *Cancer Nursing, 1*, 373–378.

Mishel, M., & Braden, C. J. (1988). Finding meanings: Antecedents of uncertainty in illness. *Nursing Research, 37*, 98–103.

Noddings, N. (1989). *Women and evil*. Berkeley: University of California Press.

Parkes, C. M. (1971). Psychosocial transitions. *Social Science & Medicine, 5*, 101–115.

Pine, V. R. (1986). The age of maturity for death education: A sociohistorical portrayal of the era 1976–1985. *Death Studies, 10*, 209–231.

Pridonoff, J. A. (1990). Professional development opportunities. *The Forum Newsletter, 14* (1), 4–5. (Available from Association for Death Education and Counseling, 638 Prospect Avenue, Hartford, CT 06105.)

Quint, J. C. (1963). The impact of mastectomy. *American Journal of Nursing, 63,* 88–92.

Quint, J. C. (1964). Mastectomy: Symbol of cure or warning sign? *GP, 29,* 119–124.

Quint, J. C. (1965). Institutionalized practices of information control. *Psychiatry, 28,* 119–132.

Quint, J. C. (1966). Awareness of death and the nurse's composure. *Nursing Research, 15,* 49–55.

Quint, J. C. (1967). *The nurse and the dying patient.* New York: Macmillan.

Quint, J. C. (1968). Preparing nurses to care for the fatally ill. *International Journal of Nursing Studies, 5,* 53–61.

Quint, J. C., & Strauss, A. L. (1964). Nursing students, assignments, and dying patients. *Nursing Outlook, 12,* 24–27.

Reed, P. G. (1986). Death perspectives and temporal variables in terminally ill and healthy adults. *Death Studies, 10,* 467–478.

Saunders, C. (1969). The moment of truth: Care of the dying person. In L. Pearson (Ed.), *Death and dying* (pp. 49–78). Cleveland: Western Reserve University Press.

Schorr, R. M., & Zimmerman, A. (1988). *Making choices, taking chances: Nurse leaders tell their stories* (pp. 15–22). St. Louis: Mosby.

Sudnow, D. (1967). *Passing on: The social organization of dying.* Englwood Cliffs, NJ: Prentice Hall.

Tornberg, M. J., McGrath, B. B., & Benoliel, J. A. (1984). Oncology transition services: Partnerships of nurses and families. *Cancer Nursing, 7,* 131–137.

Volkart, E. M., & Michael, S. T. (1957). Bereavement and mental health. In A. H. Leighton, J. A. Clausen, & R. N. Wilson (Eds.), *Explorations in social psychiatry* (pp. 281–304). New York: Basic Books.

Weisman, A., & Hackett, T. (1961). Predilection to death: Death and dying as a psychiatric problem. *Psychosomatic Medicine, 23,* 232–256.

Worcester, A. (1935). *Care of the aged, the dying and the dead.* Springfield, IL: Charles C Thomas.

Two

Chronic Illness, the Health Care System, AIDS, and Dying

Anselm Strauss

Anselm Strauss is professor emeritus of sociology, School of Nursing, University of California, San Francisco. He received his B.S. degree in biology (1939) from the University of Virginia, and his M.A. and Ph.D. degrees in sociology (1942 and 1945) from the University of Chicago. He taught at Lawrence College (1944–1946) in Wisconsin, then at Indiana University (1946–1952), the University of Chicago (1952–1958), and at his current position from 1960 to 1987. He has been a visiting professor at various universities, including the University of Cambridge, the University of Paris, the University of Manchester, and the University of Adelaide. He is a fellow of the American Associations for the Advancement of Science (1980). His books have been translated into various languages.

Strauss's main research activities have been in medical sociology and in work/professions. His research program in medical sociology and the problems of health goes back over three decades and includes studies on dying in hospitals, the management of pain in hospitals, the impact of medical technology on the care of hospitalized patients, and the problems of living with and giving service to chronically ill patients. His publications include Psychiatric Ideologies and Institutions *(1964, with coauthors),* Awareness of Dying *and* Time for Dying *(1985 and 1968, with B. Glaser),* The Politics of Pain Management *(1977, with S. Fagerhaugh),* Chronic Illness and the Quality of Life *(1975, revision in 1984, with coauthors),* The Social Organization of Medical Work *(1985, with coauthors),* Unending Work and Care *(1988, with J. Corbin)* Shaping a New Health Care System *(1988, with J. Corbin),* Hazard in Hospital Care *(1987, with coauthors),* Discovery of Gounded Theory *(1965, with B. Glaser),* Qualitative Analysis *(1987), and* Basics of Qualitative Research *(1990, with J. Corbin).*

Taking literally the editors' invitation to think about changes in chronic illness, including dying, that have occurred since I began to do research on its behavioral and management aspects, and to give some implications of those changes, I shall address these issues in two separate but related sections. The first narrates a brief saga touching on my personal and research experiences (they are closely linked). The second section addresses five glaring gaps in U.S. health care that chronic illness has made increasingly apparent.* Many critics of our health care system have written about two of these gaps; two have received far less attention, and one no attention at all. In a final section, I shall offer some thoughts about the gaps in the care of the dying in our health facilities, again linking this with the implications of contemporary chronic illness.

My understanding of the immense significance of chronic illness and its prevalence came very slowly. In 1957, I spent three months studying residents and interns in a university hospital—and barely noticed their patients. For the next three years, my research associates and I studied the staff and patients in a large state hospital, and also in one small private mental hospital for the acutely ill (Strauss et al., 1964). At the time, the "chronically ill" meant to me only the unfortunates housed on the "chronic wards" of the state hospital whose fates were never to be seen by a psychiatrist (who worked only on the acute wards). Most of these chronically ill were destined to live out their years on those back wards.

From 1960 until about 1967, I was preoccupied with studying and thinking about dying in hospitals (Glaser & Strauss 1965, 1968), scarcely noticing the other patients; besides, though I recognized that people were dying from cancer, heart disease, and other incurable illnesses, this fact signified nothing special to me about the nature of chronicity. It was on the staff's management of terminal care that we were focused. Two years later, I published a policy paper titled "Medical Ghettos" (see Strauss, 1970): It was about the inequities of the U.S. two-track system of medicine and the consequences for the health of poorer Americans. I was concerned there only with the issue of medical inequity, not at all with chronicity.

Not until the very end of our study of hospitalized dying did I finally ask: Who are all those patients who aren't dying, and what's life like for them between their hospitalizations? Answering those questions led to interviews and observations of ill people at their homes and in clinics by my students. This research led also to teaching nursing students about chronic illnesses in a course instituted during the spring of 1971. I was surprised at the 10 students who showed up on its opening day. A year or two before, there would have been far fewer students in attendance, since nurses then were not focused on chronic illness but only on particular diseases that just happened to be incurable. In other words, they were not thinking in terms of chronicity but of particular types of disease.

---

*The second section of this chapter was written in consultation with my associates on our AIDS research project. They are Shizuko Fagerhaugh, Barbara Suczek, and Carolyn Wiener. It has been our practice on this and a previous research project to list multiple authors, but I have not done so on this chapter since the editors requested a more personally reflective paper and one written by me.

Four years later, Barney Glaser and I published *Chronic Illness and the Quality of Life* (Strauss & Glaser, 1975), a book written for health practitioners. This offered a framework for thinking about the social aspects of living with chronic illness and also included several research papers by our students. It is surely a clear indicator of the steady rise of professional awareness of chronicity, reflecting too on the vastly increased public recognition of its significance, that this book has continued to sell approximately the same number of copies year in, year out, unlike most books whose readership drops off after a very few years. (It was not until 1986 that Ilene Lubkin's edited volume on chronic illness appeared, the first book by a nurse that focused on the social and economic aspects of chronic illness rather than mainly the physiological. It did take that long for full recognition of chronicity to sink in.) This rise of awareness and interest in chronicity was paralleled in the number of students who attended my class on chronic illness, the count rising to 70 or 80 by the early 1980s. Meanwhile, my more intimate knowledge of living with chronic illness, at least with cardiac disability, had been much furthered by a myocardial infarct (MI) in 1972. This helped in writing the foregoing book, as well as in helping me to make better sense of students' reports about themselves and their friends, parents, and patients.

Near the end of the 1970s, I began to wonder how the chronically ill were faring in our highly technologized hospitals. Professional staffs there viewed their patients as "acutely ill," whereas by then I conceived of them as mostly chronically ill—hospitalized for treatment there during emergency or acute *phases* of their long-term illnesses. This insight led to another intensive field study and a book titled *The Social Organization of Medical Work* (Strauss, Fagerhaugh, Suczek, & Wiener, 1985). In it my colleagues and I discussed in detail the impact of medical technology and sophisticated medical/nursing procedures on the care of hospitalized patients—most of them, of course, chronically ill and destined after hospitalization to return home to juggle their regimens, symptoms, and lives as best they could.

Near the end of 1980, while in the middle of this research, I had further problems with my heart and so got additional insight (the hard way!) into the work of managing both emergency and routine care of a severe chronic illness. Then shortly after, a research associate and I began to study the work of partners (spouses or otherwise) when one or both partners were chronically ill. As a result of that study (Corbin & Strauss, 1988), we became convinced that most management of chronic illness was actually done—and needed to be done—at home. Consequently, the health care system needed, we believed, radical reform. Home care ought to be at the center of a reshaped system, but linked complexly with the various health care facilities (Strauss & Corbin, 1988). Again, it is a measure of how far thinking about chronic illness has come if I report that in 1989 the National League for Nursing asked me to give a major presentation at their annual meetings about home care, to be based on this policy book. The League officers believed their members should quickly and strongly move—politically as well as clinically—toward home care, as well as play an educated role in its regulation.

When AIDS began to come into public notice as an incipient epidemic, I was first involved with it through a friend, Pat Biernacki, one of the pioneers in outreach prevention street work. At the time, I remember saying that for a few years the nation's concern would understandably be with AIDS mortality and prevention, but that the major long-run problem, at least in the United States, would be the massive impact of AIDS on our health care system—as a chronic illness. It did not take much prescience to foresee that with improved treatment, people with AIDS would be living longer and, like others of the chronically ill, would be treated and cared for both at home and in the health facilities—but probably in greatly increasing numbers because of the extent of the epidemic. Sadly, the newspapers are currently full of the strain on the facilities because of AIDS. They are also full of assertions, by people of moderate as well as activist views, that AIDS will probably lead to great and beneficial changes in our health care system, despite the initial disastrous impact on it. With that in mind, I turn to the second section of this chapter.

Gaps in the Health Care System

Inequity

There is scarcely need to dwell here on the medical inequity engendered by our health care system. Like all such national systems, it reflects national characteristics: class differentiations, demographics, cultural values, and political constituencies. Since early in this century, both professional and lay critics have written about the unequal access to health facilities of our population and the unequal access to quality care. Some of the inequity is because of regional differences; much of it, of course, is because of income differences by class and ethnicity. (See, for example, Dutton 1986, and her extensive bibliography on social class, health, and illness.) Medical inequity is just part of the larger pattern of economic deprivation, poor housing, inadequate diet, and so on. As Sidel and Sidel (1977, p. 11) remark, "Most of the factors influencing the health of a people lie outside what is conventionally defined as the responsibility of... 'health care.'" Yet this does not exonerate the nation for its markedly differential treatment of poorer citizens, with consequential differential rates of mortality and well-being. AIDS has simply increased the impoverishment of people who, like their counterparts with Alzheimer's disease or costly cancers or the unemployed cardiac ill, have become poorer because of their illness and less able to get adequate care because of this.

Home Care

Critics of the health care system have long since pointed to its extraordinary emphasis on acute care, with most of its resources going into treatment, research, and training directed at acute care. Experts in long-term care, rehabilitation, and gerontology have been particularly vocal and their criticisms especially astute. With respect to long-term care, they point to failures of continuity, flexibility, and responsiveness to and respectfulness for the ill themselves. (Some instances of these criticisms include Brody, Pulshock, & Masiocchi, 1978; Feldman, 1974; La Porte & Rubin, 1979; Cluff, 1981; Vladeck, 1985; & Brody, 1987.) Though agreeing with the general tenor of these criticisms, Juliet Corbin and I pointed out (1988) that these are views of health professionals, trained and experienced *as* professionals, seeing policy and practice largely from professionalized perspectives: "These are somewhat intellectualized, they are often focused sharply on the present, and they generally take a top-down (an administrator's or practitioners') rather than a grass-roots (an ill person's) perspective." We went on to criticize the critics for not differentiating among the several phases of long-term illness and so not providing an adequate conceptualization for organizing care in relation to medical/nursing and everyday requirements of the different phases (including crisis, acute, recovery or comeback, physiological or at least symptomatic stability, instability, deterioration, and dying; of course, not every ill person experiences all of these phases).

In our book, we offered a trajectory model for thinking about and organizing management of long-term illnesses, with *home care* at the center of such care. It perhaps would be effective here to quote some of what we said about that model:

1. Home is the central site—the major workplace—where lifelong illness is managed on a daily basis.
2. The major concern of the ill and their families is not merely nor primarily managing an illness, but maintaining the *quality of life*, as defined specifically by them, despite the illness.
3. Lifelong illness requires lifelong work to control its course, manage its symptoms, and live with the resulting disability. At home, the work is principally done by the ill themselves, if possible, and by family members, abetted perhaps by agency or purchased services. In health facilities, the work is done primarily by the staff, although even here patients do their share of the work.

4. ...Any course of illness will proceed through one or more of several phases.

5. Each of these phases calls for different kinds of combinations of work in different proportions by all participants: that is, work varies with the phase of the illness....

6. At home, there is an interplay of three major types of work: the work of managing illness; the everyday work of keeping a household and life in general going; and "biographical work"—the work associated with maintaining one's mental and psychological concerns as one would like them to be despite the impact of the illness and its management. This work is done chiefly by the ill and their families.

7. Within the context of home and family life, the central feature of illness management is the establishment and maintenance of arrangements. These arrangements enable the illness work to be more or less effective. Most arrangements involve organizing the time and effort of the ill person in conjunction with those of family members and sometimes those of relatives, friends, and neighbors.

8. These arrangements are almost always revised and reorganized in accordance with changes in illness phase....

9. Maintaining these necessary arrangements, and making workable rearrangements, for carrying out the three types of work are continuous.

10. The work of health practitioners feeds into this continual and daily work. This work is frequently essential.... In short, the work of health practitioners is usually very much a part of the overall illness management, but it is only a part.

11. Its effectiveness in relation to long-term management depends not only on its technical efficiency and quality, but on how well it supplements and is incorporated into the ongoing management work of the ill and their families. (Strauss & Corbin, 1988, pp. 47–49)

To the foregoing, perhaps I need only add that home care is very much part of the climate of today's health politics. Private medical corporations are much interested in the potential profits of home care; and both the American Hospital Association and the National League for Nursing—and perhaps many more contenders—are vying for a share of the regulatory power over home care. The great danger is that regulation will be minimal and aimed at a relatively low level of quality care, with profits the predominant motive.

AIDS, of course, has thrust home care increasingly into the daily newspapers. Without going into the details of the nation's policy on the handling of AIDS, suffice it to say that the burden of caring for the AIDS ill has rested primarily on volunteers and community agencies. In San Francisco, for example, numerous special organizations have sprung up to care for the ill at home, and the middle-class gay community is widely recognized to have cared for its very sick and dying members in their own homes. All this has served to underscore the glaring deficiencies of the U.S. health care system with regard to the financing and servicing of both the dying and chronically ill if they wish to be or must be cared for at home. So, AIDS both threatens to increase the deficiencies of the system in this regard and promises to force changes in the system.

Care for People without Homes

Among the major social problems now regarded by most Americans is homelessness. Besides those people who are without housing, countless others live in inadequate housing, including tiny rooms in skid-row hotels and overcrowded small apartments in ghettos. Add to this the number of people who live alone, even if they live in "family" houses, especially the elderly and the aged. In this context, the health care issue is not only how to deliver care to those populations (mostly ill with multiple chronic illnesses) but how to devise ways to improve their health despite the many environmental and health system obstacles that currently block this.

The problem is twofold. In the first place, health facilities, primarily centered in hospitals and clinics, are not organized to reach out to where these people live (and die). Institutional outreach, it is true, has somewhat increased in the last decade (probably thanks to shrinking hospital and clinic finances) but falls far short of supplying adequate health care to these populations. Conversely, the institutionalized or systematic ways of getting emergency or acutely ill poor people *to* the facilities is woefully lacking. If indeed they do get there, then they are treated by staff members who are generally drawn from higher up in the socioeconomic scale and who have little knowledge or interest in conditions that interfere with their patients carrying out necessary regimens after leaving the facilities.

AIDS is just beginning to highlight this deficiency in our health care system. I say "just" because until very recently this was not so. As the homeless and other poverty-stricken people develop AIDS, they too come to professional and public notice. Yet, since they count for very little in the U.S. hierarchy of values, and since servicing them adequately would call for considerable reorganization of health care arrangements—if not the facilities themselves—then both recognition and action are still rudimentary.

It is notable that outreach programs do not include many (if indeed any) health components. (Most outreach programs are funded as AIDS projects to discover and demonstrate ways of preventing AIDS, not as projects to handle the actual health aspects after AIDS is contracted or HIV seropositivity is diagnosed.) In San Francisco, there is only one health outreach team of which I am aware; I assess its work as effective. This team (Froner

& Rowniak, 1989) visits and diagnoses the ill in their lodgings and on the street, persuades or makes arrangements for them to be seen at health facilities, steers them through the institutional maze once there, and does some follow-up work too. In short, this team operates on a case management basis. The team's social worker contributes time voluntarily, and the nurse receives a salary as an AIDS liaison public health nurse with the Department of Public Health, although he has never really had full departmental backing. Neither the city nor any government agency would fund their work directly, although some officials in the local Department apparently respect this team's work—yet they are in a real sense outside "the system." I make special note of this health outreach team because they provide, I estimate, an effective service that nonetheless has not been funded nor made an official part of the city's health care system.

Professionals and government officials need to understand the need for these new kinds of health care arrangements. This particular health team aside, that kind of "connecting work" needs to be done for a very great number of Americans, AIDS may turn out to be the experimental ground for such necessary work and its associated arrangements. Without this reorganization, the health care system will continue mostly to fail these less fortunate citizens.

Addicts and the Mentally Ill

It has been my observation that in clinics and hospitals, drug and alcohol addicts are far from welcomed by the staff when they are known as addicts. Of course, they also are patients and so staffs are either obliged or committed to give them adequate care. Nevertheless, the common terminology about patients being good or bad, cooperative or uncooperative that is heard so often in these facilities extends also to addicts. Now, to the staff's frequent perceptions of them as truculent or uncooperative or irresponsible or unpleasant, even violent, add the evident lower socioeconomic status of some addicts. The "social value" of these particular patients becomes quite low. Uncooperative ones tend to get less attentive care—all the more so because the personnel "know" (sometimes from sound experience) that these patients will soon be back since they will not follow their regimens. Likewise, when patients who are not so obviously mentally ill as to be sent to mental hospitals or clinics come to medical facilities, they tend to be labeled as "difficult" patients. Hospital personnel have relatively little if any training in handling such mental symptoms, and so are likely either to keep as much distance as possible from them or to call on psychiatrists or chaplains for help in managing them. (In fact, this is one of the main functions of liaison psychiatrists.)

What this tells a sociologist is that, again, a considerable and seemingly increasing portion of the ill are getting less than adequate care. But why?

Not simply because of staff attitudes but because of how the facilities are organized—including how their personnel are (not) trained to work with addicts and the mentally ill, and how little value is placed on working with them in the facilities. After all, these organizations are focused on giving acute care, not managing the chronically ill. In the instance of drug addicts, this is partly a matter of poverty-generating national conditions and partly a national obsession with the evil character of drug addiction, derived from many years of media blowup and propaganda efforts by government agencies (Lindesmith, 1965).

New Phases of Illness

In our study of medical work (Strauss, Fagerhaugh, Suczek, & Wiener, 1985), my colleagues and I were much struck by a new phenomenon. The very effectiveness of contemporary medical technology and medical/nursing procedures had led to people living with a great number of illnesses from which previously they would have died. As everyone knows, this does not mean the survivors are always physically comfortable or without grave symptomology. The more usual pattern is that new developments and new symptoms in the illness appear. With time, the clinicians discover how to handle these further developments, using, for example, new drugs evolved for this very purpose. Alas, these too may produce side effects that perhaps require additional drugs or other technologies to manage, which then may lead to further side effects. Such new phases of illness call with some frequency for multiple therapies (cancer therapies are an example). And then, the chronically ill often have multiple illnesses—each illness perhaps moving into previously unknown phases.

In our book, we noted how these ill persons, when hospitalized, could sufficiently "discombobulate" the usual organization of care in such ways that they could accurately be described as producing a "cumulative mess." The mess was organizational *and* clinical. Some of the flavor of a cumulative mess and the difficulty of coordinating care can be gathered from the following account of a couple dealing with the wife's dementia:

> Coordination of care is a central issue when managing and shaping cumulative mess trajectories. The simplest component of rearticulation [of the work] which is a continual necessity, consists of decisions to *revise* protocols (drug dosages mainly) or to take *additional* action (mainly tests and procedures, but also surgery)—"simplest" because they depend on standard operating procedure. Staff then takes familiar action, draws on usual resources, and follows established forms of making arrangements with servicing departments. The *novel* arrangements, however, rest on ad hoc conferences, much negotiation and persuasion among the staff—even between staff or husband and the patient—calling in consultants, dovetailing the division of labor of a psychiatrist or the

special personnel (the sitter who will watch over potential fire hazards from the patient's smoking) and setting up unusual articulating actions.

Revisions in physicians' orders and the derived protocols (mainly changes in the medications) are called for mainly because of reassessments of new developments (positive or negative) in the course of the illness, although some revisions are precipitated by the patient's actions. Additional tasks are called forth by other kinds of illness developments, which are conceived as necessitating further diagnostic tests and treatments not originally envisioned. Each of those...tasks require further articulation into the ongoing stream of staff work.... Over the staff's novel work of rearticulation there hangs the dust of battle—battle with the patient but frequently also among the staff members as they debate what to do next.... The patient's spontaneous refusals to undergo or continue with specific procedures or drug dosages will also temporarily disarticulate the procedures or operational tasks that seemed otherwise to be under no particular threat. Repeated disarticulation of this kind ("hassles") leads to staff's annoyance, disruption of their flow of work, and if it continues long enough will result in the staff's withdrawal or other consequences negative to their work and their medical and nursing care of the given patient.

[There is also] the staff's heightened feeling that they have lost control over the evolving trajectory.... The staff's query, "How can we get this illness under control?" gradually gets transformed into the increasingly weary and desperate "Will we ever get this illness under control?" Part of the staff's response is certainly related not just to loss of control over the illness itself but their inability to keep coordinated even the associated medical and nursing work, what with all the tests, treatments, consultants streaming in and out...minor and major interferences with their medial and nursing plans, and the obvious disintegration of interactional and work relationships with [the patient]. (Strauss et al., 1985, pp. 179–180)

Such cases of cumulative mess, when we studied them, were an aggregate phenomenon. That is, care for individual patients could develop into cumulative mess patterns, but only occasionally did the disruptions become this extreme. Nevertheless, the organizational fabric of hospitals was being stressed by more or less extreme disruptions because of new illness phases.

What AIDS is likely to do is to produce collective rather than merely aggregate disruptions and strains. AIDS will do this for two reasons. First, as with other chronic illnesses, the therapies are producing—and will produce—untoward side effects that will need to be controlled with still other therapeutic actions. Second, AIDS also produces multiple physiological breakdowns, so that symptoms and associated therapies multiply. But this will happen on wards where *many* AIDS patients are housed, so the accumulative organizational strain has a collective source rather than deriving from an occasional physiologically (and interactionally) difficult patient.

In short, I see hospitals, and perhaps clinics too, as eventually at hazard. They will need to reorganize themselves and retrain their staffs for this new kind of organizational danger. I only add that this development is not at all simply the danger that flows from an increasing number of patients; rather, it is an increasing number of very sick people with new and particularly difficult kinds of previously unencountered physiological and behavioral developments. People who are concerned with the U.S. health care policy would be wise to think about this particular deficiency in our health system too. It will not be eased by thinking of how only to improve acute care. Surely it must be linked with a much broadened conception of chronic illness and how best to manage it, in and out of the health care facilities.

Chronic Illness and Care of the Dying: Another Partial Failure

In the early 1960s, when my research associates, Jean Quint (Benoliel) and Barney Glaser, and I studied terminal care in hospitals, there was not yet a death and dying movement. Jeanne, a compassionate nurse, sometimes despaired, "What good will our research ever do? Will it ever change anything?" At the time, we found that we could not talk about our data or experiences with either our nursing and sociologist colleagues because of their openly expressed anxieties when we tried to tell about these. By the end of the decade, however, attendance at death and dying workshops was massive. Sometimes the "regulars" (Kubler-Ross, White, Feifel, and a few others) and I would be addressing 800 or 900 avid listeners—mostly nurses and social workers, with a sprinkling of psychologists and psychiatrists. For a while, I was hopeful that dying as a process would be widely recognized and confronted, and thus the care of the dying would be much improved. Obviously, there have been changes for the better, among them the development of grief counseling, the widespread influence and institutionalization of hospice philosophy, legislation and organizational regulations about living wills, and of course media focus on the dilemmas attending the end of life due to advances in medical technology. As we say about other topics, death is here to stay—it is out of the closet, as compared with two decades ago.

At those early workshops, I noticed two developments with some unease. The emphasis was all on teaching and urging the audience—as individuals—to come to terms with their own fears and anxieties about death. I thought, "That's all very well as a first step," but as a social scientist, and one who had studied organized care of the terminally ill, I wondered at the almost total lack of attention paid to the group, collective, or organizational aspects of managing—or living with—other people's dying. After all, the audience consisted of professionals who worked with clients, and indeed most of the nurses were from hospitals or clinics. My second unease was aroused by the other speakers' intense focus on long-term dying, such as from cancer. Occasionally, I would speak to the point that many people died at far speedier rates, and that their problems, and those of their kin (and the staff's), were greatly affected by this. In the audience, heads nodded, but the message was overwhelmed by the more terrifying images of torturous dying.

At the time, the larger implications of my unease quite escaped me. Two or three years later, I suffered a myocardial infarct. Shortly thereafter, I gave my last public lecture about dying, and later shifted research and teaching interests to chronic illness and other health issues. My subsequent personal and research experiences in hospitals led me to realize that these organizations had not changed much in their giving of terminal care. It is true that, among the nurses at least, the movement's messages of "know thyself" and "you really can talk with dying patients about their deaths" were evident, as conveyed mainly through some of the literature (mostly Kubler-Ross, perhaps) and collegial conversation. It is my impression that few classes ever were, or are, taught about death and dying in schools of nursing; virtually none at all are given in medical schools. Where the death and dying movement took hold in hospitals was through individual nurses (mainly) who, imbued with some of its philosophy, acted with more sensitive self-consciousness toward the dying and their kin.

Doing field observations on a cardiac recovery ward in the late 1970s, I once saw a scene that should illustrate my point:[1]

A very elderly and very ill lady scheduled for surgery the next day was sitting up in bed, glasses on her nose, writing on a clipboard, absorbed in her writing. Her daughter stood on her right, helping to hold the clipboard. When the nurse left the room, I asked her what this scene was all about. With some passion, she told me the patient had been facing whether to die or to go through a fourth operation. The nurse had told her it was her own option to decide. Now the daughter is angry at the nurse for saying this, but the nurse questions whether it makes sense for the patient to go on living, for she is bleeding into her lung. The patient had written on the clipboard: "I have decided to die. The doctor says I have only a fifty-fifty chance, and that makes no sense."

I glanced back into the patient's room, where the physician and daughter were urging her to have the operation. She finally consented. They left, and a resident began to enter to insert a longer tube into her lungs; otherwise, he explained to the nurse, the blood would flow from one lung into the other. The nurse angrily said, "No," that the patient had just been through a "dramatic scene." He convinced her that at least they should move the current tube down a bit further. She reluctantly agreed.

Immediately after, the nurse cued the resident to the patient's live-or-die dilemma and they entered the room together and stood on opposite sides of her bed. The nurse said gently but passionately to the patient that the decision was up to *her*, and the young physician agreed. The next afternoon, the nurse told me sadly that the patient had died in surgery.

This scene is all the more striking because on this ward, and indeed in the entire hospital, there was no teaching or planned organizational structure about managing the care of terminally ill patients except for its technical aspects.

Even more telling is that staffs in hospitals all over the United States are giving medical and nursing care to people destined soon to die. Many of the ill and their kin are quite aware of impending death—how could it be otherwise, since it is chronic illness from which they are dying? Some have had long illness careers, complete with self-management of symptoms and emergencies, and perhaps facing death more than once. Increasing numbers of them, but still a small minority, are signing living wills, aware of the horrors that can be created by overuse or unwise use of technology and by grimly determined hospital staffs. These chronically ill people fill our hospitals because, as the saying goes among staff members, "Patients here are sicker than ever." Chronic illness sends to clinics a steady flow of the very ill but not yet dying, and they visit repeatedly. Clinic staffs are equally untrained in the special interaction that is need with people who have thought about their not-so-future deaths; nor have the clinics, any more than the hospitals, reorganized their structures to meet the issue raised by increasing numbers of the chronically ill.[2] More Americans are living longer—but with multiple chronic illnesses as they pass through their sixties and seventies, and nowadays eighties and nineties. Not all chronic illness is, of course, fatal and not all people with potentially fatal diseases die from them, either because of improved technology or genetic luck; nevertheless, the chronically ill are more likely to be closer to death than other Americans.

So, this is another of the major implications of chronic illness prevalence. If we put this together with the continued focus of hospitals (and even many clinics) on acute care, then we have a prescription for a considerable measure of failure to face with sensibility and sensitivity one of the great dramas of human existence. I doubt if this situation is much different in nursing homes—not much different anywhere except where hospice personnel are at work or where kin and other intimates are naturally wonderful during the last phases of the living-dying process. Again, AIDS points up this deficiency in our health care system.

There is need for a great deal more openness about and training for these last years, months, weeks, and days. Once, some time ago, I visited a Scottish hospital and listened to a group of elderly village women talk easily and naturally about dying and death (more at ease, no doubt, than the younger and more citified nurses). Although we certainly cannot go back to that mentality—given a totally different era, different institutions, and differently constructed persons—there is still a lesson to be learned there. Industrialized countries face a major problem in what to do about a fully expectable increase of *long*-end-of-life existence on the edge, more or less, of death. The issues involved are quite obviously moral at core, and the death and dying movement has taught us also that the issues are also psychological and medical/psychological. But they are also *organizational*. "Organizational" does not mean impersonal or bureaucratic; it means effective rationality in arrangements that will make life easier, less tortured, and more acceptable for the dying and their intimates.

Perhaps the experiences of rapidly increasing numbers of middle-aged children (mostly daughters) who bear the heavy burden of care for aged parents in the months or weeks before they die, and who watch with horror some of the worst kinds of bodily disintegration before the actual death— perhaps when they themselves get to be that age they will opt for specific legislation and changed customs about dying. They may request long beforehand that when they think there is no sense to living longer, someone will act or help them act sensibly about this business of dying. It is devoutly to be hoped, I believe, having my own set of personal images about these ordeals, that this more rational perspective will occur before new generations confront their own deaths.

Endnotes

1. These paragraphs are a slightly different worded version of the case described in *The Social Organization of Medical Work* (Strauss et al., 1985, pp. 28–29).
2. Two months after writing these sentences, a graduate student and experienced nurse, Gilly West (1991), has reported in an extensively researched thesis about the experiences of patients with breast cancer, conclusions similar to those I have expressed in the foregoing sentences.

References

Brody, S. (1987). Strategic planning: The catastrophic approach. *The Gerontologist*, 27, 131–138.

Brody, S., Pulshock, S., & Masciocchi, C. (1978). The family caring unit: A major consideration in the long-term care support system. *The Gerontologist 18*, 555–561.

Cluff, L. (1981). Chronic disease, function and the quality of care. *Social Science and Medicine, 34,* 299–304.

Corbin, J., & Strauss, A. (1988). *Unending work and care: Managing chronic illness at home.* San Francisco: Jossey-Bass.

Dutton, D. (1986). Social class, health and illness. Reprinted in P. Brown (Ed.), *Perspectives in medical sociology.* Belmont, CA: Wadsworth, 1989, pp. 23–46.

Feldman, D. (1974). Chronic disabling illness: A holistic view. *Journal of Chronic Disease, 27,* 287–291.

Froner, G., & Rowniak, S. (1989). The health outreach team: Taking AIDS education and health care to the streets. *AIDS Education and Prevention, 1,* 105–118.

Glaser, B., & Strauss, A. (1965). *Awareness of dying.* Chicago: Aldine.

Glaser, B., & Strauss, A. (1968). *Time for dying.* Chicago: Aldine.

La Porte, V., & Rubin, J. (Eds.). (1979). *Reform and regulation in long-term care.* New York: Praeger.

Lindesmith, A. (1965). *The addict and the law.* Bloomington: Indiana University.

Lubkin, I. (1986). *Chronic illness: Interventions for health professionals.* Boston: Jones and Bartlett.

Sidel, V., & Sidel, R. (1977). The health of the people. Reprinted in P. Brown (Ed.), *Perspectives in medical sociology.* Belmont, CA: Wadsworth, 1989, pp. 11–33.

Strauss, A., (1970). Medical ghettos. In A. Strauss (Ed.), *Where medicine fails* (pp. 11–29). New Brunswick, NJ: Transaction.

Strauss, A., Bucher, R., Ehrlich, D., Schatzman, L., & Sabshin, M. (1964). *Psychiatric ideologies and institutions.* New York: Free Press.

Strauss, A., & Corbin, J. (1988). *Shaping a new health care system.* San Francisco: Jossey-Bass.

Strauss, A., & Glaser, B. (1975). *Chronic illness and the quality of life.* St. Louis: Mosby. Second Printing, 1984.

Strauss, A., Fagerhaugh, S., Suczek, B., & Wiener, C. (1985). *The social organization of medical work.* Chicago: University of Chicago.

Vladeck, B. (1985). The static dynamics of long-term health policy. In M. Lewin (Ed.), *The health policy agenda.* Washington, DC: American Enterprise Institute.

West, G. (1991). *Having cancer.* Doctoral thesis, Department of Social and Behavioral Sciences, School of Nursing, University of California, San Francisco, California.

Three

Finding a Way to Give Hospice Care
A Nurse's Diary

Florence Wald

Even though Florence Wald is now retired, she continues to be active in the hospice field as volunteer caregiver and author. Writing about the tug-of-war that goes on in a reform movement and about the spiritual needs and resources of caregivers, she also continues on the long-term project of writing her diary as a caregiver. Presently, she is studying the mental anguish of patients and families along with the interventions that provide relief. She is available as a resource to the staff at the Connecticut Hospice when they are looking at clinical problems.

Each member of her family has made contributions to the world of hospices. Her husband, Henry J. Wald, prepared the feasibility study of the Connecticut Hospice; her son, Joel Wald, did the earliest literature search; and her daughter, Shari Vogler, is the Volunteer Director of Hospice Services in the Northwood Center for the elderly in Halifax, Nova Scotia. Willie is a member of the canine support staff at the Connecticut Hospice.

In terminal illness, two of life's critical moments happen at the same time. The patient's body fails to function, and the patient and the family face final separation—an event in life at least as important as birth, marriage, or bringing up a child. Even if one has the secret hope to face the end of life with courage, equanimity, competence, a sense of responsibility, a sense of achievement, a sense of humor, and the hope of giving support and comfort to one's survivors, in the act, most of us are caught unprepared when that time of life appears.

What nurses and doctors do, and the way they relate to patients and families, will determine the way life comes to a close, especially when the patient dies in a hospital or hospice setting.

From the beginning of my professional education as a nurse, I was taught to view the patient not just as a sick body but as an individual with an illness surrounded by a circle of family and friends, and as a human being with thoughts, feelings, and an idiosyncratic way of life. Among the doctors, nurses, and social workers with whom we worked, we student nurses could always find a few mentors who shared this viewpoint and helped us do it in the care we gave even when the rules and regulations of the institution hampered these efforts.

In the 1940s, there was a rapid change in methods of diagnosis and treatment as laboratory equipment became more sophisticated and surgical techniques promised hitherto undreamed of reprieves from death. Cardiac catheterization, automated monitoring devices, radioactive isotopes, electron microscopes, and flame photometers to measure electrolytes provided new tools for diagnosis, and caregivers looked at and listened to patients and their families less and concentrated on laboratory findings and machines more. Organ and tissue transplants; plastic and steel prosthetic devices; new techniques for replacing body fluids, and implanting pacemakers, valves, and blood vessels; new drugs; the discovery and development of antibiotics—all drastically changed the course of the illness. Now the challenge was to keep abreast of new medical procedures and to become skilled in using them. The temptation to escalate treatment became irresistible. Medical centers became galaxies of specialized units functioning independently and with little coordination. There were many who, like myself, held to the importance of bringing out the patient as a human being, and who felt powerless and rudderless to practice what we believed in.

Control over an individual's medical fate had shifted from the patient and the family to the institution and its workers. Pathology rather than people became the focus of education and practice for doctors, nurses, and social workers. Scientific method and technical competence demanded objectivity and detachment. Our heroes and heroines of medicine, nursing, and social work—William Osler, Florence Nightingale, Helen Hull— were neglected and the focus was no longer on the social context of health and illness. In large teaching hospitals and medical centers where the per diem costs for a hospital bed were escalating year by year and where medical faculty wanted patients with diseases and treatments important for medical students to see, patients' stays in hospital came to be determined by institutional and pedagogical concerns rather than by patients' needs.

The young intern was expected to be the detached, scientific physician who knew what was best and would decide on the action. Medicine had become so complex and sophisticated that patients and families lost whatever self-confidence they might have had in selecting a course of action and instead became dependent on the doctor, relying on the physician's judgment. Diagnosis was based primarily on laboratory tests; assessing the patient's total situation became tangential. Treatment of the disease was vigorous and persistent. By 1968, just before we undertook our study, Dr. Raymond Duff, a physician, and a sociologist, August Hollingshead, reported the pressure that physicians received from their colleagues when discontinuing treatment was proposed: "People ask you, 'What, you aren't going to operate on this cancer?... What kind of doctor are you and what kind of hospital is this?'" (Duff & Hollingshead, 1968). The doctor who abandoned intensive treatment and allowed nature to take its course was regarded as a quitter.

The nurse, as the doctor's assistant, monitored the complex instruments, collected data on the patient's progress, and organized records; she had little time to minister to patients directly, make them comfortable, or give them the information or the emotional support they needed. Nursing care was divided between professional and nonprofessional nurses so that nursing tasks could be done as quickly and as inexpensively as possible. Patients rarely saw the professional nurse responsible for their care. Nurses learned to avoid the repeated, direct, and urgent questions that patients asked, because the custom was "doctors answer questions." This caused nurses to complain bitterly that doctors were tying the nurses' hands. Student nurses, taught by their instructors to deal with terminally ill patients' questions and feelings, didn't find nurse practitioners doing it in practice (Quint, 1967).

Doctors, nurses, and patients appeared to expect physical and psychologic pain to be borne silently. Prescriptions were limited to a small selection of analgesics sparingly used. Concern about drug addiction and fear that the patient's increasing pain would lead to an unmanageable end prevailed. But caring professionals were agonized by witnessing the physical suffering and degradation of self that resulted from never-ending intensive treatment.

Social workers were often overlooked when vital decisions were being made. When a patient was dying, only the family was offered an opportunity to plan for and cope with the approaching death, thus reinforcing the patient's isolation. There was continual pressure to discharge patients hurriedly, at the expense of adequate planning and continuity of care, so that the bed could be used for the next patient. The family-patient relationships were caught in a reluctance to share communications.

Saving life had been the goal; quality of life was overlooked. But in the mid-sixties, certain questions began to surface: What was the cost in dollars and what happened to families whose savings were depleted? Did the treatment take more than it gave in the course of the disease? Were choices presented? Were choices understood? Were the side effects of treatment worse than the disease itself?

Rumblings of dissatisfaction became audible. Nurses began to encourage patients to express their feelings. Ida Jean Orlando (Pelletier), faculty member of Yale's School of Nursing, taught student nurses to pay attention to patients' words and gestures, be sensitive to patients' perceptions of reality, and refrain from deciding for the patient. She helped patients to emerge as sentient beings able to express their needs (Orlando, 1961).

In Virginia Henderson's view, the responsibility of nurses was to act on the patient's behalf in reaching for health, recovery, or a peaceful death if the patient could not do it unaided, but always with the intent of sustaining and augmenting the patient's independence (Henderson, 1966). She layed the foundation for recognizing the patient's autonomy.

The problems of those facing catastrophic illness began to emerge (Cancer Care, Inc., 1971) as the United States seemed to advance toward a national health service.

Dr. Max Pepper, another Yale colleague, was responsible for planning a regional mental health center adjacent to the Yale-New Haven Medical Center. In his work, he focused on patients' lifestyles and those who could help: family members, friends, and neighbors. He underlined the concept that a patient should not be considered alone but in the context of a patient-family with neighbors and community able and willing to help.

It was in this environment that Cicely Saunders brought her approach to those facing dying. When Dr. Saunders first came to Yale University's School of Medicine in 1963 to visit Dr. Bernard Lytton on the Medical School Faculty, she agreed to present a talk to some of the medical students. She captivated the sophisticated and often impassive medical students. The lively interest she aroused on that occasion was so moving that the medical students gave what was unheard of for them—a standing ovation. Her photographs of patients in the last days of life, looking comfortable, relieved of pain, alert, and active, enthralled the audience. She used color slides to illustrate the pharmacological management of pain and the humane care given by the nursing nuns in the care of terminally ill patients at St. Joseph's Hospice in Hackney, London. Two things stood out: First, Dr. Saunders's program for treatment of terminally ill patients opened a new and effective approach and, second, our medical students and nurses were greatly interested (or was that first?).

Dr. Saunders diagnosed chronic pain in a broad framework. Encompassing the physical and psychologic situation of the patient and family, she prescribed medications to assuage pain while keeping the patient alert. The synergistic effects of one drug on another was a key element in symptom management. The enhancing effect one drug had on another and the rate drugs were absorbed and sustained in the body made it possible to prevent pain rather than treat it. In her clinical experience, she found people with chronic pain used drugs differently than those who abused them.

While St. Christopher's was being planned and built in the early 1960s, Dr. Saunders came frequently to the United States to gather ideas from institutions long established in the care of the dying—among them, the

Dominican Hawthorne Sisters, Cancer Care, Inc., City of Hope, and You-ville Hospital—and also from medical centers where intensive curative therapy was practiced. She was soon flooded with invitations to talk about hospice care. In 1966, she came as an Annie W. Goodrich visiting professor to the Yale University School of Nursing. At the end of her stay, a work-shop was held, bringing together about 30 people who were known to be actively working with dying and bereaved persons. Some of these had corresponded with one another, but few had ever met. Dr. Elisabeth Kubler-Ross of the University of Chicago was one of the participants. Dr. Colin Murray Parkes, a psychiatrist on the staff of the Tavistock Institute of Human Relations in London was at Harvard University as a visiting fellow that year; he joined it too. He was examining the American experience of bereavement. Zelda Foster, a social worker, Dr. Ray Duff, the Rev. Edward Dobihal, and Leo Simmons met for the first time.

During her Yale visit, Dr. Saunders took part in the clinical rounds of medicine, pediatrics, psychiatry, in seminars at the nursing school, and addressed the Greater New Haven health care community at large. By this time, my interest was so strong that when my second term as Dean ended I decided to resign so that I could return to patient care using Cicely Saunders's approach. How I would go about doing it was uncertain but a sabbatical year allowed ideas to jell. At age 48, it seemed I had little enough time left to return to my first professional love of clinical nursing.

The course Cicely Saunders took had begun 20 years earlier. Little by little, she revealed her thinking and her approach.

Her education as caregiver began in nursing but a bad back made physical work difficult, so she then took training as an almoner. By 1948, her interest focused on patients with advanced cancer. Having seen such patients at St. Thomas Hospital in London as a student nurse and St. Luke's Home for the Dying in Bayswater where she volunteered, it became clear to her, that if she wanted to provide patients with the kind of care she envisioned, she should be in charge and she would need a setting of her own. This meant she needed the credentials and skills of a physician and an administrator, so she went to medical school. At St. Luke's she had found that chronic pain could be controlled with careful and constant manage-ment of medication; she then spent a year in expanding her knowledge and clinical skills in the pharmacologic management of pain. With the profes-sional degrees of nurse, social worker, and doctor, and added training in administration, she had a broad and solid base of knowledge and experience in care. She was sensitive to how the several professions viewed the patient and their work. She also had the credentials needed in a leader of such a radical new approach.

In 1959, Dr. Saunders felt it was time to act. Her daily reading of *Daily Light* opened one day to the passage, "Commit thy way unto the Lord, trust also in him and he shall bring it to pass" (du Boulay, 1984, p. 85). There were two more years of discussion with friends, family, colleagues, and mentors in the Church of England that went into the certificate of corporation, but du Boulay notes that Cicely Saunders sought and used the help of many as she was able and did make decisions herself.

Dr. Saunders did not talk about her spiritual approach in the beginning, or if she did, I didn't appreciate her profound Christian foundation from which she addressed the emotional and spiritual needs she considered as essential as expert knowledge of modern medicine. Christ's crucifixion and the resurrection are central images in St. Christopher's Hospice: "When Christ was facing death in the Garden of Gethsamane, He said to His disciples, 'Watch with me.' This is the attitude of mind and heart in which we must approach the dying so that we may try to learn from them and give to them" (Saunders, 1965).

She often said without *her* spiritual foundation she could not have embarked on this work. She encouraged others to have some form of spiritual support, although it need not be the same as hers. Dr. Saunders respects the knowledge of medical science as a valuable instrument, but regards quality of life of the patient-family as whole human beings the goal. Shirley du Boulay makes the spiritual component in her care clear and traces the spiritual themes in Dr. Saunders's life from her entrance into "the evangelical stream of Christianity" in 1945 through the drafting of St. Christopher's Articles of Association in 1964:

> Legally St. Christopher's is both a religious and medical foundation, there has never been any doubt about that. The Articles of Association undertake to promote the relief of suffering, "By providing or assisting or encouraging the provision of spiritual help and guidance for any persons resident (either as patients or otherwise) or working in any such home or homes as aforesaid." To this end they promise, "To provide or arrange for a building or premises to be used by the Association as a church or chapel available for Christian worship."
>
> These few lines, which result from so much thought in the very early sixties, hardly reflect the place religion has at St. Christopher's. They hardly could. A religious approach to life has permeated every aspect of the Hospice since before its conception. An agnostic St. Christopher's would be like bread without salt.
>
> The first breath of religious inspiration was, in a sense, in 1945, when Cicely asked what she should do with her life in gratitude for her conversion to Christianity. During the three years she had to wait for the answer and the nineteen years working to create a context for its expression, this wind was always behind her back, inspiring her and those she gathered around her. Before the first spit was dug the Bishop of Stepney articulated their aim, "so to minister to the whole personality that those whom we shall serve may be able to lose their fear of death and to find in it, not primarily a end of life in this world, but the beginning of a fuller life in the world to come." A bare two days after the Hospice had been

officially opened, Cicely wrote to the Bishop, "Today we are having our first Communion Service, with two patients down from the wards in their beds, so we have really gone straight on with the important things." (du Boulay, 1984, p. 160)

St. Christopher opened its doors in 1967. A year later, Dr. Saunders arranged for me to have a month as a work visitor at St. Christopher's in August of 1968. My husband and I took our children for a month's holiday beforehand in Europe. From the time we left France behind and crossed the Channel for England, until I faced the threshold of St. Christopher's, I had qualms. What had I committed myself to? Our vagabond sightseeing had been such a treat, I felt out of tune and ill equipped to be reincarnated as a nurse taking care of seriously ill people. Settling into a little house we had rented for the month made each of us feel all thumbs. It had a lovely well-groomed garden in the back—but no telephone. The tiny kitchen with skimpy stove, skimpier refrigerator, a hot water heater that couldn't supply the bath water, laundry water, and dishwater we needed in one day made us feel like giants in a midget's house. Letting two 14-year-old girls and a 16-year-old boy loose on London seemed very risky. Changing from driving ourselves to using the complicated bus and underground diminished our self-confidence. Crossing the streets, let alone driving on them, was unnerving. The flower-filled bay windows of St Christopher's Hospice failed to cheer me.

I stumbled into a new world. Once through the door, something happened. At the far end of the room, Peggy, the receptionist, made me feel the guest they had all been waiting for. The tide had turned and I became completely engaged in life at St. Christopher's. The week on each of the three wards and another week with other backstage offices allowed me to take part in hands-on care and to see the administrative workings behind the scenes. The hospice building had the same meager mechanical equipment as our rented house did; plumbing rudimentary by our standards, little closet space, lighting that was skimpy, and, worst of all, beds that were without a crank, let alone a motor to raise the head of the bed. I didn't have the sense of a germ-free environment but these crude material things soon slipped into the realm of the unimportant. The presence of colleagues always on the ready to help lift a heavy patient was far nicer than a gatch. The nurses weren't just willing to help one another, they seemed to anticipate what was about to be needed and be there to help. The patients, the families, the kitchen help, the dustmen, and the volunteers had the same spirit. Since most rooms had four patient beds and lots of space for visitors around them, it was easy to see what was needed, to offer help, and to recognize when I could be an intrusion.

I had expected to see patients comfortable, active, and with lots of visitors, but the spirit of give and take—allowing people to be themselves—

made individuals stand out. Getting to know the patients was easily done while helping them eat, sitting with them in the garden, and meeting their families. Doctors expected nurses to make rounds with them from bed to bed. The four-bedded rooms meant patients and families had space to become friends, but the individual spaces were large enough to allow them to be alone when that was needed by drawing curtains.

Situated on the hill of London's Crystal Palace and in a middle upper-class suburb, St. Christopher's Hospice has a sweeping view of London, with St. Paul's dome in the center. In a neighborhood of large residences with gardens surrounded by brick walls, the garden at St. Christopher's is patterned after their neighbors'. Over one wall, a branch of a neighbor's pear tree drops pears into St. Christopher's garden. The child day-care center on the first floor brought children into the dining room and they used the garden's flagstone walks to ride their trikes. In good weather it's a favored spot for everyone to have afternoon tea, including the children.

The chapel is seen first as one walks from the parking lot to the door. Through large windows there is a triptych with Christ on the cross, above the altar. The paintings of Marian Bohusz are hung throughout the public rooms. The intense colors in strong strokes give life to Christ as caregiver.

On the next floor is a pub, serving tea in the afternoon and drinks in the evening for patients, families, and staff. What happens there varies from reading racing forms, betting, knitting, listening to the "tellie," and talking politics. The environment in itself is supportive and therapeutic to create a sharing community of patients, families, and caregivers that inspires helping one another in the physical and spiritual work to be done. Could such a setting be transported across the Atlantic and re-created in a medical metropolis such as the Yale-New Haven Medical Center?

Fortunately, reform was in the air on my return from St. Christopher's. Protests against the war in Vietnam, as well as the movements for civil rights, women's rights, and patients' rights, were gathering momentum. Human values and medical ethics were at last being discussed in medical centers and were bringing theologians, philosophers, social scientists, physicians, and nurses together. The need for interdisciplinary collaboration was coming to the surface. Limitless technological possibilities of medical science were now being examined for short-term and long-term effects on the quality of life.

Dr. Edmund Pellegrino's writings on medical ethics and humanistic treatment had influenced my thinking for 30 years. In a recent article, he calls for a practice of clinical medicine that "seeks a right and good healing decision and action for a particular patient" that looks to choosing "what *ought* to be done" from among the many things that can be done for an individual patient in a particular clinical circumstance (Siegler, Pellegrino, & Singer, 1990).

Duff and Hollingshead's *Sickness and Society* (1968) had described what happened when patients were dying in our own medical center. Of the 161 patients they studied, 25 percent died. In most cases, the physician and family decided to keep the sick person from knowing the truth about his or her condition and its expected outcome. Often it was a family member who initiated this approach, instructing the physician not to tell the patient the truth. Protecting the patient from the diagnosis and prognosis of his or her illness gave rise to complicated maneuvers to keep the sick person from knowing the truth. Physicians controlled decision making by withholding information about treatment alternatives as well as prognosis from both patients and families, and were usually reluctant to discontinue intensive treatment even though patients were getting worse: "With rare exceptions, the physicians continued, long after death was imminent, to apply treatment measures to combat disease, offering hope to the patient and the family that 'in this instance' they might be effective. They did not tell the patients that there was little hope" (Duff & Hollingshead, 1968, p. 313).

Patients and spouses pressed physicians to persist in treatment in the hope of arresting the ravages of the disease. The pressure on the doctors was so strong that "even when a patient was dying they offered the *image of hope*" and used therapies they knew had little value.

Duff and Hollingshead (1968) described the strained relationships that ensued between the dying person, the family members, and the professional caregivers. Lack of involvement, evasion, deception, fear, frustration, and general dissatisfaction pervaded in the final days of the patient's life. The medical staff concentrated on the development of the disease and discussed the patient's situation and the treatment in scientific terms. As the patient's condition worsened, many doctors and nurses were so involved in the techniques, procedures, and machines to keep the patient alive that they seemed to be a committee with its attention focused on "the disease in the body in the bed."

When death came, even though it had been expected for days, weeks, or months, a reaction of "shock, depression, relief, grief, or even hysteria" engulfed the group. Physicians, nurses, technicians, and aides concentrated their attention on the tasks to be done to make the room ready for the next patient (Duff & Hollingshead, 1968, Chapter 15). Just before his book was published, Ray Duff feared he had risked his academic tenure for his candid view of patients' lives in our hospitals. Although there were sharp criticisms from his colleagues, the book met national acclaim. He was reappointed although considered a rebel.

What a sharp contrast this was to the care I had witnessed at St. Christopher's. Was it feasible to change our way of care? How could it be done? Who could be counted on to join such a project? These thoughts were in my mind one day as I came to a street crossing of the Yale-New Haven Medical Center. Serendipity, fate, chance, or a divine being must have brought Dr. Duff, Dr. Morris Wessel, the Reverend Edward Dobihal, and myself to that spot at the same time. It was noon and we went to lunch.

There, I told them what was on my mind. That lunch led to weekly lunch meetings over the next few months. We made it our business to ask nurses on the clinical settings which doctors stood by their dying patients; the names of the oncologist and breast surgeon, Dr. Ira Goldenberg and Dr. Robert Scheig, a specialist in liver disease, were given again and again. They joined the luncheon club.

The approach we settled on was an exploratory study. By giving care ourselves within the settings available—outpatient clinic, in the home, in the hospital, or in a nursing home—we could see how much we could change the settings that Duff and Hollingshead described. If we experienced obstacles of dying patients in the existing system, we would then have our own experiences as evidence that a more radical approach was needed, such as a setting as St. Christopher's.

As we talked about the problems colleagues faced in caring for terminally ill patients, somewhat to our surprise, they talked more about situations of a terminal illness in their personal lives than in their professional work. Even those who were in a position of power in the medical institution or the Yale community were not successful in persuading those who care for a friend or relative to stop intensive therapy when it was no longer effective. Dr. Goldenberg's account of his brother's death was typical:

> My brother died in a hospital a couple of years ago, and what a cold and austere reception greeted us when we arrived at the hospital after he had died. He was in critical condition for a long time and it didn't come as any surprise, but it didn't make it any easier, of course. He died after we had left the hospital for the evening, and then on the phone I was told that he had died and we came back in. The doctor wasn't there, the house staff wasn't there, and the nurses had just changed shifts and the one who was on didn't know what had really gone on, and it was a pretty upsetting kind of thing. I don't think I will ever forget that experience. Now I make it my business to be sure to sit and talk with the family at length after the patient has died. (taped discussion)

During the next three months, our luncheon club became a small, interdisciplinary team consisting of three doctors (a surgeon, a pediatrician, and an internist), the chaplain, and myself, a nurse. We shared our experiences, reviewed the literature, and planned an approach. To reproduce St. Christopher's seemed too grand and difficult a beginning. We decided to work for change within the existing health care system and to keep a running record of our efforts to get a sense of what was possible, what and who could help, sense the barriers, and how to get over them.

Our questions came from our experience as clinicians. A memorandum Morris Wessel wrote at the time set the stage for the study. He felt our focus should be on *our* experience:

Never mind the literature at this point.... Patients and families have needs not clearly understood by the professionals; care, and consequently communication break down. I don't think anyone thinks that they are doing the best job possible. They don't have any training in what the job is. If the primary goal is to cure, maybe we should emphasize the other job in terminal situations—to comfort.... Maimonides said: Cure when possible, comfort always.

Do all professionals have the same understanding of goals, needs and how to meet them?

Why is it that no one sees the family afterwards? Is it that the doctor doesn't extend himself? Is it because the family feels so keenly that the doctor failed that they don't want to see him?

Is there a way we could allow a doctor or nurse to accept feelings, sometimes hostile and sometimes angry, because the patient died, yet still stay in the picture by calling, writing or talking? I think the professional can still "be nice" to the family no matter how the family feels towards him. It will go a long way in establishing that we care enough to comfort them. We need to ask why the families are not comforted by the physician.

I don't think there is a lack of wish to help the family but rather a lack of know-how. Callousness is a defense stemming from ignorance. What is the doctor trying to do? No one ever told him or showed him how to do it. It is not only doctors. When a priest baptizes a premature infant, I can rarely get him to go and chat with the mother. His job is done, he has "saved the baby." The mother, in most instances, is not his parishioner.

Dr. Goldenberg felt we could improve the situation for patients in the acute tertiary medical center by an intensive, single-handed effort. In his experience, when a terminally ill patient in his care arrived at the hospital, he made it his business to get there as quickly after arrival as possible to smooth over rough spots: Admitting the patient, starting intravenous fluids, and getting chest films were part of his usual routine in settling the patient in by supper time. He said, "It's amazing how much more comfortable the patients become... knowing that there is someone they can turn to." He recognized, however, that it would be hard to change staff attitudes and described a physician's account of the staff response in admitting a patient. He noticed the ward secretary's unsympathetic response, "Oh, Mrs. So and So is coming back again, what's wrong *now*?" He felt the antagonism was not on the part of the secretary alone, but a reflection of the attitude prevalent among all hospital caregivers. Often it was the intern who grumbled on hearing that a terminally ill patient was coming back, "Oh, my God, is she coming in again? What for this time?" Dr. Goldenberg said, "It was as if there was something evil about being sick or that these people just get in the way. In the way of what, I'm not sure, because it seems to me that every one of these patients has something to offer insofar as the learning experience of the house officers is concerned, and God knows these people need the house officers to help."

We soon agreed on his proposal that we could recommend change from a position of greater strength if we could cite our problems and our experience in attempting to solve them within our own institution.

We expected to face such questions as: When medicines do not alleviate pain, can we find more effective ones or more appropriate dosages to keep the patient comfortable, yet aware and alert? We wondered whether we could find substitutes for heroin and cocaine. Would we be able to include families in the total picture? Could we make the experience of dying not just tolerable but a time of accomplishment for the patient, the family, and the professional? How could we keep in contact with the survivors and help them? How much leeway could there be in the rules and regulations of hospitals, nursing homes, and home care services? How well could an "extra" team function in an institution, and how well would the team members work with one another? If there were conflicts, how would they be resolved?

We considered those facing terminal illness in a broad sense—not only the patient with a disease that does not respond to curative treatment but a cluster of people, including those involved professionally, those involved as family members, and those involved in any other way in the patient's orbit. We reached for the focal point that Cicely Saunders inspired in us: "It is the patient who is, or who should be, in the center. The question is *his* because it is his situation and he is the person who matters" (Saunders, 1969).

Focus on the patient and family meant being sensitive to the patient's lifestyle and attuning our care to fit that lifestyle. We needed the patient's thoughts and feelings as well as our own. Ida Orlando had developed the manner of nurse and patient working together: listening to the patient's words and inflections, observing the patient's looks and gestures, and making sure the nurse had heard correctly before deciding on the way to go (Orlando, 1961).

We wanted maximum freedom to have a new look at a familiar situation, going into it with as few preconceptions as possible. Our goal was to describe the situation in which patients found themselves, to learn what they wanted for themselves and their families, and to follow our instincts and judgment in providing for those needs and then to see what happened.

To collect the data, we kept a log and diary, giving us recall to our actions, thoughts, and feelings. We decided on an exploratory and descriptive field study with ourselves as participant-observers. We presented ourselves to patients and families as an interdisciplinary team, available to join in their care. They were told that we were engaged in a study, were keeping diaries, would want access to their clinical records, and that once the study was finished, it would be published. (Their names would not be used; we would use pseudonyms). In exchange, we gave them assurance they could call on us to help where and when they needed our care. The physician of the team, Dr. Goldenberg, served as the patient's physician in all except two cases. Ultimately, there were two nurses, the hospital chaplain, and two Catholic priests on the patient care team, as well as the physician.

Fitting ourselves as best we could into the settings in which the patients were being cared for, the team shared the work with the doctors, nurses, social workers, and chaplains already involved with the patient in each setting.

In addition to the nurses' diaries, the Catholic priests taped their conversations with patients. All materials were transcribed, typed, and kept in chronologic order. For the monthly interdisciplinary research team meetings, a stenotypist gave a verbatim record of discussions. The pool of data filled 16 volumes of observations, actions, and thoughts—a permanent record that can always be delved in. We committed ourselves to two years of work. The study proposal was sent to the Nursing Resources Division of the United States Public Health Service, requesting funds for the Yale University School of Nursing as sponsor, myself as principal investigator, and other members (Dobihal, Goldenberg, and Wessel) as coinvestigators.

I was ready to don my white uniform and cap and to roll up my sleeves. In January 1969, we felt so confident and eager that we began without waiting for the grant to be in hand. Dean Margaret Arnstein, my successor in the Deanship, gave interim support from a faculty research development fund. In August, *A Nurses Study of Care for Dying Patients* (U.S.P.H.S. 1-R21-NU-00352-01) was awarded $31,209 for each of two years. The American Nurses Foundation awarded another $4,200. In my eagerness to begin and my concern to have the means to cover costs, I presented a budget that was predictably inadequate.

We did not think of the work as scientific; we had no hypotheses to test or relationships to search. The question was: Can a mode of care for dying patients coexist in a health system geared to cure? We wanted a record of what we did to see if and how it helped. An attempt to put them into action in the existing system could shed light on policy decision: Where and how can we meet the needs of those facing a terminal illness?

Did the standard practice of physicians to pursue curative treatment when the illness progressed relieve or cause suffering not only because of the disease but also because of the iatrogenic effects of treatment? Could communication and participation in reaching decisions between patients, doctors, nurses, social workers, and family members be improved? We knew it was usual for the doctor to make decisions without discussing the possible options or the likelihood of success and the treatments undertaken. We knew patients were moved from one institution or agency to another, depending on their condition and treatment—acute, recuperative, chronic, hopeless. Could continuity of care be achieved?

When medical treatment no longer checked the progress of a degenerative disease such as cancer, did nurses and physicians feel as helpless as their patients and as unhappy with their care? Could a group of professionals from different disciplines share the work so that the patient and family were supported as whole human beings, not just as a sick individual? What pharmacologic methods were customary in relieving pain? Would it be difficult to change attitudes and practice toward palliation? Did we have the skills to help?

For questions such as these, we needed to describe what we saw and if in our clinical judgment we believed an action or approach was not appropriate, we had the freedom to make a change. We realized academic colleagues would fault descriptive data as loose and unreliable, but my years as caregiver and nurse educator made me confident in nursing notes as a source of data. While we knew the participant observer role evokes the criticism of nonobjectivity, we were willing to accept that limitation of the study, realizing that there is a limitation to the nonparticipant observer who also sees something "wrong" being done and is unable to correct it.

From the beginning, we assumed that the relationship between caregiver and patient would influence how much and from whom help was "help" and that the relationship between colleagues would also affect our success. We found it more difficult to recall and analyze our failures than our triumphs. Struggle for control, mistrust, biases, and aversions came as a surprise. Our ideals were so lofty! Seeing ourselves in true light led us to matching patient and caregiver.

Kathy Klauss, attractive, young, quiet, and proficient in her physical care, was well suited to the self-contained patient. Those who expressed their thoughts or feelings were more likely to work with me. Dr. Goldenberg appeared much more at ease with the well-dressed, better educated, middle- to upper-class patient, leaving to Kathy or myself those who were tearful or depressed and those who needed more time, patience, support, and instruction.

Patients knew not to break into tears in front of Dr. Goldenberg. However, we were touched when patients burst out (as many did), "All Dr. G. has to do is walk into the room and I feel better!"

In four instances, patients and their families were little more than strangers to us because there was so little time. Two patients died within 48 hours, one lived 10 days but was in a coma most of the time. Another patient, the first, lived 10 days. My time with her involved so many tests and treatments (which were new to me) that we had little time for getting to know one another but staff nurses ordinarily have less.

Nurses have a rich opportunity to listen and observe, although they may not take it or may be robbed of it in managing a service or when there are too few nurses to care for too many patients. In the study, Kathy Klauss and I were free of those impediments; we were special nurses who assumed the responsibility for only a few patients at the same time. Caring for patients in their own homes was the best way we came to know the patients. They were on their own "turf," surrounded by objects that had special meaning to them and where their friends and relations were around them helping or not helping. It wasn't long before we realized we were missing two important episodes in the case histories of terminally ill patients: what had been happening before it was noticed that something was wrong and how they came to realize they were ill. We retrieved that information by asking each patient to recollect, which they did gladly. Loss and hard times were apparent in every case but one—loss of someone close who had died, of a home, a job, a neighborhood. The 13-year-old son of a patient who had been widowed for three years put us on the search. He said, "I wish my Mom would marry again. Married women don't get cancer so much."

The patients' remembrances of how it had dawned on them that something was wrong and how long it was until those fears were shared and confirmed had bearings on the doctor-patient relationship throughout the illness. Trust, blame, and guilt in the beginning could be felt at the end. A patient's premonition was not enough evidence to doctors; it was feeling a lump that moved them to act. From the time of diagnosis to surgery was a time of suspense and pressure to take action. The quality of the time from surgery to talking about what was found varied. If patients and doctors were able to be open with one another or if patients and doctors were not able to or interested in talking about the illness, the relationship went well. If patients wanted to be told and the doctor didn't want to tell, there was trouble and lingering misgivings.

Talking about the illness was a rich area to study, not only in the many issues it raised but also in how we ourselves engaged in it. We caught ourselves omitting the words *cancer* and *dying*. We felt how hard it is to give bad news, but before the study was over we had the opportunity to improve in our telling of the truth and to recognize when patients didn't want to hear or talk about bad news. Considering the changes being made in medical and nursing practice in the mid-sixties and the patients' right to know, doctors and nurses were learning a new way to speak and act—one that had not been part of their professional education.

The patients' lives while in our care were filled with uncertainty. Hearing their ways of expressing it seemed so accurate, we chose not to use higher conceptual language. "What's coming next?" "Am I slipping?" "Will the money last?" "Where will it end?" were their expressions. The battle with helplessness was a challenge to them and to us. We learned to wage that war together. For some patients, it was more difficult than others.

Even though the patients were referred to us because they were thought to be dying, 6 of the 24 patients agreed to vigorous curative treatment. The term used was "furor therapeuticus." Seeing a patient through such treatment was very painful. The patients seemed too frail for cryosurgery, laminectomy, radiation, and chemotherapy. It seemed as if the physicians couldn't keep from doing something, even on the downhill course. When at last such therapy was ended, all six patients "collapsed." One died, two went into coma but rallied when allowed to rest, and two had more unpleasant symptoms after the treatment than they had before. One patient spent four months in the hospital using every possible cure offered to her. She had one day at home and then was admitted to the medical intensive care unit where she died within hours.

We were not successful in persuading the doctors to take a palliative approach for these patients. We did not allay their fears or lower their resistance in using morphine.

Despite that, patients, families, and caregivers had more good times and success in getting comfortable than we had expected. It was good times on the run. Keeping an open eye to see the funny side, having long talks, helping the patient and family members to be open with each other, and advising patients to pace themselves were strategies of comforting that made up for the primitive pharmacologic techniques of pain control.

Facing the unknown took time and courage. Patients asked: "What's coming next"? "How long will it be?" "What's to become of me?" These were easy questions to understand and opened the way to discussing tangible worries. It was harder when patients had dreams or spoke in metaphor. Speaking in metaphor was often seen by patients' families as confusion but they could help us in deciphering the message. For example, "The square under the tree with only four bicycles" turned out to mean "The family cemetery plot has only four grave sites; we need more for my family alone."

To our surprise, few of the people for whom we cared had witnessed a death. They needed support and guidance in this experience, whether they were patients or families. They felt "the gulf getting wider" and thought "I have nothing to hold on to." Being there and helping patient and family to "hang on" or "let go" seemed very much like the midwife's role in labor and delivery.

The caregivers had little experience in helping survivors through loss to recovery. It was nothing we had done as professionals, but having been in such close communication with families through the illness, we felt the loss and could anticipate what they might need.

The diaries are full of observations and comments on the relationships among the caregivers and the settings in which we worked. The meetings of the interdisciplinary and research teams were taped. Our attempts to work together harmoniously and effectively were, on the whole, successful in our judgment, but it wasn't easy. We began with a sense of trust but often found ourselves lacking trust. Trust needed constant cultivation. Struggles for leadership were difficult between myself, an ex-Dean now in the role of a nurse practitioner, and Dr. Goldenberg, a full Professor and the patients' doctor.

We came away from the study still a team, with four of the members as founders and incorporators of the Board of the Connecticut Hospice. The planning of the hospice took three years until the beginning of home care services and nine years before the inpatient building opened its doors.

References

Cancer Care, Inc. of the National Cancer Foundation. (1971). *Catastrophic illness in the seventies: Critical issues and complex decisions.* New York: Cancer Care, Inc.

du Boulay, S. (1984). *Cicely Saunders, the founder of the modern hospice movement.* London: Hodder & Stoughton.

Duff, R. S., & Hollingshead, A. B. (1968). *Sickness and society.* New York: Harper & Row.

Henderson, V. (1966). *The nature of nursing.* New York: Macmillan.

Orlando, I. J. (1961). *The dynamic nurse-patient relationship.* New York: G. P. Putnam's Sons.

Quint, J. C. (1967). *The nurse and the dying patient.* New York: Macmillan.

Saunders, C. (1965). Watch with me. *Nursing Times,* Nov. 26.

Saunders, C. (1969). The moment of truth. In L. Pearson (Ed.), *Care of the dying person.* Cleveland: Case Western Reserve Press.

Siegler, M., Pellegrino, E. D., & Singer, P. A. (1990). Clinical medical ethics. *The Journal of Clinical Ethics, 1.*

Four

Attitudes toward Death: A Personal Perspective

An Interview with Herman Feifel, Conducted by Inge Corless, 1991

Herman Feifel

For more than 30 years, Herman Feifel has been a pioneering researcher in the area of death and dying. His work challenged the entrenched taboo that had previously discouraged scientific study in this area, and earned him his well-justified international reputation as "the founder of modern death psychology." Two generations of colleagues and students have been influenced by his perspectives and thinking, which have been a prime force in altering cultural regard and orientation concerning dying, death, and bereavement. In these and the related areas of gerontology, personality, psychotherapy, and religious experience, his publications encompass two major books and more than 100 articles and chapters, including his groundbreaking volume, The Meaning of Death. *The American Scientist has characterized Dr. Feifel's work "as basic and foundational on the psychological and philosophical meaning of death in contemporary society." The fact that his work has been published in the scholarly journals of medicine, nursing social work, history, religion, and in the popular media, clearly documents the importance of his research, as well as the success of his efforts throughout his distinguished career to "reach out" and make psychology relevant in society at large.*

He has received various honors and awards, among which are the Distinguished Scientific Achievement Award of the California State Psychological Association, appointment as a National Lecturer by Sigma Xi, the Harold M. Hildreth Award from APA's Division of Psychologists in Public Service, Special Commendation from the Chief Medical Director of the VA, the Distinguished Human Service Award from Yeshiva University, designation as Distinguished Practitioner of Psychology by the National Academies of Practice, and honorary Doctor of Human Letters from the University of Judaism, and the Distinguished Service Medallion from the Los Angeles County/University of Southern California Medical Center. He has served as consultant to the governments of Israel and Canada and, in recent years, has delievered invited keynote addresses at international conferences in England, Sweden, Israel, and Canada.

Herman Feifel (HF), a prime force in the modern death movement, kindly consented to be interviewed via telephone for this book by one of the editors, Inge Corless (IC). The remarks below capture the essence of his responses to a number of broad questions posed to him.

IC: When did death and dying become a field for scholarly inquiry?

HF: Although there were a number of preceding fitful summer lightening flashes, I think it was the events of World War II and their aftermath that served as the major impetus for what we term the "modern death movement." That war brought with it an intensified awareness of life's transience, as did the advent of the A-bomb with its threat to the future of humanity, history, as well as society. In the context of millions of dead people, the Holocaust, and potential for future mega-death, issues of meaning, purpose, and redemption became reawakened in a generation heretofore distanced from robust philosophic and religious beliefs that could transcend death. These considerations were additionally fueled by the failing gods of Freudianism and Marxism, and disillusionment with the liberal belief of the inevitability of progress. Reexamination of the purpose of life and presence of death became more impelling in this context. A burgeoning humanism and growing receptivity to the philosophy of existentialism, with its emphasis on death as close to the center of the human condition, also kindled interest in the problem of death.

More germane on the scientific side, there was growing regard for the pulsation of human life, and changes in the notion of what the scientific enterprise should be about. Challenges to worship of a mathematical physics paradigm began to permit more meaningful room for a model that would deal with the richness of life; with humanity instead of a machine; that would encompass greater representation of the future—and death—along with the past and present, in comprehending personality, psychopathology, and behavior. And, certainly, not to be slighted, were advances occurring in medical technology that were transforming the nature and place of death. Death from degenerative rather than acute infectious diseases in the big hospital was now becoming the characteristic mode of departing from life. A principal spinoff of this development was an elongation factor in the dying process, forcing society to look at death more steadily and unwaveringly. Indeed, the very definition of death became a matter of contention.

To answer the question more concretely, many scholars attribute provenance of the modern death movement to a symposium I organized titled, "The Concept of Death and Its Relation to Behavior," which was presented at the 1956 annual convention of the American Psychological Association in Chicago. The symposium served as a basis for the book *The Meaning of Death*, which was published in 1959 by McGraw-Hill.

Other nourishing elements in this frame were a revival of consumerist, populist, and ethnic dispositions during the 1960s and 1970s that attempted to recapture greater governance over one's life—including the sectors of dying, death, and grief. A net result of these attitudes was a quickening perception that dying and death were issues of legitimate concern to the scholarly community and could be a fertile venture.

A personal note in this regard—and one that may be of some psychobiographical pertinence. In 1945, I was stationed on the island of Tinian in the Marianas, in readiness for an anticipated invasion of the Japanese mainland. This was the island from which the *Enola Gay* took off in August, 1945, to bomb Hiroshima and usher in the age of megadeath. In the Feifel family album, there is a picture of me in shorts snapped two days after the bombing standing next to the *Enola Gay*.

IC: Were the 1956 symposium proceedings published, as well as your book?

HF: I don't think the proceedings were published, although they were privately shared with interested individuals. The essence of what was said in the symposium, however, was incorporated in the book, *The Meaning of Death* (1959). Participants in that 1956 historic symposium were Irving E. Alexander, of Duke University; Jacob Taubes, a philosopher of religion who gravitated to East Germany a few years later; Arnold Hutschnecker, an internist-psychosomaticist and author of the then best-selling book *The Will to Live*; and myself. The symposium was further graced by the insightful remarks of our discussant, Gardner Murphy, then Director of Research at the Menninger Foundation.

IC: What are the issues today as compared with when the field began?

HF: In a fundamental sense, the issues are pretty much the same: What is death doing in our midst and how do we relate to and cope with it? Each generation struggles to generate its own responses.

At the beginning, a salient issue was to establish the validity of the field and to cultivate hospitality to our efforts. This was not easy because of the general cultural avoidance of and gingerness toward the topic due to, as I have already intimated, an impoverishment of religious beliefs and philosophic concepts with which to transcend death, and a regnant logical positivistic model of the scientific task at theoretical levels. The latter meant favoring problems and areas that yielded easily to concrete operations that were repeatable or public. Unfortunately, positivism leaned toward splitting the world of science and the world of man. Consequently, receptivity to thanatological issues by the scientific community was not exactly overwhelming.

Among the initiates, investigations such as the presence or absence of death fear and anxiety in people held sway. This was pursued in differing populations—for example, terminally ill patients compared to healthy persons, religiously inclined individuals versus those of more materialistic bent, etc. There was also examination of the kinds of attitudes toward death that people held. A little later, studies focused on such dimensions as psychosocial aspects, empowerment of the patient in decision making, rehumanizing the orientation of health care providers toward the terminally ill and survivors, and elevating recognition by health care givers of the powerful and authentic contribution that comfort and care could make in treatment of the dying when cure was not in the cards. Dying was promulgated as a constitutive part of living and not a time to foster "social death" in the terminally ill. The hospice movement, of course, became an exemplar of this orientation.

Although a number of these perspectives are still not completely integrated by some health professionals, there is no doubt that endeavors of the thanatological community are resulting in expanded interest in and acceptance by the scholarly community, arts and humanities, media, and general public, of such matters as dying, death, and mourning.

Currently, there is much greater appreciation that death is multisplendored and requires an interdisciplinary approach to command the richness and fullness of what death means to people and how they deal with its existence. Manifestly, we now possess a corpus of knowledge and methodological sophistication not available to us in the early days. We realize that attitudes toward death are not unitary or monolithic, and that covert as well as overt attitudes exist. Research suggests that in the face of death, the human mind apparently operates simultaneously at various levels of reality, or finite provinces of meaning, each of which can be somewhat autonomous. The challenge is now to tease out and define oscillating feelings about death which many of us hold.

Also, the importance of ethical, legal, economic, and spiritual dimensions presently loom much larger as relevancies compared to the old days. Moreover, there is enhanced realization that death is for all seasons—operative throughout the life-span, not just lodged in the ken of the old and dying, combat soldier, or suicidally inclined person. Attention to the impact of death on siblings, survivors, organizations, and the community is also on the agenda. We are currently more sensitive to the significance of the future and concepts of death in our prototypes of personality, psychopathology, psychotherapy, and behavior. Most models pay tribute to the past—to the importance of the early years of life in steering later adult conduct—note the Jesuit outlook, psychoanalysis, and the psychologist John B. Watson's view in this respect. The movement is now a bit more worldly wise in this sphere. We realize that the past is consequential in influencing behavior but that we must additionally appraise the present life situation of the individual—for example, ongoing relations with an employer, spouse, and peers. However, to fully grasp what human beings are about, and what motivates behavior and relationships, we must meld in the meaning of the future. In this purview, thanatology is indicating the potent role of the meaning of death for people. A person's philosophy of death is a large part of a philosophy of life. Indeed, one of the most distinguishing characteristics of the human species is our singular capacity to conceptualize the future and, along with it, inexorable death.

We are also more wary of developing a coercive orthodoxy of how to die and grieve—that what is considered "appropriate" and "proper" is more variegated than heretofore assumed, and that individual differences have to be considered more mindfully. Further, the role of dying and death and its association to such urgent social and political issues as abortion, euthanasia, capital punishment, war, and to such self-destructive behaviors as alcoholism, drug abuse, and certain acts of violence is more evident in our range of study these days. Additionally, in a shrinking world, it is being understood that cross-cultural views concerning dying, death, and bereavement may provide us with an additional entryway to enriching understanding of and bonds between peoples. Finally, in this shift of climate, a vigorous death education movement is emerging which perceives its mandate as altering cultural orientation, not just achieving a palliative denouement.

IC: Has the field had an influence on the social context or vice versa?

HF: This reminds me somewhat of the heredity-environment controversy. Both are intertwining and dovetail. As indicated in my response to your first question—the spinoff from two World Wars, development of atomic weaponry, and advances in medical technology, all had a marked steering impact on the emergence and rise of what we refer to today as the thanatological community. On our side, we, in the modern death movement, have been responsible for brushing aside curtains of avoidance and silence surrounding death, and are assisting in clarifying the nature of human beings. We have stirred the arts and humanities, prodded medicine to humanize its relationships with patients and survivors, and cautioned against truncating the grieving process. We have elevated collegial and civic consciousness that dying is not just a biological happening but a human one as well; even goaded governmental legislation in this area. Additionally, in responding to the dying and bereaved, we are pointing out the need to address the soul as well as body. We are underlining that, in the final analysis, the greatest democracy of all is death and that we are all linked to a common humanity. In summation, both social context and the death movement have been mutually impregnating.

IC: Let's go back to the notion of empowering patients. Are you really saying that individuals have the right to make a choice as to the timing of their own death?

HF: More or less, yes. But this is not a simple matter. The patient certainly should be a main player in this decision making. Nevertheless, there are other considerations that conjoin—impact on the family, violence to one's cultural and religious philosophy, etc. True, the individual may feel, "It's my life. I don't care what anyone else thinks." Still, it is as a pebble being dropped into water where ripples can go far. Obviously, placing the timing of one's death exclusively in the hands of the individual poses a thorny bedeviling situation of conflict between individual and society. Power of decision and direction of action will reflect such varying factors as personality, situational context, cultural and religious beliefs, societal demands, even epoch. What is still required at this stage, I think, is that the patient's input concerning treatment, mode of death, and manner of burial have to be enlarged and genuinely considered.

Plainly, one of the primary controls society possesses is its ability to "give" death to, and to "remove" its possibility from, people. The physician, for example, who finds himself in a position of managing death is constrained by the state and religion: "non nocere" and "you shall not murder." As citizens, we are informed that we cannot kill a person just because we don't relish his comments. Control over death in our society is zealously guarded by the state and religion. The state says, "I shall punish or kill you if you murder someone else." You can do so only when I give permission, for example, in "carrying out your duties as a policeman" or "as a soldier during war." Religion likewise proscribes personal taking of one's life by indicating that since life is a gift of God, only God should take it. The suicidal individual proclaims that the time of death will occur "when I decide." I think this is why the act of suicide can be so unsettling for many of us. Outside the usual guilt it invokes and rent in the social fabric it can occasion, it signals that dominion over death is being eroded for the state and religious authorities. In a related way, some of the violence of our times may be conceptualized as an active response to an unmastered dread of death. The ideological attempt is made to transform death from an internal inevitability against which one is helpless, to an external threat over which one has some influence. Death is then understood as resulting mainly from the hostility of others. Violence is used to vitiate or destroy the person or institution viewed as threatening injury or death. Violence furnishes certain individuals with a type of ascendancy— control if you will—and sense of triumph in enabling them to decide when and under what conditions they can inflict injury, murder others, or kill themselves.

Patently, this is an issue that impinges on a multitude of moral, ethical, legal, economic, and social aspects, in addition to our more specific patient/family/health care focus. We are now witness to an expanding dialogue and evaluation between health care givers and the community at large. Perhaps a new ethos, or more innovative options of response, will emerge that are more attuned to ongoing advances in medical technology and to changing social realities.

IC: What are some key current conceptual and methodological issues in the field?

HF: The key conceptual issue at this time is to probe the association between a person's weltaunschauung, or "world outlook," and its ties to the meaning of personal death. Understanding the linkage between the nature of man—who we are and what we are about—to dying, death, and bereavement is an essential master key. And this search will have to be carried out in settings that supersede the limitations of parochial disciplinary knowledge, and in which craftsmanship does not divorce itself from horizons.

Deeper scrutiny is also required of suggested connections between attitudes toward death and such vexing social issues as abortion, AIDS, euthanasia, and capital punishment, and to such behaviors as alcoholism, substance abuse, and certain forms of violence. After all, life-threatening behaviors involve possible injury or ultimate death to self and others. This approach could further instruct us about such dispositions as "partial death," "symbolic death," and grief over loss other than life, and to such experiences as stress, trauma, and disaster.

We need to consider more expansively the steering force of death at all age levels in the life-span, between child and hospice patient, and in differing populations. More longitudinal study is called for. A major base of our current data is cross-sectional and informs us more about "differences" rather than "changes" concerning death attitudes. Moreover, we have to be more cognizant of dissembling guises that fear of death can assume, for example, insomnia, depression, various psychosomatic symptoms, and even certain psychotic manifestations. At the beginning of my mushrooming scientific interest in the field, I remember noting how certain mentally ill patients defended themselves against anxiety of mortality by perceiving themselves to be God: "I am omniscient and all-powerful, therefore I am immune to death." Others stated, "I'm already dead." They had beaten death to the punch. "If you're already dead, you can't die, can you?" And, of course, we are not exactly suffering from a surfeit of generative theory-based formulations.

Our opportunity here is that we can "wear out" rather than "rust out."

IC: What are or were mistakes and pitfalls in the field? Have we learned anything from those errors?

HF: As I have indicated, we shall not do full justice to the field if mere accuracy and reliability become our icons and the ensuing information is irrelevant to the fundamental problem of "what is man." We must beware of venerating naked fact at the expense of meaning. This in no way signifies any denigration of efforts to improve the validity of our measuring instruments, and the field's requirement for more "hard" data. We have tended to become, however, a bit too beguiled by presumed "stages of dying" and "phases of mourning," imputing to them an ill-advised intimidating authority. Fortunately, a renewed awareness of individual differences and personhood is reentering our reflections.

Somewhat disquieting, also, has been the continuing stance by a number of health care providers that truth and hope have to be mutually exclusive. Just recently the dying Emperor of Japan, Hirohito, was shielded from knowledge of his oncoming death because in Japan this kind of truth is not to be shared with patients. This is not to deny the mental hygienic value of denial, and the supporting niche it offers in helping some of us cope with the stress of serious and terminal illness. Nevertheless, we must be cautious in letting this approach become self-defeating. Truth can be gentle and merciful. And it can help us in establishing priorities, shaping life goals, and in resensitizing us to the uniqueness and preciousness of life—in a way not available to us if we completely adopt an avoidance and denial posture. Another bothersome development is the entrance into the field of a number of dabblers and dilettantes which, I trust, will be a passing fancy.

In a certain sense, I think the movement has been fortunate from the beginning in avoiding a fixation on parts and on the diseased organ at the expense of the humanity of the patient. Indeed, this has been one of the salutary contributions that thanatology is providing to health care providers and to the general community.

In sum, we have wandered into some cul-de-sacs and lost some innocence in our progression into adulthood, but it appears that our growing maturity generally fits us well. But there is still much room for the prophet as well as priest.

IC: Have the media and "pop" psychology enhanced the field or created obstacles to the rigorous investigation of death and dying phenomena?

HF: The answer is both. As is the case with much knowledge, it can be used for good or evil, for enlightenment or for misleading purposes. The record has been a mélange. It has been good in the sense that it has brought to the consciousness of many people a perspective, along with information about dying and bereavement, that would otherwise not have occurred. A cheering upshot has been support for the rights of the terminally ill, and enhanced understanding of people in grief. One thinks of such recent television productions as "The Story of Brian" and "Bang the Drum Slowly."

On the other hand, in Janus-faced fashion, they have served to feed denial of death along with providing enhanced familiarity. Death has been given considerable but unrealistic portrayal via irenic and antiseptic Hollywood expirations, in the gothic fantasies of horror films, and in derivative television renditions. Death has also been depicted in a cops-and-robbers manner, where although one is killed, you show up in another television production or movie a few months later, resurrected and in good health. Even when realistic death is offered, as in deaths resulting from the recent Gulf War or deadly cyclone in Bangladesh, it presents itself too often as a type of fictive experience. We watch these reported events in the evening while eating our TV dinners. There is an inescapable trivializing of death in this process. Death becomes not really death. It's akin to the potential suicide who imagines that after he has committed the deed, he'll be able to look down from above and see the tears of sorrow and guilt his act has brought to the survivors. You're dead, but not really so.

In similar vein, a marked element of "pop" psychology tends to defang the penetrating significance of death for us. In its presentation, we become as rapid falcons in a snare enacting the flitting of a bat. The knowledge that "from the moment we are born we are old enough to die" becomes veiled. The great scandal that death poses for consciousness and life inclines toward interpreting it as fortuity or bad luck rather than as the predestined future of human beings. Domestication rather than fortitude and moral strength becomes our striving set.

IC: What do you think of the new near-death movement?

HF: As I have stated in a previous forum, the reported phenomena by a number of patients involved in clinical death merit scrutiny and recognition of their role in our psychic economy. What is somewhat disconcerting is the claim by some that this "proves" the existence of an afterlife. There may well be life after death, but vaulting to that conclusion from these narrated near-death experiences discloses more a leap of faith than well-advised scientific evaluation. This in no way disparages the reality of these occurrences for the people who declare them. I just think that in weighing the evidence in this area, we possess less farfetched and more parsimonious explanations within the canons of science to interpret these episodes. What strikes me about many of these out-of-body accounts is the hunger for meaning and purpose they suggest in an age of faltering faith. One may also view many of these narrations with their mostly propitious outcomes as a kind of personal reassurance that death is really "a gentle night," "a compassionate mother," or "family reunion" rather than "a devouring tiger" or "a cold and lonely realm."

IC: If you had to select three key questions or policies which you think are central to the field at this juncture, what would they be?

HF: I am still captured by the concept of how each one of us relates to and deals with the knowledge that death is inescapable—that it is a key issue for life. Throughout history, the idea of death has posed the eternal mystery which lies at the core of philosophy and religion. And, I think, it is not just conceptual caprice that suggests that recognition of death may be the prototype of human anxiety, that any loss may represent total loss. The notion of death offers us a royal entryway to stretching and enriching our comprehension of human conduct. I cannot envision definitive theories of personality and psychopathology that do not incorporate the guiding component of death in their deliberations.

Plainly, as emphasized in some of my previous remarks, this outlook must be grounded in a theory-based milieu linked to a methodology integrating alertness to multilevels and multimeanings, and emanating from varying ages and populations under differing conditions. Valid data, after all, constitute central material without which, as Gardner Murphy once commented, "all else is diluted and derivative." Furthermore, we must continue to involve ourselves with the interacting factors of the biological, psychological, and religious-cultural in our system of ideas about death.

I am also becoming persuaded that more earnest attention has to be accorded to stirrings for establishing a type of National Institute that would represent the thanatological community in the domains of health care and public policy. We now possess a ripeness of knowledge and readiness that are sufficiently firm to contribute to the *pro bono publico* in a unified and systematic way. A major caveat in this notion, however, is that we not become mesmerized by the world of politicians and lobbyists at the price of distorting and undercutting the humanity of persons, and that we persist in speaking to the soul along with sustaining the body.

IC: What sage advice do you have for readers of the book?

HF: That's a gracious sentiment, Inge—one with which I won't cavil too much. From my experiences in the field, what comes to mind are a number of Henny Youngman one-liners. I trust they won't sound overly bromidic:

Science equips but does not guide us. We should take to heart Thoreau's admonition that we not end up using improved means in the service of an unimproved end.

The best teachers and educators are not necessarily those who impart masses of information but those who help us to think and to comprehend the world in fresher and more discerning ways.

We should avoid dogmatic adherence to a pressuring orthodoxy of thinking that leads us to disregard evidence or indications that cannot be readily embraced by our dominant canons or beliefs. This type of accommodation may provide us with an equanimity of sorts but the passivity of imperious knowledge is indecent in a mysterious universe. Fancy words, perhaps, but we all know of prevailing modes of conceptualizing and treating the dying and bereaved where ashes rather than the fire is being extolled at the altar.

We should differentiate between what we know and what we don't; between performance and public relations—albeit the latter has its place.

I guess, in summation, our mandate is to amplify our sense of how death can serve life.

IC: How did you personally come to the field?

HF: I suppose it was a confluence of personal and professional reasons. I was reared in a religious household where matters of meaning and redemption were not alien. Achievement, a level of excellence, and contribution to the community were also implanted. And, of course, growing up meant establishing one's own identity. Early on, I grasped that somehow death represented the big veto to many of these deeds and possibilities.

As an adolescent, I remember the comforting impact of the movie, "Death Takes a Holiday," wherein death becomes humanized in the form of the young Frederic March and, even better, when he walks off with the apple-cheeked heroine Evelyn Venable, even though she knows what he represents and who he really is. Love conquers death. It provided me with a wishful de-demonizing of death. Apparently, apprehension about death was already a presence for me. There is the memory of my taking subway rides from deep in Brooklyn to make an early 8:00 A.M. class at the City College of New York, which was located in upper Manhattan—and during that ride, coming to the relieving deduction that I was probably the youngest person (I was then about 16 years of age) on that morning journey. Most of the riders going to work in that subway car would most likely have to die before me, so I was shielded for the time being. A tentative mastery over fear of death was being constructed.

And then, of course, there was the oncoming reality of World War II. It was not so much that I feared being found wanting in courage or acquitting myself decently, but the thought troubling me was that it could bring a terminus to my unassayed tasks and dreams. Events of the Holocaust and the legacy of my personal proximity to the B-29 planes that bombed Hiroshima and Nagasaki further stoked my concern with thanatological issues.

Perhaps more overriding, on a personal plane, was the death of my mother, the first parent to die. My regard for death was now irrevocably changed. The impact was quite different than even when I was on the receiving end of shots being fired against me not exactly in love. My wall of protection against death had now been breached. I could no longer command the intellectual illusion of my magic bullet-proof vest that would guard me and sustain the Psalmist's promise that, "though a thousand fall at your side, and a myriad at your right hand, it shall not come near you." I had now become emotionally vulnerable. For the first time, death was now truly in my gut. My mother died in 1952; my first article dealing with death was published in 1955.

On the professional side, my war experiences and the state of the post-World War II world sharpened second thoughts I was harboring concerning the authority of logical positivism in defining the scientific enterprise, particularly as it applied to psychology, my home territory. There was a growing conviction on my part that a vital psychology must be rooted in people, not in a mathematical physics paradigm, and that psychology was neglecting the existential richness of life. Accompanying this recognition was expanded realization that the role of the future in molding present behavior was being slighted, and that data explicating "stress," in which I had become interested, had concentrated mainly on contrived laboratory situations rather than on *in vivo* situations. All these aspects coalesced for me in the early 1950s and resulted in my organized focus on what we now refer to as thanatology. I judged this new path as one that would yield additional dimension and depth to my original interest and choice of psychology as a discipline—namely, to understand human conduct and what shapes it.

IC: If you had to do it all over, would you choose the field again?

HF: Despite the various vicissitudes I had to contend with, I probably would. Our closeness to and familiarity with the field makes many of us underestimate the sterling contributions we have made not only to professional health care but to a more meaningful cultural perspective about dying, death, and bereavement. As a movement, we have undergirded respect for the sanctity and meaningfulness of life at all ages, underscored our common humanity, and are providing a comprehension and images more adapted to contemporary death and mourning.

I personally am grateful to my residence in the thanatological household because it has broadened my grasp of who we are as persons, and who I am myself. And, certainly, one of the most precious by-products for me has been the resulting collegial friendships with an inspiring and committed bunch of characters. I truly don't know of a kindred group more perceptive of the human condition, and so full of quips and pranks, zest, and the juices of life (there must be something to this counterphobic "death water" business). An auspicious time may emerge in the future when we can "give" away the thanatological imperative to medicine, the behavioral sciences, and humanities. In the meantime, may we go from strength to strength.

Five

Society and the
Imperative of Death

Robert Fulton

Robert Fulton is Professor of Sociology and Direc-
tor of the Center for Death Education and Research at
the University of Minnesota. He has been involved in
the study of the sociology of death for over three de-
cades. In 1963, he conducted the first seminar on death
to be offered at an American university. In 1955, he ed-
ited Death and Identity, *a book that integrated and in-*
terpreted the significant social science research done
to that date in the area of death, grief, and bereave-
ment. The third revised edition of the book will be
published in 1993.

Fulton has participated in symposia and seminars
on grief and bereavement both nationally and interna-
tionally, and has contributed widely to the literature
on death. From 1970 to 1973, he served as the first as-
sociate editor of Omega, *the international journal on death. In 1978, he edited the book,*
Death and Dying: Challenge and Change, *in conjunction with The Course by Newspaper*
Project, which he coordinated under the auspices of the National Endowment for the Hu-
manities. This newspaper course on death and dying was taught in over 350 colleges and
universities and had a newspaper readership of over 12 million.

In 1985, Fulton was recipient of the Outstanding Achievement Award presented by
the National Forum for Death Education and Counseling in recognition of his outstanding
contributions to the field of Thanatology. In 1988, he was recognized by the National Cen-
ter for Death Education for his pioneer contributions and dedication to the field of Death
Education. In 1990, the Sociological Practice Association honored him with their Distin-
guished Career Award. Since 1971, he has been acknowledged by Who's Who in America
for his efforts on behalf of death education.

The image of death is anthropomorphic, and understandably so. It is the
individual who takes ill, sickens, and dies. It is the individual who is killed,
either intentionally or unintentionally. And it is the individual who ends
his or her own life or dies by misadventure.

But the fact of death confronts not only the individual; it is also a
challenge for society. This challenge, moreover, is not merely one of dealing with replacement, i.e., of taking measures to assure that there are a

sufficient number of human beings to carry out the duties and tasks of maintaining the social order; nor is it only one of meaning, rationale, or eschatology. The challenge for a society is far more critical, for death poses a threat to the very existence of society itself.

I have reference not to the mortal conflict that a society will engage in to defend the integrity of its soil or its people or to the threat posed by environmental disasters. If either of these phenomena is of sufficient magnitude, it can, of course, destroy a society. But these are usually perceived as external threats, and their occurrence elicits a conscious response. I have in mind, rather, the ontology, largely unreflected and unrecognized, that defines a society's essence, structures its institutions, and informs its relationship to the unknown.

In a modern society, such as the United States, where relationship with the unknown ("God" or "the impersonal forces of life") is at best ambiguous, if not ambivalent, the cultural myths and social traditions that have grown up around the phenomenon of death play a mostly unacknowledged but nonetheless significant role.

This significance has not gone entirely unnoticed, however. Anthropologists especially have long recognized the importance for society and the individual of death and its dramaturgy. Scholars such as Durkheim (1954), Van Gennep (1961), Radcliff-Brown (1952), Malinowski (1954), Hertz (1968), Evans-Pritchard (1965), Geertz (1957), Mandelbaum (1976), and others have emphasized the role of ritualized behavior in facilitating and preserving social life in the face of oblivion.

For Malinowski, death is a "centrifugal force" in a society, evidenced by fear, dismay, and demoralization. Funeral customs, he argues, powerfully counteract this destructive influence. The ritual drama of the funeral and other death-related ceremonies, as part of the sacralizing institution of religion, restore a society's weakened solidarity and reestablish its shaken morale (Malinowski, 1954, pp. 52–53). Van Gennep, moreover, would assign great importance to mortuary customs, because he finds those penitential ceremonies that incorporate the dead into the next world to be characteristically the most elaborate (Van Gennep, 1961, p. 146).

Sociologists, too, have noted how death affects the social fabric, though they have a different estimate of mortuary customs as they pertain to modern social life. Robert Blauner (1978), for example, in his influential essay, "Death and Social Structure," challenges Van Gennep's assessment of funerary rites. It is Blauner's contention that while many nonmodern societies organize their social life around the ever-present reality of death, modern societies need not. Increased life expectancy and other demographic shifts in society, secularization, medical bureaucratization, along with the isolation of the ill and dying person from family and community, all serve, as a consequence, to mute the grief experience of death. Rituals and mourning practices become more restrained, and the grief experience rationalized. The change in social organization found in large, complex societies, Blauner would argue, has not only relocated the setting of death but has also changed its social meaning and psychological valence to the extent that heretofore integrating funeral rituals and practices, despite their diminished place in social life, can, in fact, introduce discord and controversy (Blauner, 1978, pp. 35–39).

The late Talcott Parsons would concur with Blauner's assessment of the situation regarding modern responses to death, but he would accord a greater role to the individual in the direction and character that these responses have taken. Belief in the scientific tradition, acceptance of one's mortality within an eschatology that promises an afterlife, personal privacy, and social fluidity combined with "apathy," explain, he argues, modern society's reaction to personal loss and the modern encounter with death (Parsons, 1963, pp. 61–65).

But the sociological issue raised here transcends the pragmatic questions of how modern society confronts death or how and why an individual responds to loss. Death compels us to ask many other questions besides the quintessentially instrumental ones. For instance: Why and for what purpose do we human beings exist? To whom or to what are we responsible? Why does a particular society exist? How did it come into being? To whom or to what is it responsible? What must be done, or who or what must be served or placated in order that we or it may continue? What errors of omission or commission may precipitate our or its demise? What is the nature of the relationship between the body politic and the incorporeal spirit? What is the cosmological and historical significance of a society, and on what ultimate principle does it rest?

In the modern, secular world, when questions of this nature are raised, they are typically asked on behalf of the individual. On the other hand, when society's survival is questioned, as we have seen with Parsons and Blauner, the discussion is usually a functional one, secularly based and institutionally focused.

It is within the realm of the ontological question, however, that the nonpragmatic and the nonrational answer is paramount. In modern Japan, for example, the Emperor, Akihito, the 125th heir to the Chrysanthemum Throne, recently observed a 1300-year-old annual ceremony of planting grains of rice in a hallowed plot of ground to assure the survival and well-being of the Japanese people. Such behavior strikes many Westerners as quaint. A *New York Times Magazine* article on this occasion observed that even most Japanese "regard the Emperor as irrelevant" but that, on the other hand, "they expect him to behave in an exemplary fashion and maintain the institution as a repository of culture and tradition" (Weisman, 1990, p. 29).

In modern Western societies, much ritual behavior today is either dismissed out of hand as anachronistic or viewed as a cultural artifact among the myriad of customs and traditional practices that enliven societal diversity. Yet, such acts and their spiritual and existential implications constitute the very essence of a society's relationship with the unknown and its confrontation with the imperative of death.

Mardi Gras, the pre-Lenten festivities in New Orleans, is a Western example of such a custom. The bullfight is another. And the funeral is yet another. These customs and rituals, by enveloping the participants in a panoply of attitudes and ritual actions, beliefs and celebratory behaviors, capture the inextricable relationship between humans and the incorporeal. Mardi Gras, the bullfight, and the funeral practices of a primitive and a modern society, as will be discussed in this chapter, provide insight into certain broad thanatological issues that presently confront modern society, both illustrating and embodying, as they do, the universality of human-kind's struggle to maintain existence and fathom life's imponderable mysteries.

Mardi Gras

At first blush, the carnival called Mardi Gras strikes an observer in much the same way as our contemporary celebrations of Thanksgiving and Christmas—that is, as a ritual reenactment of an historic or spiritual event whose significance has been diminished by time, commercialism, or license. Mardi Gras, however, is more than meets the eye.

Mardi Gras, or "Fat Tuesday," which is held annually in New Orleans prior to the beginning of Lent, is generally seen as a time of unabashed fun and public merriment. Revelers, disguised in masks and costumes, put aside the normal rules of propriety and social intercourse in exchange for days and nights of drunkenness, nudity, sexuality, and sometimes violence. In a word, it would appear to be the devil's workshop, in which law and order are absent and passion and self-indulgence prevail (Kinser, 1990). But there is another side to Mardi Gras: the recognition and celebration of the life of society.

To begin, Mardi Gras is sponsored by semi-secret social clubs, called Krewes, that are established along religious, social, racial, and class lines. While Krewes are oftentimes organized by neighborhoods, membership in the most prestigious Krewes is, for the most part, a function of social status. The prestige of a Krewe is reflected in the order of precedence it enjoys in the parades that are held during Mardi Gras. The most prestigious is the King Rex Krewe, whose parade is held on the evening of Shrove Tuesday, the day prior to Ash Wednesday—the first day of Lent.

Preparation for Mardi Gras by Krewe families begins months and even years before the particular parade and pageant that will include or feature the sons or daughters of Krewe members. Mothers and daughters make forays to shopping meccas—New York, London, Rome, and Paris—in search of the wardrobes necessary for the many different occasions and functions to which the young scions and debutantes of New Orleans society will be invited and presented (Shane, 1962).

In the meantime, the Krewe organizers arrange for the purchase from Italy, France, and elsewhere of thousands of dollars worth of trinkets and favors that are to be thrown from the Krewes' floats at the time that the parade winds through Old New Orleans—Vieux Carre—to the civic auditorium. In addition, large truck trailers must be rented to haul the floats, a pageant must be planned and rehearsed, a queen and her court must be elected, social engagements must be arranged, and invitations delivered. These are but a few of the innumerable details demanded by this yearly social occasion. These arrangements are very time consuming and demanding, but of paramount importance to a participating family is the ability to pay. For instance, it has been reported that parents virtually bid thousands of dollars to assure their daughters a place in the queen's court while securing their social position in the larger society (Shane, 1962).

A Krewe parade, like the Mardi Gras festival itself, has its own order of precedence. First to appear in the narrow, gas-lit streets of Vieux Carre, illuminating the procession with lanterns hanging from large wooden crosses and moving forward in a swaying, snakelike manner, are the "lumieres," black men who have been employed for the occasion. As the lumieres sashay down the street, the spectators throw coins onto the cobblestones. The lumieres, without breaking step, reach down and pick up what coins they can while holding their large, heavy burdens upright.

Hard on the heels of the lumieres are the "mummers," the adult male members of the Krewe, who, hooded and berobed in flowing white, ride imperiously on their Arabian stallions.

The mummers are followed by the elaborately decorated floats. The richly costumed queen and her court wave and receive the applause of the curbside spectators as they pass. Other floats in the parade carry the wives, children, and other relatives and friends of the Krewe members. Smiling and tossing favors and trinkets, they shower their largesse on the importunate and scrambling spectators. Slowly, the procession makes its way from Old New Orleans to the steps of the Civic Auditorium. Here, a different but related social drama unfolds.

Upon arrival at the auditorium, the celebrants change into formal dress for the evening's pageant and ball. After the queen and her court and their escorts are presented, they stage a dramatic presentation, following which, the traditional ball begins. It is the obligation on the part of a young man honored with a dance to present a young woman with a small gift, usually of silver.

Following the ball, the celebrations are continued at private parties and receptions. For many young men and women who will receive invitations to several such events, this series of activities will be repeated every evening until the conclusion of Mardi Gras, which is dramatically climaxed with the symbolic killing of the Prince of Misrule (the devil), precisely at midnight on Shrove Tuesday.

Mardi Gras is followed by the 40-day fast of Lent. During this time, the celebrants abstain from foods such as meat and dairy products, from activities such as the theater, from sexual intercourse, and from holding marriage ceremonies; they intensify their religious observances: perform penances, such as wearing hairshirts; flagellate themselves; walk without shoes or on their knees; make pilgrimages to shrines, climb holy stairs, and increase their attendance at religious ceremonies (masses, prayers, vespers, matins); give alms to the poor and otherwise atone for their sins—as well they might.

Mardi Gras, in its full, dramatic richness, embraces two significantly different but related human themes. First, the orgiastic festivities of Mardi Gras express in the most vivid way possible what the world is like when it is ruled by the devil. Superficially, it is a world of excitement, fun, and pleasure, but beneath the glitter and the festivities it is a world awash in the deadly sins of pride, envy, anger, jealousy, sloth, gluttony, and lust. Ultimately, it is a world of chaos and darkness that needs to be rejected if the individual, or indeed society itself, is to perdure. The Prince of Misrule must, perforce, be killed. In the burning of his effigy, society expresses its willingness to turn away from such a world and receive a resurrected God's mercy.

The second theme, more obscure, addresses the structure of the social order itself. The pageantry of the parades, with their largesse of gift giving, is complemented, in turn, by the curbside spectators throwing coins at the lumieres. This indirect exchange of gifts, at the same time that it recognizes the superior and inferior roles that are being played out on the part of the New Orleans Krewe members and the spectators, confirms the subordinate place of the lumieres. Since the lumieres do not participate in the gift exchange, they have their place at the bottom of the social order both defined and acknowledged (Kinser, 1990, pp. 307–318, passim).[1] The different Krewe parades and the other social activities, public and private, spell out in colorful fashion the hierarchical character of social life in New Orleans and the place of class and caste in its public affairs (Kinser, 1990, pp. 119–199, passim).

The issue of continuity, as it relates to the social order, can also be seen in the courtship rituals that take place during Mardi Gras. At the invitation-only civic auditorium dance and in the private parties and family receptions that follow, the scions of the most distinguished families of New Orleans are presented and introduced to one another, with the expectation that from their loins will arise the next generation of social leaders and responsible citizens.

The Bullfight

The traditional bullfight shares, albeit indirectly, many important themes that Mardi Gras articulates and dramatizes. The primary theme is, of course, the fundamental struggle between order and chaos, between that which is conscious, purposeful, and life giving and that which is mindless, indifferent, and annihilating. It should not come as a surprise, therefore, that the annual cycle of bullfights, in Mexico and in the other parts of the world in which this sport is still pursued, usually does not commence until after the Easter celebration of Christ's resurrection (Hemingway, 1932, p. 508).

The drama of the bullfight, the *corrida de toros*, like the pageantry of Mardi Gras, is as controlled in its orchestration as it is explosive in its violence. The stages of the bullfight follow each other with the same orderly progression as that of a symphony or a Mass. First trumpet: the ceremonial march of the matadoros; second trumpet: the bull is released into the ring; third trumpet: the picadores appear mounted on blindfolded horses and carrying eight-foot long spiked poles; fourth trumpet: the banderilleros parade into the arena carrying two-foot long thick wooden sticks, decorated with frills of colored paper and ending in a steel harpoon point; fifth trumpet: the confrontation, the faena, of the two protagonists—the matador and the bull (Tynan, 1955, pp. 1–2).

Each participant plays his role. The picadores on their horses stab the bull in order to weaken its shoulder muscles. The banderilleros also pierce the bull's neck and shoulders with their beribboned darts further to exhaust its strength. Running and pirouetting, they consecrate the bull to the sacred use of the community, like the religious celebrants of ancient Minos, who cavorted with and somersaulted over the back of the celebratory bull 30 centuries ago (O'Dwyer, 1988, p. 19). And finally, the matador, with sword and cape, executes a series of traditional maneuvers that could be likened to devotional religious dances, until he finally stands alone before his adversary. With consummate control, he arches his body over the horns of the motionless animal, and with one skillful thrust of his short sword strikes it dead instantly. To miss his mark means his death. The courage of the matador, the aesthetic quality of his movements, both those of his body and of his cape, and the swift death of the bull determine how his performance is received and rewarded by the aficionados.

Following the death of the bull, it is dragged ignominiously from the ring by a team of gaily decorated horses and its flesh is given to the poor of the community. In turn, the aficionados spontaneously shower the triumphant matador with gifts of their own—hats, scarves, wine flasks, and the like. More ceremoniously, however, special parts of the bull's body—ear, hoof, and tail—are presented to the matador by the president of the fiesta brava to acknowledge the matador's bravery and artistry and to express the spectators' appreciation of his performance. The faena has ended.

The triumph of order over chaos, of good over evil, declared by this ancient dramaturgy is, however, short-lived. With a blare of trumpets, a new bull appears in the center of the ring, and a new corrida begins, one of six that will take place that Sunday and every Sunday afternoon throughout the season in a continuous and never-ending cycle, imitating the struggle between life and death itself.

Like Mardi Gras, the bullfight embraces historic religious themes that are both apparent and subtle. The matador's preparation for combat with the bull, for instance, requires not only a lifetime of physical preparation and training but a religious regimen as well. Prior to his appearance in the bull ring, the matador attends Mass and, in the same formal fashion as a priest will vest before services, ceremoniously dons his "suit of lights," thus declaring his priestly role in the cause of life (O'Dwyer, 1988, p. 33; Marvin, 1988, p. 17).

The role of the matador as life's champion is symbolized, moreover, by his unique costume, particularly his headdress, with its accompanying tuft of hair (the anadado—an imitation pigtail). The matador's costume informs the spectators that the mortal battle about to begin is, in fact, between two bulls—one black and one white. Their encounter gives expression to, as well as is generative of, the struggle for life.

The significance of the bullfight has much greater import than its limited occurrence or its present status as tourist entertainment in Europe and Latin America would suggest. The drama that portrays ancient cosmogony and that illuminates human confrontation with the raw, brute threat of extinction celebrates the human spirit and its courage in defying death. In doing so, it transforms the encounter into an aesthetic experience. Death and life, before one's very eyes, perform a cosmological pas des deux.

While a ritual such as the bullfight can be characterized as one that dramatizes the struggle between life and annihilation, and Mardi Gras can be viewed as a ritual that celebrates the quiddity and renewal of society, they, nevertheless, have two motifs in common: survival and sufferance. Intrinsic to both rituals is humankind's implicit understanding that the Creator demands sacrifice from the creature. Societal survival, or individual salvation, is the prize; pain or penance is the price. Mardi Gras and the bullfight are twofold in their essence: They dramatize the human condition while enacting it. They do so, however, from profoundly different points of focus. Mardi Gras involves the entire community—the fate of one is the fate of all. The bullfight, on the other hand, involves essentially but one actor—he who champions our human cause—the matador. Christ-like, he is prepared to die that others might live.

The Dani

In order to pursue further the meaning of the two ceremonies so far discussed, and in order to see their significance for our own construction of reality, let us turn to a pastoral people of New Guinea: the Dani. These people came to our attention as a result of the highly publicized death of Michael Rockefeller, who disappeared off the coast of New Guinea after filming a documentary of their lives. The existence of the Dani as neolithic warrior farmers would otherwise have been of little interest to the modern world, except for anthropological reports of their exotic customs, such as the practice of severing the fingers of young girls as a sign of mourning (Mead, 1969, p. viii).

Simply and briefly put, these people live in a mountainous region of New Guinea. Their diet consists mainly of ground crops and domesticated pigs. The men assist the women in agriculture and undertake large-scale irrigation projects, although, for the most part, until it was outlawed by colonial authorities, they historically occupied themselves in ceremonial warfare with neighboring tribes. Men and boys would array themselves in feathered headdresses and, armed with bows and arrows and spears, engage in battle. Sundown or the injury or death of a combatant would suspend the hostilities (Gardner & Heider, 1969, pp. 135–144, passim).

What is of interest and importance for our analysis is the behavior of the community that followed upon the death of a combatant. The deceased was returned to his village and the procession greeted by wailing tribeswomen. His body was placed in the center of the village and wrapped in banana leaves; there was much crying and display of grief over the corpse. Mourners, many of whom came from great distances, brought gifts for the bereaved: prized nets, woven with great manual skill, for the female relatives, and ornaments made of valued cowrie shells for the male relatives.

The female survivors painted themselves with white ash as a mark of their grief. The deceased was placed in a chair constructed of bamboo. Wood was collected and placed around the chair. Depending on the relationship of the deceased to the bereaved and the deceased's status in the tribe, pigs were brought and sacrificed in his honor. After the funeral feast of steamed sweet potatoes and pig, the body was ceremoniously anointed in the grease of the slaughtered animals, and the pyre ignited.

The following day, the village shaman met the young girls who had been chosen by their families to donate fingers as gifts to the deceased's family. Each young girl was brought forward, and her elbow struck sharply, numbing her arm; her hand was placed on a large board, and one or more fingers were severed at the joint. Her hand was then wrapped in banana leaves (Gardner & Heider, 1969, p. 96).

Although such a ritual can be perceived as brutally sadistic and cruel, this practice nevertheless informs us once again of how humankind has thought about the relationships among ourselves, as well as our relationship with our gods and their expectations of us. That is, humankind over and over again demonstrates its total belief in the gods and, despite any and all calamaties and evidence to the contrary, solicits their good will. Such expressions of commitment, more often than not, involve infliction of pain or mutilation of the body. Simply stated, the relationship that Job had with his God would appear to be an archetypal model for humankind.

But we need to look beyond pain, penance, and mortification if we are to understand the full implications of these celebratory activities. These behaviors need to be viewed both within the context of the communal life and world view of the Dani and their overarching cosmogony.

The Dani live in small, tribal communities. In the best of times, they live at the level of subsistence. Relationships are basically a function of gender. In brief, while men occasionally assist with heavy, laborious tasks, women do most of the domestic labor, including the growing of crops. Most importantly, women also raise the pigs, which are the community's primary source of protein. In the light of this fact, the relationship between the simple but dramatic act of severing a young girl's fingers as a sacrifice to the dead and her life-long obligations as a mother and wife takes on new significance. The young girl is, of course, a living memorial to the deceased. She must, however, continue to participate in family and community life; that is, to marry, bear children, and perform her share of family and communal activities. This is so, despite the fact that over the years, she may be obliged to submit one or more times to these mutilating rituals (Gardner & Heider, 1969, p. 96).

I have before me the image of a Dani woman in middle age, in possession of only her thumbs, pensively smoking her pipe. There is an air of resignation about her, mixed with what I perceive to be contentment. She has given all her eight fingers to the gods. She has been a good daughter, wife, and mother, and has become a revered icon of the dead. This woman, nevertheless, still takes care of the pigs.

Let me propose a schema that will, I hope, cast light on the behaviors and rituals I have described. The scenario acted out among the Dani, for as long as human memory serves, makes the beneficence of the gods hinge on the courage and prowess of the men in their violent, ritualized encounters with neighboring tribes. The killing of the pigs for the funeral feast not only gives expression to the grief of the villagers and allows them to come together and share food and reassure themselves that the community still survives, albeit diminished, but it also permits them to propitiate the gods. The killing of the pigs, moreover, promises a leaner tomorrow. The sacrifice of the fingers of the young girls, who must be kept alive and nurtured, is an act of mortification that greatly increases the difficulty with which the women perform their tasks of providing for their warrior husbands and fathers.

The upshot of the confrontation with death for the Dani is this: Not only does a man die—a man who was a husband, a father, a brother, a warrior, and a laborer—but his death essentially jeopardizes the community's future. That is, not only are the resources of the community squandered at his funeral, but the amputation of the fingers of the oncoming generation of village women makes life even more difficult and puts the community at even further risk. Heider's estimate that, over a generation, upwards of 20 percent of the male population will be killed from such ritual skirmishes adds poignancy to the message that a man must be a brave and courageous warrior and kill before he is killed if the community is to survive, (Heider, 1970, pp. 128–129).[2]

While such beliefs and behaviors strike us perforce as exotic and dysfunctional, if not destructive, contemporary analogues to these practices can be found in the United States, as well as in other modern societies throughout the world. It is to this aspect of our own modern culture that we now turn.

Funeral of President Kennedy

David Kertzer, in his book, *Ritual, Politics and Power*, observes that the importance of political drama and pageantry in social life is as pervasive on the U.S. scene as it is neglected by the scholars who might be expected to analyze it. This failure to appreciate the significance of political rites and social rituals, he says,

> is understandable, since our own rites, our own symbols, are the most difficult to see. They seem like such natural ways of behaving, such obvious ways of representing the universe, that their symbolic nature is hidden. Here, indeed, is one of the sources of power of rites and symbols, for insofar as they become dominant they create a convincing world; they deflect attention from their contingent nature and give us confidence that we are seeing the world as it really is. (Kertzer, 1988, p. 184)

The state funeral of President John Kennedy illustrates Kertzer's observations as it serves to concretize the preceding discussion. The funeral also demonstrates the pervasive and overriding power of belief in immortality as well as its attendant burdens—mortification and sacrifice.

The funeral involved not only the American public but indeed the entire allied world. It is estimated that more than half a billion persons viewed on television the proceedings of the four melancholy days leading to President Kennedy's burial in Arlington National Cemetery. Important for our discussion is that despite the fact that his death initially was feared to be the result of the political conspiracy of a foreign power and a precursor to a violent confrontation, 92 representatives of sovereign governments, including 8 heads of state and 10 prime ministers from allied countries and friendly nations of the world, accompanied by their military attaches and other dignitaries, came to the nation's capital. Representing the United States were the newly sworn-in President Lyndon Johnson, the members of the cabinet, the members of the Supreme Court, the members of Congress, and many other dignitaries and leaders from throughout the nation (Mossman & Stark, 1971, p. 201). All assembled, not only in the same country or the same city but all under a single roof of the rotunda of the Capitol, to pay their respects to the dead president at a time that was considered perilous. One can hardly imagine what one atomic bomb or even one well-placed conventional bomb could have done to change the character of American society and indeed the course of world history. The fact that no bomb was dropped and that the funeral was concluded without incident in no way diminishes the act of faith demonstrated by the mourners who gathered together on November 25, 1963.

In addition to the funeral proper, other prescribed acts were carried out that served both to express a world's respect for the dead president and in a variety of ways to testify to faith in the benificence of the Creator and the efficacy of sacrifice and supplication. For example, all the major ships of the allied nations fired 21-gun salutes, squadrons of jet aircraft flew overhead, and thousands of soldiers stood at rigid attention along the funeral course (Mossman & Stark, 1971, p. 195). Outside the capital, millions of citizens attended prayer services, and Masses for the dead president were held throughout the country—indeed, throughout the world. The nation's children were dismissed from school, and the overwhelming majority of the employed citizens of the United States were released from their respective workplaces by proclamations declaring that day a legal holiday (World News Digest, 1963, p. 409).

The principles that governed President Kennedy's funeral are, I believe, fundamentally no different from those that inform the Dani funeral rites: acceptance of one's fate and submission to the gods—a principle of oblation that can also be seen in the Kaddish, the hymn of praise to the Deity that Jewish mourners recite (Kaufman, 1967).

Submission is also expressed, as we have observed, in the sacrifice of wealth to evoke a god's favor. The survivors' expenditure of resources to honor the dead, we know, can be in sharp contrast to their possible need of those same resources. During our Colonial period, for example, the General

Court of Massachusetts as well as the Virginia Assembly passed laws prohibiting "extraordinary expense at funerals" (Habenstein & Lamers, 1955, p. 212). It may also be recalled that the best-selling book of 1963 was no other than Jessica Mitford's critique of extravagant American funeral practices, *The American Way of Death.*

Though newspaper accounts of the Kennedy funeral described it as "simple" and "restrained," the expense of the funeral was actually considerable, matching at least the cost of the Taj Mahal, the famous memorial tomb built in Agra, India, in the 1600s. It is estimated that the construction of the Taj Mahal in 1963 U.S. dollars cost approximately $2 billion (Burton-Page, 1971, p. 701). A simple calculation based on that year's gross national product of $560 billion shows that the cost of dismissing the millions of U.S. workers from their places of employment on the day of the president's funeral resulted in approximately $2 billion lost in wages, products, and services (U.S. Bureau of the Census, 1962, 1975). The expense to the country, along with that associated with the military display and funeral pageantry, compares readily to the memorial the emperor, Shah Jahan, built to honor his beloved wife. Moreover, an additional $1,841,026 was provided by the government for improvements to the 3.2 acres set aside in Arlington National Cemetery by the Secretary of the Army to honor the memory of the president. Furthermore, the Kennedy family personally paid $632,634 toward the decoration of the grave site (Superintendent, Arlington National Cemetery, n.d.).

In an economy as large as that of the United States, the cost of President Kennedy's funeral was miniscule, nevertheless, for millions of workers to leave their offices, workbenches, and assembly lines at such a portentous moment amounts to a significant act of faith on the part of the whole country. Such behavior permits us to recognize the role of the nonrational in our public as well as our private affairs. For a people who otherwise see themselves as pragmatic and penultimately rational, this collective response to President Kennedy's death obliges us to recognize, and perhaps even acknowledge, how much we inhabitants of the modern world have in common with people who are considered "primitive," especially in regard to the primordial response to death.

The review of Mardi Gras and the bullfight, and the two examples of funeral practices, show us how as human beings we respond to the fundamental challenges of existence. In brief, these different rituals and customs inform us that human cosmogonies include ideas of a Creator and a creation, of good and evil in perpetual conflict, of individual and societal struggle for survival, of human death and immortality, and of mortification and sacrifice.

We have observed as well that rituals and ceremonies concretize ideas and beliefs about the structure and character of social life and at the same time dramatize our individual places and relationships as well as our relevance as members of society. What message, then, does President Kennedy's funeral set forth to citizens of our democratic society? President Kennedy's state funeral, conducted in the national tradition of honoring an American dignitary, served to "salute his accomplishments in life" as well as "demonstrate the Nation's recognition of a debt owed for his services" (Resor, 1971, p. iii).

It was the most widely viewed funeral ceremony in history. A montage of images of the funeral continues to have the power to stir our emotions and to remind us again of that tragic time: Jacqueline Kennedy kneeling at the side of her husband's flag-draped casket with her daughter Caroline; John, the president's son, standing in brave salute; the solemn procession down Pennsylvania Avenue; the heavy casket borne gracefully and respectfully by both black and white members of the armed services; and six matched grey horses pulling the casket-laden caisson, followed by a spirited black stallion. President Kennedy's funeral served to declare not only that he was dead but also that order had once more been restored in the nation.

Death evokes powerful emotions within us that need to be vented or calmed. This was made evident when the nation mourned openly not only as solitary citizens but also together as a society. As a society, it observed public as well as private expressions of grief; it participated in a funeral to which the whole world paid heed.

Public evidence of the private reactions to President Kennedy's death is available. At least 39 different surveys were conducted at varying intervals following his assassination. Although the studies were manifestly different in design and intent, certain common reactions were discernible. These reactions are best shown by the study of the National Opinion Research Center in Chicago, which polled a representative national sample of 1,400 adults within a week of the assassination. The study showed the following results:

1. Preoccupation with the death was almost total.
2. Nine out of ten people reported experiencing one or more of such physical symptoms as headache, upset stomach, fatigue, dizziness, or loss of appetite.
3. Two-thirds of the respondents felt very nervous and tense during the four days.
4. A majority of the respondents confessed to feeling dazed and numb.
5. Most people—men and women—cried at some period during this time.
6. The event was compared most often to the death of a parent or close friend or relative.
7. There was a tendency to react to the assassination in terms of personal grief and loss rather than in terms of anxiety for the future or of political or ideological concern.

As the researchers described it, the reactions of the American people during the four days following the death of President Kennedy appeared to have followed a well-defined pattern of grief familiar to clinical practice. The funeral of the president channeled that grief and gave it poignant expression. In acknowledging the death of the president and dramatizing the nation's continued viability, as it provided a vehicle for the expression of loss, the funeral successfully met the challenge of the imperative of death (Wofenstein & Kliman, 1965, passim; Bureau of Social Science Research, 1966, passim)

Funerary rituals, however, as was earlier observed, can also be dysfunctional, even if a society, as Blauner and Parsons would argue, is so structured as to deflect the centrifugal force of death. The anthropologist Clifford Geertz cites, for example, the case of a funeral in a Javanese town, in which insistence on traditional practices disrupted the sense of community rather than restoring it. He explains that the traditional rites, which were suited to an agricultural, village folk milieu, were inappropriate and caused much dissension and confusion among the villagers who were transplanted to town life, where the economic, social, and political orientations differed from those of the village (Geertz, 1957, pp. 32–54).

Mandelbaum also gives an example from the Kota, a hill people of South India, where typically the traditional funeral ceremony aggravates the sorrow of the mourner and provokes social discord. During one stage of the Kota funeral, at what is termed the "dry funeral," there is a juncture when all Kotas who are present at the ceremony come forward one by one to give a parting bow of respect to the relics of the deceased. This phase of the funeral initiates a time of great tension and conflict. Mandelbaum describes it as follows:

> Around this gesture of social unity, violent quarrels often rage. When kinsmen of a deceased Kota are fervent supporters of one of the two opposing factions in Kota society, they may try to prevent a person of the other faction from making this gesture of respect and solidarity. This is tantamount to declaring that those of the other faction are not Kotas at all—a declaration which neither side will quietly accept. Thus a ritual action which symbolized concord has frequently triggered a good deal of discord. (Mandelbaum,1976; see also Gluckman, 1954, pp. 1–36)

President Kennedy's funeral, I believe, along with the aforementioned ingredients of social affirmation and national unity, also contained an element of dysfunction. Following the graveside service, after the 3rd Infantry battery fired a 21-gun salute and Cardinal Cushing pronounced the benediction, after the bugler sounded "Taps," after the U.S. Marine Band played the hymn "Eternal Father, Strong to Save," Cardinal Cushing stepped forward and blessed a flame. A taper, lighted from that flame was then handed to Mrs. Kennedy, the president's widow, who ignited the torch that would become the "eternal flame" at the head of the president's grave. This ceremony, conducted at the state funeral's conclusion, was held at the behest of Mrs. Kennedy, and was not a part of the nation's prescribed conventions for civil and military funerals (Mossman & Stark, 1971, p. 202).

The symbol of the eternal flame represents the most transcendent of human values. In France, Portugal, and other European countries, where it burns before the tombs of their unknown soldiers, the flame testifies to their belief in freedom, equality, and human dignity. Significant as the tradition has been in Europe, it is important to observe that there is no eternal flame before the Tomb of the Unknown Soldier in Arlington National Cemetery. In addition, it is also important to note that no other U.S. president—not Washington, the "father of the country," nor Jefferson, the "framer of the country," nor Lincoln, the "savior of the country" (who also was assassinated while in office)—has been so honored.

The placing of an eternal flame before President Kennedy's grave has political implications that cannot be pursued here, challenging as they are. Rather, I would like to suggest one possible implication of the flame for our modern society, as it concerns our changing ideas about dying as well as death.

At the same time that the eternal flame burns at the head of President Kennedy's grave and his death continues to evoke universal sympathy, as indicated by the millions of people from all over the world who visit his grave annually, an increasing number of U.S. citizens who die each year are, on the other hand, disposed of in a singularly different manner.

In San Diego County, California, which also includes the city of San Diego, a contemporary scenario for the disposition of the dead, now observed in almost one-sixth of all deaths, is as follows: Upon the declaration of a patient's death, the body is removed to the hospital morgue. An organization called Telephase is notified. The body is picked up at the morgue and enclosed in a rubberized bag; it is transported in an unmarked station wagon to a crematorium. The body is cremated and the ashes are placed in a cardboard or plastic container for storage, dispersal, or delivery to an assigned recipient. No obituary is published. The legal survivor is later billed (Crean, 1982, p. 145).

Similar contractors are now operating in other cities of the United States. In Vancouver, British Columbia, Canada, a vehicle capable of transporting 12 such bodies to a crematorium is now utilized. Across the United States, moreover, the San Diego scenario is serving increasingly as a model for the disposition of human remains (Finlay, 1985, p. 548; Sawyer, D., 1982, p. 530).

What, then, is implied by this stark contrast between the anonymous death and impersonal disposal of a growing number of U.S. citizens and the magnificent setting, chosen by the president's widow, of President Kennedy's grave, which has become a place of pilgrimage for millions annually? Standing as it does on the steep ground below the Custis-Lee Mansion, one of the most dramatically visible and historic residences in Washington, and in direct alignment with the Lincoln Memorial, the Washington Monument, and the nation's Capitol, the gravesite, sanctified by its eternal flame, declares the apotheosis of the 37th president of the United States.

How might we interpret the distinction that we observe among U.S. citizens when we dispose of their bodies? The state funeral for the president of the United States, whose office serves as a symbol of national unity, appropriately, as we observed, provided a ceremony that reestablished the political and moral order that had been interrupted by death. However, thought needs to be given to the social and political implications of a low and sombre black wall, densely engraved with the names of more than 58,000 Americans who gave their lives in the Vietnam War, contrasted with a single 3½-acre gravesite upon which a usurped symbol burns.

I believe that the placing of the eternal flame before President Kennedy's grave not only achieved the apotheosis of President Kennedy but it also provided the basis for a new *zeitgeist* for America that contributes to this separation between principle and practice. In the usurpation of a symbol that historically has served to honor the nameless dead, the placing of the eternal flame over the grave of President Kennedy was both a grandiose and dysfunctional act.

In the 30 years since President Kennedy's funeral, U.S. society has experienced many significant changes related to the life and death of its citizens. The development of the kidney dialysis machine in Seattle, Washington, for example, brought the issue of who should live and who should die into distressingly sharp focus for U.S. citizens. Nonmedical criteria (e.g., educational level and property ownership) initially were established conjointly with medical considerations to select the first dialysis patients (Simmons & Fulton, 1973, p. 174; see also Katz & Proctor, 1969). Such a basis for selection of the first patients not only contradicted our traditional democratic philosophy but also said, in effect, that some persons have a more legitimate claim to life than others. Of course, it has always been true that the wealthy have had access to better medical care than the poor, but it has never been an official medical position that those with property or higher education or superior social status have a prior claim to life.

It was, however, established by an anonymous committee of seven, known portentously as the "Life and Death Committee," that one's right to a life-sustaining machine was in part a function of his or her potential or actual contribution to society. The doctor, the lawyer, the executive on the way up, it was implied, has a greater claim to life than the unskilled, the unemployed, or the unwanted. The past few years have seen the production of large numbers of kidney machines, as well as the development of new kidney transplant techniques that benefit thousands, but many of the moral and ethical issues generated by these technological advances and medical procedures still wait to be resolved.

Moreover, in this era of AIDS, the issue of triage (forced choice decision making) now extends into every aspect of care of the sick and elderly. These difficult challenges are, I believe, weighted and burdened even more so by a seemingly dispirited American electorate that increasingly abdicates its responsibility to participate in the political process[3] and by a public that, in the past 40 years, has reversed its stance on euthanasia and is in serious disagreement, if not conflict, in regard to other critical life and death matters. What must be recognized is that the moral, political, and intellectual environment within which we now live and work has changed over these past three decades, and significantly so.

It is for us as citizens to note these changes and respond creatively to them. In part, such response means overcoming an electronic image of a life transcendent that a grieving widow, through the exercise of her personal will, has left us. The interjection/introjection of an eternal flame into a funeral ceremony intended to express a nation's grief and restore its integrity created a standard against which other citizens have come to judge themselves. Such a standard heretofore had been left to God or to the unknown powers to which President Kennedy's funeral ceremonies were dedicated. When U.S. citizens are called on to address social issues such as dying, euthanasia, abortion, or AIDS, it is not enough simply to be medically informed nor morally principled. They need also to understand what has been designated as the "archotic tradition" (La Barre, 1984, p. 130)—those beliefs and assumptions, rooted as well as expressed in ritual and ceremony, that serve to describe social reality and ultimately our perceived place in it.

As citizens of a democratic society, we would be well advised to take to heart what Gladstone, a former prime minister of England, once asserted: "Show me the manner in which a nation or community cares for its dead, and I will measure with mathematical exactness the tender sympathies of its people, their respect for the law of the land, and their loyalty to high ideals."

Endnotes

1. In this regard it should be reported that the African Americans in New Orleans hold a parade of their own called the King Zulu Parade. These celebrants, with their own colorful floats, also make their way through the streets of New Orleans during Mardi Gras and also throw gifts to bystanders. In this case, however, the gifts are coconuts and other objects that serve to express the anger and resent-

ment of the New Orleans African-American population toward their white counterparts (Kinser, 1990, pp. 307–318, passim).

2. Heider is very much aware of the difficulties in ascertaining any accurate figure of the number of Dani men who may be killed over any period of time. His estimates, however, provide some idea of the number of lives that are lost to these ritual wars. It is his estimate that 0.48 percent of the population is killed yearly in such contests, and that "28.5 percent of the males and 2.4 percent of the females, die bloody, rather than natural, deaths." See also Bromley, who estimates that between 1954 and 1956, the Aso-Logobal Confederation of the southern Grand Valley lost 1 percent of its population per year through war (Bromley, H. Myron, "The function of fighting in Grand Valley Dani Society," in *Working Papers in Dani Ethnology*, No. 1. Bureau of Native Affairs, Hollandia-Kota Baru).

3. Only 50.2 percent of eligible voters participated in the 1988 presidential election, down from 62 percent in 1964 (United States Bureau of the Census, 1989, pp. 109, 258).

Acknowledgments

I would like to acknowledge the significant contribution that Ms. Rafael Tilton has made to this chapter, not only in meeting the secretarial demands that such a project requires but also in addressing its substantive content. R. Evan Fulton and Eric Silverman need also to be acknowledged for their bibliographic assistance and useful comments and suggestions. Finally, I am deeply indebted to Inge Corless for her good counsel and encouragement throughout the preparation of the manuscript.

References

Blauner, R. (1978). Death and social structure. In R. Fulton (Ed.), *Death and identity* (rev. ed.) (pp. 35–39). Bowie, MD: Charles Press Publishers.

Bureau of Social Science Research. (1966). *Studies of Kennedy's assassination.* Washington, DC: Author.

Burton-Page, J. (1971). "Taj Mahal." *Encyclopaedia Britannica.* Chicago: Encyclopaedia Britannica, Inc.

Crean, E. (1982). Personal communication, Vancouver, B.C. Cited in R. Fulton et al., Loss, social change and the prospect of mourning. *Death Education, 6,* 137–150.

Durkheim, E. (1954). *The elementary forms of religious life* (J. Swaine, Trans.). London: Allen and Unwin.

Evans-Pritchard, E. E. (1965). *Theories of primitive religion.* Oxford: Clarendon Press.

Finlay, B. (1985, July). Right to life vs. the right to die: Some correlates of euthanasia attitudes. *Sociology and Social Research, 69* (4), 548–560.

Gardner, R., & Heider, K. G. (Eds.). (1969). *Gardens of war: Life and death in the New Guinea stone age.* New York: Random House, pp. 135–144 (passim).

Geertz, C. (1957). Ritual and social changes: A Javanese example. *American Anthropologist, 5a,* 32–54.

Gluckman, M. (1954). *Rituals of rebellion.* Manchester: University Press, pp. 1–36.

Habenstein, R. W., & Lamers, W. M. (1955). *The history of American funeral directing.* Milwaukee, WI: Bulfin Printers.

Heider, K. G. (1970). *The Dugum Dani.* New York: Wenner-Gren Foundation for Anthropological Research, pp. 128–129.

Hemingway, E. (1932). *Death in the afternoon.* New York: Charles Scribner's Sons.

Hertz, R. (1968). *Death and the right hand.* (R. Needham, Trans.). Glencoe, IL: Free Press.

Katz, A., & Proctor, D. (1969, July). *Social psychological characteristics of patients receiving hemodialysis treatment for chronic renal failure: Report of questionnaire survey of dialysis centers and patients during 1967.* Washington, DC: U.S. Government Printing Office.

Kaufman, D. (1967). *Dictionary of religious terms.* Westwood, NJ: Fleming H. Devell Co.

Kertzer, K. (1988). *Ritual, politics and power.* New Haven, CT: Yale University Press.

Kinser, S. (1990). *Carnival, American style.* Chicago and London: The University of Chicago Press.

La Barre, W. (1984). *Muelos: A stone age superstition about sexuality.* New York: Columbia University Press.

Malinowski, B. (Ed.). (1954). *Magic, science, and religion and other essays.* New York: Doubleday.

Mandelbaum, D. G. (1976). Social uses of funeral rites. In R. Fulton (Ed.), *Death and identity* (pp. 39–45). New York: Wiley and Sons.

Marvin, G. (1988). *Bullfight.* United Kingdom: Basil Blackwell.

Mead, M. (1969). Introduction. In R. Gardner & K. G. Heider (Eds.), *Gardens of war: Life and death in the New Guinea stone age* (pp. vi–vii). New York: Random House.

Mori, T. (1962). *The dysfunction of rituals.* Paper presented at the I.S.A. Fifth World Congress of Sociology, Washington, DC.

Mossman, B. C., & Stark, M. C. (1971). *The last salute: Civil and military funerals, 1921–1969.* Washington DC: Department of the Army.

O'Dwyer, J. (1988). *The art of the matador.* Glendale, CA: Arthur H. Clark Co.

Parsons. T. (1963). Death in American Society—A brief working paper. *The American Behavioral Scientist, 6,* 61–65.

Radcliffe-Brown, A. R. (1952). Taboo. In *Structure and function in primitive society* (pp. 131–152). London: Cohen and West.

Resor, S. R. (1971). Foreword. In B. C. Mossman & M. C. Stark. (Eds.), *The last salute: Civil and military funerals, 1921–1969.* Washington, DC: Department of the Army.

Sawyer, D. O. (1982). Public attitudes toward life and death. *Public Opinion Quarterly, 46* (4), 523–533.

Shane, P. (1962, Feb.). Personal communication.

Simmons, R. G., & Fulton. J. (1973). Ethical issues in kidney transplantation. In C. A. Frazier, (Ed.), *Is it moral to modify man?* (pp. 171–188). Springfield, IL: Charles C. Thomas.

Superintendent, Arlington National Cemetery. (n.d.). *The Kennedy graves in Arlington National Cemetery.* Arlington, VA: Author.

Tynan, K. (1955). *Bull fever.* London: Longmans.

United States Bureau of the Census. (1962). *Historical statistics of the United States.*

United States Bureau of the Census. (1975). *Historical statistics of the United States. Colonial Times to 1970* (Vol. 1). Bicentennial edition.

Van Gennep, A. (1961). *The rites of passage* (M. B. Vizedon & G. L. Caffee, Trans.). Chicago: University of Chicago Press.

Weisman, S. R. (1990, August 26). Japan's Imperial Present. *The New York Times Magazine, 139,* 29–30.

Wofenstein, M., & Kliman, G. (Eds.). (1965). *Children and the death of a president.* Garden City, NY: Doubleday and Co.

World News Digest Staff. (1963). *Facts on File, 23.*

Six

Historical and Contemporary Theories of Grief

Margaret Shandor Miles

Alice Sterner Demi

Margaret Shandor Miles is Professor and Chair, Health of Women and Children Department, School of Nursing, at the University of North Carolina at Chapel Hill. She teaches in the master's program in pediatric nursing and in the doctoral program in nursing.

She has her diploma in nursing from Mercy Hospital, Pittsburgh, a BSN from Boston College, an MN in pediatric nursing from the University of Pittsburgh, and an MA and PhD in Counseling Psychology from the University of Missouri–Kansas City. She was the founding member of the Society of Pediatric Nurses, a national association concerned with improving the health and nursing care to children and their families.

Miles is well known for her clinical work and research related to dying children, parental grief, and parenting the infant or child with a life-threatening illness. Her clinical work with the bereaved has focused primarily on couples experiencing pregnancy or infant loss and bereaved parents. Her booklet for grieving parents was pivotal in focusing on the special needs of bereaved parents. Miles's current research focuses on parenting the medically fragile infant, parental caregiving with HIV-infected infants, and the responses of bereaved families to organ donation. As a member of the Carolina Consortium on Human Development, she has begun to apply principles of developmental science to research related to parenting and grief. Miles has worked with the American Nurses' Association to develop a number of position papers related to death and dying. She is also the Director of a center focusing on health behaviors in vulnerable youth.

Alice Sterner Demi is Professor of Psychiatric/Mental Health Nursing at Georgia State University, Atlanta, where she teaches family theory, family therapy, and nursing theory at the graduate level. Demi received a diploma from Monmouth Medical Center, New Jersey, a Baccalaureate degree from Incarnate Word College, Texas, a master's degree from University of Texas, Austin, and a doctorate from the University of California, San Francisco. She is a Fellow of the American Academy of Nursing, an honor which was bestowed upon her for her pioneering efforts in hospice nursing.

Demi has conducted research on widowhood and on survivors of suicide. She has also collaborated with

Dr. Miles in a number of studies, including guilt in bereaved parents, parameters of normal grief, rescue workers' reactions to disaster, and nurses' roles in disaster. She has used her research findings on bereavement to spur development of bereavement programs, such as the Survivors of Suicide outreach program in Marin County, California, and the Grief Education Institute in the Metro-Denver area.

Demi is continuing her bereavement work in the Atlanta area. Recently, she collaborated with members of the Coalition for Prevention of Youth Suicide and the Link Counseling Center to develop and implement an outreach program for survivors of suicide.

Freud began publishing his thoughts about mourning in the latter part of the last century (1893–1895/1955), Eliot noted the paucity of research on family responses to grief in the 1930s (Eliot, 1930, 1932), and Lindemann published his well-known paper on acute grief in 1944, however, it was not until the 1970s that intense and sustained interest in understanding the process of grief developed. The reasons for this neglect may be the result of taboos in our culture regarding death. In addition, psychological theories of the mid-twentieth century discouraged interest in emotions such as grief (Averill, 1979). During the 1940s and 1950s, emotions were often treated as intervening or "drive" variables and were not the variables of interest. In the ensuing years, however, interest in bereavement grew as the effects of World War II (Hoopes, 1977; Lifton, 1974), the results of clinical work and research with the bereaved (Lindemann, 1944; Parkes, 1970), and the theorizing of key leaders in psychiatry and psychology (Averill, 1968; Bowlby, 1960, 1961; Caplan, 1964; Gorer, 1967; Engel, 1961) led to the conclusion that the grief process was long and painful and that a wide range of somatic and psychological problems occur during bereavement.

The focus on grief in the 1970s paralleled the increased interest in death and dying fostered by the writings of Feifel (1959), Glaser and Strauss (1966, 1967), Quint (1969), Kubler-Ross (1969), Kastenbaum and Aisenberg (1972), Becker (1973), Weisman (1972), Shneidman (1973), and others. The hospice movement, which centered around issues of terminal illness, also served to focus attention on the grief process as it related to terminal illness (Stoddard, 1978). The numerous groups for the bereaved that emerged from the hospice movement and the self-help movement in the 1970s created further public and professional awareness about the needs of the bereaved (Lieberman & Borman, 1979).

This chapter reviews some of the major conceptualizations of grief and bereavement developed during the twentieth century. The review is not comprehensive; the emphasis is on theories that explicate the normal or so-called usual experience of adult grievers. The review does not include the literature related to childhood bereavement responses, which requires a separate intensive review. In addition, the review does not focus on the vast, diverse, and fragmented body of literature related to abnormal or pathological grief, which also deserves a treatise of its own (Demi & Miles, 1987; Lazare, 1979).

Psychoanalytic Views on Grief

The views about grief have been heavily influenced by Freud's psychoanalytic explanations about mourning. Although widely quoted, Freud really wrote very little about mourning in comparison to the volumes he wrote on other topics. Many of the papers in which he mentions mourning relate to case studies of individuals whom he was treating and who had also experienced a major loss. In these essays, he attempted to differentiate in various ways normal grief responses from mental illness, especially hysteria, neurosis, and melancholia. Freud's ideas were undoubtedly influenced by his own personal experiences with grief and by the events surrounding World War I (Pollock, 1961).

In one of the earliest discussions on grief, Freud identified acute hallucinatory amentia as a pathological abberation of mourning (1896/1966). In *Studies on Hysteria* (1893–1895/1955), Freud attempted to differentiate the hysteria of Elizabeth von R, who had nursed her father until death and who also experienced the sudden death of a sister and her unborn child, from the situation of another woman who had cared for three dying family members. This latter woman, who vividly recalled and wept over scenes of the illness and death of these family members, experienced what Freud considered normal recollections of the deceased and the death experience, especially on anniversary dates, whereas Elizabeth von R's hysteria was a result both of her grief response to the deaths she had experienced and to other complicated psychodynamic aspects of her identity. In another case study of a young man with obsession neurosis, Freud (1909/1955) noted that his illness intensified after his father's death and was a pathological expression of grief. In this essay, Freud pointed out that a normal period of mourning would last one to two years, whereas a pathological response would last indefinately.

In a lecture on psychoanalysis (1910/1957) and in a later lecture on neurosis (1917/1963), Freud suggested that it was normal for the bereaved to have a period of affective fixation to the deceased for a time. This fixation can lead to an abandonment of interest in the present and future for a time but is still not a neurosis. In contrast, however, a fixation that continues years later indicates an abnormal attachment and may indicate neurosis.

Later, in "Totem and Taboo" (1913, 1953), Freud suggested that bereaved individuals may be overwhelmed with tormenting doubts as to whether or not they were responsible for the death of a loved one through carelessness or neglect. This guilt response could lead to a pathological form of mourning, especially if there was ambivalance in the relationship with the deceased that prevented the normal transference of the libido from that person to a new object. Instead, the libido invested in the lost object is introjected by a process of identification, and hostile feelings toward the deceased are manifested in self-reproach and self-accusations. Thus, Freud suggested that mourning has the specific psychical task of detaching the survivors' memories and hopes from the deceased. When this has been achieved within the course of normal mourning, the pain grows less intense and with it the associated remorse and self-reproach.

Freud struggled to conceptualize how grief might differ from melancholia (clinical depression) in his classic paper "Mourning and Melancholia" (1915/1957). He suggested that grief was a normal reaction to the loss of a loved person, or an abstraction that has taken the place of a loved person. Both mourning and melancholia involve profoundly painful dejections, cessation of interest in the outside world, loss of capacity to love, inhibition of activity, and delusional expectations of punishment. In grief, resolution is accomplished through the slow process of reality testing in which the loss of the individual is verified and the withdrawal of the libido from the attachment is accomplished. Freud hypothesized that however painful mourning may be, mourning does come to a spontaneous end with the passage of time. Although melancholia has some similarities to mourning, it also involves narcissistic identification and ambivalence in the relationship with a lowering of self-regard and self-reproach. In this essay, Freud (1915/1957, p. 246) stated, "In mourning it is the world which has become poor and empty; in melancholia it is the ego itself." Pollock (1961) conjectured that this treatise on mourning was heavily influenced by the death of Freud's father and brother; by the severing of his relationship with Adler, Jung, and other colleagues; and by his sons' involvement in World War I.

Freud's last treatise of any consequence on grief was published in 1926 (1926/1956), six years after the death of his daughter and three years after his favorite grandson's death. In this essay, Freud continued to try to understand the intense pain of grief and attempted to differentiate pain, anxiety, and mourning as different responses to loss. He reiterated the fact that mourning occurs in response to a real loss and that it involves cathexis of longing toward the lost object and an undoing of the ties that bind him to the deceased. In a letter to Binswanger (1929/1960), nine years after the death of his daughter and six years after the death of her youngest son, his favorite grandson, Freud poignantly discussed the long-term impact of grief from a personal perspective:

> Although we know that after such a loss the acute state of mourning will subside, we also know we shall remain inconsolable and will never find a substitute. No matter what may fill the gap, even if it be filled completely, it nevertheless remains something else and actually this is how it should be. It is the only way of perpetuating that love which we do not want to relinquish. (Freud, 1929/1960)

A number of psychoanalytic followers of Freud, although not directly writing about normal grief, commented on various aspects of the grief process primarily in order to understand melancholia. In her classic paper, "Absence of Grief" (1937), Deutsch stated that unmanifested grief will be expressed either in clearly pathological ways or in disguised forms such as obsessions, schizoid responses, or depression. Klein (1940), in her treatise on mourning and its relation to manic depressive states, proposed that the mourning person goes through modified and transitory manic depressive states that are gradually overcome with the support and sympathy of others. She compared the mourning processes to the infantile crisis of childhood, in which the ego is forced to develop methods of defense against pining for the mother's breast that was lost. Furthermore, she suggested that there is no difference between grief over the loss of an infant and grief over loss of a beloved adult such as a spouse. For a more complete discussion of psychoanalytic views about grief, the reader is referred to papers by Pollock (1961) and Siggins (1966).

In 1961, Pollock revised Freud's views about guilt in the bereaved and incorporated Bernard's theory of adaptation, Cannon's principle of homeostasis, and Darwin's concepts of phylogenetic evolution. Pollock viewed the mourning process as an ego-adaptive process that occurs in an attempt to maintain the constancy of the internal psychic equilibrium. The mourning process involves refocusing from the internal psychic response to an altered external environment where the deceased individual no longer exists. For Pollock, the process of mourning involves both an acute and a chronic stage. The acute stage results from the sudden upset in ego equilibrium, causing narcissistic mortification and loss of control. The responses during acute grief involve shock, acute regression, and immobilization. These immediate responses are followed closely by grief responses such as hyperactivity, deep despair, sorrow, anxiety, energy impoverishment, and intense psychic pain. The acute stage gradually progresses to the chronic stage in which object decathexis occurs and adaptive mechanisms help to integrate the experience of loss with reality. Pollock further notes that while mammalians and birds may experience acute grief, only humans experience the chronic grief stage, which requires the mature ego to detach itself from the object.

Grief as an Acute Crisis

Lindemann (1944), in his widely quoted publication "Symptomatology and Management of Acute Grief," poignantly described the symptomatology of normal grief based on psychiatric interviews with 101 patients. These patients have been mistakenly thought to be relatives of those who died in the Coconut Grove fire disaster. However, subjects also included psychoneurotic patients, relatives of deceased hospitalized patients, and relatives of servicemen who died in World War II. An earlier publication by Cobb and Lindemann (1943), however, focused directly on the responses of 32 survivors of the Coconut Grove disaster who had been admitted to the hospital. In this paper, the authors began to describe the syndrome of acute grief based on their interviews with 7 of these survivors who had experienced severe grief related to the death of one or more close relatives in the fire. These observations were developed further and elaborated on by Lindemann in the 1944 paper. Lindemann's views were also influenced by his psychoanalytic background and by the attack on Pearl Harbor, which killed over 2,200 people, and the war that followed.

Lindemann (1944) described acute grief as a definite syndrome with both psychological and somatic symptomatology. He identified five striking features of grief: somatic distress, preoccupation with thoughts of the deceased, guilt, hostility, and loss of usual patterns of behavior. The somatic distress particularly included sighing respiration, lack of strength, exhaustion, digestive symptoms, as well as a feeling of tightness in the throat, choking, and shortness of breath. The duration of normal grief is dependent on the success of the "grief work," which he described as the emancipation from the bondage to the deceased, readjustment to the environment in which the deceased is missing, and formation of new relationships. A major obstacle to this work was described as avoidance of the intense distress connected with grief, particularly noted in men. Lindemann stated that treatment of an uncomplicated and undistorted grief reaction could be accomplished in 8 to 10 interviews lasting a period of four to six weeks. Based on his work with women whose husbands were involved in the war, Lindemann also proposed that grief could be experienced in anticipation of a loss.

Lindemann was particularly interested in acute grief because of its potential impact on mental and physical health. Thus, he suggested that grief could be distorted or delayed; distorted grief reactions included overactivity without a sense of loss, experiencing symptoms similar to the deceased, development of a frank medical disease such as ulcerative colitis, alteration in the relationship to friends and relatives, furious hostility, absence of emotional display, lasting loss of patterns of social interaction and patterns of conduct, and agitated depression. Delayed grief responses may be brief or long lasting; in the latter case, expression of the unresolved grief may be precipitated by another loss or salient event in the individual's life years later.

Lindemann's views about grief were based on his clinical observations and psychotherapy with patients and not on research. In his paper, he did not provide data about the frequency of the interviews, the time span following bereavement in which he saw these bereaved individuals, or the frequency of the syndromes described. He also largely ignored both the social context and individual personal factors that may influence bereavement responses. Lindemann's paper, however, was seminal and continues to be the most widely quoted paper on grief.

Caplan (1961, 1964), in the develoment of "crisis theory," built on Lindemann's work and proposed that bereavement, along with other life events, could trigger a crisis that is generally resolved in four to six weeks.

He suggested that individuals who were not improved in this time be referred for psychiatric care. Caplan (1964) also proposed that the outcome of a crisis is determined by the balance of stressors and resources. A crisis is a turning point for an individual and may lead to either improved or worsened health, and during a crisis, the individual has a heightened desire for help and is more susceptible to the influence of others. Caplan's crisis theory, along with Lindemann's paper, erroneously gave the impression that the grief response was short-lived; this had a dramatic influence on the research and clinical treatment of the bereaved. Caplan (1974), however, subsequently revised his concept of grief as a single crisis that resolved in six to eight weeks to a series of crises called "life transitions," which are resolved over a much longer period of time.

Grief as a Major Life Transition

Parkes, noted for his ongoing research and theory development in the area of widowhood, was influenced by his associations with both Caplan and Bowlby. Parkes first viewed grief as an acute stress response but later identified grief as a major life transition—a period of challenge and readjustment (1972a, 1975a; Parkes & Weiss, 1983). Thus, for Parkes, grief is "a complex time-consuming process in which a person gradually changes his view of the world and the places and habits by means of which he orients and relates to it" (Parkes, 1970, p. 465). Grief involves a process of realization—making psychologically real an external event that is not desirable and for which coping patterns do not exist (Parkes, 1972a).

One of Parkes's major contributions is his systematic descriptions of the painful emotional, behavioral, and physical manifestations of grief. In his first book, Parkes (1972a) described "pangs of grief"—acute episodes of severe anxiety and psychological pain in which the lost person is strongly missed—and "pining"—a persistent and obtrusive wish for the person who is gone, along with preoccupation with thoughts of the deceased. Parkes proposed that pining leads to intense searching behavior in an attempt to recover the lost love object. He noted that two opposing tendencies are experienced: an inhibitory tendency that tends to hold back or limit the painful stimuli, and a facilitative or reality-testing tendency that enhances the perception and thoughts of disturbing stimuli. Common mitigating behaviors in the early months that maintain the feeling that the deceased person is still nearby include searching for the lost person, achieving in dream and fantasy a reunion, and identifying with the deceased. As these attempts fail, the bereaved experience intense psychological pain, separation anxiety, anger, guilt, depression, and aimlessness (Parkes, 1970, 1972a). Parkes also delineated other characteristics of grief: emotional symptoms, behavioral changes, and numerous physical reactions such as sleep disturbances, aches and pains, loss of energy, and appetite changes (Glick, Weiss, & Parkes, 1974; Parkes, 1970, 1972a, 1972b).

Parkes (1970) identified several phases in the grief process: numbness, yearning and protest, and disorganization; subsequently, he added a phase of reorganization. Although he varied the terminology used for the phases, in his later publications he consistently maintained the presence of four phases. In his view, however, the transitions from one phase to another are seldom distinct, and features from one phase of grief often persist into the next (Parkes, 1972a).

Parkes and his colleagues also hypothesized antecedent, concurrent, and subsequent variables that influence grief resolution and tested these hypotheses in ongoing research (Glick, Weiss, & Parkes, 1974; Parkes, 1972a, 1972b, 1975a, 1975b; Parkes & Weiss, 1983). These variables included antecedent variables such as past childhood experiences, personality, religious beliefs, the relationship with the deceased, and the mode of death; concurrent factors such as other life crises, age, and socioeconomic status; and subsequent experiences such as social support, secondary stresses, and emergent opportunities. In research, Parkes and his colleagues found that a lack of forewarning of the loss, low socioeconomic status, multiple life crises, and early reactions of severe distress were particularly important predictors (Parkes, 1975a, 1975b; Parkes & Weiss, 1983).

The collective work of Parkes and his colleagues has been extremely important in describing the manifestations of grief and in identifying risk factors related to selected mental and physical health outcomes. It is interesting to note, however, that Parkes, whose work is extensive and based on relatively normal samples, is not quoted as often in the bereavement literature as Lindemann, who published only one paper based on clinical observations of a relatively small group of patients who were seeking help during their bereavement experience. This may be because of the extensive number of Parkes's publications, the changing nature of his conceptualizations about grief, and the lack of a single publication that synthesizes these evolving views.

Attachment Theory and Grief

During the 1960s and 1970s, Bowlby (1960, 1961, 1969) made major contributions to the conceptualization of loss and grief through his studies on attachment. His ideas were culled from his background as a physician, scientist, and child psychoanalyst, were rooted in psychoanalysis, neurophysiology, ethology, and information theory, and were based on extensive clinical observations of animals and humans. The basic premise of Bowlby's work is that attachment is a protective biological mechanism that serves to ensure the survival of the individual and the species. Thus, attachment is a fundamental form of behavior with its own internal motivation distinct from the drives previously identified in psychoanalytic theory (Bowlby, 1969, 1982). His astute observations of infants and young children separated from their mothers led Bowlby to identify the "separation response syndrome," in which separation from a significant other evokes behavior patterns that function to restore proximity of the lost love object. The separation response syndrome entails three phases: protest, despair, and detachment (Bowlby, 1960, 1969, 1973). Separation anxiety was considered the usual response to a threat of loss of an attachment, whereas mourning was considered the usual response after a loss actually occurred (Bowlby, 1982). Bowlby hypothesized that childhood loss has a major impact on personality development.

In his later works, Bowlby (1980, 1982) extended his attachment theory to incorporate the grief response of bereaved adults. Building on the growing body of research about the bereaved, especially the work of Parkes, Bowlby depicted the emotional distress of grief as breaking the bonds of attachment. Bowlby (1961) originally conceptualized bereavement responses as falling into three phases: urge to recover the lost object (yearning and searching), disorganization and despair, and reorganization. He subsequently added a fourth phase, numbing, which preceded yearning and searching (Bowlby, 1980). Bowlby also identified five classes of variables affecting the course of mourning. These included the identity and role of the deceased, the age and sex of the bereaved, causes and circumstances of the loss, social and psychological circumstances surrounding the loss, and the personality of the bereaved. He concluded that personality of the bereaved has the greatest influence on the course of mourning (Bowlby, 1980).

Bowlby's work was pivotal in providing insight into the experiences of attachment and loss in children and was influential in the development of programs and policies related to child care, hospitalization, and interventions with children experiencing short- and long-term losses. Bowlby's theories of adult responses to loss appear to be built on the research and practice of colleagues, especially Parkes. As a result, it is difficult to distinguish his ideas on adult bereavement from those of his contemporaries. In addition, his work evolved over time and, as changes were made, he has not clearly and concisely explicated his evolving theory. Nevertheless, his ideas influenced his contemporaries and continue to be an important theory of attachment and loss.

Psychophysiological and Biological Aspects of Grief

Expanding on Bowlby's work on grief as a behavioral phenomenon, Averill (1968) analyzed bereavement behavior from biological, cultural, and psychological perspectives. He hypothesized that bereavement has significance beyond the well-being of the individual and suggested that it fulfills an evolutionary societal need—namely, the maintenance of the long-term social bonds needed for survival of the species. Averill differentiated bereavement into two components: mourning and grief. Although both components serve to reinforce the social structure, mourning is the conventional pattern of responses dictated by the mores and customs of society. Grief, on the other hand, is a set of commonly experienced physiological and psychological reactions of biological origin (Averill, 1979). Although his ideas about bereavement were similar to Bowlby's with regard to the biological basis for grief and mourning, he rejected Bowlby's psychoanalytic interpretations and placed more emphasis on culture. In his treatise, Averill does not discuss all of the factors influencing bereavement behaviors nor does he attempt to incorporate grief into existing models. Neither Averill nor Bowlby's views about the biological evolutionary nature of bereavement have been widely accepted.

In 1961, Engel, a physician, challenged medicine by raising the question of whether grief was a disease occurring in response to the trauma of loss and therefore similar to the response of an individual to a physiological stressor such as a burn. His purpose in raising this challenge was to legitimize grief as a proper subject for study by medical scientists. Building on the views of Freud and Lindemann, Engel (1964) proposed that grief had biochemical, physiological, and psychological dimensions and suggested that grief responses occurred in a sequence of stages: shock and disbelief, developing awareness, restitution, and resolution. Until recently, Engel's views about the biochemical and physiological aspects of grief have had limited influence on the study of normal grief. However, advances in research on the biochemical aspects of behavior and on the immune system's response to stress have redirected attention to the biochemical and physiological consequences of grief.

Grief as a Stressful Life Event

Most of the conceptualizations about grief are psychodynamic, focusing primarily on the psychological responses to the loss itself; few authors have conceptualized the grief response within a broader stress framework. Yet, in all the major conceptualizations about stressful life events, grief is viewed as a major cause of stress (Stroebe & Stroebe, 1987). Pearlin (1989), however, views grief within a stress paradigm and suggested that the death of a spouse leads to other stressful events, such as economic hardships or social isolation, that may be stronger antecedents of the response to death than the death itself. Thus, he suggested that an individual's response to the death of a significant other must be considered in the total context of the individual's life, and that manifestations of grief are found at every level of functioning. He further suggested that the influence of mediators such as coping skills and social support are extremely important considerations in the eventual reduction of bereavement related stress (Pearlin, 1982).

Demi (1987, 1989) has proposed a model of bereavement that synthesizes grief, life transition, and stress and coping theories; the model provides a guide for understanding the interaction of multiple variables and their influence on bereavement processes and outcomes. Building on the work of Parkes, Caplan, and others, Demi suggested that the bereaved experience at least three crisis periods during bereavement; these periods are comparable to Parkes's stages of numbness and yearning, disorganization, and reorganization. The outcome of each crisis is a potential turning point that may lead to improved health and greater maturity or to poorer health and psychosocial deterioration. Adaptation is influenced by the balance of intrapersonal and sociocultural stressors and resources. Individual developmental stage and the developmental stage of the family also are considered as mediating variables. While this model is comprehensive and builds on other conceptualizations of grief, it has not been tested empirically.

Stroebe and Stroebe (1987) recently developed a Deficit Model of Partner Loss, which applies general psychological stress models to conjugal bereavement. The model offers an analysis of the situational demands characteristic of widowhood and of the coping resources needed to deal with these demands. Demands in this model include the loss of emotional and instrumental support and the loss of social identity; resources include both intrapersonal and interpersonal resources. Stroebe and Stroebe suggested that this model accounts for individual differences in both psychological and physical reactions to loss. The authors hypothesized that the closer the relationship between the partners, the greater the role differentiation within the marital group, the more central the marriage is to social identity, and the less warning the individual had of the loss, the greater the demands. However, individuals with a stable personality and with emotional support available may appraise the loss as less demanding and may cope better. Based on a thorough review of the bereavement research literature as well as their own studies, the authors also concluded that concurrent negative life stressors, gender, age, forewarning of the loss, and social support are critical in determining the course and outcome of grief.

A cognitive-emotional view of grief within a psychoanalytic framework has been conceptualized by Horowitz, who considers the response to death to be a general stress-response syndrome (Horowitz, 1982; Horowitz & Kaltreider, 1979). Based on Freud's observation of reminiscence and compulsive repetition following a traumatic event, Horowitz suggested that a major loss requires a change in one's inner psychic models. This change occurs slowly since it takes time for the integration of reality and for the development of new schemata to occur. During this process, the bereaved exhibit painful emotional responses such as vulnerability, rage, guilt, and sadness. Because these emotional states are powerful, controls are activated to prevent unendurable anguish, or "flooding." Thus, the response to death includes an outcry stage, which is replaced by a vacillation between "denial or numbing," in which reality is avoided and blocked, and "intrusion," in which the reality is faced. As the reality and schemata are integrated, the stress-response syndrome is resolved.

Horowitz redefined the conceptualization about pathological grief; he suggested that an excess in avoidance of the pain of grief or an excess in intrusion of the pain of grief may be caused by the reemergence of latent self-images and role relationships that may predispose one to pathology (Horowitz, Wilner, Marmar, & Krupnick, 1980). Horowitz's model is closely related to the DSM-III diagnosis of posttraumatic stress disorders (Horowitz & Kaltreider, 1979). The model is unique in its conceptualization of avoidance and intrusion as primary aspects of grief. Having evolved out of a clinical intervention program for the bereaved, the model has relevance for clinical work with the bereaved (Horowitz & Kaltreider, 1979; Horowitz et al., 1984). However, the model is only a partial model and does not account for many aspects of the grief response nor variables that may have an impact on the process.

Predictive Models of Grief

As research on bereavement has evolved, many factors have been found to influence both the grief process and grief resolution. Thus, there is a continual need to revise existing models of grief or to create new models of grief that incorporate these discoveries. A number of multivariate models have been developed to guide research; in these models key factors thought to influence bereavement reactions are identified. These factors include selected antecedent experiences, the background of the bereaved individual, illness- and death-related factors, and concurrent bereavement reactions. Many of these models tend to be partial models that focus on only one set of variables or on selected subconcepts; most of them are not clearly tied to previous conceptualizations of grief.

In his Human Grief Model, Bugen (1977) asserted that the intensity and duration of grief is best predicted by a combination of two key variables: the degree of closeness of the relationship (central or peripheral) and the level of perceived preventability of the death. Thus, if the bereaved had a close or central relationship to the deceased, the grief will be intense. If the bereaved survivor believes that the death was preventable and feels responsible, the grief process will be prolonged; however, if the death was perceived as unpreventable, the mourner is absolved of responsibility and guilt, thereby shortening the grief process. Bugen also proposed that the relationship with the deceased must move to a peripheral position for grief to be resolved.

Bugen's conceptualization about grief represents a partial model focusing only on a narrow aspect of the grief experience. Multiple factors such as suddenness of the death, personality of the bereaved individual, and ambivalence in the relationship should also be considered. Although the model has been useful in pointing out the importance of the closeness of the relationship and the perceived preventability, a major limitation is that Bugen conceptualizes these two variables as dichotomous and static rather than continuous and fluid.

A number of conceptualizations have identified social support or the social milieu as an important but often overlooked factor in bereavement responses. Dimond (1981), who has studied the grief of elderly widows and widowers, supported the notion of adjustment to the loss of a spouse as a period of psychosocial transition rather than an acute crisis. Dimond postulated that the adaptation of elderly widows and widowers depends on the interaction of three critical intervening factors: the support network, concurrent losses, and coping skills. Walker, MacBride, and Vachon (1977) in their studies of widows and widowers applied support networks concepts to the crisis of bereavement. They suggested that distress is caused by a lack of fit between social and psychological needs of the individual and the individual's social network. Maddison and his colleagues also asserted that the social network is an extremely important predictive variable in the widowed (Maddison & Raphael, 1975; Maddison & Walker, 1967). They also identified concurrent crises, mode of death, and preexisting problems in the marriage as important variables influencing outcomes in widows.

Clinical Models of Grief

Worden (1982) has proposed a scheme for understanding the grief process that synthesizes the work of many other theorists and researchers and builds on his own experiences with the Omega Project—a longitudinal study of the responses of individuals and families to life-threatening illness and suicide. Worden proposed that four "tasks of mourning" must be completed in order to resolve grief: accepting the reality of the loss, experiencing the pain of grief, adjusting to an environment in which the deceased is missing, and withdrawing emotional energy and reinvesting it in another relationship. In addition to describing manifestations of normal grief, he also provided clues to diagnosing complicated grief responses and identified key determinants influencing grief outcomes: role of the deceased, nature of attachment, mode of death, historical antecedents, personality, and social variables. Worden further proposed that grieving individuals need to take action, and that grief resolution can be influenced by intervention. Worden's book was written as a guide for clinicians working with the bereaved and, as such, was not proposed as a theory. Although he clearly described aspects of the grief experience and identified important variables influencing grief, he has not synthesized these variables into a comprehensive model of grief.

Therapeutic tasks of grief have also been identified by Shuchter and Zisook (1987) in their "multidimensional model of spousal bereavement." These tasks were developed to provide a framework for clinical interventions with the bereaved. The first two tasks involve developing the capacity to experience, express, and integrate the painful feelings associated with grief and to use the most adaptive means to modulate the painful aspects of these feelings. The third task involves integration of the continuing relationship with the deceased spouse. The fourth task involves maintaining one's health and ability to function. As the authors are particularly interested in "pathological" grief, they outline pathways in which both psychological and physiological manifestations occur related to this task of grief. The fifth task involves successful reconfiguration of relationships with others, and the last task involves achieving an integrated, healthy self-concept and stable world view.

The conceptualizations put forth by Shuchter and Zisook are directly tied to clinical intervention with bereaved widows and widowers. Research has been done by the authors on the topic of unresolved grief. It is not clear, however, how this work is tied to the model described above; one can assume that unresolved grief occurs when the tasks of grief are not completed adequately. On the other hand, Zisook (1987) suggested that most, if not all, of the bereaved never totally resolve their grief, and that significant aspects of the process go on for years after the loss, even in otherwise normal individuals.

An Integrative Theory of Bereavement has recently been proposed by Sanders (1989). The model is based on empirical research and psychodynamic theories including those of Freud, Bowlby, and Parkes. Her model includes five phases of bereavement: shock, awareness of loss, conservation-withdrawal, healing, and renewal. Each phase is characterized by a wide variety of responses that affect three levels of functioning: emotional, biological, and social. She proposed that at the end of the phase of conservation-withdrawal, the bereaved individual makes a decision, conscious or unconscious, to survive or to remain in perpetual bereavement. The decision to survive is not the end of the bereavement process; the bereaved must be motivated to implement enormous changes to reach renewal. According to Sanders, the inclusion of motivation is what differentiates her theory from preceding models of grief. Sanders further proposed that internally and externally moderated variables interact during the bereavement process and have a significant effect on outcome. This model is a useful step toward an integrative theory but falls short because it is a linear model, is logically inconsistent in some areas, and the key component—motivation—is not adequately defined or integrated into the model.

Another recent model, developed by Schneider (1984), incorporates a growth-oriented framework. For Schneider, the manifestations of grief are holistic and include physical, cognitive, emotional, spiritual, and behavioral responses. Schneider set forth nine assumptions about grief and identified three tasks of grief: limiting awareness, acceptance, and reformulation. The shifts from one task to another represent key turning points in the grief process. The model consists of a number of phases: initial awareness, limiting awareness, awareness, gaining perspective, resolving loss, reformulating loss, and transforming loss. Schneider also identified factors affecting the response to loss: type of loss, attachment, number of losses, existing relationships, personality, suddenness or anticipation of the loss, preventability, and time since death. In attempting to provide a holistic and comprehensive treatise on grief, Schneider's model becomes so complicated that it is difficult to follow. The model has not been widely used in either clinical practice or research.

An explanatory model of grief following unnatural death has been tentatively proposed by Rynearson (1987). He developed his model based on clinical research with the bereaved survivors and views the model as a potential basis for therapeutic intervention. Rynearson hypothesized that unnatural dying directly influences the nature and course of bereavement because the bereaved must adjust not only to the death but also to specific aspects of the unnatural elements of the death. Rynearson put forth four tentative propositions. First, the adjustment to unnatural death involves a variable combination of violence, violation, and volition; homocidal, suicidal, and accidental dying, in particular, involve these elements in a characteristic pattern. Second, the adjustment to unnatural death is a complex state that involves a balance between acceptance and denial of these dissonant variables. Each variable is associated with a compensatory psychological responses: "violence with postraumatic stress, violation with victimization, and volition with compulsive inquiry" (Rynearson, 1987, p. 82). These responses are specifically associated with unnatural dying and occur independent of antecedent factors. The third proposition is that the adjustment to unnatural death is positively correlated with the degree of identification with the victim. Fourth, the adjustment to an unnatural death is influenced by the sociocultural consequences of violence, violation, and volition.

Rynearson's overall proposition is that individuals adjusting to unnatural versus natural dying would experience a greater incidence of symptoms of posttraumatic stress, victimization, and compulsive inquiry. As this is a relatively new conceptualization about bereavement, there is little research or clinical validation of the model. However, the author invites others to test and expand on his ideas.

Parental Grief

Most of the conceptualizations about grief have been based on or focused on the grief of widows and widowers. These views about grief are fairly broad and universal, and help us to understand the grief of parents. However, there are elements of the parental role that are thought to lead to different manifestations and outcomes of grief. Thus, several authors have focused specifically on the grief process experienced by bereaved parents.

Miles (1984) has proposed a conceptual model for understanding parental grief. The model, based largely on the work of Parkes, describes the responses experienced by bereaved parents during three overlapping phases of grief: numbness and shock, intense grief, and reorganization. Reactions during the phase of intense grief include loneliness and emptiness, which lead to intense yearning and searching; helplessness, which leads to anger, guilt, and fear; physical symptoms such as appetite and sleep changes, somatic distress, and the onset of health problems; and behavioral changes, including depression, difficulty concentrating, confused thought processes, disorganization, and abuse of drugs and alcohol. Miles suggested that the "search for meaning" is a critical element in the grief process (Miles & Crandall, 1983). In addition, Miles, along with her colleague, Demi, have proposed a conceptual model of parental bereavement guilt (Miles, 1984; Miles & Demi, 1983–84, 1986). The authors hypothesized the process through which guilt feelings are developed in bereaved parents, identified key factors that may impact on guilt responses, and proposed a typology of guilt feelings. This model was expanded to encompass the grief experienced following any death and is presented in a separate chapter in this volume (see Chapter Eleven).

Miles's conceptualizations about parental grief were developed from observations grounded in clinical practice and were the basis of a publication used for over a decade by Compassionate Friends to help bereaved parents understand and cope with their grief (Miles, 1980). The model has not been developed further or tested empirically. The conceptual model of parental bereavement guilt, however, has been tested and revised (Miles & Demi, 1986; Miles & Demi, submitted).

Based on his extensive clinical experiences with bereaved parents, Klass (1988) also has conceptualized the unique aspects of parental grief when a child dies. Klass's model of grief is based on the previous psychoanalytic and psychodynamic models of grief. Klass views the death of a child as unique because parental bonds to a child are strong and deeply rooted in the parent's own history and psychological structure and because parents closely identify with their children.

For Klass, parental grief is represented as two disequilibria: a social disequilibrium and a psychic disequilibrium. Thus, bereaved parents must reestablish equilibrium between the self and the social environment and within their inner selves. A new social equilibrium is achieved when the parent establishes new patterns of interaction and sources of gratification that can provide the stability to function in a social environment that has been radically changed by the death of the child. The new social self is not a return to the old self, for the parents' lives have been drastically changed by the death. New psychic equilibrium is achieved as the inner representations of the child are reformed and incorporated into the bereaved parents' ongoing psychic life. The majority of bereaved parents internalize the dead child by introjection—that is, by keeping a sense of the child and of their emotional bond with the child intact while transforming the inner representation of the child in such a way that it brings solace (Klass, 1988).

The strength of Klass's model of parental bereavement is his attempt to tie the parents' responses to the death of a child to the overall parental role. In doing so, he has described some unique struggles experienced by bereaved parents. The theory is heavily rooted in psychoanalytic theory, and, as such, makes generalizations about the process of grief without clear validation of these views. Although Klass provides an explanation about why the process and experience of grief in bereaved parents may differ from the grief of other survivors, many of the experiences and processes he describes are equally applicable to grief following the loss of any close relationship.

A "two-track model" of parental grief was proposed by Rubin (1981), who suggested that the experience of loss has a broad impact on the bereaved that involves both a loosening of the affective bond with the deceased and personality changes. The first stage in the reaction to loss requires acceptance and a beginning loosening of affective attachments to the deceased. The following stage, the mourning period, involves a subdued process of detachment from the deceased and subtle changes in personality. At the final stage, a resolution is achieved with the conclusion of the detachment process and the stabilization of personality changes. Rubin tested his model with research with parents whose infants died of Sudden Infant Death Syndrome. The cross-sectional nature of the study and the measurement of "personality change" limit the generalizations that can be made from the study.

Littlefield and Rushton (1986) have proposed a sociobiology of bereavement. Building on the basic tenets of sociobiology, they proposed that the death of a child is difficult largely because children are the vehicles through which DNA is propagated into the next generation. They proposed that the degree of both genetic investment and loss should be proportional to the propagation potential and related meaning of each child. Thus, some children would be grieved for more than other children and some family members would grieve more than others. The authors put forth 10 hypotheses related to these tenets and then proceeded to test them in a study of bereaved parents. According to the authors, the findings supported many of their predictions and suggested that modern evolutionary theory is of value in helping to understand the ultimate significance of this and other human emotions. As noted by the authors, however, alternative theories also could be used to interpret the findings of the study and there are limitations in the design. The propositions of this model are not supported by the vast literature on parental grief that suggests that the intensity of parental grief is not greatly affected by the the presence of handicaps or other health problems that affect the child's future ability to parent a child.

Summary and Discussion

This review of past and contemporary theories about grief demonstrates both consistent and divergent views about grief. The models tend to be derived from *either* clinical practice or research. The clinical models are primarily concerned with describing the manifestations of grief and understanding the bereaved's responses in order to provide effective interventions. The research models have been developed to guide research in the field; they tend to identify key variables affecting grief responses but often do not adequately address the grief responses themselves. It is evident from reviewing the literature that clinical practice with the bereaved, bereavement research, and changes in other fields, such as psychology and medicine, have influenced views about grief and, at times, caused major shifts in the understanding of the bereaved.

As theoretical perspectives and research in the area of bereavement have evolved, some general concepts have emerged as salient. For example, most authors agree that there is an early period of numbness, shock, disbelief, and acute distress in the first few hours, days, or weeks following a major loss. There is also agreement that grief responses continue for many months and even for years, and that manifestations of grief include emotional, cognitive, social, and behavioral responses. The symptoms and behaviors described as common during grief, however, vary. In addition, many symptoms formerly thought to denote pathological grief are now recognized as normal components of the grief process. There is less acknowledgment and knowledge about the physical symptoms and physiological responses; consequently, these are often given insufficient attention.

Although there is widespread agreement on the normalcy of many grief manifestations, there is little agreement about what constitutes complicated or abnormal grief (Demi & Miles, 1987). In a preliminary review of the literature on this topic, we noted the widely divergent nature of this literature. For example, many of the early papers about pathological grief categorized individuals as abnormal based on behavioral or emotional responses that we currently consider normal. A comprehensive analysis and synthesis of this literature and some hypotheses regarding the parameters of normal and complicated or abnormal grief responses is clearly needed.

Throughout the twentieth century, conceptualizations of the duration of the grieving period have been continually revised. Early in the century, authors considered the grief response to be a long-term process (Freud, 1909/1955, 1913/1953). Grief was conceptualized in the middle of the century as an acute, short-lived crisis (Lindemann, 1944; Caplan, 1961, 1964). In the 1970s, theorists returned to the view that grief is long-term process (Caplan, 1974; Click, Weiss, & Parkes, 1974), a view that is currently widely accepted.

The changing conceptualizations about grief duration have greatly influenced bereavement research and practice. Today, a greater emphasis is placed on the importance of studying the bereaved for a longer period of time. In addition, clinicians working with the bereaved are increasingly aware of the potential need for long-term follow-up and recognize that intermittent therapy may be needed at critical junctures. This understanding of normal grief as a long-term process has also influenced the widespread acceptance of bereavement support groups that provide help to the bereaved over extended periods of time. There is, however, a gap in the conceptualizations about grief and in grief research in understanding how a major loss is experienced throughout life and how the event influences the life course of the bereaved individual. More longitudinal studies of the bereaved using a life-span developmental perspective are needed.

An important advance has been the identification of the many factors influencing the grief process and grief outcomes. Among the most important variables identified across the models are personal and family characteristics such as socioeconomic background, other concurrent stressors, and the availability of social support; relationship factors, including the role with the deceased, ambivalence in the relationship, and level of attachment; and aspects of the death, such as the type of death (violent, illness related, etc.), degree of forewarning of the death, and perception of preventability or responsibility for the death. Although there is general agreement about many of these variables, they are frequently conceptualized and/or measured differently in various studies.

Most of the models of grief are based on individual, psychodynamic views of personality. Several models, however, also incorporate biological and bioevolutionary views of grief, and interest has emerged in understanding grief from a psychoneuroimmunologic perspective. Another perspective that is not well developed is interpreting grief from a stress and coping perspective. Major loss and the resultant grief responses have not been well integrated into other broader theories about personality and human development. Furthermore, there is a great need to conceptualize how grief impacts on the family unit and how major or frequent losses in a family affect individuals and the family across generations.

In summary, most of the theories reviewed are partial models that explain limited aspects of the bereavement experience. Some focus on the process and manifestations of grief, while others focus on the variables influencing the process and outcomes. Most models, however, neglect the family, social, cultural, and ecological contexts that influence the bereavement process. Clearly, there is a need to integrate these contextual factors into a comprehensive theoretical model of grief.

References

Averill, J. R. (1968). Grief: Its nature and significance. *Psychological Bulletin, 10* (70), 721–748.

Averill, J. R. (1979). The functions of grief. In C. E. Izard (Ed.), *Emotions and personality and psychopathology* (pp. 339–367). New York: Plenum Press.

Becker, E. (1973). *The denial of death.* New York: Free Press.

Bowlby, J. (1960). Grief and mourning in infancy and early childhood. *Psychoanalytic Study of the Child, 15,* 9–52.

Bowlby, J. (1961). Processes of mourning. *International Journal of Psychoanalysis, 42,* 317–340.

Bowlby, J. (1969). *Attachment and loss, Vol. I: Attachment.* New York: Basic Books.

Bowlby, J. (1973). *Attachment and loss, Vol. II: Separation—Anxiety and anger.* New York: Basic Books.

Bowlby, J. (1980). *Attachment and loss, Vol. III: Loss—Sadness and depression.* New York: Basic Books.

Bowlby, J. (1982). Attachment and loss: Retrospect and prospect. *American Journal of Orthopsychiatry, 52,* 664–678.

Bugen, L. (1977). Human grief: A model for prediction and intervention. *American Journal of Orthopsychiatry, 47* (2), 196–206.

Caplan, G. (1961). *An approach to community mental health.* New York: Basic Books.

Caplan, G. (1964). *Principles of preventive psychiatry.* New York: Basic Books.

Caplan, G. (1974). Foreword. In I. Glick, R. Weiss, & C. M. Parkes, *The first year of bereavement* (pp. vii–xiv). New York: Wiley and Sons.

Cobb, S., & Lindemann, E. (1943). *Neuropsychiatric observations. Annals of Surgery, 117* (6), 814–824.

Demi, A. S. (1987). Hospice bereavement programs: Trends and issues. In S. Schraff (Ed.), *Hospice: The nursing perspective* (pp. 131–151). New York: National League for Nursing.

Demi, A. S., (1989). Death of a spouse. In R. Kalish (Ed.), *Midlife loss: Coping strategies* (pp. 218–248). Newbury Park, CA: Sage.

Demi, A. S. & Miles, M. S. (1987). Parameters of normal grief: A Delphi study. *Death Studies, 11,* 397–412.

Deutsch, H. (1937). Absence of grief. *The Psychoanalytic Quarterly, 6,* 12–22.

Dimond, M. (1981). Bereavement and the elderly: A critical review with implications for nursing practice and research. *Journal of Advanced Nursing, 6,* 461–470.

Eliot, T. D. (1930). Bereavement as a problem for family research and technique. *Family, 2,* 114–115.

Eliot, T. D. (1932). The bereaved family. *Annuals of the American Academy of Political and Social Science, 160,* 184–190.

Engel, G. L. (1961). Is grief a disease? A challenge for medical research. *Psychosomatic Medicine, 23,* 18–22.

Engel, G. L. (1964). Grief and grieving. *American Journal of Nursing, 64,* 93–98.

Feifel, H. (Ed.). (1959). *The meaning of death.* New York: McGraw-Hill.

Freud, S. (1953). Totem and taboo. In J. Strachey (Ed. and Trans.), *The standard edition of the complete psychological works of Sigmund Freud* (Vol. XIII, pp. 18–74). London: Hogarth Press. (Original work published in 1913).

Freud, S. (1955). Case histories. In J. Strachey (Ed. and Trans.), *The standard edition of the complete psychological works of Sigmund Freud* (Vol. II, pp. 22–181). London: Hogarth Press. (Original work published 1893–1895).

Freud, S. (1955). Some obsessional ideas and their explanations. In J. Strachey (Ed. and Trans.), *The standard edition of the complete psychological works of Sigmund Freud* (Vol. X, pp. 185–186). London: Hogarth Press. (Original work published in 1909).

Freud, S. (1956). Inhibitions, symptoms, and anxiety. In J. Strachey (Ed. and Trans.), *The standard edition of the complete psychological works of Sigmund Freud* (Vol. XX, pp. 77–178). London: Hogarth Press. (Originally published in 1926).

Freud, S. (1957). Five lectures on psychoanalysis. In J. Strachey (Ed. and Trans.), *The standard edition of the complete psychological works of Sigmund Freud* (Vol. XI, pp. 20–63). London: Hogarth Press. (Original work published in 1910).

Freud, S. (1957). Mourning and melancholia. In J. Strachey (Ed. and Trans.), *The standard edition of the complete psychological works of Sigmund Freud* (Vol. XIV, pp. 243–258). London: Hogarth Press. (Originally published in 1915).

Freud, S. (1960). Letter to Binswanger. In E. L. Freud (Ed.), *Letters of Sigmund Freud* (p. 386). New York: Basic Books, Inc. (Originally published in 1929).

Freud, S. (1963). General theory of neurosis. In J. Strachey (Ed. and Trans.), *The standard edition of the complete Psychological works of Sigmund Freud* (Vol.

XVIII, pp. 243–463). London: Hogarth Press. (Original work published in 1917).

Freud, S. (1966). Extracts from the Fleiss Papers. In J. Strachey (Ed. and Trans.), *The standard edition of the complete psychological works of Sigmund Freud* (Vol. I, pp. 220–232). London: Hogarth Press. (Original work published 1896).

Glaser, B., & Strauss, A. (1966). *Awareness of dying.* Chicago: Aldine.

Glaser, B., & Strauss, A. (1967). *A time for dying.* Chicago: Aldine.

Glick, L. O., Weiss, R. S., & Parkes, C. M. (1974). *The first year of bereavement.* New York: Wiley and Sons.

Gorer, G. (1967). *Death, grief, and mourning.* New York: Anchor Books.

Hoopes, R. (1977). *Americans remember the home front: An oral narrative.* New York: Hawthorn Books.

Horowitz, M. J. (1982). Stress response syndromes and their treatment. In L. Goldberger & S. Breznitz (Eds.), *Handbook of stress: Theoretical and clinical aspects.* New York: Free Press.

Horowitz, M. J., & Kaltreider, N. B. (1979). Brief therapy of the stress response syndrome. *Psychiatric Clinics of North America, 2* (92), 365–377.

Horowitz, M. J., Weiss, D. S., Kaltreider, N., Krupnick, J., Marmar, C., Wilner, N., & DeWitt, K. (1984). Reactions to the death of a parent. *Journal of Nervous and Mental Disease, 172,* 383–391.

Horowitz, M. J., Wilner, N., Marmar, C., & Krupnick, J. (1980). Pathological grief and the activation of latent self-images. *American Journal of Psychiatry, 137,* 1157–1162.

Kastenbaum, R., & Aisenberg, R. B. (1972). *The psychology of death.* New York: Springer.

Klass, D. (1988). *Parental grief: Solace and resolution.* New York: Springer.

Klein, M. (1940). Mourning and its relation to Manic Depressive states. *International Journal of Psychoanalysis, 21,* 125–153.

Kubler-Ross, E. (1969). *On death and dying.* New York: Macmillan.

Lazare, A. (1979). Unresolved grief. In A. Lazare (Ed.), *Outpatient psychiatry: Diagnosis and treatment.* Baltimore: Williams & Wilkins.

Leiberman, M. A., & Borman, L. E. (Eds.). (1979). *Self-help groups for coping with crisis.* Washington: Jossey-Bass.

Lifton, R. L. (1974). *Death in life: survivors of Hiroshima.* New York: Random House.

Lindemann, E. (1944). Symptomatology and management of acute grief. *American Journal of Psychiatry, 101,* 141–148.

Littlefield, C. H., & Rushton, J. P. (1986). When a child dies: The sociobiology of bereavement. *Journal of Personality and Social Psychology, 51,* 797–802.

Maddison, D., & Raphael, B. (1975). Conjugal bereavement. In B. Schoenberg, I. Gerger, A. Wiener, A. H. Kutscher, D. Peretz, & A. C. Carr (Eds.), *Bereavement: Its psychosocial aspects* (pp. 26–40). New York: Columbia University Press.

Maddison, D. C., & Walker, W. L. (1967). Factors affecting the outcome of conjugal bereavment. *British Journal of Psychiatry, 113,* 1057–1063.

Miles, M. S. (1980). *The grief of parents.... When a child dies.* Compassionate Friends, Inc., P.O. Box 1347, Oak Brook, IL 60521.

Miles, M. S. (1984). Helping adults mourn the death of a child. In H. Wass & C. Corr (Eds.), *Children and death* (pp. 219–241). Washington, DC: Hemisphere.

Miles, M. S., & Crandall, E. K. (1983). The search for meaning and its implication for growth in bereaved parents. *Health Values: Achieving High Level Wellness, 7,* 19–23.

Miles, M. S., & Demi, A. (1983–84). Toward the development of a theory of bereavement guilt. *Omega, 14* (4), 299–314.

Miles, M. S., & Demi, A. C. (1986). Guilt in bereaved parents. In T. Rando (Ed.), *Parental loss of a child: Clinical and research considerations.* Champaign, IL: Research Press.

Miles, M. S., & Demi, A. C. (1991). *Guilt in parents bereaved by accident, suicide, and chronic disease.* Manuscript submitted for publication.

Parkes, C. M. (1970). The first year of bereavement: A longitudinal study of the reaction of London widows to the death of their husbands. *Psychiatry, 33,* 444–467.

Parkes, C. M. (1972a). *Bereavement: Studies of grief in adult life.* New York: International Universities Press.

Parkes, C. M. (1972b). Health after bereavement: A controlled study of young Boston widows and widowers. *Psychosomatic Medicine, 34,* 449–461.

Parkes, C. M. (1975a). Determinants of outcome following bereavement. *Omega, 6,* 303–323.

Parkes, C. M. (1975b). Unexpected and untimely bereavement: A statistical study of young Boston widows and widowers. In B. Schoenberg, I. Gerber, A. Weiner, A. Kutscher, D. Peretz, & A. Corr (Eds.), *Bereavement: Its psychosocial aspects.* New York: Columbia University Press.

Parkes, C. M., & Weiss, R. S. (1983). *Recovery from bereavement.* New York: Basic Books.

Pearlin, L. I. (1982). The social contexts of stress. In L. Goldberger & S. Breznitz (Eds.), *Handbook of stress: Theoretical and clinical aspects.* New York: Free Press.

Pearlin, L. I. (1989). The sociological study of stress. *Journal of Health and Social Behavior, 30,* 241–256.

Peppers, L. G., & Knapp, R. J. (1980). *Motherhood and mourning: Perinatal death.* New York: Praeger.

Pollock, G. H. (1961). Mourning and adaptation. *International Journal of Psychoanalysis, 42,* 341.

Quint, J. (1969). *The nurse and the dying patient.* New York: Macmillan.

Rubin, S. (1981). A two-track model of bereavement: Theory and application in research. *American Journal of Orthopsychiatry, 51* (1), 101–109.

Rynearson, E. K. (1987). Psychological adjustment to unnatural dying. In S. Zisook (Ed.), *Biopsychosocial aspects of bereavement*. Washington, DC: American Psychiatric Press.

Sanders, C. M. (1989). *Grief: The mourning after*. New York: Wiley & Sons.

Schneider, J. (1984). *Stress, loss and grief: Understanding their origins and growth potential*. Baltimore: University Park Press.

Shneidman, E. (1973). *The deaths of man*. New York: Quadrangle/The New York Times Book Co.

Shuchter, S. R., & Zisook, S. (1987). The therapeutic task of grief. In S. Zisook (Ed.), *Biopsychosocial aspects of bereavement*. Washington, DC: American Psychiatric Press.

Siggins, L. D. (1966). Mourning: A critical survey of the literature. *International Journal of Psychoanalysis, 47*, 14–25.

Stoddard, S. (1978). *The hospice movement: A better way of caring for the dying*. New York: Random House.

Stroebe, W., & Stroebe, M. S. (1987). *Bereavement and health: The psychological and physical consequences of partner loss*. New York: Cambridge University Press.

Walker, K. N., MacBride, A., & Vachon, M. L. S. (1977). Social support networks and the crisis of bereavement. *Social Science & Medicine, 11*, 35–41.

Weisman, A. D. (1972). *Death and denial*. New York: Behavioral Publications.

Worden, J. W. (1982). *Grief counseling and grief therapy*. New York: Springer.

Zisook, S. (1987). Unresolved grief. In S. Zisook (Ed.), *Biopsychosocial aspects of bereavement*. Washington, DC: American Psychiatric Press.

Part Two

Concepts Central to the Study and Practice of Thanatology

Seven

Is There an Ideal Deathbed Scene?

Robert Kastenbaum

Robert Kastenbaum has contributed to the study of death-related experiences for more than three decades. "Time and Death in Adolescence," his first paper, was published in Herman Feifel's groundbreaking (1959) book, The Meaning of Death. *Current and recent publications include* Death, Society, & Human Experience, *fourth edition (1991), and* The Psychology of Death, *revised edition (1992). He serves as editor of* Omega, Journal of Death & Dying, *and the* International Journal of Aging & Human Development. *Other interests include the study of communication and creativity across the total life-span.*

Having worked his way through school as a newspaperman, Kastenbaum started graduate studies in philosophy, received his degree in psychology, became director of a geriatric hospital, and is currently professor of communication at Arizona State University.

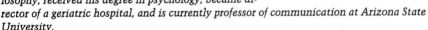

There have been numerous idealized deathbed scenes throughout human history. The brave warrior dies in stoic dignity. The aged patriarch blesses his family. The youthful martyr embraces death rather than deny her faith. The gasping sinner is released from guilt and anxiety by a sign of salvation. These and other idealizations of the deathbed scene were expressions of broader cultural themes and dynamics. Within some contexts, the idealized death was simply one that did not call much attention to itself or violate expectations. The men who rode with Attila, for example, were free to curse, scream, laugh, or remain silent as they exchanged lethal blows with their adversaries. Dying abed, attended by a priest and a loving family, did not figure in their expectations. They would die as they had lived, falling in battle or from exhaustion and disease.

More rare but highly influential have been the inspirational deaths of individuals who either affirmed or challenged cultural values at the cost of their own lives. The Dakota brave leads his companions into battle with the invitation that this is a good day to die. The Kamikaze pilot (having left his cherished American-made baseball glove in the care of a buddy) guides his dive bomber into the superstructure of an enemy cruiser. The physician exposes himself to a virulent disease to test his theory of its mode of transmission (Bean, 1952). The civic gadfly drains the cup of hemlock when he could have escaped with his life but not his philosophy intact. These exemplary deaths may be taken as instruction for the rules of living as well as dying.

Idealizations of the deathbed scene suffered a partial eclipse as the Industrial Revolution and the cult of progress made their way. Hardship and poverty were not new to the human condition, but overcrowding, pollution, appalling slums, and joyless labor seemed to deprive both life and death of their dignity for those who were not fortunate enough to catch the brass ring of success. Consider just one telling example: In 1832, the British parliament finally enacted a reform act to provide physicians with cadavers needed for research and training. The gallows had been the only legitimate source, but they did not keep up with demand. Furthermore, this forward-looking measure was intended to eliminate the practice of murdering people for their corpses or robbing freshly dug graves (Richardson, 1987). How was this reform to be accomplished? By consigning the bodies of poor-house residents to the surgeons! Already ground into ruins by the harshness of nineteenth-century industrial society, the miserable residents of the poor houses now faced the ignomy of being treated as though they were capital offenders and their bodies subjected to barely imaginable indignities. It was no exaggeration to say that the medical specimens-to-be were terrified at the prospect. Within this context, the deathbed scene held no promise of comfort or redemption; it was merely the prelude to another ordeal. (And, yes, the financial side of this reform measure was highly favorable to the medical establishment—cheap supplies were now guaranteed.)

Even so, the eclipse was not complete. Again, we must be content with a single example: Tuberculosis was a major scourge throughout the nineteenth century and well into the twentieth century. Although the parallel is limited, tuberculosis was in some sense the AIDS of earlier generations—young people inexorably wasting away while others stood helplessly by, often at a protective distance. Like AIDS, "consumption" was (1) contagious, (2) a progressively debilitating condition, (3) associated with "unclean" conditions, and (4) likely to cause death by snatching one's breath away. Nevertheless, a distinctive kind of idealized deathbed scene emerged. This was the image of a feverishly alert, strangely joyful, volatile, and creative person who seemed more alive at the point of death than did many others who were in full health. In their classic investigation of tuberculosis, Rene and Jean Dubos (1952/1987) observed that "the wasting and emaciation...added to the glamour of many of the romantic artists and poets." A new idealization of the deathbed scene had entered society's repertoire: life blazing up just before it is extinguished. There were some elements of reality here, but soon this image drifted away to pursue its own career through literature, drama, and anecdote.

The "romantic" deathbed scene often featured the tragic demise of a beautiful young woman by tuberculosis. Watching the final act of plays and operas, audiences could moisten their eyes as still another woman paid the wages of sin for having dared to love (the typical undertext). Women were also the favorite victims of suicide, self-sacrifice, or murder in the romantic deathbed scene: Madame Butterfly and Carmen continue to meet their doom in matinee and evening performances to this day. Whether through tuberculosis or some other means, the deathbed scene became an almost obligatory element in the assertion of romantic sentiments against the unsettling, impersonalizing forces of modernization. Alarmed by the accelerating demystification of self and world, many also felt an urgent desire to confirm survival after death. Deathbed visions (best known through Barrett's 1926 retrospective) were regarded by some as proof that spirits no longer of this earth may comfort us as we depart. The ideal deathbed scene, then, might be one that either expressed the drama of intense romantic individuality versus cruel fate or demonstrated the soothing balm of immortality on the dying brow.

In reality, deathbed scenes were far from attractive. Hospitals were regarded by the public as places to die—miserably. Deaths at home were often ordeals as well. Wealth allowed one to purchase the services of physicians who were more likely to increase suffering through the ignorant aggressive medicine of the day. Poverty meant watching a family member die by inches in a crowded flat or tenement. Symptom relief was rudimentary—a shot of whiskey was perhaps the best thing going, although some over-the-counter elixirs contained powerful drugs (the use of which is now heavily regulated).

By the middle of the twentieth century, the deathbed scene had lost much of its luster. Both physicians and chaplains were generally conspicuous by their absence. Distant and pseudo-objectivistic attitudes were sytematically instilled in medical training. "By the time he is in medical school, he is ready to call human skeletons 'Max' or 'Agnes'; and he can slap a cadaver on the backside as if it were a window-display dummy.... Does it need to be said that this bravado is largely counterphobic?" (Kasper, 1959, p. 261). Many clergy were also provided with little in the way of instruction for their encounters with the dying and grieving. "I saw my first dying patient today," a young chaplain told me in the early 1960s. "I was the one who was scared!" Although there were notable individual exceptions, neither the physician nor the chaplain seemed to regard the deathbed scene as a situation that demanded all that they could bring to it from their disciplinary knowledge and personal resources.

Within more recent years, the hospice movement has transformed concepts and practices of terminal care. The history, philosophy, aims, and methods of hospice care have been well described elsewhere (e.g., Gilmore, 1989; Kastenbaum, 1991; Manning, 1984; Phipps, 1988; Saunders, 1967; Stoddard, 1978). The effectiveness of hospice care has been evaluated repeatedly (e.g., Mor, 1987; Mor, Greer, & Kastenbaum, 1988). The overall pattern of results has been positive, especially with respect to sparing the patient from intrusive and useless diagnostic and treatment procedures, and protecting the patient-family primary support unit.

At a turning point in the hospice movement some recognition was given to the deathbed scene as such. Participants in an international conference agreed that most hospital deaths seemed to follow hidden standards such as the following:

1. The successful death is quiet and uneventful. The death slips by with as little notice as possible; nobody is disturbed.
2. Few people are on the scene. There is, in effect, no scene. Staff is not required to adjust to the presence of family and other visitors who might have their own needs that would upset the well-routined equilibrium.
3. Leave-taking behavior is at a minimum.
4. The physician does not have to involve him or herself intimately in terminal care, especially as the end approaches.
5. The staff makes few technical errors throughout the terminal care process and few mistakes in medical etiquette.
6. Strong emphasis is given to the body during the care giving process. Little effort is wasted on the personality of the terminally ill individual.
7. The person dies at the right time, that is, after the full range of medical interventions has been tried out, yet before the onset of an interminable period of lingering on. (Kastenbaum, 1975)

The conference participants—including Dr. Ciceley Saunders and other leading clinicians and researchers—articulated these hidden standards with the purpose of renouncing and replacing them with a more enlightened approach. The new standards proposed by this group eventually became the credo of the National Hospice Organization and were enshrined in the federal regulations that govern hospice operations and reimbursements. However, as time has gone by, there has been a tendency to overlook the deathbed scene itself. Hospice programs have had to work strenuously to muster the resources necessary to provide their services, educate the professional and lay public, and comply with the paperwork demands made on all health-related organizations. We have continued to learn about pain relief, staff stress, and many other important aspects. Meanwhile, though, the hospice deathbed scene has gone largely undocumented and neglected as a topic for systematic reflection.

In what follows, I offer some exploratory observations and comments on deathbed scenes within the current hospice era. A more extensive treatment of the subject with a different set of case histories has also been prepared (Kastenbaum, 1992).

Idealizations and Realizations

The interactive dynamics of idealizing and realizing deathbed scenes can perhaps best be conveyed through examples. I have chosen one example for detailed presentation, followed by briefer selections from the experiences of other individuals. Some details have been withheld or slightly altered to protect confidentiality.

The Entertainer's Final Performance

Mr. B. J. had a long and successful career in show business. A brochure reprinted a reviewer's comments: "A folksy, friendly, funny man, B. J. has never failed to captivate his audience." He was a solo instrumentalist and singer who could also banter amusingly and tell a good story. Although seldom the top name on the marquee, he often appeared in conjunction with the most celebrated performers of the day. Mr. B. J. was an elfin and lively person who seemed to thoroughly enjoy his life and career. Although his marriage had dissolved some time ago, he retained more family ties than might have been expected for a person who was so often on the move. There were seven grandchildren, four great-grandchildren, and a great-great-grandchild in the picture, along with a daughter, son, and other relations.

He and his much younger woman companion had been living with his sister and brother-in-law. But now, at age 73, Mr. B. J. was losing his struggle with cancer. He preferred to die where he was living, so he called on the services of a local free-standing hospice organization. Effective symptom management was established and maintained, and it was obvious that he had abundant interpersonal support from his at-home companions as well as the benefit of hospice expertise.

When it seemed as though death was but a short time away, he dictated a letter that was faithfully taken down and typed by his young companion:

Dear Friends:

I wish I could write you all individually but I haven't time. You all fall into a beautiful category, and yet together you become the sun in my life. Each of you, like a ray of light, that lit up my trail. And I hope that somewhere, along this line, I have brought you a ray of sunshine of my own.

I thank each and every one of you. Not one above the other, but all together. This has to be my last word. I never was good at communicating, but those of you that I've known, I'm so happy to have met.... So I bid you all goodbye for now and if you believe as I do, we'll all meet again and hopefully on the same shore and that I'm worthy to be with you. I say this with all the love in my heart.

Bless each and every one of you. Goodbye for now, but not forever. I'm going to play a bigger show. It's a long-term engagement, I hope. And I've been practicing a long time for this. So I hope that when I go on stage there that I'll be able to please you all again.

Your friend, BJ

The letter was to be accompanied by the lyrics to one of his own songs.

This deathbed message was not to be his final communication. It was the first of three "performances" in the kind of "farewell tour" that some entertainers so enjoy that they repeat them at regular intervals. But Mr. B. J. knew that this was to be his last "tour" and, characteristically, did not want to miss a moment.

The second farewell occurred several days later as he felt the hand of death even closer upon him. This time, he just let his thoughts roam where they would, but took care to see that his companion had her tape recorder handy. There was now a more personal, reflective, and questing character to his observations:

My mind and your mind is opening up to only sensitive communication and we must cast out any outside thoughts that would interrupt the words. We don't ask but we receive all ideas without question and all we have to do is keep these ideas within us, the reasons why we say them. And we do not interject the way He says them. It may seem illogical, upside down, for He speaks to us backwards, knowing that we can interpret them if need be....

This is the way of communicating the divine ideas through us to them to make them materialize in this babbling world of fools. We don't have to explain why. We use our minds directed by Him to bring the idea to those who can reform to a realization and to be trained that we might also interpret. As we see them (the ideas) progress into a meaningful interpretation within ourselves and as a dry, clear-eyed idea of what He is speaking, we don't have to keep babbling them out to the others....

As we become a finished product, a channel, both ways, then we become the overseers of His divine thoughts.... For this is the clear eyes of a baby who now [can] see and hear.... Then we become the channel, the communication between God and his lower self.

The concluding section of these deathbed thoughts was expressed in a rapid, unpunctuated, but decisively accented speech that perhaps bears comparison with the idiosyncratic genius of the Irish poet, Gerard Manley Hopkins. In our own vernacular, Mr. B. J. was "on a roll."

> Gradually becoming as Christ, the son of God, now molding itself into the man and cleansing each and every soul. It has nothing to do with us, the few before us and the few after us, will bring his new thoughts into the world, with no hardening of the heart. The hardness of the diamond idea; self by self, idea by idea, that is the diamond, the pearl, til the final great wonderful pearl of great force shining with all the pinnacle—the pearl of great price, eternal.

> We don't have to question anymore, for the first Christ is the pinnacle, the peak of perfection which we see born of every eye, ear, feeling, sensitivity. And all of God's will becomes the hardness, clarity, view, and truth of God's world. And man must more and more come to this final conclusion. (pause)

> It is finished.

> Thank you father. Amen. All men into one, his only begotten idea, his only begotten son, one in all, all in one. Indestructible, omnipresent, omnipotent. All powerful, all presence.... Go from here in peace. Amen.

> Thank you.

This rush of inspiration would have served very well as an exemplary deathbed scene—but there was another scene yet to come.

The next day, Mr. B. J. was very tired and wanted only to sleep. Nevertheless he perked up when he learned that it was lasagna for dinner. This was followed by a perilous episode—"a seizure of some type," according to hospice records. He could not speak for a while. As soon as he recovered the use of his voice, Mr. B. J. motioned for the tape recorder that now "was always kept by the bed for dictation purposes." ("Agnes" is his sister; "Chantele" is his companion.)

Chantele: Go ahead.... Want a drink of water? Here you go, take a drink. Baby, you gonna wake up?

B. J.: I'm awake.

Chantele: Agnes..Agnes, can you come here?

B. J.: To everybody..To all... Got a mike?

Chantele: Yeah, right here.

B. J.: To all... B. J. to all... Don't squeeze me, don't squeeze. (Chantele had put her arms around him, and Agnes was holding his hand.) To B. J....to me, from me...from me to all... In case... From me to all... Love, I love you.... Bye, bye, all is well... Forever... In case... All, everybody, it's been great. I

love you... you've all been good. I'll see you again.... One more time...I
love you all....OK

He dies.

This sequence of farewells together frame an extended deathbed scene
that occurred over a period of about four days. A selective summary-
analysis suggests:

1. Mr. B. J. was terminally ill for months, and dying for weeks, but the
   deathbed scene, as such, was introduced by his own initiative in
   dictating a farewell letter.
2. The dying man was keenly aware of his situation.
3. He played the dominant role in determining the character and tone
   of the deathbed scene.
4. Mr. B. J. was well prepared to construe his situation as the "last
   act" of a continuing series of performances he had given throughout his life. This was accompanied by a superior ability to impro-
   vise, shape, and communicate.
5. Through a combination of good fortune and his own ability to form
   and maintain intimate relationships, the dying man had the attention and support of two of the people who most mattered to him.
6. The social value of his last words was affirmed by the presence of
   listeners, a tape recorder, and a willing typist. And, in turn, the
   evident value of his last words affirmed that he had lived a worthy
   and interesting life.
7. His farewell letter imagery made no reference to physical or emotional distress. Instead, he opened with a nature metaphor ("sun,"
   "ray of light") that conveyed the impressions of warmth, clarity,
   and certainty, as distinguished from the possibilities of confusion,
   doubt, and fear in the fog-night-storm. The imagery concluded by
   assimilating his impending death with his career in show business.
   This bridging metaphor ("a long-term engagement, I hope") reduces
   tension by its light humor and sense of continuation. Nothing in
   the text suggests a dreaded fall off the edge of the world (or stage).
8. The blessing theme ("each and every one of you") is also a powerful
   component for an ideal or exemplary death. The dying person could
   be perceived as closer than the rest of us to the mysteries of
   existence, creation, and destruction. The dying person is also more
   dependent and vulnerable. From this enigmatic position of weakness and power, Mr. B. J. could offer something precious to those
   who would survive him. Apart from the spiritual implications, this
   rhetorical gesture helps to balance the social exchange that occurs
   in and around the deathbed scene: You have given devoted care; I
   give you the parting gift of one who must travel on.

9. The second farewell differed in content and structure, as it also differed in purpose and audience. The old entertainer was no longer standing in center stage taking his leave, but he was still in the wings, confiding in his supporting cast. His stream-of-consciousness remarks deserve more attention than can be given here. It is obvious, however, that Mr. B. J. was engaging in an inner dialogue with his sense of deity at the same time that he is attempting to report the results to his intimate companions. It is also obvious that there is an obverse to his friendly, folksy, audience-focused orientation: "this babbling world of fools." Just as the show business metaphor allowed him to bridge his life and death, so does his dialogue with God provide the opportunity to encompass both his persona and the disappointments and bitter memories that have been kept concealed from public recognition.

10. "It is finished" (how similar to Tolstoi's *Ivan Ilych*!!) refers not to his life but to his quest for understanding and resolution. The presence of an attentive companion might have been a key factor in his ability to reach this serene outcome. And, once reached, this mindset allowed him to return more securely to the blessing theme: "Go from here in peace."

11. The "final final scene" is beset and truncated by Mr. B. J.'s rapid physical decline. Syntax gives way, but the struggle for communication continues. Although very weak, he remains in command ("Got a mike?... Don't squeeze..."). Limited to the most essential of utterances, the old entertainer again bestows the gift of praise and absolvement. His survivors need have no self-doubts or regrets: "You've all been good" (by implication: "You've been a terrific audience!").

12. The very last word again expresses the consistent frame that Mr. B. J. was able to carry through his life to his death. Having attempted his final encore ("One more time..."), he offers his final "I love you"—and then, seasoned pro that he is, puts the whole performance into perspective: "OK." His observing self remains with his performing self to the end.

We will return to Mr. B. J. after some contrasting material is introduced. It should be noted, though, that these comments about "final act" and "performance" should not be taken to imply insincerity or superficiality on his part. At some points he was speaking more in his public voice; at other times, in his private voice. But he was thoroughly aware of his situation and strongly linked with his companion and sister. Unlike most other people, he came to his deathbed with a highly polished and dominant view of self that happened to prove well suited to the occasion.

Other Voices, Other Experiences

Much more briefly, we will expand our sample to include several other sets of observations and experiences that can contribute to our understanding of the exemplary or idealized deathbed scene.

A college student reflects on two types of experiences with deathbed scenes:

> Television movies or soap operas portray a romanticized portrait of the dying person. In the dying scene there is usually a very nice looking "dying" person carrying on a conversation with someone at their bed side. The words flow nicely, then suddenly the sick person gets weaker, closes his/her eyes and dies. Such a sweet scene. Even when it's an accident (or some other violent occurrence), the dying person again gets to say semi-sweet words. Again and again, death is treated as a small intrusion. It comes quietly and leaves quietly.

Her observations of the typical movie/soap opera version of the death-bed scene have been supported by those made by many other students and myself during our media-monitoring exercises. But now she speaks of a much more personal experience:

> My brother died last week. He died of cancer. The illness was diagnosed... last year and quickly progressed. His strength gradually went and his weight also. His handsome looks deteriorated and he looked so much older. Most movie characters... remain looking as great as ever with just a little touch of [dark] make up under their eyes to indicate illness. The last week of my brother's life was confined in bed. Although his mind was clear, he was in and out of consciousness and at times disoriented. Three days before he died, he couldn't eat, only took water from a spoon. Even swallowing the liquid was difficult. Pain was constantly with him, not one area in his body that didn't hurt. Those last three days he spoke very little and then with great effort. He closed his eyes, and six hours later his shallow breathing stopped. His family surrounded him. He died in his house as he wanted.

"The Hollywood version" of the deathbed scene bears little resemblance to the real thing (with some notable exceptions, especially in recent years). But the same can be said about the "educated young American" version. Students enrolled in two death education courses were asked to describe their own prospective deathbed scenes as they expected these scenes to actually happen—and then to alter these scenarios in both a positive and a negative direction (Kastenbaum & Normand, 1990). The resulting scenarios were compared with data from the National Hospice

Study (Mor, Greer, & Kastenbaum, 1988) and from a review of symptom control literature (Levy, 1987–1988). The deathbed scenes expected by the students were almost completely symptom-free and near-idyllic. (Even those who anticipated being killed in an accident did not expect physical or emotional suffering.) Despite their intentions to comply with the instructions, most students immediately transformed the expected into the desired. This phenomenon showed up clearly when they experienced great difficulty in altering the expected deathbed scene in a positive direction: "I guess I already said what I hoped is going to happen." Interestingly, even those students who already had significant experience as health care providers created deathbed scenes that were much closer to the Hollywood version than to those they had actually witnessed.

There is reason to believe that many people possess alternative visions of the deathbed scene. An idealized scene can coexist with a more realistic assessment. Veteran oncological nurses wept luxuriously over the sentimentalized deathbed scene in the novel and movie, *Love Story*. But the next day they would again cope resolutely with the hard realities encountered in their work.

It is possible that further research will indicate that both best case and worst case scenarios often supplement and even dominate our most realistic expectations. For example, a strong and cohesive family was providing excellent home care to its patriarch, supported by the services of a local hospice program (Kastenbaum, 1992). But the hospice nurse sensed that a powerful undercurrent of anxiety existed within this family and threatened to overwhelm them. It turned out that the family had been operating with the too-painful-to-express fear that the old man would "bleed out" as he died. Even in imagination, this event was highly stressful. Once she learned of this worst case scenario, the hospice nurse was able to offer the family assurance that this would not happen (and it didn't). While attempting to do what it could—realistically—to provide loving care for the dying person, the family was beset both by visions of a storybook finish and a catastrophic nightmare.

The actual death of the student's brother, described earlier, is much closer to the "normative" deathbed scene than either the Hollywood/Pollyannish or catastrophic visions. The young man was able to stay at home with his family and there were times when he could communicate meaningfully with them. Yet he did suffer many of the deteriorative physical changes associated with the dying process. It was one thing for his sister and other family members to share the impact of this ordeal—but it was an additional source of distress to be exposed to the mass media's distortion of the deathbed scene. She adds: "Movies avoid the ugly sounds of death. They avoid the 'baddies' of dying and use only the 'nicies' of the act. It reminds me of how drunkards are humorously portrayed on screen when in reality they're usually obnoxious or rude.... Wouldn't it be nice if death really were gentle, like it is usually portrayed in movies and TV?"

The Deathbed Scene and the Caregiver: A Few Questions

Studies of the human encounter with death have contributed some knowledge and understanding but have also been accompanied by the uncritical acceptance of "findings" that are little more than slogans. Systematic research into the contemporary deathbed scene has barely started and we do not need another set of premature conclusions to soothe, agitate, or confuse. However, one can offer a few guiding questions that might be of interest to family and professional caregivers.

1. *Can we find a balance between expectation and desire, hope and and dread?* Many of us have difficulty in resisting the images of both a catastrophic deathbed scene and one that is transfigured into a sublime spiritual experience. The passage from life has been neoromanced by some "pop-death" authors and lecturers. This has promoted a fantasy of "healthy dying" (Kastenbaum, 1979) in which, at an extreme, people are expected to be more actualized on their deathbeds than ever before in their lives. Such fantasies represent a flight from fears of unimaginable deathbed suffering as well as a displacement of the "ever onward and upward" theme that dominated our society during more optimistic times. Can we be tolerant of fantasies and fears—our own and others—while still keeping our focus on the realities of this unique person in his or her unique situation?

2. *Can we communicate openly, clearly, and flexibly with all the people who may have a role in the deathbed scene?* A positive answer would require our ability to select a language for mutual discourse that is not overloaded with technical terms or vague symbolisms. It would also require us to learn and respect the other person's viewpoint. This is not easy when the other person has both a background and a stake in the situation that is quite different from our own—or when custom has made us unduly deferential or persnickety to "that kind of person." Have we developed the ability to engage in that intense activity known as active listening? Can we decenter from our own concerns and anxieties in order to respond to the needs of others? These are among the factors that will either improve or impair communication around the deathbed scene.

3. *Can we sense the tides and tones, the overall shape of the deathbed scene?* As a successful performer, Mr. B. J. could grasp the signifi-

cance of a particular moment in his last phase of life. He could make the most of this moment and offer useful cues to his companions. Can we also be adept at recognizing where matters are heading, and when it is time to put everything else aside and speak? Listen? Touch? Pray? An excessive attention to details and routines could distract us from realizing what the moment requires. Can we align ourselves both with the details of care and the whole sweep of feelings and events?

4. *Can we participate in both an idealized and realized deathbed scene?* Yes, I think, but probably not at the same time. It is not likely that we will sense much of the "ideal" during the course of the terminal care process. There are uncertainties, setbacks, complications, intrusions, disappointments, and doubts. But we may later have the repose and perspective to discern that in realizing his or her own death, our dying companion was also approaching an ideal as well. The ideal, the perfect, the completed—all these related concepts require a pause from the onrushing stream of time. For a precious moment, the dying person and his or her companions may reach a place together that is not engulfed by the current. But for the most part, we will be holding on—to our companions, to ourselves—until time has slipped away with its prize. Later, in memory, in whatever repose life can offer, we are more apt to appreciate how this departure realized an immanent ideal for this one, unique, irreplaceable person. Does not the ideal grow from the actual, and is it not most at home where all ideals flourish?—in the expecting, in the recalling, in the sharing, in not the moment's pangs but the spirit's reflection?

References

Barrett, W. (1926/1986). *Death-bed visions.* Wellingborough, Northamptonshire: Aquarian Press.

Bean, W. B. (1952). Walter Reed. *Archives of Internal Medicine, 89,* 171–187.

Dubos, R., & Dubos, J. (1952/1987). *The white plague.* New Brunswick: Rutgers University Press.

Gilmore, A. (1989). Hospice development in the United Kingdom. In R. Kastenbaum & B. K. Kastenbaum (Eds.), *Encyclopedia of death* (pp. 149–152). Phoenix: Oryx Press.

Kasper, A. M. (1959). The doctor and death. In H. Feifel (Ed.), *The meaning of death* (pp. 259–270). New York: McGraw-Hill.

Kastenbaum, R. (1975). Toward standards of care for the terminally ill. *Omega, Journal of Death and Dying, 6,* 289–290.

Kastenbaum, R. (1979). "Healthy dying": A paradoxical quest continues. *Journal of Social Isssues, 35,* 185–206.

Kastenbaum, R. (1991). *Death, society, and human experience* (4th ed.). Columbus: Charles E. Merrill.

Kastenbaum, R. (1992). *The psychology of death.* New York: Springer.

Kastenbaum, R., & Normand, C. (1990). Deathbed scenes as imagined by the young and experienced by the old. *Death Studies, 14,* 201–218.

Levy, M. H. (1987–1988). Pain control research in the terminally ill. *Omega, Journal of Death and Dying, 18,* 265–280.

Manning, M. (1984). *The hospice alternative.* London: Souvenir Press.

Mor, V. (1987). *Hospice care systems.* New York: Springer.

Mor, V., Greer, D. S., & Kastenbaum, R. (1988). *The hospice experiment.* Baltimore: Johns Hopkins University Press.

Phipps, W. E. (1988). The origin of hospices/hospitals. *Death Studies, 12,* 91–100.

Richardson, R. (1987). *Death dissection, and the destitute.* London: Routledge and Kegan Paul.

Saunders, C. (1967). *The management of terminal disease.* London: Hospital Medical Publications.

Stoddard, S. (1978). *Hospice movement—A better way of caring for the dying.* New York: Stein & Day.

Eight

Physiological Characteristics of Dying and Death

Ida Martinson

Virginia Neelon

Ida Martinson, R.N., Ph.D., F.A.A.N., is Professor in the Department of Family Health Care Nursing at the University of California, San Francisco, School of Nursing. She is most well known for her pioneering study providing home care for children dying from cancer before hospice care became established in the United States. She is active in supporting the option of hospice care for children throughout the United States and the world. For 20 years she has studied families who have or had a child with cancer in the United States and recently in Taiwan, China, and Korea. With her doctorate work in physiology, the physical and psychological aspects of dying have been of a long-standing interest.

Virginia Neelon is an Associate Professor of Nursing and Director of the Biobehavioral Laboratory at the University of North Carolina at Chapel Hill. She received her undergraduate degree in nursing from Duke University School of Nursing, her master's degree in nursing from the University of California at San Francisco, and her Ph.D. in physiology and pharmacology from Duke University. Her physiology research has been in the area of membrane transport with a focus on the effects of aging on gastrointestinal transport of nutrients.

Neelon's nursing research and clinical interests are in the area of aging, taking both a physiological and behavioral approach to understanding problems of elders. She is coprincipal investigator with Dr. Mary Champagne in the study of acute confusion in hospitalized elders, funded by NIH and the National Center for Nursing Research. With Dr. Champagne and Ms. Eleanor McConnell, she has developed the Neecham Confusion Scale, an instrument for rapid and unobtrusive assessment of normal information processing and acute confusional behavior of hospitalized patients. Neelon and her coworkers were the first recipients of the Mary Opal Wolanin Research Award for their work in assessing acute confusion in the hospitalized elderly.

Overview

Historical Definitions

In the past, few difficulties existed in defining the concepts of *dying* and *death* with clear, simple, commonly accepted explanations. For example, Hippocrates (1849, p. 236) referred to the process of dying by observing that "signs of the worst" were "a sharp nose, hollow eyes, collapsed temples, cold contracted ears with the lobes turned out, forehead skin rough, distended and parched, and a green, black, livid or lead coloring of the face." The event of death was further described as "when the eyelids were contracted, livid, or pale; the lips and nose were livid or pale; and the other signs prevailed, then death was close at hand. The 'mortal sign' was relaxed, pendant, cold or blanched lips."

Later, Munk (1887, p. 55) offered a description of "dying persons" by utilizing similar anatomical descriptions, but varying the number, combination, and order of appearance of the specific characteristics. For example "signs of the dying act" were described as including glazed, half-closed eyes, dropped jaw with open mouth; blanched, cold, and flaccid lips; cold, clammy sweats on the head and neck; hurried, shallow respirations or a slow stertorous breathing with a rattle in the throat; irregular, unequal, weak, and immeasurably fast pulse; position supine sliding down toward the foot of the bed; arms and legs extended, tossed about in disorder; and hands waving in empty air, fumbling and picking.

Current Definitions

Contemporary attempts to define *dying* and *death* have become increasingly complicated with varying and sometimes conflicting interpretations arising from differing disciplinary approaches, especially in the disciplines of law, theology, biology, and in the clinical disciplines. Adding further complexity is the fact that health professionals tend to focus on different dimensions when defining these concepts.

In addition, while there has been a resurgence of interest in helping individuals and families understand and cope with psychological and spiritual concerns surrounding the dying process, there have been relatively few new developments (since the early 1970s) in our understanding of the physiological process of dying, despite some significant advances in the biological understanding of cell and organ function, of cell injury, and of the prevention of cell death.

Circulatory Changes.   A focus on changes in the circulatory system during the dying process is exemplified by several studies that have emphasized changes in the circulatory system to describe the dying process. Garvey's

(1952) investigation utilized such vital signs and other circulatory indicators as a rise in pulse, a fall in blood pressure, a rise or fall in oral temperature, a rise in rectal temperature, periodic or Cheyne-Stokes respirations changing to grunting and rattling, cold extremities, pallor, and mental cloudiness. Mottled skin and cyanotic lips and nails attributed to a reduced blood supply were signs seen by Walker (1973) during the last hour before death. Lewis (1965) claimed a slowed circulation predisposed the patient to complications. A decrease in peripheral circulation during the dying process was acknowledged by Worcester (1940). To this he attributed a drenching sweat and cooling of the body surface, regardless of the temperature of the surrounding air. The sweat was described as most profuse on the upper parts of the body and on the extensor rather than the flexor surfaces. As the surface cooled, the inward temperature increased instead of lessening.

Kirk (1968) viewed the terminal phase as resembling shock, except that in shock, the person retained a certain degree of consciousness. His description of clinical signs emphasized a rise in temperature and pulse, a fall in blood pressure, pallor, hollowed cheeks, pointed nose, dry tongue, dull corneas, sunken eyes, a cold sweating forehead, a loss of consciousness, a decrease in muscle tone so that the jaw sags and the mouth opens, and audible, rattling breathing going to shallow, inaudible, to Cheynes-Stokes respirations.

While recognizing circulatory changes, others have also commented on additional aspects, such as muscle dysfunction. For example, Worcester (1940) noted that dying is a progressive process, usually proceeding from the feet toward the head, resulting in the sensation of losing power of motion and reflexes, first in the legs and eventually in the arms. In addition, anal sphincters relax. The stomach tends to become distended because peristalsis ceases while swallowing and salivary secretions continue. Worcester also noted that sucking and breathing are the last instinctive actions and thirst the last craving. There is currently a debate about the extent to which a dying person experiences or suffers from thirst; systematic data are not available.

Other Changes.   Additional dimensions of dying have been explored by Rodstein and Borstein (1970), who revealed the electrocardiogram pattern of the dying heart, and Exton-Smith (1961), who documented geriatric patients' perceptions of such symptoms and discomforts as pain, nausea, vomiting, dysphasia, dyspnea, confusion, and awareness of dying. In addition, Carrington (1921) focused on the smell associated with the dying process. The so-called smell of death was described as the smell of musk, the source of which was claimed to be the development of ammonia in decomposing blood. Although the source is unknown, nurses have also reported a characteristic smell associated with the dying patient's room.

There are few objective and systematic studies published on the distress of dying. Rees (1973) found that only 26 percent of patients dying at home or in the hospital did not have one or more symptoms that were distressing, including vomiting, bedsores, and fecal or urinary incontinence. More than half of the subjects in this sample experienced pain of varying severity and experienced some anxiety. More than a fourth of them had severe or very severe pain, and severe or very severe respiratory distress. Some 40 percent of the subjects were depressed. Rees's results did not specifically corroborate studies by Hinton (1963) and Exton-Smith (1961) in terms of the frequency of various distressing problems but methodologic differences—differences in types of patient and the environment for dying—were obvious. Both of the earlier studies, however, did document the common distress and discomforts suffered by those who were dying. They also documented that as death became imminent, there was an increasing awareness by patients that they were dying.

Definitions of Death

Although there are many ways to approach definitions of *death* and *dying*, this chapter will focus on the physiological and biological aspects of dying. As such, *dying* will be defined as a series of irreversible biological events over time (which precede death) experienced by patients not expected to recover (Schusterman, 1973). The outcome of the dying process is *death*, which more precisely is a cumulative cell death that culminates in somatic death.

Somatic death, or death of the body as a whole, is defined as a cessation of the functioning of vital organs—the heart, lungs, and/or brain. With the collapse of any one of these vital organs, cell death rapidly proceeds, albeit unevenly, in the rest of the body, resulting in cessation of cell life throughout the entire organism. Rapid somatic death is thought to occur most often when cardiac functioning ceases. A number of serious events follow the cessation of heart beat (e.g., a fall in temperature which leads to cooling and stiffening of the body, clotting of the blood, discoloration of tissues, and structural and functional changes in red blood cells). Body temperature falls slowly rather than rapidly. By 24 hours after death it usually equals the temperature of the surrounding air. With infectious causes of death, body temperature may continue to rise for a period of time after death.

Muscular structure and chemical changes also occur, resulting in muscular rigidity and eventually autolysis of tissues. Because muscle relaxation requires energy, as ATP stores in the muscle are depleted, muscles contract and stiffen, and so-called rigor mortis sets in. The time frame for rigor mortis varies with the status at the time of death, but the entire body is usually affected by these changes within 12 hours after death. This is soon followed by diminishing of stiffness as necrosis and lytic dissolution occur. Similarly, failure of brain and lung function is equally destructive. Malfunctioning of these three organ systems and how they relate to somatic death will be explored more fully in the following section.

Cell death is the permanent cessation of life functions of the cell. Cell death can occur as a physiologic, energy-dependent event (apoptosis) as a means for the body to eliminate unwanted cell populations or as a means of regulating cell size. The cell disintegrates into membrane-bound bodies easily phagocytosed and degraded by adjacent cells. Since this process is a physiologic mechanism, it does not provoke inflammatory or connective tissue responses (Cawson et al., 1989). In contrast, pathologic cell death is characterized by mitochondrial swelling, disruptions of intracellular and nuclear membranes, and lysis with leakage of degradative and inflammatory enzymes into the surrounding tissue. Pathologic cell death, depending on the location and degree, may cause symptoms such as pressure, cramping, irritation, nausea, and so on.

In terminal illness, the primary mechanisms leading to cell death are by hypoxic or ischemic injury and by cytolytic destruction of cells by microorganisms, immune mechanisms, or chemical toxins. In hypoxic injury to cells there is depletion of oxidative-dependent cellular energy supply. Membrane transport processes fail and cells swell. Anaerobic glycolysis lowers intracellular pH and depresses metabolic functions. Ischemia involves not only hypoxic injury but further impairs the removal of toxic metabolites, particularly those resulting from anaerobic metabolism.

Microorganisms kill cells by direct cytolytic attack or provoke injury by initiating a host immune response. Certain injured cells/tissues (pancreatic cells) and some microorganisms can release powerful lytic enzymes that cause further necrosis of surrounding tissue. By all these mechanisms, in the terminal state, necrotic cells initiate a cascading process of further tissue destruction marked by swelling, inflammation, hemorrhage, and obstruction, both to blood supply and passage of body fluids and wastes.

Whenever cell death occurs, there is a termination of the functions of individual cells or groups of cells. Sometimes a particular vital activity comes to a halt before others. For example, the heart may continue to beat for a short time after respiration has stopped. Also, when cellular respiratory mechanisms are destroyed, other activities may continue briefly. Disassociation of vital functions at the cellular level makes it extremely difficult to be certain of the precise moment of cell death. In other words, cell death can occur without somatic death and somatic death can occur with cells continuing to live for short periods. The system does not fail all at once. Organs stop their operations at different modal rates, and possibly even at differing rates for each individual.

Cancer: A Case Example Demonstrating Physiological Symptoms of Dying and Death

Although a paucity of information exists that clearly identifies subjective and objective indicators of the dying process, two specific exceptions to that lack of information are *respiratory cell* and *cerebral cell death*. The first is recognized as an absence of respirations and the second as an absence of brain waves. One example of the dying process and the outcome of death has been documented by Inagaki and colleagues (1974) in studying the incidence of infection, organ failure, and hemorrhage, as revealed during autopsy of cancer patients. This study concluded:

> Infections in our patients were mostly due to the mechanical or pathological effects of the underlying malignancies.... More vigorous antibiotic therapy is needed before adequate control of these complications can be accomplished.... Twenty-five percent of the patients in this study died from organ failure which was usually caused by the underlying malignancy. Other factors producing organ failure in these patients were mainly arteriosclerotic in origin and occurred in the elderly population. Iatrogenic liver and renal failure were rarely seen as a terminal event.... The incidence of hemorrhage as the terminal event in leukemic patients has significantly decreased since the introduction of platelet transfusions. In our study fatal bleeding occurred in only 7% of the patients and was mainly related to tumor factors.... Finally, in a group of 83 patients with advanced disease, a specific cause of death could not be determined. All these patients had extreme degrees of debilitation, malnutrition, and electrolyte imbalance which led to death. At postmortem examination, their malignancy was disseminated to almost all vital organs and consequently they were considered as dying of "carcinomatosis." (Inagaki et al., 1974, p. 573)

Since cancer has been identified as among the major causes of death, this particular disease will be utilized to discuss some of the signs and symptoms of dying and death. Data underlying the present discussion are based on reports of physiological changes during dying as well as autopsy reports following death from cancer.

Death of Cells

As described earlier in this chapter, cell death results from a combination of influences. It is becoming increasingly clear that dying does not induce general cellular changes equally throughout the body, either on a morphological or biochemical level. Rather, the type and severity of the changes, consequent to dying, appear to vary considerably from cell to cell, as well as from tissue to tissue, within the same organism. In other words, dying of the cell may be ascribed to alterations in the setting of the control mechanism that regulates the functional activity within and between cells.

Physiological Changes During Dying

Although theories on the nature of the dying process are not numerous, and dying is not a simple discrete phenomenon but rather a series of complex interrelated cellular changes that occur over time, much of what is known of the dying process is related to the underlying disease processes. Much has yet to be learned, however, concerning cellular transformations associated with dying from a disease such as cancer, as opposed to those associated with dying that has resulted from aging. In addition, little study has been done to address the question of whether there are physiologic differences in the dying process that are related to genetic and racial differences,.

In an attempt to further explore the process of dying from disease, the following will focus on the three main mechanisms of dying: failure of the brain, heart, and lungs. Simply stated, the series of events leading to death are:

1. The brain ceases to supply information vital for controlling ventilation, heart action, or muscular tone of arteries.
2. The lungs are unable to supply adequate fresh air for gas exchange with the bloodstream.
3. The heart or blood vessels are unable to maintain adequate circulation of blood to vital tissues.

Prior to recent medical technological advances, the heart, lungs, or brain frequently failed in a rapid synchronous manner, regardless of which was initially mortally affected. Current technology can support the cardiopulmonary functions for long periods of time, maintaining cerebral performance and thus rendering inconsequential the temporal order of organ failure. Although the original intent of this life-support technology was to maintain the functioning of these organ systems during a period of crisis from which recovery might otherwise be expected, the utilization of such means to support vital functions in terminal patients regardless of age or disease may become inappropriate.

Cardiovascular System.   Proper circulatory function is maintained by a delicate balance between cardiac output and the venous return of blood to the heart. When blood volume is reduced, as in hemorrhage, hypovolemia results in a fall in venous pressure, and venous return to the heart may be inadequate. The compensatory response is an increase in veno-motor tone, which decreases the capacity of the venous system and its distensable bed, resulting in an increased venous pressure.

During the dying process, the heart as a pump can fail and all cells of the body are affected by insufficient blood flow, resulting in ischemia. If cardiac failure occurs slowly, some compensation occurs with dilatation of the heart and increased venous pressure. As the failure progresses, the venous pressure becomes too high and compensation can no longer occur. Signs of decompensation may include myocardial ischemic pain, liver congestion and distention, and pulmonary congestion. Other signs of circulatory disruption may be a decrease in skin temperature and a change in skin color resulting from insufficient peripheral blood flow.

In addition, cardiac failure causes changes in respiration. Slowing of the circulation can lead to the development of rapid Cheynes-Stokes respirations. The most common cause of Cheynes-Stokes breathing is a decrease in circulation time between the lungs and brain. Cheynes-Stokes breathing is initiated by a more rapid respiratory rate and deeper respirations. This, in turn, causes a decrease in PCO_2 in the pulmonary blood. Later (depending on circulation time), the pulmonary blood reaches the brain, the decreased PCO_2 affects the respiratory control center in the brain, and respiration is depressed or slowed again, leading to another cycle. In order for Cheynes-Stokes oscillation to occur, sufficient time must elapse during the hyperpneic phase for the body fluid PCO_2 to fall considerably below the mean. This decrease in PCO_2 initiates the apneic phase of respiration, which must last long enough for tissue PCO_2 to rise high above the mean. During hyperpneic phases, increased load on the heart (due to lowered blood pressure and increased ventricular filling) may cause cardiac failure if it is not already present. During apneic phases, the inability of chemoreceptors (in the aortic arch, carotid body, and medulla) to initiate respiration because of repiratory center asphyxia may lead to respiratory failure.

Central Nervous System Alterations.   An additional physiologic consideration directly influencing dying and death is the functioning or malfunctioning of the brain. Hemorrhage or growing brain tumors may interfere with other bodily functions, depending on which structures in the brain are affected. For example, if the temperature-regulating center in the brain is affected, uncontrollable fever may occur because the temperature-sensing regulation center itself is malfunctioning. This interrelationship is further exemplified by the existence of brain tumors, which may result in bleeding and damage to a portion of the brain, potentially influencing malfunctioning of any system of the body.

The complicated communication network of the central nervous system may break down in a variety of ways during the dying process. Infection of the lining of the brain seriously disrupts normal brain functioning due to the inflammatory swelling response. Blood flow disruption to various portions of the brain can be interrupted by moving clots of blood or tumor. Bleeding within the cranium causes pressure that may seriously damage brain function. Cerebrovascular episodes are a common cause of death when major vessels within the brain are occluded and circulation to the brain is impaired sufficiently. Malignant tumors within the brain, whether slow or fast growing, will be destructive of brain tissue because of their direct infringement. Metastatic lesions from a number of other primary malignancies can spread to the brain and cause similar damage.

Metabolic changes can seriously affect normal brain function by interfering with the integration of vital functions. Disorders of acid-base balance—such as renal, hepatic, or pancreatic failure—represent examples of destruction of brain function. Insufficient hormone secretion by the thyroid, adrenal, or pituitary gland also influences brain function through biofeedback mechanisms mainly through the hypothalamus. In addition, an overdose of barbiturates, tranquilizers, or other medications may markedly depress cerebral functions leading to decompensation.

Classic signs of brain decompensation indicating changes in consciousness include confusion or inability to orient to place, person, or time. More serious decompensation is characterized by lethargy, a state of apathy with reduced ability to perform simple cognitive functions; attention can only be stimulated or gained by tactile, auditory, or visual stimuli. Later, a state of sleep (stupor) prevails, in which there can be withdrawal or purposeless movement in response to touch, sound, or other stimuli, but no arousal or wakefulness occurs. In semicoma, movement can be elicited only in response to deep pain. In coma, the last stage of consciousness, no communication is possible at all.

In the early stages of central nervous system decompensation, pupil constriction becomes sluggish. When one side of the brain is compressed more than the other side, the corresponding pupillary light reaction may become more sluggish, but eventually both pupils lose their reactivity to light and dilate into a fixed position. Opiates like morphine can produce pinpoint pupillary constrictions. As brain hypoxia becomes worse, the pupils become dilated.

Inadequate cerebral blood flow may be indicated by the following behavioral characteristics: (1) disorientation to place, time, and event; (2) anxiety as evidenced by tone and pitch of voice, inappropriate laughter, picking at bed clothes, and darting of eyes from one object to another; and (3) stupor (i.e., slow responses in speech and manner with unusual stimuli required for arousal).

Respiratory Alterations.   Pulmonary failure is not uncommonly a cause of death. Simply stated, pulmonary failure is the inability of the pulmonary system to adequately supply oxygen and remove carbon dioxide from the bloodstream. In mild pulmonary failure, inadequate oxygen supply is observed first. Only much later does excretion of carbon dioxide become a problem; then carbon dioxide accumulates in the blood in the advanced stages of pulmonary failure. Interestingly, the early signs and symptoms of hypoxia or hypercarbia are rather similar. They include confusion, hyperexcitability, irritability, and a sense of fear ranging from mild anxiety all the way to a feeling of impending doom. In the beginning of respiratory failure, shortness of breath and an increased respiratory rate and depth occur with heavy exertion. As the process continues, shortness of breath occurs with even less exercise until finally it may occur at rest.

The four major causes of pulmonary failure are: (1) interruption of pulmonary vascular supply (pulmonary thromboembolism); (2) emphysema; (3) alteration of the chest wall; and (4) central nervous system alterations. The lungs act as a remarkably good filter, preventing all particles traveling in the bloodstream larger than red and white blood cells from reaching the systemic circulation. This sieve-like function is very useful for straining out abnormal intravascular material. In some situations, however, large blood clots from venous thrombi in the vessels of the lower extremities can cause death. Pulmonary thromboembolism is the third most common mechanism of death.

Structural changes in the lungs and chest can also create serious respiratory alterations. Chronic obstructive lung disease destroys pulmonary alveoli so the net surface area for air-blood exchange of gases is progressively reduced. Pneumonias caused by viral, bacterial, fungal, or other agents result in impaired gas exchange because they involve a significant inflammatory reaction that impedes oxygen transfer. Fluid or air accumulation in the pleural space prevents complete lung expansion. Common causes of such fluid accumulation in the dying person include congestive heart failure, infection, or cancer metastasis. Extreme muscle weakness such as that which occurs with some degenerative neuromuscular diseases may severely hamper respiration. Depression of the respiratory centers in the lower medullary portion of the brain can lead to all the characteristics of pulmonary failure and ultimately to death.

Near-Death Terminal Physiological Events, Signs, and Symptoms

Physiological events commonly occurring near the time of death include hemorrhage, cardiac alterations, pulmonary infection, or sepsis. Cardiopulmonary failure is a frequent final cause of death. Therefore, often the best indicators of imminent death are likely to be cardiac and respiratory signs.

During the last hours before death, signs and symptoms may be due to hypoxia. Signs and symptoms of anxiety may be present and may be primary or secondary to the hypoxia. A full-volume pulse means death is probably several hours away, whereas an irregular weak pulse suggests death is close. In patients with light-colored skin, mottling or blueness of the skin suggests shutdown of peripheral circulation and approaching death. In patients with dark skin, circulatory shutdown can better be detected by the color of nailbeds, the mucous membranes of the mouth, and the soles of the feet. Most patients become unconsious only for the last hours of life, although there are many exceptions. For instance, the person dying with a brain tumor may be unconscious for several days. Responsiveness to touch (e.g., eyelids flicker at touch) may mean a higher level of responsiveness.

Other signs of impending death include decreased urine output, mottled skin, agitation/distress, dyspneic cyanosis, decreased mental alertness, or sleepiness and apathy. Vital sign changes are variable with the underlying pathophysiology but often include decreased temperature, increased heart rate/irregular pulse, rise in respirations, periods of apnea, and fall in blood pressure.

When the patient's extremities become cold and cyanotic, breathing becomes irregular with periods of apnea, and perfusion parameters become weak, death may be impending within an hour or two.

Conclusion

The actual course of dying is indeed complex. Prior to technological advances, the heart, lungs, and brain frequently failed in a rapid synchronous manner, regardless of which organ was first mortally affected by what disease. Current technology, however, can support cardiopulmonary functions for long periods of time, maintaining cerebral perfusion and thus rendering inconsequential the temporal order of organ failure and cell breakdown.

Understanding the physiological interrelationships between cell death, somatic death, and failure of vital organs is an important step but only a first step in better understanding the dying process. Knowledge of underlying physiological changes during dying can enhance our ability to prevent needless discomfort, maximize symptom management strategies, and enhance the quality of remaining life.

References

Carrington, H. (1921). *Death, its causes and phenomena*. New York: Dodd & Mead.

Cawson, R. A., McCracken, A. L., Marcus, P. B., & Zaatari, G. S. (1989). *Pathology: The mechanisms of disease*. St. Louis: C. V. Mosby.

Exton-Smith, A. N. (1961). Terminal illness in the aged. *The Lancet, 2*, 304–308.

Garvey, C. J. (1952). *The management of the "hopeless" case*. London: H. K. Lewis.

The genuine works of Hippocrates (F. Adam, trans.). (1849). London: Sydenham Society.

Hinton, J. M. (1963) The physical and mental distress of the dying. *Quarterly Journal of Medicine, 32,* 1–21.

Inagaki, J., Rodriguea, V., & Bodey. (1974). Causes of death in cancer patients. *Cancer, 33,* 568–573.

Kirk, J. E. (1968). Premortal clinical biochemical changes. In O. Bodansky & C. P. Stewart (Eds.), *Advances in clinical chemistry, 2,* New York: Academic Press.

Lewis, W. (1965). A time to die. *Nursing Forum, 4,* 7–27.

Munk, W. (1887). *Euthanasia: Or medical treatment in aid of an easy death.* London: Longmans & Green.

Rees, W. D. (1973). The distress of dying. *The American Heart Journal, 86,* 141–142.

Rodstein, M., & Borstein, A. (1970). Terminal ECG in the aged. *Geriatrics, 25,* 91–100.

Schusterman, L. R. (1973). Death and dying—A critical review of the literature. *Nursing Outlook, 21,* 465–471.

Walker, M. (1973). The last hour before death. *American Journal of Nursing, 73,* 1592–1593.

Worcester, A. (1940). *The care of the aged, the dying, and the dead.* Springfield, IL: Thomas.

Nine

Psychosocial Variables
Cancer Morbidity and Mortality

Mary L. S. Vachon

Mary L. S. Vachon received her diploma in nursing from the Massachusetts General Hospital, School of Nursing. Her Bachelor of Science degree was obtained from Boston University. She then moved to Toronto, Canada, where she was employed by the Clarke Institute of Psychiatry for over 20 years. Currently, she is Consultant in Psychosocial Oncology at Sunnybrook Health Science Centre/Toronto Bayview Regional Cancer Centre. She obtained an M.A. in Sociology from the University of Toronto and a Ph.D. in Sociology from York University.

Vachon is an Associate Professor in the Departments of Psychiatry and Behavioural Science at the University of Toronto and is Clinical Co-Director of Wellspring, a community-based center for people with cancer. In addition, she is a consultant to Princess Margaret Hospital and the Palliative Care Team of St. Elizabeth Visiting Nurses Association. She is a psychotherapist, researcher, and educator who has focused her work in the areas of life-threatening illness, bereavement, and occupational stress. Most recently, she has completed a large study: A Needs Assessment of People Living with Cancer in Three Canadian Provinces. She has published widely, has lectured throughout the world, and is the recipient of several awards, including the Mara Morgenson Flaherty lectureship of the Oncology Nursing Society and a Citation of Merit from the Canadian Cancer Society.

Interest in the subject of the psychosocial aspects of cancer dates back at least to the second century and the work of Galen, who stated that "cancer was much more frequent in 'melancholic' than 'sanguine' women" (Stolbach & Brandt, 1988, p. 3, references in original). In the eighteenth and nineteenth centuries, authors suggested that women who were prone to develop cancer were sedentary and melancholic and they suffered from depression and/or deep anxiety. In addition, such women were thought to have experienced numerous disasters, losses, or reversals of fortune in their lives. These factors often resulted in feelings of grief (Stolbach & Brandt, 1988, references in original).

In the twentieth century, interest in the subject of psychosocial issues and cancer has been renewed. The focus has gradually shifted from an emphasis on the psychosocial factors that were hypothesized to be associated with the development of the disease (Evans, 1926; LeShan & Worthington, 1956; LeShan, 1959, 1966; Blumberg, West, & Ellis, 1954; Bacon, Renneker, & Cutler, 1952), to the psychosocial factors associated with the experience of the disease and its progression (Cassileth et al., 1985; Derogatis; Abeloff, & Melisaratos, 1979; Temoshok, 1987; Weisman & Worden, 1975; Worden, Johnston, & Harrison, 1974), to programs of intervention designed either to alter the distress associated with the disease or even to alter the course of the disease (Cunningham, 1988; Cunningham et al., in press; Cunningham & Tocco, in press; Grossarth-Maticek et al., 1984; Siegel, 1986; Spiegel et al., 1989). One of the difficulties of some of the programs that purport to alter the course of the disease is that the researchers may well be working with biased samples, thus their results must be viewed with caution (Morgenstern et al., 1984). Recent work by Spiegel and colleagues (1989), whose sample was more carefully controlled than most others, is therefore particularly important.

This chapter will review some of the current controversies in the cancer literature in an attempt to synthesize some of the findings on the psychosocial factors that are at this time thought to possibly be associated with the disease and/or its progression. The focus will be primarily on the most commonly discussed psychosocial variables: stressful life events, personality, and social support. There will also be a brief review of programs of intervention.

There are two basic premises that I make in this chapter. First, cancer is seen as being a biological disease that would continue to exist even if it were possible to alter the impact of stressful life events, transform personalities, and change social support systems at the individual level. (Whether cancer would continue to exist if we were able to alter the psychosocial factors involved with such variables as environmental carcinogens, dietary habits, smoking, sexual behavior, poverty, and heredity is beyond the scope of this chapter.)

The second premise of the chapter is that cancer, like any other disease, does not occur in a vacuum. The person living with the disease has a personal history that may or may not be relevant to the current illness experience. However, in the course of one's history, one has developed personality characteristics and coping mechanisms that may be helpful or unhelpful in dealing with the current illness situation.

In addition, most individuals are members of a social network. The manner in which an individual's significant others respond to the person and his or her illness may in part determine the individual's response to the disease. An individual's process of adaptation to disease will in part also be determined by a number of other variables, including one's age and stage of family development, the nature of the disease, and the trajectory or pattern of the illness. A diagnosis of widely disseminated breast cancer in a young woman with dependent children is obviously a different disease requiring a different response from that of an older retired man diagnosed as having localized prostatic cancer.

It must also be remembered that both the person with cancer and the others involved in the illness experience will respond differently, depending on whether the illness is perceived as having been "cured," whether it is a chronic disease, or whether the disease fairly rapidly progresses to death (Vachon et al., 1977).

Finally, the assumption is made that if the needs of the person with cancer and the significant others are handled reasonably well from the early stages of the disease, then even if the final outcome is death, the problems associated with this outcome will be fewer and less complicated than would be the case if there were numerous unresolved problems during the early stages of the illness.

Given that it is impossible to review all of the data available on the psychosocial factors associated with illness and death from cancer, this chapter will deal primarily with the issues of psychological factors that may be associated with the development and/or progression of the disease; personality; social support; and psychosocial interventions.

Because of the nature of this book, the focus will tend to be on the more life-threatening forms of cancer that are somewhat more likely to lead to death, rather than on the issue of survivorship. That does not mean, however, that the number of people who do survive and lead a full life after the diagnosis of cancer should go unrecognized. The reader who is interested in the subject of survivorship is referred to some of the literature in this area (Wiscombe, 1988; Cella, 1987; Cella & Tross, 1987; Fobair et al., 1986; Fraser & Tucker, 1988; Mullan, 1985; Quigley, 1989).

Psychosocial Factors and Life-Threatening Illness

Some of the major questions with regard to the issue of psychosocial factors and cancer are whether or not (1) there are certain stressful life events or personality characteristics that predispose one to develop cancer, (2) psychosocial factors are associated with long- or short-term survival with cancer, and (3) by discovering any connections, a difference can be made in either the development or the course of cancer.

The Biology of Cancer

Before discussing the psychosocial aspects of cancer, it is important that the reader has a basic knowledge about the biology of the disease so that psychosocial aspects can be placed into perspective.

Using breast cancer as an example, Hu and Silberfarb (1988) state that it must be recognized that there are many stages in the development of a cancer. The simplest model proposes a two-step process. The first step is the *initiation* of the disease. In this step, "cells are irreversibly changed into potentially neoplastic cells by an alteration in the genetic material of the cell" (p. 31). The second step is *promotion,* in which "agents act that facilitate the altered growth of the already initiated cell line [Pitot, 1985]" (p. 31).

Drawing on the work of Yarbo (1985), Beckmann (1989) says that the etiologic agents that act either as initiators or promoters of cancer produce genetic mutations at the

> cellular level which subsequently activate oncogenes that lead to malig-
> nant transformation and cell proliferation.... Because more than one mu-
> tation is required to transform a normal cell into a malignant one, several
> oncogenes or oncogene sets are involved in the transformation process.
> At some point in the process the contribution of the etiologic agents
> becomes unimportant. What is important is the cells' capacity to acquire
> a vascular supply, survive the body's own immunologic defenses, and
> proliferate in local and distant sites.

The process of the establishment of the disease takes varying lengths of time, depending on the type of cancer involved. To again use the example of breast cancer, the doubling time of different types varies from 8 to 15 years before a breast cancer becomes clinically evident (Hu & Silberfarb, 1988, quoting Devitt, 1976 & Fournier et al., 1985).

The Interaction Between Biological and Psychological Factors

The length of time it takes between the time of the initiation of a tumor and its development to the clinically recognizable level implies that if a researcher were to be looking for an association between the onset of disease and any specific incident or emotions that might be associated with the development of the disease, then, depending on the tumor type involved, one must look for events and traits from at least a decade before the diagnosis was made. "And any event that exerted an effect for only a short period would not appreciably decrease the time it took for a cancer to become evident and therefore would not increase the risk of cancer" (Hu & Silberfarb, 1988, p. 32).

In the specific instance of breast cancer, Hu and Silberfarb (1988) conclude that if psychologic factors are involved in the development of breast cancer then they probably operate as promoters of the disease, rather than as initiators.

> That being so, if they do affect the manifestation of breast cancer, they
> probably affect the progression of breast cancer in the same way, i.e. *the
> questions of whether psychological factors can influence the develop-*

ment of cancer and whether they can affect the prognosis of breast cancer are the same question. [italics in original] (p. 33)

Given the fact that promotion is clinically important in the manifestation of breast cancer, the authors state that stress as a promoter could in fact be clinically important in the manifestation of breast cancer. However, this is probably the case for only a subset of the breast cancer population and therefore one would not expect the finding to be consistently replicated in an unselected population. In addition, such an event would generally have occurred several years prior to the disease becoming clinically evident.

Stressful Life Events

One of the major controversies in the psychosocial oncology literature today is whether or not there are predisposing specific stressful life events, stressors, or personality characteristics that might be associated with the development of cancer. Hu and Silberfarb (1988) state that psychological factors, such as stress, could *potentially* act as promoters of cancer and could conceivably exert very powerful effects on the genesis and growth of clinical cancer. They state that with breast cancer in particular there is strong evidence that promotion plays a very important role in the expression of the neoplasm. They cite as evidence the fact that there is a much higher incidence of neoplastic mammary cells than is ever manifest clinically. Autopsy studies have shown that 25 to 30 percent of *all* women have either in situ or invasive breast cancer on autopsy. Obviously, this is far in excess of the number of women who are ever diagnosed as having breast cancer. Even metastatic cells do not necessarily lead to the development of metastatic disease. "Obviously, then, there are body conditions that are more and less conducive to the growth of breast cancer, and it would be reasonable to suppose that psychological factors could have an effect on these" (Hu & Silberfarb, 1988, p. 32).

Baltrusch and Waltz (1986) suggest that chronic stressors, such as loneliness, loss, problems in living, and/or an inability to cope with stressful life situations, might be implicated in the initiation and development of cancer. They suggest an association with parental rejection and/or lack of concern in the early family environment (see also LeShan & Worthington, 1956; Thomas & Greenstreet, 1973; Thomas, Duszynski, & Schaffer, 1979; Vachon, 1985, 1987). Such an early environment, it is posited, may in turn influence the personal and social environments one has in adulthood.

In addition, it has been hypothesized that chronic stressors may alter the

host environment, so as to favor the neoplastic transformation of normal cells or to lower antitumor resistance. Individuals with particular personal and social characteristics may have immunological malfunction due to

an abnormal neurohormonal regulation, which could weaken their defenses against oncogenesis, as Berczi [reference in orignal] and Dilman
[reference in orignal] suggest. (Baltrusch & Waltz, 1986, p. 264)

Osterweis, Solomon, and Green (1984) have reviewed the literature on
bereavement and cancer and point out a number of methodological flaws in
the literature that associate bereavement with cancer, especially cervical
cancer, leukemia, and lymphoma. They state, however, that a number of
studies have suggested that bereavement might predispose one to develop
cancer. This might be particularly true with hormone-sensitive cancers,
because there are observed changes in the hormonal milieu following
bereavement. Osterweis, Solomon, and Green state that estrogen-depen-
dent breast cancers and testosterone-dependent prostatic cancers might be
particular cases in point. They state that further studies are needed in the
areas of ovarian, testicular, and adrenal cancers.

Personality Characteristics and Cancer

A number of studies have explored the association between personality and
cancer. Again, one must be cautious in interpreting the results of such
studies. Baltrusch and Waltz (1986, p. 266) point out that "early losses,
rejection, and a feeling of social disconnectedness are very probably associated with trait anxiety and depressiveness, and the inordinate use of repression as a defence mechanism."

In addition, it is thought that early deprivation and loss may lead to
early immunological malfunction due to abnormal neurohormonal regulation. This might then weaken the body's normal host resistance "so as to
favor the neoplastic transformation of normal cells or to lower antitumor
resistance... [and] weaken their defenses against oncogenesis" [references in
original] (Baltrusch & Waltz, 1986, pp. 263–264). It has also been suggested
that there is an association between chronic stress in adulthood and a
tendency to react to stress with hopelessness and depression. It is hypothesized that these responses may be possible psychological precursors of
neoplasms (Baltrusch & Waltz, 1986).

Levy and Wise (1988) note that in attempting to understand the role of
psychosocial variables in the course of cancer, it makes sense to study
cancers in which psychosocial variables might be thought to have a substantial role (i.e., cancers in which biological factors might not account for
the total outcome variance). They have researched melanoma and breast
cancer because in their intermediate stages both of these cancers have fairly
unpredictable courses. "Very early and very advanced stages, as well as all
stages of more virulent malignancies such as lung or pancreatic cancer,
rarely deviate from their expected course. Thus, it is less likely the host's
behaviour will have a significant impact on disease course in the latter
cases" (p. 78).

Temoshok (1987) and her colleagues (Temoshok & Heller, 1984; Temo-shok & Fox, 1984), as well as Morris and Greer (1980) and Greer and Watson (1985), have proposed a Type-C coping style, in contrast to the Type-A behavior pattern hypothesized to be associated with cardiac disease. The Type-C personality has been hypothesized to be "cooperative and appeasing, unassertive, patient, unexpressive of negative emotions (particularly anger) and compliant with external authorities, in contrast to the hostile, aggressive, tense and controlling Type A individual" (Temoshok, 1987, p. 548). The Type-C personality has been associated with more prognostically unfavorable initial lesions in cutaneous malignant melanoma and breast cancer (Temoshok, 1987).

Cassileth and associates (1985) found no such association between psychosocial factors and disease progression in patients with advanced cancer. In an attempt to put both sets of findings into perspective, Temoshok (1987) proposed a process model of coping style and psychological-physiological homeostasis in which three groups of factors were considered: Type-C coping style, emotional expression, and helplessness/hopelessness. She hypothesized that the Type-C personality may be considered to be nice, friendly, and helpful to others. He or she seldom gets into fights and arguments and is helpful to have around. Psychological esteem derives from reflected acceptance and social rewards that come from the environment and the person feels psychologically balanced. Temoshok states, however, that what might happen over time is that the person might come to chronically block all needs and feelings and this might result in negative biological and psychological consequences. The person might come to be totally unaware of many physical and psychological needs and this may result in chronic feelings of hopelessness and helplessness. This attitude is often not consciously recognized because the person feels it is useless to express one's needs as they cannot or will not be met by the environment. The individual then feels helpless to change the situation. All of this is hidden under a mask of normalcy and self-sufficiency.

It is hypothesized that while this pattern may not be problematic for everyone with these personality characteristics, it may lead some to a numbing of biological and physical pain. In the presence of increasing stressors, even stronger Type-C mechanisms may arise. The person may begin to feel depressed. This depression is not linked to a specific stressor but is the cumulative burden of unexpressed needs and feelings that have not been adequately expressed or dealt with. This situation *may* set the stage for the promotion of disease.

Temoshok (1987) hypothesizes that the Type-C individual eventually develops a coping style that involves suppressing conscious recognition and even the perception of feelings and biological needs. In what she admits is a highly speculative theory, she hypothesizes that "cancer arises from situations that are chronically accommodated at a lower level of organization (than cardiovascular disease)—at the mental level of perception, which has as its biological substrate immunomodulatory neuropeptides" (p. 560).

The hypothesis goes on to state that at some point the accumulated stressor load becomes too much, particularly when a severe stressor is introduced. At this time, the individual has three choices: to marshall resources and develop a more stable and adequate coping style, to experience the breakdown of the Type-C facade and to confront the chronic but hidden feelings of hopelessness, or to continue to cope, using the Type-C style, but with more stress on the system.

If needs are expressed consciously, then the individual's social support system is hypothesized to improve and biological and psychological equilibrium are achieved. Intervention may be effective at this point in helping the individual to alter long-standing behavioral and cognitive patterns. "On the other hand, conscious hopelessness and learned helplessness are hypothesized to contribute to unfavorable health outcomes, as the individual gives up trying to achieve equilibrium in any area, and the previous state of chronic biological disequilibrium is exacerbated" (Temoshok, 1987, p. 561).

Temoshok (1987) posits that the reason why some studies have found the Type-C style to be associated with cancer outcome, while other studies have found helplessness and hopelessness to be associated is related to the time in the cancer and coping process that the psychological assessment was conducted.

> When these psychological variables are assessed after the traumatic event of cancer diagnosis, some individuals will be at the breaking point, while others will be tending towards either hopelessness or a more adequate coping style. On the other hand, long-term prospective studies are more likely to find Type C-like characteristics associated with cancer outcome. [references in original] (pp. 561–563)

One of the potential problems associated with the current theories linking stressful life events or personality to the initiation or progression of cancer is the potential to "blame the victim" (Sontag, 1977). The individual can come to be seen as being consciously or unconsciously responsible for the development of the disease and for the success or failure of efforts made to alter the course of the disease. Ruth Shereff (1989), a journalist who was diagnosed as having advanced ovarian cancer at age 44, writes of the distress a person can experience when well-meaning friends give the message that the individual is responsible for the disease. Such friends often supply the person with books that give overt or covert messages that, by following certain techniques, the patient may be able to alter the course of the disease. If one follows the techniques and the disease does not at least go into remission, then one may be seen as being to blame for the recurrence of the disease either because one has not worked hard enough or because one consciously or unconsciously has "chosen" to die of the disease. Shereff quotes the prominent psychiatrist Dr. Jimmie Holland as saying that this type of thinking may lead patients to fear that if at any point they get depressed or "down in the dumps," then they may be causing their tumors to grow. Dr. Holland is also quoted in the same article as saying, "People with a fighting spirit... often do better because they demand the right treatments and maintain good nutrition. There is no 'mysterious internal mechanism. It's just common sense'" (Shereff, 1989, p. 30).

In concluding this section, it is important to always remember that

> the major determiners of cancer outcome are biological: tumor type, how far the cancer has progressed before treatment is begun, and the biological treatments available for such tumors. But for some cancers, if behaviour matters—and we see evidence that it does—this is important because behaviors can be changed. Again, whether such change would affect the course of established disease is the next question to be answered. (Levy & Wise, 1988, p. 92)

Social Support and Life-Threatening Illness

Levy and Wise (1988) have found evidence of a link between social support and the increased risk of developing cancer. They state that the three factors that emerge from the literature and research studies on increased biological risk of developing cancer include "inadequate social support, cognitively generated helplessness, and inadequate expression of negative emotion" (p. 90). They posit a causal role for perceived social support in decreasing risks associated with cancer in that

> social support could operate cognitively, with other persons modeling and reinforcing active coping solutions during situational crises. Successful coping may enhance self-esteem and affect the causal attributions a person makes such that more credit is assumed for positive events and less blame is assumed for negative outcomes. Successful coping may reduce the physiological concommitants of stress, allowing neuroendocrine and immune functions to return to homeostatic balance. This balance might be protective in relation to disease outcome. (pp. 91–92)

They further suggest that when social support is effective, resulting in more effective coping, then the individual might be able to avoid the negative emotional and behavioral sequelae of failed coping experiences and thereby avoid the helpless/depressed symptom cluster. This might then affect the long-term outcome of the disease process.

Alternatively, Levy and Wise (1988) posit that social support might act on emotional expressiveness as one learns the acceptability of expressiveness from the members of one's social support system. This would be similar to Temoshok's suggestion that at a particular time the Type-C personality might be able to express needs verbally and consciously and thus receive help and support from the members of the social network. "Optimal social support may facilitate expression of distress in time of crisis, and also provide a higher likelihood that the distress will be dealt with and constructively resolved" (p. 92).

Support for the latter hypotheses was found in earlier work by Vachon and her colleagues (1979). They interviewed 162 women diagnosed with breast cancer and followed them for two years after the initial diagnosis. Eight years after the initial interviews, they accessed the hospital records to ascertain whether there were psychosocial variables that were associated with long-term survival. They found that women who had high distress (as measured by the 30-item Goldberg General Health Questionnaire) and high perceived social support were significantly more apt to still be alive eight years after diagnosis (68 vs. 46 percent, $p < .05$). When they controlled for the biological effects of the disease by excluding those who had developed a recurrence within the first year after their diagnosis, they found that 81 percent of those with high distress and high social support were still alive versus 56 percent of others ($p < .05$). The group that was most apt to be dead were those with high distress and low social support (49 percent dead vs. 19 percent of those with high distress and high social support). Similar findings in a larger New York study were reported by Marshall and Funch (1983). It may well be that the ability to express distress to a social support system that listens and cares may be associated with longer-term survival.

It has also been suggested that social support might work in other ways such as by acting to enhance compliance with a medical regimen (Levy & Wise, 1988). This may partially explain the finding by Vachon and colleagues (1979) that the women in the study who were rated as having good perceived social support reported being satisfied with the support they received from family, friends, and professionals.

Components of Social Support

Because social support is a crucial component in adaptation to life-threatening illness, it is important to understand its various components. Social support can be seen as a transactional process requiring a fit between the donor, the recipient, and the individual circumstances for its appropriate provision (Heller & Swindle, 1983; Shinn, Lehmann, & Wong, 1984). Social support is comprised of emotional support, appraisal support, informational support, and instrumental support (House, 1981). Emotional support involves actions that are self-esteem enhancing. Appraisal support provides feedback on one's views or behavior. Informational support entails giving advice or information that promotes problem solving. Finally, instrumental support is the provision of tangible assistance.

Social support is a process with multiple components. The "goodness of fit" between donor activities and the needs of recipients is governed by the amount, timing, source, structure, and function of social support. There must be an adequate balance between the amount of support offered and the perceived threat engendered by a particular situation. In addition, the type and amount of support most useful to distressed individuals may change over time. Support that is offered may not correspond with the circumstances of the individual (Heller & Swindle, 1983; Shinn, Lehmann, & Wong, 1984; Vachon & Stylianos, 1988).

The amount of support needed may vary not only with individuals but also with the stage of the disease. In a study of persons with either breast or colon cancer, Dunkel-Schetter (1984) found that, in general, the greater the amount of social support amongst those with a good prognosis, the more positive their affect and the higher their self-esteem. However, among those with a poor prognosis, that was not necessarily the case. Dunkel-Schetter suggests that individuals in the fairly passive role associated with advanced disease may feel that by receiving extra support, they incur debts that they will never be able to repay. This can be threatening to some individuals who are not used to being in the role of receiver. In addition, when one's well-being is threatened in multiple ways by a poor prognosis, social support cannot ward off all threats.

A Perceived Lack of Social Support and the Person with Cancer

The sensitivity to a perceived lack of social support that may be found in persons in either an acute or chronic stress situation, such as may occur with a diagnosis of cancer or in the process of living with the disease, may lead people to being vulnerable to what they feel is the wrong type of support. The so-called wrong type of support may involve the wrong timing—offering information about prognosis before the person is ready to hear it, for example—or the source of the support may be wrong. Research has shown that if support comes from the wrong person, if it is the wrong kind of support, or if the person feels rejected, then feelings of stress may be exacerbated (Dunkel-Schetter, 1984; Heller & Swindle, 1983; Shinn, Lehmann, & Wong, 1984; House, 1981; Vachon & Stylianos, 1988; Wortman & Dunkel-Schetter, 1979).

Dunkel-Schetter (1984) found that while a piece of advice might be rejected if it came from family and/or friends, the same advice coming from health care professionals might be accepted. In her study, she found that emotional support and tangible assistance were reported as being equally helpful whether received from family, friends or medical personnel, whereas information and advice were perceived as being helpful generally only if they were provided by medical personnel. When family and friends tried to provide information or advice, their attempts were resented and disliked regardless of the nature of the advice offered.

Individuals may feel embarrassed and more anxious when in a stressful experience—they feel they are being devalued by the experience or by others (Heller & Swindle, 1983). Suggestions from family and friends might be perceived to be criticism, whereas the same or similar suggestions made by professionals may be viewed as a neutral expression of helpful concern. The perception of disapproval from one's family and friends may become a source of ongoing strain or conflict that may generate shame or guilt, anxiety, frustration, and despair (Shereff, 1989; Thoits, 1985; Vachon & Stylianos, 1988).

Lehman, Ellard, and Wortman (1986) suggest that part of the difficulty that may occur between someone who is going through a crisis and a member of his or her support system is that while people know hypothetically what to do and say, the tension inherent in actual face-to-face interactions impedes the delivery of those strategies that would have been effective. This may be because of the anxiety about interacting with victims of life crisis, inexperience, as well as the fear of doing the wrong thing. The authors suggest that potential supporters may be so uncomfortable that natural expressions of concern cannot be expressed. Therefore, the helper acts primarily in a way that minimizes his or her anxiety (Lehman, Ellard, & Wortman, 1986; Vachon & Stylianos, 1988; Wortman & Lehman, 1985).

The lack of supportiveness may be particularly marked in those closest to the person going through the life crisis because these are the persons who feel most affected by the distress and feel most responsible for decreasing or alleviating the distress. This is not always possible. This problem might be most acute in persons who have what is called a "dense" social network in which most of the members know one another and hold similar ideas as to how the person "should" be coping with the problem at hand.

Social support serves a variety of functions. It may be important to have particular types of social support for certain problems or phases of the disease process (Vachon, 1986). Rook (1987) has found that those exposed to major life events require help provided by others (social support and social exchanges providing recreation, humor, and affection) that contributes to a sense of companionship and foster feelings of well-being. Support may protect people from the debilitating effects of life stress, but companionship protects them from the emptiness and despair associated with loneliness (Vachon & Stylianos, 1987; Rook, 1987).

Psychosocial Intervention

Christ (1984) has proposed a model of intervention in cancer that utilizes different interventions at nodal points in the cancer experience, such as diagnosis, treatment induction, treatment side effects, treatment termination, normalization, recurrence, research treatment, terminal illness, and bereavement. She suggests specific psychosocial interventions aimed at helping patients and families complete predictable, practical, social, and emotional tasks. These interventions include resource provision; education; cognitive skills training, including behavioral techniques; crisis intervention; supportive intervention; and insight-oriented intervention (Christ, 1984, as quoted in Vachon, 1988).

Interventions may be done by professionals or by skilled volunteers who may also have been or be cancer patients. Interventions may be done individually or in groups and may be offered to patients and/or families. This section will highlight a few of these types of interventions.

Individual and Family Intervention

Tarnower (1984) wrote of psychotherapy in the care of the person with cancer and said that psychotherapy may be seen either as a preventive measure or as a treatment for mental illness. When seen as a preventive measure, psychotherapy may

> enhance the individual's ability to cope with the extreme stresses, anxiety and depression that accompany the diagnosis and treatment of cancer.... Such preventive therapy might include individual work for the patient and/or family or pastoral counselling. Preventive therapies are used to avoid such serious emotional difficulties as incapacitating anxiety, disorganizing anxiety, chronic anger, fear, seclusiveness or an altered life pattern with undesirable relationships or destructive outcome. (Tarnower, 1984, as quoted by Vachon, 1988)

Psychotherapy for mental illness would include treatment of persistent signs of mental disturbance that seriously interfere in a person's functioning at home, work, or in social settings. Such intervention might also be necessary to confront issues involving confrontation with the reality of death.

There are comparatively few studies that attempt to look at the efficacy of psychotherapeutic intervention, particularly with persons with a limited life expectancy. An important exception to this is the work of Linn, Linn, and Harris (1982). They did a controlled study of 120 terminally ill men not being treated who were in a hospice setting. Patients were seen in a counseling relationship several times a week. Efforts were made to develop a trusting relationship in which the man could relate freely. "Efforts were made to reduce the patient's denial, but to maintain hope. Feelings of control over the environment were stressed. Patients chose whether or not to complete unfinished business, plan for their children, or decide about treatments" (Linn, Linn, & Harris, 1982, as reported in Vachon, 1988). Patients were encouraged to continue meaningful activities as long as possible and to perform a life review to attempt to reinforce life accomplishments, develop a sense of meaning, and provide for increased self-esteem and a sense of life accomplishments. Families were seen if and when the patient wanted them to be seen.

The results of the study were that at three months after referral, depression was less in the experimental group than in the control group and life satisfaction and self-esteem were increased at 3, 6, 9, and 12 months for the experimental group. In addition, those in the experimental group showed less alienation and more internal control. Controlling for one-year survivors, the experimental group had a better quality of life. Three months after the intervention started, the experimental families were better able to accept the diagnosis, offer more emotional support, and discuss the diagnosis more freely with the patient (Linn, Linn, & Harris, 1982, as quoted in Vachon, 1988).

Group and Family Intervention

Social support allows for comparison with others. When confronted by new and or ambiguous experiences, people tend to compare themselves with others in similar situations. Self-help or mutual aid groups allow for someone in a new and unaccustomed role to have a group of peers for social comparison (Shinn, Lehmann, & Wong, 1984). Dr. Phyllis Silverman (1980, p. 9), who has made a significant contribution to the mutual aid literature, defines *self-help* as a "personal search which need not involve a group, but rather, which usually involves the person's learning to use information and expert knowledge to cope with the problem.... [Such groups] can be and, generally speaking are, offered by professionals who may or may not have personal experience with the problem, but who use their training and expertise to help their clients care for themselves."

One of the most exciting examples of such a program is that conducted by Spiegel and colleagues. (1989). Spiegel states that he grew tired of hearing that psychosocial intervention could prolong life and decided to do a 10-year follow-up study on women with metastatic breast cancer whom he and his colleagues had treated with a 1-year program of supportive group therapy and self-hypnosis for pain. When he did the follow-up, he was surprised to find that those in the experimental group had lived twice as long as those in the control group (36.6 months for intervention group vs. 18.9 months for control group).

The Role of Persons with Cancer Providing Support to Other Persons with Cancer

The role of persons with cancer (PWCs) as providers of support has been researched and debated. For some PWCs, contact with another PWC may not be helpful (Rofe, Lewin, & Hoffman, 1987), whereas for others it may be most important. Van Den Borne, Pruyn, and Van Den Heuvel (1987) reviewed the literature on the effects of contacts between cancer patients and concluded that most of the studies did not satisfy the methodological conditions necessary to draw firm conclusions, nor were they grounded in theory. "Supporters of self-help claim that contacts between cancer patients will lead to a decrease in psychosocial problems. Opponents are convinced that such contacts increase uncertainty and anxiety and will lead to a decrease of self-esteem, for instance, in the case when a fellow sufferer dies" (p. 34).

Brown and Griffiths (1986) are persons living with cancer who have been involved in mutual aid programs in the United Kingdom. They say that while the models of mutual aid programs may differ, they all have a common thread of desiring to improve the lot of persons affected by cancer. They see the broad aims of these interventions as being to provide opportunities for support, participation, learning, and empowerment. The authors see two major types of groups. The first type is concerned primarily with the emotional and practical well-being of persons with cancer and their family members. These groups are not dogmatic and extend acceptance to people regardless of the manner in which they cope with their cancer. The second type informs people about a range of approaches that may either enhance their quality of life or are believed to have the capacity to affect the cancer itself. These groups teach people to help themselves through such strategies as relaxation, visualization, and nutrition. The efficacy of this type of approach is currently being studied in Canada by Dr. Alistar Cunningham (1988, 1989, 1991) at Princess Margaret Hospital. Other programs try to provide both types of intervention. Generally, the groups are primarily supportive rather than confrontative.

Efficacy of Mutual Aid Interventions

Taylor and colleagues (1986) reviewed the literature and concluded that most of the studies that have been done on support groups of a variety of types for PWCs have found similar results in that those who participated reported significantly less tension, less confusion, more vigor, less fatigue, fewer maladjusted coping responses, and fewer phobias without necessarily having a significant decrease in depression. However, she concluded that in some cases findings were ambiguous due to the lack of longitudinal design or to absent comparison groups.

Two important large studies of PWCs who did/did not participate in support groups have recently been reported (Taylor et al., 1986; Van Den Borne, Pruyn, Van Den Heuvel, 1987). In order to gain insight into the effectiveness of aftercare by "fellow sufferers," Van Den Borne, Pruyn, and Van Den Heuvel (1987) carried out a longitudinal and quasi-experimental, nonequivalent control study in the Netherlands. They found that regular contacts between fellow PWCs decreased negative feelings of depression, anxiety, and psychological complaints and increased self-esteem. This was particularly true for those under treatment and those whose disease had returned. Women with breast cancer reported that regular contacts with other women with the disease decreased their feelings of uncertainty, especially if they had not received relevant information from their physicians. Uncertainty was also reduced in those with Hodgkin's who indicated receiving relevant information from their physicians. However, for those with Hodgkin's who indicated they had not received relevant information from their physicians, having only a few contacts with others with the disease led to an increase in feelings of uncertainty.

Taylor and associates (1986) studied Southern California PWCs who had/had not participated in a support group. The sample was recruited through oncologists and support groups. Of the 1,068 potentially eligible PWCs, 61 percent responded. The median age was 58 years; 22 percent were males, 93 percent were white, and 62 percent had at least some college education, making this a rather biased white middle- to upper middle-class population. The results indicated that whereas the majority of respondents had found their family and friends to be supportive, 55 percent wished they could talk more openly with their family members and 50 percent wanted to talk more openly with friends. This study provided only marginal support for the idea that communication problems led people to join support groups. Those in support groups were marginally more apt to feel that their families didn't understand what they were going through and that family members expected too much of them. Although attenders were generally likely to be satisfied with the medical care provided by their main physician, they were significantly more likely than nonattenders to report a bad experience with the medical community during their medical experience. These experiences generally consisted of cold or callous treatment or a perceived error in medical judgment. Attenders were also marginally more apt to have other problems in addition to cancer.

The authors concluded that support group attenders were generally more apt to be users of resources of all kinds. They were more likely to have shared their concerns with their friends and spouses, to have consulted with mental health professionals, to have read books in order to solve their problems, and to have previously attended a support group for a problem other than cancer. They were also more likely to have been participants in religious, social, and cultural groups. They suggested that support groups were not meeting the needs of minorities, the working class, and males. They presented some evidence that males generally were more receptive to social support groups if the groups had an educational model and if their wives participated.

Summary

In summary, this chapter has attempted to provide a broad overview of some of the psychosocial issues that must be taken into consideration in caring for persons with cancer. Cancer has been seen as a biological disease to which some people may be more or less susceptible, depending on previous life experiences, stressful life events, personality, one's immune system, and one's social support system. There may be ways of altering behavior and/or increasing perceived social support. It is possible, but not yet conclusively shown, that these types of intervention *may* be effective in increasing life expectancy, particularly in diseases such as breast cancer and melanoma.

References

Bacon, C. L., Renneker, R., & Cutler, M. (1952). A psychosomatic survey of cancer of the breast. *Psychosomatic Medicine, 14,* 453–460.

Baltrusch, H. F., & Waltz, M. E. (1986). Early family attitudes and the stress process—A life-span and personological model of host-tumor relationships: Biopsychosocial research on cancer and stress in Central Europe. In S. B. Day (Ed.), *Cancer, stress and death* (2nd ed., pp. 241–283). New York: Plenum.

Beckmann, J. H. (1989). *Breast cancer and psyche.* Odense, Denmark: Ideas International.

Blumberg, E. M., West, P. M., and Ellis, F. W. (1954). A possible relationship between psychological factors and human cancer. *Psychosomatic Medicine, 16,* 277–286.

Brown, T., & Griffiths, P. (1986). Cancer self-help groups: An inside view. *British Medical Journal, 292,* 1503–1504.

Cassileth, B. R., Lusk, E. J., Miller, D. S., Brown, L. L., & Miller, C. (1985). Psychosocial correlates of survival in advanced malignant disease. *New England Journal of Medicine, 312,* 1551–1555.

Cella, D. F. (1987). Cancer survival: Psychosocial and public issues. *Cancer Investigation, 5,* 59–67.

Cella, D. F., & Tross, S. (1987). Death anxiety in cancer survival: A preliminary cross-validation study. *Journal of Personality Assessment, 51,* 451–461.

Christ, G. (1984). Support networks. In American Cancer Society, *Proceedings of the Fourth National Conference on Human Values and Cancer.* New York: American Cancer Society.

Cunningham, A. J. (1988). From neglect to support to coping: The evolution of psychosocial intervention for cancer patients. In C. L. Cooper (Ed.), *Stress and breast cancer* (pp. 135–154). London: Wiley & Sons.

Cunningham, A. J., Edmonds, C. U. Z., Hampson, A. W., et al. (1991). A group psychoeducational program to help cancer patients cope with and combat their disease. *Advances: The Journal of Mind-Body Health, 7* (3), 41–56.

Cunningham, A. J., & Tocco, E. K. (1989). A randomized trial of group psychoeducational therapy for cancer patients. *Patient Education and Counselling, 14,* 101–114.

Derogatis, L. R., Abeloff, M. D., & Melisaratos, N. (1979). Psychological coping mechanisms and survival time in metastatic breast cancer. *Journal of the American Medical Association, 242,* 1504–1508.

Devitt, J. E. (1976). Clinical prediction of growth behaviour. In B. Stoll (Ed.), *Risk factors in breast cancer.* Chicago: Year Book Medical Publishers.

Dunkel-Schetter, C. (1984). Social support and cancer: Findings based on patient interviews and their implications. *Journal of Social Issues, 40* (4), 77–98.

Evans, E. (1926). *A psychological study of cancer.* New York: Dodd-Mead.

Fobair, P., Hoppe, R. T., Bloom, J., Cox, R., Varghese, A., & Spiegel, D. (1986). Psychosocial problems among survivors of Hodgkin's Disease. *Journal of Clinical Oncology, 4,* 805–814.

Fournier, D., Hoeffken, W., Junkermann, H., Bauer, M., & Kuehn, W. (1985). Growth rates of primary mammary carcinoma and its metastases. In J. Zander & J. Baltzer (Eds.), *Early breast cancer—Histopathology, diagnosis and treatment* (pp. 73–86). New York: Springer-Verlag.

Fraser, M. C., & Tucker, M. A. (1988). Late effects of cancer therapy: Chemotherapy-related malignancies. *Oncology Nursing Forum, 15,* 67–77.

Greer, S., & Watson, M. (1985). Towards a psychobiological model of cancer: Psychological considerations. *Social Science and Medicine, 20,* 773–777.

Grossarth-Maticek, R., Schmidt, P., Vetter, H., & Arndt, S. (1984). Psychotherapy research in oncology. In A. Steptoe & A. Matthews (Eds.), *Health care and human behaviour* (pp. 325–341). London: Academic Press.

Heller, K., & Swindle, R. W. (1983). Social networks, perceived social support, and coping with stress. In K. Heller & R. Swindle (Eds.), *Preventive psychology: Theory, research and practice.* New York: Pergamon.

House, J. S. (1981). *Work, stress and social support* Reading, MA: Addison-Wesley.

Hu, D., & Silberfarb, P. M. (1988). Psychological factors: Do they influence breast cancer? In C. L. Cooper (Ed.), *Stress and breast cancer* (pp. 27–62). London: Wiley & Sons.

Lehman, D., Ellard, J., & Wortman, C. (1986). Social support for the bereaved: Recipients' and providers' perspectives on what is helpful. *Journal of Consulting and Clinical Psychology, 54,* 438–446.

LeShan, L. (1959). Psychological states as factors in the development of malignant disease: A critical review. *Journal of the National Cancer Institute, 22,* 1–18.

LeShan, L. (1966). An emotional life history pattern associated with neoplastic disease. *Annals of the New York Academy of Sciences, 125,* 780–793.

LeShan, L., & Worthington, R. E. (1956). Personality as a factor in the pathogenesis of cancer: A review of the literature. *British Journal of Medical Psychology, 29,* 49–56.

Levy, S. M. (1986). Behavior as a biological modifier: Psychological variables and cancer prognosis. In B. L. Andersen (Ed.), *Women with cancer: Psychological perspectives* (pp. 289–306). New York: Springer-Verlag.

Levy, S. M., & Wise, B. D. (1988). Psychosocial risk factors and cancer progression. In C. L. Cooper (Ed.), *Stress and breast cancer* (pp. 77–96). Chichester: Wiley & Sons.

Linn, M. W., Linn, B. S., & Harris, R. (1982). Effects of counselling for late stage cancer patients. *CA, 49,* 1048–1055.

Marshall, J. R., & Funch, D. P. (1983). Social environment and breast cancer: A cohort analysis of patient survival. *Cancer, 52,* 1546–1550.

Morgenstern, H., Gellert, G. A., Walter, D., Ostfeld, A. M., & Siegel, B. S. (1984). The impact of a psychosocial support program on survival with breast cancer: The importance of selection bias in program evaluation. *Journal of Chronic Diseases, 37,* 273–282.

Morris, T., & Greer, S. (1980). A "Type C" for cancer? Low trait anxiety in the pathogenesis of breast cancer. *Cancer Detection and Prevention, 3* (1), Abstract 102.

Mullan, F. (1985). Seasons of survival: Reflections of a physician with cancer. *New England Journal of Medicine, 313,* 270–273.

Osterweis, M., Solomon, F., & Green, M. (1984). *Bereavement: Reactions, consequences and care.* Washington, DC: National Academy Press.

Pitot, H. C. (1985). Principles of cancer cell biology: Chemical carcinogenesis. In V. T. DeVita, S. Hellman, & S. Rosenberg (Eds.), *Cancer—Principles and practice of oncology* (pp. 79–99). New York: Lippincott.

Quigley, K. M. (1989). The adult cancer survivor: Psychosocial consequences of cure. *Seminars in Oncology Nursing, 5,* 63–69.

Rofe, Y., Lewin, I., & Hoffman, M. (1987). Affiliation patterns among cancer patients. *Psychological Medicine, 17,* 419–424.

Rook, K. S. (1987). Social support versus companionship: Effects on life stress, loneliness, and evaluation by others. *Journal of Personality and Social Psychology, 52,* 1132–1147.

Shereff, R. (1989). Wish me well. *Ms., 18* (4), 26–30.

Shinn, M., Lehmann, S., & Wong, N. W. (1984). Social interaction and social support. *Journal of Social Issues, 40,* 55–76.

Siegel, B. S. (1986). *Love, medicine and miracles.* New York: Harper & Row.

Silverman, P. R. (1980). *Mutual help groups: Organization and development.* Beverly Hills: Sage.

Simonton, O. C., Simonton, S. M., & Creighton, J. L. (1978). *Getting well again.* New York: Bantam Books.

Sontag, S. (1977). *Illness as metaphor*. New York: Farrar, Straus & Giroux.

Spiegel, D., Bloom, J. R. , Kraemer, H. C., & Gottheil, E. (1989, October 14). Effect of psychosocial treatment on survival of patients with metastatic breast cancer. *The Lancet*, 888–891.

Stolbach, L. L., & Brandt, U. C. (1988). Psychosocial factors in the development and progression of breast cancer. In C. L. Cooper (Ed.), *Stress and breast cancer* (pp. 3–24). London: Wiley & Sons.

Tarnower, W. (1984). Psychotherapy with cancer patients. *Bulletin of the Menninger Clinic, 48*, 342–350.

Taylor, S. E., Falke, R. L., Shoptaw, S. J., & Lichtman, R. R. (1986). Social support, support groups and the cancer patient. *Journal of Consulting and Clinical Psychology, 54* (5), 608–615.

Temoshok, L. (1983). Emotion, adaptation and disease: A multidimensional theory. In L. Temoshok, C. Van Dyke, and L. S. Zegans (Eds.), *Emotions in health and illness: Theoretical and research foundations* (pp. 207–233). New York: Grune and Stratton.

Temoshok, L. (1987). Personality, coping style, emotion and cancer: Towards an integrative model. *Imperial Cancer Research Fund 1987, 6* (3), 545–567.

Temoshok, L., & Fox, B. H. (1984). Coping styles and other psychosocial factors related to medical status and to prognosis in patients with cutaneous malignant melanoma. In B. H. Fox & B. H. Newberry (Eds.), *Impact of psychoendocrine systems in cancer and immunity* (pp. 86–146). Toronto: C. J. Hogrefe.

Temoshok, L., & Heller, B. W. (1984). On comparing apples, oranges and fruit salad: A methodological overview of medical outcome studies in psychosocial oncology. In C. L. Cooper (Ed.), *Psychosocial stress and cancer* (pp. 231–260). Chichester: Wiley.

Thoits, P. A. (1985). Social support and psychological well-being: Theoretical possibilities. In I. G. Sarason & B. R. Sarason (Eds.), *Social support: Theory, research and applications* (pp. 51–72). Dordrecht: Martinus Nijhoff.

Thomas, C. B., Duszynski, K., & Schaffer, J. (1979). Family attitudes reported in youth as potential predictors of cancer. *Psychosomatic Medicine, 41*, 287–302.

Thomas, C. B., & Greenstreet, R. L. (1973). Psychobiological characteristics in youth as predictors of five disease states: Suicide, mental illness, hypertension, coronary heart disease and tumor. *Hopkins Medical Journal, 132*, 16–43.

Vachon, M. L. S. (1985). Psychotherapy and the person with cancer: One nurse's experience. *Oncology Nursing Forum, 12* (4), 33–40.

Vachon, M. L. S. (1986). Models of group intervention for cancer patients and families. In S. Day (Ed.), *Cancer, stress and death*, (2nd ed., pp. 203–206). New York: Plenum.

Vachon, M. L. S. (1987). Unresolved grief in persons with cancer referred for psychotherapy. *Psychiatric Clinics of North America, 10* (3), 467–486.

Vachon, M. L. S. (1988). Counselling and psychotherapy in palliative/hospice care. *Palliative Medicine, 2* (1), 36–50.

Vachon, M. L. S., Freedman, K., Formo, A., Rogers, J., Lyall, W. A. L., & Freeman, S.J. J. (1977). The final illness in cancer: The widow's perspective. *Canadian Medical Association Journal, 117*, 1151–1154.

Vachon, M. L. S., Rogers, J., Lyall, W. A. L., Cochrane, J., & Freeman, S.J. J. (1979, September 26). *Longitudinal adaptation to breast cancer.* Paper presented at the Canadian Psychiatric Association Annual Meeting, Vancouver, British Columbia.

Vachon, M. L. S., & Stylianos, S. (1988). The role of social support in bereavement. *Journal of Social Issues, 44* (3), 175–190.

Van Den Borne, H. W., Pruyn, J. F. A., & Van Den Heuvel, W. J. A. (1987). Effects of contacts between cancer patients on their psychosocial problems. *Patient Education and Counselling, 9*, 33–51.

Weisman, A. D., & Worden, J. W. (1975). Psychosocial analysis of cancer deaths. *Omega, 6*, 61–75.

Wiscombe, J. (1988). Surviving: A growing legion looks to tomorrow. *Coping, 2*, 12–16.

Worden, J. W., Johnston, L. C., & Harrison, R. H. (1974). Survival quotient as a method for investigating psychosocial aspects of cancer survival. *Psychological Reports, 35*, 719–726.

Wortman, C. B., & Dunkel-Schetter, C. A. (1979). Interpersonal relationships and cancer: A theoretical analysis. *Journal of Social Issues, 35* (1), 120–155.

Wortman, C. B., & Lehman, D. R. (1985). Reactions to victims of life crisis: Support attempts that fail. In I. G. Sarason & B. R. Sarason (Eds.), *Social support: Theory, research and applications* (pp. 463–489). Dordrecht: The Netherlands.

Yarbo, J. W. (1985). Breast cancer. The new biology in conflict with the old dogma. *Seminars in Oncology Nursing, 1* (3), 157–162.

Ten

Denial, Acceptance, and Other Myths

Stephen R. Connor

Stephen R. Connor, Ph.D., is a licensed clinical psychologist who has been a pioneer in the field of hospice care. Since 1975 he has served as the founding director of three hospice programs in California (Monterey, San Francisco, and Kaiser Hospital Walnut Creek). In addition, he has had extensive clinical experience working with the dying and bereaved. For three years he was a hospice surveyor for the Joint Commission on Accreditation of Healthcare Organizations. Connor has done research on the use of denial by the terminally ill, the impact of bereavement intervention on use of health care services, and factors affectiong anticipatory grief. He has chaired the psychosocial work group of the International Work Group on Death, Dying and Bereavement and currently chairs the National Hospice Organization's Standards and Accreditation Committee. Connor has published on a variety of hospice-related topics and is a frequent presenter at national meetings on psychosocial and management issues in hospice care. He is presently the Executive Director of the Hospice of Central Kentucky in Elizabethtown.

"We're all dying," Sheila said. "You might get hit by a truck on your way home and die before me." A few months later, I had the sad duty of confirming for 28-year-old Sheila that she was soon to die. In her last few days in the hospital, she showed a kind of acceptance. There was a look on her face I hadn't seen before. Mainly she seemed relieved. There was no more need to maintain a pretense. Also, a self-destructive tendency that led her to having sabotaged a reasonable chance for treatment of Hodgkin's disease was being fulfilled.

Such dynamics underscore the difficulty we all have in reducing the complexities of human experience to concepts such as denial and acceptance. Perhaps we have a greater need for landmarks and labels when dealing with the mysteries of the dying process, thus we feel more comfortable and less helpless if there is a predictable road map to follow.

157

This may explain why Elizabeth Kubler-Ross's five stages of dying (denial, anger, bargaining, depression, and acceptance) became so universally accepted as *the* explanation of the dying process. Other authors (Kastenbaum, 1974; Kalish, 1978) have commented on the limitations of her model. Our response to the knowledge of impending death is not a linear one. It is characterized by vacillations in emotional and cognitive responses. Most often the human reaction is that of ambivalence—the coexistence of fearful avoidance and the desire for release.

Rather than being contradictory, ambivalence seems a natural part of the dying process. Death as the ultimate unknown is usually feared. Underneath our managed exterior is a raw terror of annihilation. In our lives we attempt to control events; at the moment of death, control is gone. In juxtaposition to fear, many grow weary of the struggle to stay alive. There may also be a curiosity as to what lies ahead. At times, death may be seen as a solution to a life's unanswered questions.

This chapter will examine various reactions to the knowledge of imminent death. Stage theories and other models will be examined. The concept of denial of death, a complex and misunderstood phenomenon, will also be explored. Emphasis will be placed on the interpersonal nature of denial. Death acceptance will be explored from both the psychological and transcendent perspective. Finally, some clinical observations on working with the dying and their families experiencing these reactions will be presented.

Reactions to the Knowledge of Imminent Death

Death defines life. It gives our lives meaning and context, yet nothing is as feared or as assiduously avoided. There are probably as many reactions to dying as there are people who die. It is really quite intriguing how individuals faced with comparable tragedies can respond so differently. One may be incapacitated with anxiety and dread; another reacts with stoic resignation. Recently, a patient said he felt that "death was like a big present with a bow tied on it." He couldn't wait to find out what was inside.

Weisman (1972) originated the concept of "appropriate death." He describes this as a purposeful death. Appropriate death should be pain free, with emotional and social impoverishments kept to a minimum. The person should be able to function as effectively as possible as long as possible before dying. Conflicts should be recognized and resolved, and remaining wishes should be satisfied. Control should be yielded to others in whom the dying person has confidence. However, what might be an appropriate death for one person might be unsuitable for another.

A considerable body of research points to the view that in adults age is negatively correlated with fear of death. Bengston, Cuellar, and Ragan (1977) studied three age groups (45–54, 55–64, 65–74). The youngest cohort expressed the most fear of death, whereas the oldest expressed the least. Similar results were found by Kalish and Reynolds (1977), Wass (1977), Devins (1979), Cappon (1978), and Kastenbaum and Aisenberg (1972).

A number of factors may account for this tendency. The elderly are confronted more often with death among their peers. Death is viewed culturally as the natural conclusion to the life cycle. Older persons are also more likely to believe in an afterlife (Kalish & Reynolds, 1977). They may be less concerned about survivors and less concerned about having additional life experiences.

Is it true that people die as they lived? In the sense that people cope with death the way they've coped with other problems in life, perhaps yes. Yet there are times when the dying process inflicts indignities that seem so inappropriate to a loving, caring person, or when death seems so easy for the hard-hearted.

Stage Theories

Kubler-Ross's (1969) five stages of dying have been most effective in entering the popular imagination. As a metaphor for dealing with all losses, many of us feel the sequence fits with human experience. She provided a new language that can be useful if not used too concretely.

Kastenbaum (1974) states that the problems with stage theories of dying are that they reckon little with the symptoms and trajectories of a particular disease state, with the person's personality, or with the person's environment. He also criticizes the lack of any scientific evidence for the existence of the five stages (Kastenbaum & Kastenbaum, 1989).

Garfield (1978) challenges the notion that all people—regardless of belief system, age, race, culture, and historical period—die in a uniform sequence. Kalish (1978) questions whether all patients go through stages and highlights the influence of the medical care system on the patient's reactions to illness. The goals of cure and rehabilitation can encourage reactions such as denial and anger. Dying persons show a variety of emotions that ebb and flow throughout their lives. These emotional reactions or stages can vary from minute to minute. We see a wide variety of emotions in dying people, some displaying a few, some a great many.

Instead of defining a universal, sequential order of stages of dying, it may be more helpful to describe phases of dying and courses of illness that demand different coping strategies at different times.

Holland (1989) describes several possible courses for the patient following a cancer diagnosis: (1) treatment leading to long survival and cure; (2) treatment leading to survival with no evidence of disease, followed by recurrence; (3) treatment with poor response and no disease free interval, followed by palliative treatment and death; and (4) no primary treatment possible, followed by palliative treatment and death. For the patient who experiences many remissions, there may be considerable uncertainty, ambiguity, and several episodes of heightened anxiety and preparation for death. There is also uncertainty as to length of remission (or "cure") and when recurrence will occur.

Another view of the phases involved in dying of a terminal illness is offered by Weisman (Pattison, 1978). These include (1) the acute crisis of knowledge phase; (2) the chronic, living-dying interval (middle knowledge); and (3) the terminal phase. Weisman (1972) adds that, given the same disease, people do not follow the same sequences and do not die at the same rate, of the same causes, or the same circumstances. There is no well-recognized succession of emotional responses that are typical of people facing death. Pattison (1978) believes that the concept of stages of dying is not only inaccurate but misleading to both the dying person and his or her helpers. Dying may be stageless.

Denial of Death

The concept of denial originates in the early writings of Freud (1924), who introduced the term *disavowal*. Originally thought of as a psychotic symptom, denial came to be viewed also as a mechanism of defense used in some neurotic conflicts (Freud, 1940).

Denial is often thought of as a process of repudiating a painful reality and sometimes replacing it with a more pleasant version. It has always been thought of as a reaction to external threats, whereas *repression* is considered the psychological mechanism for dealing with internal distress or troubling impulses. Jacobson (1957) examined the use of denial in both the internal and external world. The dichotomy between denial and repression remains though the meaning of these two terms has tended to merge.

Psychoanalytic thinkers view denial as the result of intrapsychic conflict. In the case of terminal illness, the external threat of death causes the person to feel in danger of being overwhelmed with anxiety. The individual who lacks higher functioning defenses resorts to the more primitive use of denial to survive emotionally. (See Sjoback [1973] for a thorough account of the development of the psychoanalytic concept of denial.) Others have viewed denial as a more adaptive coping process (Beilin, 1981; Beisser, 1979; Dansak & Cordes, 1978–79; Hackett & Cassem, 1970; Haan, 1965) or as a useful strategy in the early stages of response to cancer (Detwiler, 1981; Falek & Britton, 1974; Kubler-Ross, 1969; Weisman, 1972).

Some writers and researchers have focused on both the negative and positive functions of denial in the seriously ill and elderly. Becker (1973), influenced by Otto Rank, attempted to explain our inability to deal with death through the depth psychology of heroism and its failure. The hero faces death without denial. Our culture seems to have failed to inculcate the values of the hero. Weisman (1972) proposed three degrees of denial. First-order denial is the patient's obvious denial of the main facts of the illness. Second-order denial may appear after the diagnosis is accepted. It is denial of the significance or implications of the illness. Third-order denial is the patient's inability to believe that the illness will result in death. Such patients seem to believe they will remain in their incapacitated state indefinitely.

Breznitz (1983, p. 258) expanded on Weisman's concepts, proposing seven different kinds of denial "each related to a different stage in the processing of threatening information." Included are denial of (1) information, (2) threatening information, (3) personal relevance, (4) urgency, (5) vulnerability, (6) effect, and (7) affect relevance. The more denial used, the greater the reality distortion involved.

Hackett, another associate of Weisman's, in his work with heart disease and cancer, emphasized denial as arising from the social sphere (Hackett & Weisman, 1964; Weisman & Hackett, 1966; Hackett & Weisman, 1969). Hackett saw the importance of denial in preserving significant relationships. He proposed a scale (Hackett & Cassem, 1974) that classified denying patients into three groups: mild, moderate, and major. Those in the major category never acknowledged fear of death, whereas those in the mild category readily admitted fear and lacked consistent defensive tactics. Most fell into the moderate category, though the author notes the criteria were never precise.

Working in the field of stress and coping, Lazarus has contributed much to the literature on denial. Lazarus and Golden (1981) suggest that age is a major factor in how a patient responds to impending death. They conclude that "denial like processes have both beneficial and harmful consequences depending on the timing, circumstances, and pervasiveness" (p. 30). They emphasize the importance of examining how people evaluate the significance of the threat to their well-being. This notion of "cognitive appraisal" helps us to understand the diversity of emotional responses seen in patients.

Another recent author (Taylor, 1989) sees the reality distortion of denial and repression as unhealthy but explores the adaptive use of "positive illusions." These are sometimes self-deceptive ways we help get ourselves through difficult crises. "Repression and denial alter reality whereas illusions simply interpret it in the best possible light."

Acceptance

Many of us feel we have seen acceptance in dying patients. It has been variously described as "the calm before the storm," "a kind of peace that came upon the person," or a withdrawing from life and worldly things.

However, acceptance seems to be the least understood of reactions to impending death. Kubler-Ross (1969) defined *acceptance* as "a patient who does not want visitors anymore, who does not want to talk anymore, who has usually finished his unfinished business, whose hope is no longer associated with cure, treatment, and prolongation of life."

The foregoing description sounds like someone who may be more depressed than peacefully accepting. Most of what we take as acceptance is closer to resignation, a giving up or collapsing in the face of overwhelming difficulty. An accepting person would more likely be open to contact with significant people, be ready to say goodbye, and respond to but not be in need of familial support.

Resignation is what usually emerges as a terminal illness progresses. It is not acceptance. A 76-year-old man with lung cancer responds during a recent hospice intake interview, "What's the use in getting upset about it? It won't do any good." Another patient answers, "I'd like to die and get it over with"; a third replies, "What else can you do? I hope I go in my sleep." These comments do not sound like they are from people who feel their lives are complete and death is the inevitable miracle about to happen. Instead, they belie a kind of learned helplessness. The anger, attempts at mastery, and other responses have not changed the relentless course of demise. Denial is no longer possible in the face of overwhelming evidence. Enough time has passed to at least gather the strength to face reality.

Many caregivers hear acceptance in the above comments. Just to acknowledge such a painful reality without emotional distress seems like a major accomplishment, and to some extent it is especially for those who still feel they have much to accomplish with their lives.

There are others who do seem to have come to an acceptance of their death. What makes them different from those who are resigned to death? The difference may seem subtle but is more profound. George, a 72-year-old retired executive who had pancreatic cancer, always spoke of death as his teacher. Several serious illnesses had taught him to value his time and use it wisely. His main complaint was how cancer had affected his golf score. Mary, a 67-year-old homemaker with metastatic breast cancer, lived for her family. She fought her illness while her family urged her not to give up. Three days before she died, a change seemed to come over her. She called her family together and told them she was ready to die. She seemed immensely full of love as she told each of them what they had meant to her.

Acceptance seems to be a less than common occurrence in dying patients. It is a rare and beautiful experience that caps an exceptional life. Denial and resignation are the responses we usually see. Let us not be too critical of resignation, however. Imagine you are dying of cancer and you have a spouse and three young children. Accepting your death in this situation might not seem appropriate. Resignation might be the best to hope for, only after considerable painful working through of the inevitable unfinished business. Acceptance of death may also be contradictory for the person with an existential world view. Death may be inevitable but it also is the ultimate senseless act. People will cope with death the best way they can. When they do not seem to be doing well, it is best if we can try to understand with them how this is, given the context they are in and the personal issues they bring with them.

One of the most difficult questions about acceptance is its transcendent quality. Does acceptance imply a spiritual perspective? Spiritual does not mean a religious orientation necessarily. It is a perception that acknowledges a continuity to life beyond the self. Most who have seen a person accept death might say they had a transcendent or spiritual quality about them.

There is much in the popular literature about acceptance of death and what some have termed the "happy death" movement. Most present death as a spiritual journey that allows great potential for growth if done consciously. *The Tibetan Book of the Dead* (see Bardo thodol, 1975) offered perhaps the first inspiration for the importance of using the dying and afterdeath experience as an opportunity for spiritual growth. All attachments to worldly things must be abandoned. All fears, holding on, and painfulness must be faced and passed through.

In Grof and Halifax's (1978) *The Human Encounter with Death*, the history of man's struggle to find transcendental meaning in death is explored. Adapting Eastern Buddhist teaching to the West, Levine contributed a number of books on "conscious dying" (Levine, 1982, 1984, 1987). Also, Moody (1975) and others have helped to document the important similarities in the experiences of those who have had near death episodes.

Undoubtedly, many draw inspiration and comfort from these authors as others do from the Bible. What is required is faith and the ability to suspend disbelief. For those who are able, we can suppose a kind of acceptance of death. For the great majority of humans, however, doubts seem to creep in. We are not entirely sure about our faith or we do not believe in the continuation of life after death. The notion of a "conscious" death is too far removed from the present reality of distress and unfinished business. We are too caught up in the world of our making.

Working with Reactions to the Knowledge of Impending Death

One of the clichés of the death and dying field is the expression, "Meet the patients where they are." A closer examination of this truism, however, may give considerable insight. The caregiver must decide what interventions are likely to be helpful versus harmful in an emotionally laden situation.

If the patient is, in fact, accepting imminent death, the question of intervention becomes easy as no intervention is really necessary, other than our presence. The most important question becomes: Is this really acceptance? As already noted, acceptance may really be resignation or perhaps depression. At the opposite end of the spectrum is the dying person who appears to be denying. This is what challenges most caregivers. Does one support the defense/coping style or does one attempt to help the person work through and get beyond denial? Different answers are called for with different people.

As a starting point, one must always ask the question: In what service is denial being used? It may be useful to view the use of denial on a continuum. At one extreme could be intrapsychic denial used as a defense to decrease anxiety, to keep the person with limited inner-strength from feeling overwhelmed. At the other extreme could be interpersonal denial like coping, where denial is used in the service of attempting to preserve interpersonal relationships with significant people.

Patients making use of interpersonal denial are consciously aware of the circumstances of their illness and prognosis. They act as if all is well because they fear that talking about their prognosis would be too upsetting to others and might result in their being abandoned and rejected. There may also be use of denial because of guilt over the effect of their condition on others or to protect others from possible emotional distress brought about if the patient's condition is openly acknowledged.

These motivations are commonly encountered and need to be addressed if progress is to be made. The reality in our culture is much more often that *not* discussing what is really happening to the dying person is what causes distance and separation from loved ones—all this at a time when the dying person most needs support and the presence of family and friends. Experience suggests that if denial is used as a way of controlling intrapsychic conflict, then psychosocial intervention may not be helpful. However, denial employed to avoid interpersonal conflict is very amenable to intervention and intervention in such circumstances can be quite helpful.

How does the caregiver know what kind of denial is being used? Intrapsychic denial may be accompanied by overt signs of psychopathology. Other times it may be more difficult to identify. Though most patients doubt the accuracy of the diagnosis or prognosis or refuse to believe it at first, the person who steadfastly ignores reality, refuses to cooperate in treatment, and cannot be reasoned with is probably manifesting intrapsychic denial.

In contrast, the use of interpersonal denial is usually more obvious. Privately, the patient may be quite open with the caregiver about the situation. However, when family members are around, only optimism and future plans are discussed. Caregivers are also part of the patient's interpersonal world. As a patient's physician or nurse, you are looked to for support.

If the patient fears you may abandon him or her if the same outlook is not maintained, then openness may not be forthcoming. This is often referred to as the "conspiracy of silence" between patient, family, and caregivers. Everyone knows what is going on but no one will talk about it (Glaser & Strauss, 1965).

Obviously, people do not fit neatly into categories, so it may be seen that most people are motivated to varying degrees by both their inner and outer needs. Others may benefit from psychosocial intervention only after they have had enough time to gain some emotional distance and marshal their adaptive coping abilities. This brings us back to the notion of "meeting people where they are." The amount and kind of intervention should be guided by the patient's response. We have to pace our interventions based on the person's readiness to hear such information. We know when we are ahead of a patient. He or she can get angry and upset with us. Comments like "She really upset me" or "I wish he wouldn't come around talking about death all the time" let us know we have not timed our intervention correctly or that it may have been inappropriate.

Many of us view the presence of hope in a dying patient as a kind of denial. This is often not the case. Of course, there are many different kinds of hope. Hope for comfort and absence of conflict are obviously consistent with the dying patient's situation. As clinicians, we must acknowledge our limitations. We cannot divine the future. We do not know how long our patients will live. It is important to many of our patients that there may be even a small possibility that life will continue. To insist on removing even this small hope may not be therapeutic. Some studies have shown that selective use of denial is correlated with improved survival (Hersh, 1985; Pettingale et al., 1985). We need to remember that this is *their* death, not our death. What seems more useful is to begin by helping patients to acknowledge that they can maintain some realistic hope while facing the reality of their impending death. This may seem contradictory but in fact is their situation.

A dying patient who speaks only of hope and cure is often fearful that once the possibility of death is embraced, all will be lost. A positive attitude must be maintained. To live and win, all negativity must be avoided. This perspective, popularized in recent years, brings with it a number of problems. Patients whose senses tell them that the battle for health is being lost can become quite distressed. If one believes that one can overcome disease with the right attitude, then failure to do so leads to feelings of self-blame and inadequacy. Also, some believe that if one can cure disease, then it follows that one may have caused it in the first place. Not only can one feel badly for making oneself sick, one feels worse for failing to correct the situation. Other people may make demands on and criticize the patient if the correct positive attitude is not demonstrated. They may be too uncomfortable to hear patient's doubts and fears. Lazarus (1985) gives a helpful account of this phenomenon, which he terms "trivialization of distress." The medical profession's attempt to minimize the distress associated with illness and old age may be increasing rather than decreasing human misery.

Helping patients to understand that they will not get sicker or die sooner if they acknowledge the reality of their situation can lead to the development of more realistic hopes. They may also adjust better and reestablish emotional equilibrium (Billings, 1985; Mishel et al., 1984). However, we can only do these things if we are first comfortable with our own mortality. Possibly the most effective intervention one can make is to demonstrate that you, as a caregiver, can talk openly and comfortably about dying.

Conclusion

Denial is possibly the most universal reaction to the knowledge of impending death. Acceptance of impending death is less common and may sometimes be confused with depression. Caregivers are often unsure about how to respond to the various reactions seen in dying patients. Even the seemingly accepting person can be ambivalent and the denying patient can have moments of acceptance. Reactions to dying are as varied as there are people who are dying.

Stage theories offer little insight into the actual trajectories of people who are dying. Dying may be stageless. Is acceptance of death possible? Experience suggests that some people seem to accept death, either through a feeling of having concluded a meaningful existence or through some form of spiritual insight. More often, death is faced with resignation or depression, or not faced at all.

A great many coping strategies may be employed in the service of denial. What seems most helpful for the clinician is to distinguish interpersonal from intrapsychic denial. The former may respond well to psychosocial intervention, whereas the latter may best be left unchallenged. Whenever psychosocial interventions are made, they must be paced to the patient and family's readiness to deal with issues surrounding dying. Finally, we, as caregivers, can only be effective in helping others to face death if we have explored and confronted our own mortality.

References

Bardo thodol (1975). *The Tibetan book of the dead; The great liberation through hearing in the Bardo; by Guru Rimpoche according to Karma Lingpa; A new translation from the Tibetan.* (Clear Light Series) XX. Berkeley: Shambala Publications.

Becker, E. (1973). *The denial of death.* New York: Free Press.

Beilin, R. (1981). Social functions of denial and death. *Omega, 12* (1), 25–35.

Beisser, A. R. (1979). Denial and affirmation in illness and health. *American Journal of Psychiatry, 136* (8), 1026–1030.

Bengston, V., Ceullar, J., & Ragan, P. (1977). Stratum contrasts and similarities in attitudes toward death. *Journal of Gerontology, 32* (1), 76–88.

Billings, J. (1985). *Outpatient management of advanced cancer, symptom control support, and hospice in the home* (pp. 236–259). Philadelphia: Lippincott.

Breznitz, S. (1983). The seven kinds of denial. In S. Breznitz (Ed.), *The denial of stress* (pp. 257–280). New York: International Universities Press.

Cappon, D. (1978). Attitudes of the aged toward death. *Essence, 2* (3), 139–147.

Dansak, D. A., & Cordes, R. S. (1978–79). Cancer: Denial or suppression. *International Journal of Psychiatry in Medicine, 9* (3–4), 257–262.

Detwiler, D. A. (1981). The positive function of denial. *The Journal of Pediatrics, 99* (3), 401–402.

Devins, G. (1979). Death anxiety and voluntary passive euthanasia: Influences of proximity to death and experiences with death in important other persons. *Journal of Consulting and Clinical Psycholoqy, 47* (2), 301–309.

Falek, A., & Britton, S. (1974). Phases in coping: The hypothesis and its implications. *Social Biology, 21* (1), 1–7.

Freud, S. (1924). *The loss of reality in psychosis and neurosis* (p. 184). Standard Edition XIX.

Freud, S. (1940). *An outline of psycho-analysis* (pp. 144–207). Standard Edition XXIII.

Garfield, C. (1978). Elements of psychosocial oncology: Doctor-patient relationships in terminal illness. In C. Garfield (Ed.), *Psychosocial care of the dying patient.* New York: McGraw-Hill.

Glaser, B. G., & Strauss, A. L. (1965). *Awareness of dying.* Chicago: Aldine.

Grof, S., & Halifax, J. (1978). *The human encounter with death.* New York: Dutton.

Haan, N. (1965). Coping and defense mechanisms related to personality inventories. *Journal of Consulting and Clinical Psychology, 29* (4), 373–378.

Hackett, T. P., & Cassem, N. H. (1970). Psychological reactions to life threatening stress: A study of acute myocardial infarction patients. In H. S. Abram (Ed.), *Psychological aspects of stress.* Springfield, IL.: Charles C Thomas.

Hackett, T. P., & Cassem, N. H. (1974). Development of a quantitative rating scale to assess denial. *Journal of Psychosomatic Research, 18* (2), 93–100.

Hackett, T. P., & Weisman, A. D. (1964). Reactions to the imminence of death. In G. H. Grosser, H. Wechsler, & M. Greenblatt (Eds.), *The threat of impending disaster: Contributions to the psychology of stress,* (pp. 300–311). Cambridge MA: The MIT Press.

Hackett, T. P., & Weisman, A. D. (1969). Denial as a factor in patients with heart disease and cancer. *Annals of the New York Academy of Sciences, 164–182.*

Hersh, S. (1985). Psychosocial aspects of patients with cancer. In V. DeVita, S. Hellman, & S. Rosenberg (Eds.), *Cancer: Principles and practices of oncology* (2nd ed., pp. 2051–2066). Philadelphia: Lippincott.

Holland, J. (1989). Clinical course of cancer. In J. Holland & J. Rowland (Eds.), *Handbook of psychooncology* (pp. 75–100). New York: Oxford University Press.

Jacobson, E. (1957). Denial and repression. *Journal of the American Psychoanalytic Association, 5,* 61–92.

Kalish, R. (1978). A little myth is a dangerous thing: Research in the service of the dying. In. C. Garfield (Ed.), *Psychosocial care of the dying patient* (pp. 219–226). New York: McGraw-Hill.

Kalish, R., & Reynolds, D. (1977). The role of age in death attitudes. *Death Education, 1* (2), 205–230.

Kastenbaum, R. (1974). On death and dying: Should we have mixed feelings about our ambivalence toward the aged? *Journal of Geriatric Psychiatry, 7* (1), 94–107.

Kastenbaum, R., & Aisenberg, R. (1972). *The psychology of death.* New York: Springer.

Kastenbaum, R., & Kastenbaum, B. (1989). *Encyclopedia of death* (pp. 220–222). Phoenix, AZ: Oryx Press.

Kubler-Ross, E. (1969). *On death and dying.* New York: Macmillan.

Lazarus, R. S. (1985). The trivialization of distress. In J. D. Rosen & L. J. Solomon (Eds.), *Preventing health risk behaviors and promoting coping with illness* (Vol. 8), Vermont Conference on the Primary Prevention of Psychopathology. Hanover: University Press of New England.

Lazarus, R. S., & Golden, G. (1981). The function of denial in stress, coping, and aging. In E. McGarraugh & S. Keissler (Eds.), *Biology, behavior, and aging* (pp. 283–307). New York: Academic Press.

Levine, S. (1982). *Who dies? An investigation of conscious living and conscious dying.* New York: Anchor Books.

Levine, S. (1984). *Meetings at the edge.* New York: Doubleday.

Levine, S. (1987). *Healing into life and death.* New York: Doubleday.

Mishel, M., Hostetter, T., King, B., & Graham, V. (1984). Predictors of psychosocial adjustment in patients newly diagnosed with gynecological cancer. *Cancer Nursing, 7,* 291–299.

Moody, R. (1975). *Life after life.* New York: Bantam Books.

Pattison, E. M. (1978). The living-dying process. In C. Garfield (Ed.), *Psychosocial care of the dying patient* (pp. 133–167). New York: McGraw-Hill.

Pettingale, K., Morris, T., Greer, S., & Haybittle, J. (1985). Mental attitudes to cancer: An additional prognostic factor. *Lancet, 1,* 750.

Sjoback, H. (1973). *The psychoanalytic theory of defensive processes.* New York: Wiley and Sons.

Taylor, S. (1989). *Positive illusions: Creative self deceptions and the healthy mind.* New York: Basic Books.

Wass, H. (1977). Views and opinions of elderly persons concerning death. *Educational Gerontology, 2* (1), 15–26.

Weisman, A. D. (1972). *On dying and denying: A psychiatric study of terminality.* New York: Behavioral Publications.

Weisman, A. D., & Hackett, T. P. (1966). Denial as a social act. In S. Levin & R. Kahara (Eds.), *Geriatric psychiatry: Creativity, reminiscing, and dying* (pp. 79–110). New York: International Universities Press.

Eleven

Bereavement Guilt
A Conceptual Model with Applications

Alice Sterner Demi

Margaret Shandor Miles

Alice Sterner Demi is Professor of Psychiatric/ Mental Health Nursing at Georgia State University, Atlanta, where she teaches family theory, family therapy, and nursing theory at the graduate level. Demi received a diploma from Monmouth Medical Center, New Jersey, a Baccalaureate degree from Incarnate Word College, Texas, a master's degree from University of Texas, Austin, and a doctorate from the University of California, San Francisco. She is a Fellow of the American Academy of Nursing, an honor which was bestowed upon her for her pioneering efforts in hospice nursing.

Demi has conducted research on widowhood and on survivors of suicide. She has also collaborated with Dr. Miles in a number of studies, including guilt in bereaved parents, parameters of normal grief, rescue workers' reactions to disaster, and nurses' roles in disaster. She has used her research findings on bereavement to spur the development of bereavement programs, such as the Survivors of Suicide outreach program in Marin County, California, and the Grief Education Instituted in the Metro-Denver area.

Demi is continuing her bereavement work in the Atlanta area. Recently, she collaborated with members of the Coalition for Prevention of Youth Suicide and the Link Counseling Center to develop and implement an outreach program for survivors of suicide.

Margaret Shandor Miles is Professor and Chair, Health of Women and Children Department, School of Nursing, at the University of North Carolina at Chapel Hill. She teaches in the master's program in pediatric nursing and in the doctoral program in nursing.

She has her diploma in nursing from Mercy Hospital, Pittsburgh, a BSN from Boston College, an MN in pediatric nursing from the University of Pittsburgh, and an MA and PhD in Counseling Psychology from the University of Missouri–Kansas City. She was the founding member of the Society of Pediatric Nurses, a national association concerned with improving the health and nursing care to children and their families.

Miles is well known for her clinical work and research related to dying children, parental grief, and parenting the infant or child with a life-threatening illness. Her clinical work with the bereaved has focused primarily on couples experiencing pregnancy or infant loss and bereaved parents. Her booklet for grieving parents was pivotal in focusing on the special needs of bereaved parents. Miles's current research focuses on parenting the medically fragile infant, parental caregiving with HIV-infected infants, and the responses of bereaved families to organ donation. As a member of the Carolina Consortium on Human Development, she has begun to apply principles of developmental science to research related to parenting and grief. Miles has worked with the American Nurses' Association to develop a number of position papers related to death and dying. She is also the Director of a center focusing on health behaviors in vulnerable youth.

Guilt, a common manifestation of grief, varies greatly in its origins, intensity, and duration. Many theorists perceive that guilt is a normal manifestation of grief (Averill, 1968; Bowlby, 1980; Cassem, 1978; Glick, Weiss, & Parkes, 1974; Lindemann, 1944). However, many theorists also see excessive guilt as a destructive force during bereavement that is related to poor outcomes (Bugen, 1977; Glick, Weiss, & Parkes, 1974; Lieberman, 1978; Parkes, 1975; Parkes & Weiss, 1983; Raphael, 1983; Wahl, 1970). Bereavement theorists, researchers, and clinicians have demonstrated interest in bereavement guilt, but there has been little systematic theory development or in-depth research on bereavement guilt. Consequently, widely diverse views persist on the role of guilt in bereavement.

We (the authors of this chapter) previously developed a typology of parental bereavement guilt (Miles & Demi, 1983–84) that we pilot tested with 28 parents. Subsequently, we expanded the typology into a more comprehensive model (Miles & Demi, 1986) and validated the model with a sample of 128 parents, who were bereaved by various modes of death (Miles & Demi, 1991). In this model, we hypothesized the process by which bereavement guilt develops, discussed the variables that influence bereavement guilt, and described the sources of guilt in bereaved parents. The purpose of this chapter is to present a revised conceptual model of bereavement guilt, which is applicable to diverse bereaved persons (e.g., widows, parents, siblings, and grandparents) who are bereaved by various modes of death (suicide, accident, chronic disease, or acute illness).

Review of Literature

Some believe that guilt is central to human existence, that guilt is the inevitable result of the development of one's conscience, and that the conscience (and thus one's propensity to experience guilt) is developed in childhood. Psychodynamic theories propose that both an overdeveloped and an underdeveloped conscience can create psychological and behavioral problems that may be manifested as guilt proneness or absence of guilt (Freud, 1938; Mowrer, 1960). Thus, the individual with an underdeveloped conscience will experience little or no guilt following the death of a significant other, whereas the person with an overdeveloped conscience is likely to experience intense and multifaceted guilt following the death of a significant other. Individuals with a normally developed conscience are less likely to experience these extremes of guilt.

Knowledge related to guilt experienced during bereavement is limited. Research has tended to focus on the frequency of guilt in the bereaved, with reported frequency ranging from none (Yamamoto et al., 1969) to all (Sanders, 1989). Guilt has been reported to be especially frequent and problematic among bereaved parents (DeFrain & Ernst, 1978, 1982; Edelstein, 1984; Lehman, Wortman, & Williams, 1987; Miles, 1984; Rubin, 1984–85), those bereaved by suicide (Cain, 1972; Demi, 1978, 1984; Henslin, 1970, 1972; Rudestam, 1977; Van Dongen, 1990), and those who experienced an unexpected death (Demi, 1978, 1984; Glick, Weiss, & Parkes, 1974; Worden, 1982).

Several authors (Lindemann, 1944; Sanders, 1989; Van Dongen, 1990; Worden, 1982), based on research and clinical practice, have identified common sources of guilt in bereaved persons. Lindemann (1944), in his classic article on grief, proposed that guilt is caused by self-accusations such as a perceived failure to do right by the deceased loved one and negligence or exaggerated minor omissions. Worden (1982) noted that survivors may feel guilt because they didn't provide adequate medical care to the deceased, or they couldn't prevent the loved one's pain, or they didn't experience the correct amount of sadness following the death. Sanders (1989) reported that guilt may range in intensity from a small nagging remembrance of a kindness not performed to full-blown, intense, all-encompassing guilt. She found that most guilt was directly related to the death; however, her subjects also reported some survivor guilt and guilt related to experiencing pleasure. Van Dongen (1990) reported that 60 percent of suicide survivors in her study experienced guilt, and this was most common among those who retrospectively perceived clues to the deceased's suicidal intent and did not act on these clues.

Only a few researchers have specifically investigated the sources of guilt feelings and related factors influencing these feelings (Henslin, 1970, 1972; Johnson-Soderberg, 1983; Miles & Demi, 1983–84, 1986). Henslin (1970) identified five areas of guilt in suicide survivors: not being aware of the suicidal intent, feeling they should have been able to prevent the suicide, feeling they had done something to cause the suicide, noncausal actions that were regretted, and not having the "proper" feeling after the suicide. Johnson-Soderberg (1983), in a study of bereaved parents, identified three major types of guilt: personal, existential, and anticipatory.

Our model of parental bereavement guilt (Miles & Demi, 1983–84, 1986, 1991) proposes a typology of six guilt sources: Death-Causation, Illness-Related, Childrearing, Moral, Survival, and Grief Guilt. In a study of bereaved parents (Miles & Demi, 1991), guilt sources differed by mode of death. Suicide bereaved parents and accident bereaved parents were re-markably similar on Death Causation Guilt (63 and 64 percent, respective-ly) and Childrearing Guilt (51 and 52 percent, respectively). However, the suicide bereaved parents also reported considerable Illness-Related Guilt, while the accident bereaved parents reported no Illness-Related Guilt. The chronic disease bereaved parents showed a different pattern, with Childrearing Guilt being the most frequent (44 percent), followed closely by Illness-Related Guilt (41 percent), and much less frequent was Death-Causation Guilt (26 percent). Few parents in the three groups reported Grief Guilt, Moral Guilt, or Survival Guilt. However, there was a sufficient number of responses in these categories to retain the categories in the model.

Review of the literature and our previous research support the view that guilt is a particularly ubiquitous and severe phenomenon among those bereaved by suicide; that it is equally ubiquitous, but less severe among those bereaved by accident; and that it is generally less ubiquitous and less severe in those bereaved by chronic disease. Thus, it appears that unexpect-edness of the death and mode of death are related to frequency and intensity of guilt feelings.

Revised Theoretical Model of Bereavement Guilt

In our model, *guilt* is defined as a feeling that results from perceived failure to fulfill personal or societal expectations of oneself. Bereavement guilt may result from actual or imagined transgressions. These transgressions may take the form of behaviors, thoughts, or feelings, and may result from acts committed or omitted.

We assume that some guilt is a natural and normal component of the grief process, but that intense, unrelenting, prolonged guilt is outside the normal parameters of grief (Demi & Miles, 1987). Guilt generally provides few nonverbal cues to its presence, therefore one must rely on verbal expressions of guilt feelings to assess its presence. Terms commonly used to express guilt feelings are feeling sinful, remorseful, regretful, responsible, accountable, at fault, blameworthy, unworthy, in error, culpable, wrong, evil, criminal, ashamed, and deserving of punishment.

The Development of Guilt Feelings

The death of a loved one (or a loved-hated one) precipitates intense pain and distress, characterized primarily by feelings of sadness and helplessness, and, in some instances, a sense of responsibility for the deceased. The survivor may question: Why me? Why my loved one? What did I do to deserve this? As part of the bereavement process, the bereaved person is preoccupied with thoughts of the deceased, and reviews past thoughts, feelings, behaviors, and interactions with the deceased. In this life review, the individual evaluates these past experiences and may perceive violations of self or societal expectation that occurred during the loved one's lifetime, at the time of the death, or since the death. This discrepancy between self/societal expectations and the perceived performance produces guilt feelings (see Figure 11-1).

Variables Influencing Guilt Feelings

Bereaved individuals experience widely diverse intensity, duration, and sources of guilt. Many variables have been proposed as influencing the occurrence of guilt in bereavement. Based on our own research, the research reported in the literature, and our clinical experiences, we propose a number of variables that influence the occurrence of guilt during bereavement: Interpersonal, Personal, Situational, and Societal variables.

Interpersonal Variables Interpersonal variables are related to the bereaved person's role and relationship with the deceased. These variables include the intensity of the relationship, the quality of the relationship (including the degree of ambivalence), the degree of dependence in the relationship, and the adequacy of role performance. Interpersonal variables are often tied to the individual's status as a spouse, parent, child, sibling, or grandparent, and to the ages of the survivor and the deceased. Thus, a mother is likely to have a more intense relationship and to feel more responsible for a young child than for a parent or sibling and consequently experiences greater bereavement guilt. The individual's perception of how well he or she functioned as a parent, spouse, and so on, is also important. The individual

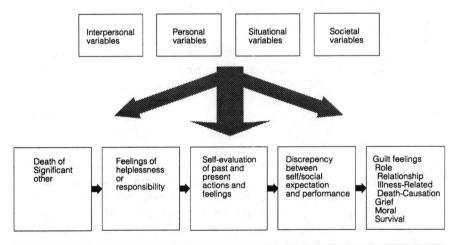

Figure 11-1   Theoretical model of bereavement guilt (© Margaret S. Miles and Alice S. Demi, 1983, 1991.)

who feels that he or she failed in many ways in the performance of responsibilities to the deceased is also likely to experience greater guilt.

Personal Variables   Personal variables include the individual's personality structure, coping patterns, and overall mental and physical health. Of particular importance are the extent of development of the conscience and the individual's level of self-esteem. Previous experiences with loss and grief also have an impact on the development of bereavement guilt.

Situational Variables   Situational variables encompass all of the circumstances surrounding the death. The mode of death, the amount of forewarning of the death, the degree of violence involved in the death, the perceived preventability of the death, the care provided by others during the illness and at the time of death, and the presence of concurrent stressors are all important Situational variables.

Societal Variables   Societal variables are related to the overall societal attitudes toward death and the amount and type of support provided to the bereaved. Societal expectations about correct behaviors and myths about ideal relationships are particularly influential. People are expected to have perfect relationships with their loved ones and to grieve "correctly" when they die. Society, in general, perceives certain types of deaths, such as suicide and homicide, as more negative, and thus provides less support and more stress to survivors of these types of death. These negative societal attitudes are often expressed as stigmatizing, blaming, and rejecting the bereaved.

Expression of Guilt Feelings

Guilt feelings may be expressed as Role Guilt, Grief Guilt, Moral Guilt, or Survival Guilt. Role Guilt encompasses three subdimensions: Relationship Guilt, Illness-Related Guilt, and Death-Causation Guilt.

Role Guilt   Role Guilt is guilt related to perceived failure to perform adequately in a complementary role to the deceased, as a parent, spouse, sibling, child, or so on. This category encompasses all aspects of the relationship to the deceased from general thoughts, feelings, and actions that occurred during the loved one's lifetime, or occasionally prior to their lifetime (Relationship Guilt), to thoughts, feelings, and actions during the loved one's illness (Illness-Related Guilt), to thoughts, feelings, and actions that are perceived by the survivor to be directly related to the loved one's death (Death-Causation Guilt).

Relationship Guilt: Relationship Guilt is guilt that results from perceived failure to live up to self or societal expectations in the overall role with the loved one, as a parent, spouse, sibling, child, lover, and so on. Each relationship carries with it certain role responsibilities that include both affective and instrumental aspects. The affective roles include giving and receiving affection. The instrumental roles include providing for physical nurturing and safety. These roles vary, depending on the particular role status (e.g., parent, spouse, child) and the individual characteristics of the two persons in the dyad (e.g., age, maturity, independence, health status). Often, individuals assume different roles from those normally expected based on a role status. For instance, a sibling may assume a parental role status and take on both the affective and instrumental roles accompanying that role status.

Relationship Guilt may be expressed as dissatisfaction with the quality or intensity of the relationship at the time of, or before, the loved one's death. This dissatisfaction may be with emotional aspects of the relationship, nurturing and disciplining practices, or physical care provided. Other sources of guilt in this category are problematic relationships with others that interfered with the relationship with the loved one (e.g., marital conflict or divorce) and personal problems that affected the quality of the loved one's life. Role Guilt appears to represent the normal guilt feelings experienced by a partner in any significant dyadic relationship. During bereavement, these normal guilt feelings may be greatly exaggerated.

Even when the bereaved survivor had a very good relationship with the deceased, and the deceased had a full and happy life, survivors often express regret for doing or not doing things that would have made the deceased's life even more happy or more fulfilled. Sometimes this guilt is fleeting and causes minimal distress, while other times it is persevering and causes intense anguish.

Statements exemplifying Relationship Guilt are the following:

I feel immense guilt at trying to get divorced and working instead of spending time with my son.

I feel guilt for not being a better husband, not loving her enough, being angry or impatient with her, not being able to reverse her accident. I feel guilty about all the things I didn't do for her or give her.

Our relationship could have been better. I could have been more understanding, less angry in some situations. I could have accepted her boyfriend more openly. I could have been more generous with her. I wish I had shown her more love and been less of a disciplinarian.

I feel guilt about not taking time to enjoy more things with him, as he died on December 23 around midnight, and I was too busy getting ready for Christmas the last few days that he lived.

Illness-Related Guilt: Illness-Related Guilt is defined as perceived failure in the caregiving role during the loved one's illness or at the time of death. Illness-Related Guilt is expressed in diverse ways, such as perceived failure to adequately address symptoms or problems, regret for agreeing to further medical therapy and thus prolonging the loved one's suffering, not being with the loved one at the time of death, making medical decisions that had a negative effect on the deceased's quality of life, and perceived failure to help the loved one cope with the illness or with related emotional consequences. Statements about directly or indirectly causing the death are specifically excluded from this category.

The following are some examples of Illness-Related Guilt:

I feel most guilty as to the quality of the last part of his life. Chemotherapy was not a good decision.

I had stayed at the hospital day and night for weeks. The only day I left to go home for a few hours, he died. I've always felt really guilty about that.

She asked me if she was going to die and I just couldn't be honest with her. Now I feel guilty because we weren't able to talk about it with her. I wonder if she would have been less scared if we had talked about it more openly.

I feel guilty about not recognizing his symptoms earlier and trying harder to find the right medical help. The thing that is most distressing to me is that he had to suffer so much—that nothing could be done for him and that I could do so little to ease his pain.

Death-Causation Guilt: Death-Causation Guilt involves attribution of the cause of death to oneself in some way (self-blame). The bereaved person may indicate a belief that he or she either indirectly contributed to or directly caused the loved one's death. These expressions of guilt may refer to imagined events or actual acts of omission or commission. This category includes guilt related to the genetic or biological origin of a familial disease or to caregiving behaviors that are perceived to have led to the death such as purchasing a vehicle that subsequently was involved in the fatal accident, not recognizing a loved one's symptoms and not seeking medical care, making the wrong medical care decisions, planning the event that led to the death, or inattention to safety.

A father whose son died in a vehicular accident expressed the following guilt feelings.

> If only I had not let him have the motorcycle. I should have said no when he wanted to buy the motorcycle. I should not have let him go riding that day. I felt he wasn't able to handle it very well and I should have followed my feelings. If I could have been with him, I could have done something.

Grief Guilt

Grief Guilt is related to the perceived failure to experience what the survivor perceives to be appropriate behavioral or emotional reactions during the bereavement period. This includes guilt related to emotional and behavioral reactions at the time of the death, and, since the death, perceived failure in relationships with others due to the grief process, the amount of grief felt (too much or too little), or enjoying oneself again.

Verbalizations that indicate Grief Guilt include statements such as, "I didn't grieve correctly," "I wasn't able to cry," "I cried too much," "I didn't give enough attention to my husband and children while I was grieving," and "I felt guilty when I enjoyed myself." Specific examples of Grief Guilt follow:

> I raised my son all his life and taught him to fish and hunt (two things I always loved). Now I can't bear the thought of having a good time because I feel guilty.
>
> Anything that I enjoy doing makes me feel guilty. Because my son had been physically and mentally ill most of his life, I've had guilt feelings because I felt a certain sense of relief when he died.
>
> I felt guilty for not breaking down—for being "strong" as I was. I felt that I should have reacted as I've seen others react during similar situations. But my friends complimented me on my strength, those who knew me well.... I feared that people thought I didn't love my son enough.

Moral Guilt

Moral Guilt is related to the belief that the loved one's death was punishment or retribution for violating a moral, religious, or ethical standard. The violation may have been related to events in the distant past or to more recent experiences. In the following example, a mother whose child died of Sudden Infant Death Syndrome expresses Moral Guilt:

> You know, I didn't really want to be pregnant. I had considered having an abortion but I'm a Catholic and have been raised believing that abortion is wrong. I tried several times to get an abortion, but then I'd chicken out at the last minute. I just couldn't do it. After my baby was born, I loved him with all my heart. When my baby died, I felt I was being punished for the thoughts I had earlier.

Survival Guilt

Survival Guilt is related to the belief that the young should outlive the old or that the more worthy should outlive the less worthy. It is often manifested by parents and grandparents who perceive that it is unnatural for a parent or grandparent to outlive a child. Parents and grandparents often express guilt for surviving when they are old and infirm, and their child or grandchild was healthy, youthful, and was destined to be a part of the future generation and carry on the genetic pool. Survival Guilt is also common after a disaster or an accident (Lifton, 1967). The survivors may feel that they were less deserving and therefore they should have died, not their loved one. The following statement of a chronically ill mother whose teenage daughter died suddenly and unexpectedly in an accident provides an example of Survival Guilt:

> I feel guilty that she nursed me through so many surgeries, and I am alive.... She should be here instead of me.... She had so much to live for and I have so little to live for.

Application of the Model

The following case examples are presented to show the multiple sources of guilt and the factors that influence guilt responses in the bereaved. These examples demonstrate the application of this model to various bereaved individuals (a widow, a sibling, a mother, a father, and a grandparent) who were bereaved by various modes of death.

Sudden Death of a Spouse

Mary Ellen, a 40-year-old community health nurse experienced the sudden, unexpected death of her 45-year-old husband, Jack. The couple had been married over 20 years and had a reasonably happy marriage until the last three years, during which time Mary Ellen considered getting a divorce.

Jack had chronic arthritis; the related pain and disfigurement made Jack depressed and irritable. He complained that Mary Elllen was too involved with her job and going to school part time, and didn't give him enough attention and affection. Mary Ellen worried about Jack's health because he had "strange symptoms." She frequently urged him to see a physician and to stop his heavy smoking.

Mary Ellen describes her thoughts and feelings:

> When he died, I was so angry with him. He was a heavy smoker and I tried everything to get him to stop smoking. As a nurse I saw so many people with cancer and emphysema. I was so afraid he'd get a chronic illness. I never suspected he'd have a heart attack.... About a year ago he went to see a psychiatrist. I asked him why he finally got some help, and he said that the last time we had a fight he had such severe chest pain he thought he was going to have a heart attack. His friends told me that I put too much stress on him. I guess I did. On the autopsy, it showed that he had a heart attack about a year ago! The psychiatrist should have picked up on his reason for seeking help, but I should have also!... He had so many strange symptoms. I kept bugging him to see a medical doctor. He finally went to see a rheumatologist and came home and told me that the doctor said he was fine except for his arthritis. We got in a fight and he yelled at me, "If you weren't bugging me about my health, you'd be bugging me about something else." Right then and there I vowed to myself that I wouldn't say one more word about his health, and I didn't.... One day we were out jogging and he said, "I don't want to die." I tried to reflect his statement and asked, "You're afraid to die?" He said angrily, "No, I'm not afraid to die!" And the conversation stopped there. I wish I could have said the right thing and gotten him to talk about his feelings....
>
> The night before he died he complained about a new pain in his left shoulder.... I should have realized it was his heart and not his arthritis. Somehow I should have made him go to the emergency room. If I hadn't made that vow not to say anything about his health, he'd be here today.... Mostly I feel guilty for being so angry at him.

Mary Ellen experienced all three types of Role Guilt (Relationship Guilt, Illness-Related Guilt, and Death-Causation Guilt) and Grief Guilt. Relationship Guilt was related to her perceived failure as a wife to make the marriage relationship more satisfactory and her failure as a nurse to facilitate his expression of his thoughts and feelings about death. She had several sources of Illness-Related Guilt—not insisting that he consult another physician and not being successful in getting him to stop smoking. Her Death-Causation Guilt was evidenced by her belief that if she had taken appropriate action the night before his death, he would still be alive. Surprisingly, her most intense source of guilt was her failure to grieve appropriately—Grief Guilt. She remained intensely angry at her husband for not taking better care of himself and then felt guilty for that feeling.

Factors that contributed to the intensity of her guilt were her ambivalence toward Jack and her sense of responsibility for his health because she was not only his wife but also a nurse.

Sibling Death in Childhood

The focus of a Sally Jessy Raphael (1990) television program was bereavement guilt. Among the panelists was a young man who had experienced the death of a sibling in childhood and who has suffered intense guilt ever since. Gary was 8 years old when his 7-year-old sister drowned. His parents were in the midst of a divorce and his father had told Gary that he needed to be the man of the house now. His grandmother and grandfather had left him and his four younger sisters on a beach while they went to get a boat. Before she left, his grandmother reminded him that he was responsible for taking care of his sisters since he was the oldest. None of the children could swim, so they played in the sand for a while and then waded out in shallow water to the dock. John picked a dead fish out of the water and laid it on the dock. His sister threw the fish back in the water. John became angry and demanded that she fetch it from the water. Obediently, she jumped in the waist-high water and went after the fish. Unfortunately, there was a sharp drop off. John jumped in and attempted to save her, but she drowned. When the grandparents returned to the beach and realized what had happened, his grandmother started screaming at him and blaming him for the accident because he had not watched his sister. Gary did not tell anyone about the dead fish for over 20 years.

> I caused her death.... It was awful. I tried to go after her but I couldn't swim. I yelled but no one came to help.... What bothers me the most is I never told my sister I loved her. I used to tease her a lot.... She was a very sweet thing.... I wondered if she knew how I really felt about her.... I should be dead right now myself. Could I have saved her? I had a hold of her hair. I wonder, did I try my best?... I didn't tell anyone about the fish. They'd think I was a murderer. It ate me up inside.... I know she's in heaven now. If I could tell her—talk to her.

Gary provides an example of several aspects of the theoretical model of Bereavement Guilt. When his sister died, he had intense feelings of helplessness and responsibility. His sense of responsibility for protecting his sister was intensified by his father and grandmother who emphasized that he was expected to take care of his sisters. He incorporated his father's and grandparents' expectations of him into his own self-concept. He then evaluated his performance based on the incorporated standards and expectations of his father and grandmother. In this evaluation, he found that he had violated both his self-expectations and societal expectations (parents and grandparents) and this resulted in intense guilt.

Gary also provides an example of the various types of guilt. He reports intense Relationship Guilt—that is, guilt related to his performance in the sibling role, not telling his sister he loved her, teasing her and treating her cruelly, and not appreciating her. He also reports intense Death-Causation Guilt. He feels certain that he caused his sister's death through both an act of commission and an act of omission. The act of commission was telling her to retrieve the fish from the water, and the act of omission was failing to pull her from the water when he had his hands on her hair. He has also experienced some Survival Guilt. He states that he should have died instead of her. He was older and he was also less worthy, therefore he should have died first. One wonders if he may also have experienced some Moral Guilt, since he expressed strong but ambivalent beliefs about God and the Devil. This boy's guilt was greatly intensified by the grandparents' and parents' behavior toward the boy both before and after his sister's death.

A Grandmother's Grief

A grandmother who had helped raise her grandson, Roger, experienced intense grief when Roger committed suicide. Roger had been living with his grandmother for the past two years while he was attending college. Roger had an argument with his grandmother and left her home abruptly. He returned the next day and said that if she would allow him to stay for three more weeks, he would then move out. She agreed but was adamant that he move out at the end of that time period. Three weeks and one day later, while still living at his grandmother's home, he ended his life.

> I can't keep from blaming myself and four other people. The child's mother left him when he was four months old, therefore he never had a fair chance. He had a daddy that drank. I feel most guilty about going away for Easter dinner; he didn't go with me because he had to go to work; instead he went to the garage [and committed suicide]. I also regret that I didn't assure him that I loved him. For nine years he was very dedicated to the church. When he started working on Sunday he couldn't attend church, so he started going to some very rough places. My minister, his daddy, and his stepmother talked to him and told him if he didn't change he would go to hell. I strongly believe he would be alive today if we hadn't tried to change him.

This grandmother had strong Relationship Guilt because of her intense and ambivalent relationship with her grandson, with whom she had developed a parental-type involvement. She believed that she had failed in her parenting and grandparenting duties. She felt responsible for his father's alcoholism and for the father's resultant neglect of Roger. She felt guilt specifically for not showing him enough love. She also expressed Death-Causation Guilt by saying he'd be alive today if she and others had acted differently.

Suicide Bereaved Parents

Many suicide bereaved parents express multiple sources of Role Guilt. While Interpersonal Guilt is extremely common, it is often intertwined with Illness-Related Guilt and Death-Causation Guilt. These parents often express guilt related to not recognizing the child's distress or intensity of the distress, or not taking appropriate action if they did recognize the distress. Following are several examples.

A mother discusses her Interpersonal Guilt and her Illness-Related Guilt after her 26-year-old daughter's suicide:

> I feel guilty for not spending more meaningful time with her all her life, not being more empathetic to her, not accepting her and loving her totally. I also feel guilt at what I did not understand about depression. I wish I could have a second chance to understand the factors of suicide so I could have known what she was leading up to. A year before her death, she broke up with a fellow she cared a great deal about. She went to college, but couldn't carry a full load and was extremely despondent over this. She became very depressed; this showed itself as stubbornness and not wanting to discuss anything. She wouldn't do anything to help herself in any way, because, I now realize, she felt so hopeless. I wish I had understood.

A 42-year-old mother describes her Interpersonal Guilt and her intense Death-Causation Guilt related to her 16-year-old daughter's suicide:

> I have felt guilty about two things. First, on a visit I made to her a few months before she died, she had been very cold and aloof at first, which hurt me tremendously. Later on in the visit she warmed up to me and we embraced and held each other. When the day came for me to leave, she asked that I come see her again. It would have meant an hour's trip on a very busy day, and I was still hurting from the first encounter so I refused to go and visit her again. I lost the opportunity to see her one more time, and I know I hurt her feelings.
>
> Secondly, while she was away, I invited a young relative to live with us as she was undergoing some family trauma herself. My mistake was letting her have my daughter's room (the only one available). I always feel that fact contributed in some way to her feeling of being displaced—having no place to go. That was a terrible mistake but, at the time, I thought I was helping my relative out. I still haven't been able to rid myself of these feelings—the agony persists for me.

Death of an Infant

Parents of critically ill infants have multiple experiences that contribute to guilt following the death of an infant. James and Marie, both 18 years old, were recently married. Their daughter was born at 24 weeks' gestation with Downs syndrome and congenital heart disease. During her time in the neonatal intensive care unit, she was continuously intubated and on a respirator, and underwent numerous procedures and surgeries. At four months of age, when her condition again worsened, her parents, after multiple consultations with the health care staff and other family members, made the decision not to continue treatments and to remove life support. Marie's reaction to her daughter's death was complicated by her feelings of responsibility for Marie's premature birth.

> I felt responsible for her early birth. My mother-in-law said it was because I continued to work. I felt it was because I had missed my doctor's appointment.

The father, James, expressed feelings of responsibility because of the infant's heart ailment.

> The congenital heart disease was what complicated things. I wonder if she got this problem because I used drugs in the past? I wonder if it was my fault?

James felt at peace with the decision to remove the respirator, but for months afterward, Marie continued to feel ambivalent about the decision. She stated:

> The doctors and the nurses talked to me. They told me she didn't have a chance, that she would be retarded, that she would never be normal. Jim agreed with them. But I had a hard time making the decision. They had to talk and talk and talk to me. Finally, I decided, but now I wonder if it was the right thing. Did I contribute to her death? Was I responsible for it?

Marie also expressed guilt about her involvement with her daughter at the time of death.

> The nurses asked me if I wanted to hold her when she was dying. My mother was there and she answered for me—she said no "because I was too distressed." I was so upset that I just accepted the decision. Now I feel so guilty. I didn't have the strength to hold my daughter while she was dying. It's like I turned down my one opportunity to really be her mother.

This example provides evidence of both Death-Causation and Illness-Related Guilt. Both the father and mother experienced Death-Causation Guilt. The mother felt responsible for the preterm birth because of her thoughts about abortion. She also felt Death-Causation Guilt because she was involved in the decision to turn off the respirator. The father felt responsible for the congenital anomaly because of his past drug use. The mother also expressed Illness-Related Guilt for not fulfilling her expectations of herself as a mother to her dying child. A number of factors influenced the parents' guilt responses. The mother was influenced by the attitudes of other family members, especially her mother, mother-in-law, and husband. The couple's immaturity and lack of experience with illness and death were additional stressors. Undoubtedly, the health care professionals' attitudes and the extended family's attitude towards the infant's diagnosis of Downs syndrome was also a factor influencing their decisions and later responses.

Implications

Clinicians working with the bereaved need to be aware of the common manifestations of guilt and to recognize that the presence of guilt is not necessarily pathological. Those with a strongly developed conscience are likely to experience guilt because of their high expectations of themselves and their perceptions that society has high expectations of them also. The bereaved need to be reassured that guilt feelings are common and a normal part of the grief process. They also need to be provided help in sharing guilt feelings. Family and friends, as well as some professionals, are often quick to say, "You shouldn't feel guilty," thereby minimizing and invalidating feelings of guilt and cutting off further expression of this painful emotion.

In working with individuals experiencing guilt, it is also important to assess and understand the factors that may influence guilt responses. It appears that guilt is more common and intense after a sudden unexpected death and after a suicide. Individuals experiencing such losses may need additional help in sharing and dealing with guilt feelings. Another factor to be considered is the level of responsibility for the health or safety of the loved one; the bereaved who perceive a higher level of responsibility may have more intense guilt. Thus, mothers who experience a pregnancy or neonatal death and parents of minor children who die may be at greater risk. Following a chronic disease, it is important to note the possibility of guilt related to the caregiving during the individual's illness and at the time of death. Ambivalence in the relationship with the deceased also appears to be a common thread that increases the possibility of guilt feelings after death.

Conclusions

In this chapter, we have proposed a conceptual model of bereavement guilt that describes the process by which guilt develops, the variables that influence the process, and the sources of guilt. We have also provided examples to demonstrate these concepts. We propose this model as a starting point for dialogue on bereavement guilt and challenge other theorists and researchers to further develop and to test this theory of bereavement guilt or to develop and test other models of bereavement guilt. Considering the relatively high prevalence of guilt in bereavement, and its potential to cause intense distress, additional research attention should also be given to investigating ways to ameliorate guilt.

References

Averill, J. (1968). Grief: Its nature and significance. *Psychological Bulletin, 70,* 721–748.

Bowlby, J. (1980). *Attachment and loss, Volume III: Loss, sadness and depression.* New York: Basic Books.

Bugen, L. (1977). Human grief: A model for prediction and intervention. *American Journal of Orthopsychiatry, 47* (2), 196–206.

Cassem, N. (1978). *Grieving for others: Practical management component of normal mourning.* Paper presented at Annual Meeting of the American Psychiatric association, Atlanta, GA.

Cain, A. (1972). *Survivors of suicide.* Springfield IL: Charles C Thomas.

DeFrain, J. D., & Ernst, L. (1978). The psychological effect of Sudden Infant Death Syndrome on surviving family members. *Journal of Family Practice, 21,* 103–111.

DeFrain, J., Taylor, J., & Ernst, L. (1982). *Coping with sudden infant death.* Lexington, MA: D. C. Heath.

Demi, A. S. (1978). Adjustment to widowhood after a sudden death: Suicide and non-suicide survivors compared. In M. V. Batey (Ed.), *Communicating nursing research* (Vol. 11, pp. 91–99). Boulder, CO: Western Interstate Commission for Higher Education.

Demi, A. S. (1984). Social adjustment of widows after a sudden death: Suicide and non-suicide survivors compared. *Death Education, 8* (Suppl.), 91–112.

Demi, A. S., & Miles, M. S. (1987). Parameters of normal grief: A Delphi study. *Death Studies, 11,* 397–412.

Edelstein, L. (1984). *Maternal bereavement: Coping with the unexpected death of a child.* New York: Praeger.

Freud, S. (1938). *The basic writings of Sigmund Freud* (A. A. Brill, Trans.). New York: Random House.

Glick, I., Weiss, R., & Parkes, C. (1974). *The first year of bereavement.* New York: John Wiley and Sons.

Henslin, J. M. (1970). Guilt and guilt neutralization: Response and adjustment to suicide. In J. D. Douglas (Ed.), *Deviance and respectability: The social construction of moral meanings.* New York: Basic Books.

Henslin, J. M. (1972). Strategies of adjustment: An ethnomethodological approach to the study of guilt and suicide. In A. C. Cain (Ed.), *Survivors of suicide.* Springfield, IL: Charles C Thomas.

Johnson-Soderberg, S. (1983). Parents who have lost a child by death. In V. J. Sasserath (Ed.), *Minimizing high risk parenting.* New Brunswick, NJ: Johnson & Johnson.

Lehman, D. R., Wortman, C. B., & Williams, A. F. (1987). Long-term effects of losing a spouse or child in a motor vehicle crash. *Journal of Personality and Social Psychology, 52* (1), 218–231.

Lieberman, S. (1978). Nineteen cases of morbid grief. *British Journal of Psychiatry, 132,* 159–163.

Lifton, R. L. (1967). *Death in life: Survivors of Hiroshima.* New York: Simon and Schuster.

Lindemann, E. (1944). Symptomatology and management of acute grief. *American Journal of Psychiatry, 101,* 141–148.

Miles, M. S. (1984). Helping adults mourn the death of a child. In H. Wass & C. Corr. (Eds.), *Children and death* (pp. 219–241). New York: Hemisphere.

Miles, M. S., & Demi, A. (1983–84). Toward the development of a theory of bereavement guilt. *Omega, 14* (4), 299–314.

Miles, M. S., & Demi, A. S. (1986). Guilt in bereaved parents. In T. Rando (Ed.), *Parental loss of a child: Clinical and research considerations.* Champaign, IL: Research Press.

Miles, M. S., & Demi, A. S. (1991). *A comparison of guilt in bereaved parents whose children died by suicide, accident, or chronic disease.* Unpublished paper.

Mowrer, O. H. (1960). *Learning theory and behavior.* New York: John Wiley.

Parkes, C. M. (1975). Determinants of outcome following bereavement. *Omega, 6,* 302–323.

Parkes, C. M., & Weiss, R. S. (1983). *Recovery from bereavement.* New York: Basic Books.

Raphael, B. (1983). *The anatomy of bereavement.* New York: Basic Books.

Raphael, S. J. (1990, December 17). *The Sally Jessy Raphael Show* (television program). American Broadcasting Co.

Rubin, S. S. (1984–85). Maternal attachment and child death: On adjustment, relationship, and resolution. *Omega, 15* (4), 347–352.

Rudestam, K. E. (1977). Physical and psychological responses to suicide in the family. *Journal of Consulting and Clinical Psychology, 45,* 162–170.

Sanders, C. M. (1989). *Grief: The mourning after.* New York: John Wiley.

Van Dongen, C. (1990). Agonizing questioning: Experiences of survivors of suicide victims, *Nursing Research, 39,* 224–229.

Wahl, C. (1970, March–April). The differential diagnosis of normal and neurotic grief following bereavement. *Psychosomatic, 11,* 104–106.

Worden, J. W. (1982). *Grief counseling and grief therapy.* New York: Springer.

Yamamoto, T., Okonogi, T., Iwasaki, T., et al. (1969). Mourning in Japan. *American Journal of Psychiatry, 125,* 1660–1665.

Twelve

Quality of Living

Diane Scott-Dorsett

Diane Scott-Dorsett is currently the founder and Director of Comprehensive Support Services for Persons with Cancer, a private practice in San Francisco. She is Associate Clinical Professor, University of California School of Nursing, Department of Physiological Nursing, San Francisco, and Attending Scientist, the Medical Research Institute, an independent research facility affiliated with California Pacific Medical Center, San Francisco. Scott-Dorsett was formerly Nurse Scientist at Memorial Sloan-Kettering Cancer Center, New York, a Robert Wood Johnson Foundation Clinical Nurse Scholar and Postdoctoral Fellow at the University of California San Francisco. She has been a Bristol-Myers Scholar, having produced and directed award-winning media programs for patient education. Her Bachelor of Science degree was earned at Rutgers University College of Nursing, and she received both an M.A. and Ph.D. from New York University. Scott-Dorsett's research examines patterns of recovery following cancer diagnosis. In addition to her practice, teaching, and research activities, she facilitates a Leukemia Society of America-sponsored Family Support Group for the northern California area and is a member of the Board of Trustees and Medical Advisory Board, Leukemia Society of America, Northern California Chapter.

A concern for quality of life has become uniquely important as a therapeutic challenge in health care. As the population ages and chronic life-threatening disease becomes more prevalent, a host of new problems are introduced into the lives of patients, and their families and into the practices of health care providers. Fundamentally, the concept of cure has been replaced by the idea of prolonged remission; the existential issues emerging from this shift, in turn, introduce the individual to a whole new world of experience initiated by an altered life trajectory. Rigorous medical treatments are accompanied by uncomfortable and distressing side effects. Life crisis intensifies problems predating the illness, providing an opportunity for their reemergence, reexamination, and resolution. Occasional acute morbidities are superimposed on the chronic illness itself. And major changes in the individual's relationships, work, and environmental organization become part and parcel of the overall transformation.

The dimensions of this new world impact heavily on the family, a major source of social support for the individual experiencing health crisis. Although the person diagnosed with the illness becomes the primary focus of treatment activity, his or her support system is a critical factor in living with life-threatening disease and must be considered integral to the plan of care.

Modern medical advances have prolonged life but with a consequent, parallel challenge invoking the development of approaches to maximize the quality of the life extended. Those professions, concerned with the care and treatment of persons diagnosed with life-threatening illness and of those who for any reason become vulnerable to death, must consider quality of life as an important aspect of therapeutics. Although medical treatment may be the foundation for cure, quality of life is the central element of care. Both entities, care and cure, are mutually dependent; in effect, they both promote the healing process.

This chapter will explore the concept—quality of life—and its dynamic form—quality of living—from three intercepting angles: (1) theoretical foundations, (2) research and measurement, and (3) clinical application. The chapter is written for practitioners in every health care discipline who concern themselves with the illness, recovery, and dying experience of patients and their families. It is dedicated to both the promotion of optimal health and, in the last analysis, life well lived.

Theoretical Foundations

The moment life begins, quality becomes its intrinsic characteristic. Indeed, on every level of awareness, human beings experience, interpret, and create their quality of life. In an operational sense, quality is multifactorial in that uncountable sources deep within and external to the person contribute to its nature; and, although recognized as having holistic essence, for purposes of understanding and measurement, social science has viewed the concept as multidimensional, composed of physical, psychological, spiritual, interpersonal, social, financial, political, and other interacting components that produce a total effect.

Definitions of quality of life have been offered since the time of Aristotle, who suggested happiness as the ultimate goal (Aristotle, 1976). Oliver Wendell Homes spoke of the complete life, implying that the highest grade is reflected by a multifaceted existence (Holmes, 1860). The World Health Organization has officially defined quality of life as "being in a state of complete physical, mental and social well-being" which extends beyond the mere absence of disease.

Certain characteristics seem to cut across all definitions of quality of life and living. First, quality of life is a perception, essentially subjective and uniquely different for each person. Second, most often quality of life is described as a feeling of well-being or as being in harmony with nature. Third, definitions generally specify a balance in several life domains— work, family, environment, for instance—and in one's sense of creative fulfillment overall. Fourth, over the past 10 years, quality of life has been considered an ongoing presence related to aims, goals, and expectations of self and others, squarely grounded in the individual's activities of daily living. And finally, quality is modified by the contextuality of life, a set of vectors that take into account not only present circumstance but past experience and future expectations (Calman, 1987). Context contains the threads of continuity inherent in change with time.

Quality of life is expressed in terms of satisfaction, contentment, happiness, fulfillment, and the ability to successfully cope with adversity. These descriptors are metaphorical in that happiness, health, long life, and control are commonly considered as good for the person and acknowledged as the physical and social bases for well-being in Western society.

There are four major themes revealed in the quality of life literature:

1. Quality is considered an attitude rooted in culturally determined beliefs and values, modified by the context of life.
2. Quality of life changes with the growth and development of the individual. Each stage and phase of existence lends itself to reprioritizing values and to a resultant transformation of self.
3. Quality of life is reflected in the individual's ongoing interpretations, feelings, and emotions, and in language and behavior. A person can evaluate his or her quality of life verbally, but every aspect of his space, relationships, and work communicates it as well.
4. Quality of life serves as a criterion by which choice among options is made.

According to deGroot (1986), quality of life as an attitude goes hand in hand with personal growth and development. As such, an individual's maturation and interchange with environment represent contextual elements while quality of life becomes the criterion by which the person conducts his or her life and makes choices among options. Thus, the infrastructure of quality of life includes one's opinions, interests, and purposes in life—cognitive elements that emerge from age, developmental stage, and cultural beliefs and values.

An individual's fundamental values are generally coherent with the fundamental values of his or her culture. This sense of coherency is directly tied to feelings and emotions, the essence of each lived moment in time. When asked to evaluate one's quality of life, in general, the response will be related to the overall sense of coherence, the reflection of a balance among the many factors important to life in a particular context, culture, and environment.

Further, the values of the person in a culture are reflected in metaphorical language. Conflict with those values produces adversity for the individual, expressed metaphorically in language. For example, chronic illness may be perceived as a threat to independence—an important value in U.S. society. In response, the individual's description of concerns may be rich in symbolism, representing loss of independence or fear of dependency.

Life-threatening illness imposes both threat and challenge to the established coping repertoire on an everyday basis. The individual experiences a host of emotions—anxiety, fear, anger, depression—that in an evolutionary sense serve to protect him or her. However, the same feelings that trigger vigilance, denial, avoidance, and other intrapsychic processes that assist the person to cope with the threat in manageable doses are nevertheless painful. The feelings will interactively color further perceptions of the illness experience, which will be evaluated in light of the individual's quality of life criteria. The result of this comparison will have a potent effect on the choices made and the coping repertoire mobilized in living those choices.

Quality of life, as a dynamic criterion by which we experience, interpret, and create our existence, develops throughout life. Although notions of quality of life change as we grow and mature, they accumulate with a style as individual as one's fingerprints. In understanding quality of life perceptions, we look to the individual's style of living, everyday routine, metaphors of language, and values that become clearly apparent in the choices made from the field of options available.

A brilliant illustration is found in Kaufman's *The Ageless Self* (1986), an ethnography of Americans over age 70. Kaufman, who sought to understand how the elderly person conceives of his or her own life, focused on the themes of the life story as told by 60 people whom she interviewed. Themes of each life story were extracted by attention to the repetition of specific words, use of language, general thought patterns, structure of the overall story, and the dominant subject matter of the account.

The theoretical framework for the study employed Erickson's Eight Stages of the Life Cycle (Erickson, 1963, 1968; Erickson, 1988) (see Figure 12–1). Specifically, Kaufman wondered how people integrate a lifetime of experience in order to achieve Erickson's final stage of identity: ego integration. Although Ericksonian theory places the ego integration stage in the later years of the life cycle, individuals who face a life-span cut short by serious illness (an altered life trajectory), at any age, face the task of ego integration as well.

Themes in the life story are, by definition, subjective interpretations of cultural heritage and personal experience. Since social beings integrate culture and experience into their sense of identity, the coherency emerging

	1	2	3	4	5	6	7	8
Old Age								Integrity vs. Despair. WISDOM
Adulthood							Generativity vs. Stagnation. CARE	
Young Adult						Intimacy vs. Isolation. LOVE		
Adolescence					Identity vs. Role Confusion. FIDELITY			
School Age				Industry vs. Inadequacy. COMPETENCE				
Play Age			Initiative vs. Guilt. PURPOSE					
Early Childhood		Autonomy vs. Shame, Doubt. WILL						
Infancy	Basic Trust vs. Basic Mistrust. HOPE							

Figure 12–1 Eight stages of psychosocial development of the human life cycle (*Source:* Reproduced from *Wisdom and the senses: The way of creativity*, by Joan M. Erikson, by permission of W. W. Norton & Company, Inc. Copyright© 1988 by Joan M. Erikson.

establishes meaning in life and the sense of self-worth. The interpretation of this process, whether by self-assessment or through other characterizations of an individual's life, communicates its quality.

Kaufman found that life story themes were influenced by structural forces, such as the socioeconomic status of childhood, family ties, education, geographic mobility, and work. These elements provided an understanding of people's limitations and opportunities as a basis for making choices and for the establishment of meaning in their lives.

Four to six themes emerged from each story categorized as either topical (marriage, work, religion etc.), defining the social structure of their lives, or interpretive (self-determination, acquiescence, disengagement) of their sense of self-worth, cultural norms, goals, expectations, and evaluation of their own performance. Themes revealed themselves in three dimensions: content, timing, and style. To illustrate, the content dimension included the central meaning of affective ties, marriage, work, social status, acquiescence, and self-determination. Timing illuminated life's flow of events, interpretive time markers and turning points, both high and low. Style revealed the person's notion of self and the evaluation of his or her performance in the larger world. The needs for recognition, perfection, and relationships were divulged as style in the themes.

In the final analysis, Kaufman further operationalized ego integration as "coming to terms." She said, "There are moments during the life course when people choose, or are persuaded by circumstance, to evaluate or become conscious of the direction of their lives. The life story is a means of comparing the life lived with the prescribed directive" (1986, p. 185), not only in old age but at any critical turning point that compromises existence.

The findings of Kaufman's study support and expand Erickson's idea that integration is at the core of the "creative, symbolic process of self-formulation" later in life. Integration is fundamental to self-formulation as well when life is threatened at any age.

The theoretical foundation for quality of life as a therapeutic dimension in clinical practice rests on the notion of a developmental demand for integration. Integration is based on a congruency among cultural values of origin, interpretation of the meaning of experience, and self-evaluation of performance in everyday life. Thus, any life event or experience that alters the individual's sense of mortality offers an opportunity to reintegrate or transform the self. This process begins with a search for the meaning of the event in the individual's life and a review and assessment, on many levels of awareness, of its quality.

In summary, quality of life is central to the transformative process accompanying change in the life trajectory. Aging, illness, major life events, unresolved issues, or any shift that compromises existence represents such an alteration. Transformation has as its goal an integration of the experience as part of the self and is dependent on the capacity of the individual to integrate diverse experience and make global statements about those experiences. Barofsky (1986) points out that quality of life is reflected as integration every time we respond to the question, How are you? Thus, we are asked to make quality of life assessments as a highly frequent event in social exchange.

In the process, quality of life is both a criterion for judgment and an attitude that serves as the individual's rudder, guiding choices and the way he or she operates in open waters. Quality of life is deeply rooted in cultural beliefs and values. In circumstances when the coherence between beliefs and values and personal experience is threatened, quality of life informs the individual's choice of options and how he or she copes with the adversity.

Ego integration is a fusion of the interpretation of the event or its meaning in life, one's sense of identity and feelings of self-worth. Simply, quality of life is an internal reference to questions of identity and meaning. As such, it is a unique, subjective, ongoing presence that responds to circumstances potentiating change or that create incongruity with basic beliefs and values. Quality of life is important to health and health care practice. As the basis of care, an understanding of the patient and family's quality of life potentiates cure; overall, quality of life is essential to healing, even in the dying process.

Research and Measurement

Health care practitioners have been evaluating the quality of the lives of their patients intuitively since the beginning of time. Sleep disturbance, changes in appetite, weakness, depression, pain, inability to work and take part in leisure activities, and disturbances in relationships have been the most obvious indicators of deterioration in quality of life. In 1985, an international workshop on quality of life assessment and cancer treatment was held in Milan, Italy, cosponsored by the World Health Organization, the Netherlands Cancer Institute, the National Cancer Institute (Bethesda), and the National Tumor Institute of Italy. Speakers and attendees were charged with awakening the "technology for assessment of quality of life" (Ventafridda et al., 1986, p. v) through the synthesis of existing data and the identification of research gaps. Although specifically focused on cancer, the results of this historic meeting are useful to the understanding and application of the concept of quality of life in both health and disease, and are important to its measurement in any illness. Moreover, cancer alone results in 1 out of 10 deaths throughout the world; and more than four million people suffer from unrelieved cancer pain. Consequently, cancer as a model for life-threatening illness illustrates that quality of life plays a critical role in human suffering that goes beyond the modern-day ability to successfully treat disease. In a global sense, reducing unnecessary mortality and managing pain and discomfort more effectively become prime objectives of any worldwide program based on quality of life maximization. The proceedings of the international workshop (Ventafridda et al., 1986) emphasized the importance of valid, reliable instruments to measure quality of life that are also practical, realistic, and applicable cross-culturally. Measurement was viewed not only as a method for clinical assessment but as a base for health policy making, the establishment of priorities in care, and resource allocation (Stjernsward, Stanley, & Koroltchouk, 1986; Yates, 1986).

The history of quality of life assessment is grounded in social science research dating back to 1930. With the advent of clinical trials in the 1970s, the concept began to be applied in health-related research. For example, an early study (National Center for Health Care Technology, 1981) of coronary bypass recipients counted the patient's return to work as a major outcome variable. In more recent times, although observable change in behavior is still the most frequently measured variable, attention to the judgment process inherent in quality of life decisions is important to the expansion of knowledge and measurement skill in this field of social science. To these ends, Barofsky (1986) has identified three approaches to assessment: (1) understanding quality of life as a judgment process, (2) basing assessments on large-scale population comparison norms, and (3) conducting psychosocial studies specific to specialty-based parameters.

Quality of life outcome analyses have largely emerged from the recognition of their relevance to care and to treatment goals at different stages of illness. Schipper and Levitt (1986) point out that quantitative studies have become the legal currency of science. The scientific method, thought to ensure reproducibility and validity in research, has been grounded in quantifiable measurement. They argue that quality of life outcome measures, although qualitative by nature, can be just as rigorously investigated because quality of life is the closest measure to the ultimate clinical outcome sought: "the ability of a patient with an illness to carry on living a life of functional and philosophic meaning" (p. 20). These investigators have recognized the following dimensions as important evaluation parameters: (1) symptom distress, (2) functional status, (3) psychological distress, (4) social interaction, (5) sexuality and body image, and (6) satisfaction with medical treatment (p. 31).

The classic approach to evaluating quality of life was developed by Karnofsky (Karnofsky & Burchenal, 1949), yet the Karnofsky Performance Rating Scale (see Figure 12–2) was not tested nor did it come into more frequent use until 30 years later. The Karnofsky is the best known assessment tool used in clinical trials in the last decade and measures the individual's ability to carry out normal activities and to work. There are three major categories (normal/able to live at home/unable to care for self) divided by degree of performance ability. Similar scales have been constructed by Zubrod and colleagues (1960), Carlens, Dahlstrom, and Nou (1970), Burge and colleagues (1975) and the World Health Organization (1979). These early scales evaluated physical performance and the need for nursing care. Although criticized for its inadequate scaling and narrow interpretation of functional status (Schipper & Levitt, 1986), the Karnofsky-type index was a beginning.

As the science of psychometrics advanced, so did the accuracy and consistency of measurement approaches to quality of life. By the mid-1970s, several investigators (Craig, Comstock, & Geiser, 1974; Morris, Greer, & White, 1977; Roberts, Furnival, & Forrest, 1972) added the psycho-social dimension to the concept of functionality. From these early attempts, several more recent versions, carefully tested over time for reliability (ability to measure with consistency) and validity (ability to measure the construct(s) purported to be measured), have been constructed. Although a fairly accurate reading of a person's quality of life can be made by

Karnofsky Rating Scale

Instructions: Please circle the percentage that best reflects the patients' abilities.

Normal, no complaints	100	Normal Activity:
		Fully Ambulatory
Able to carry on normal activities; minor signs or symptoms of disease	90	
Normal activity with effort	80	
Cares for self; unable to carry on normal activity or to do active work	70	Self-Care: Partially
Requires occasional assistance, but able to care for most of his needs	60	Ambulatory
Requires considerable assistance and frequent medical care	50	
Disabled; requires special care and assistance	40	Incapacitated: Non-ambulatory
Severely disabled; hospitalization indicated though death not imminent	30	
Very sick; hospitalization necessary; active supportive treatment necessary	20	
Moribund	10	
Dead	0	

Figure 12–2 Karnofsky Functional Assessment Tool (*Source:* Karnofsky & Burchenal, 1949.)

simply asking for a subjective rating, the response may not give enough information on every dimension of life being considered nor allow for the development of interventions designed to maximize quality of life at any phase in the continuum of an important life experience.

Measuring quality of life becomes a more valid reflection when done over time. Having some idea of baseline or precritical event status is useful to the accuracy of the overall picture. Further, when measuring quality of life, longitudinal design is most effective in getting an idea of how quality of life changes over time and in understanding the variables having the greatest impact on the process.

Currently, three types of quantitative scales are most frequently used in measuring quality of life: (1) linear analogue scales, (2) Likert-type scales, and (3) standard scales such as the Karnofsky. To gain some perspective on the complexities of quality of life research, three measurement models, characterized by five essential parameters, will be presented: Graham and Longman (Young & Longman, 1983: Graham & Longman, 1987), Padilla and Grant (1985), and Ferrans and Powers (1985, 1990). Each model will be discussed in terms of its (1) theoretical framework, (2) operational definition, (3) psychometric vigor, (4) normative base for interpretation, and (5) clinical relevance.

Quality of Life Model (Young & Longman, 1983; Graham & Longman, 1987)

The conceptual framework for the quality of life research by Graham and Longman (see Figure 12–3) focuses on four variables central to quality of life in chronic illness. Quality of life is defined as "the degree of satisfaction with present life circumstances perceived by the person" (Young & Longman, 1983, p. 220). The four variables include (1) symptom distress, or the degree of discomfort perceived by the person; (2) social dependency, or the

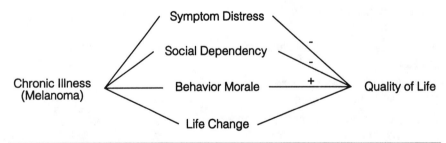

Figure 12–3 Conceptual framework for Young and Longman's Quality of Life (*Source:* Young, K. J., & Longman, A. J. (1983). Quality of life and persons with melanoma: A pilot study. *Cancer Nursing, 6* (3), 219–225. Reprinted with permission.)

extent of assistance required for activities the individual normally carries out alone; (3) behavior-morale, or the prevailing mood or spirit of the individual; and (4) life change, or the degree of change experienced in areas of daily living.

Psychometric research has established the scale's reliability (internal consistency coefficient alphas ranged from 0.82 to 0.95) and its validity. In a study of 60 adults between the ages of 20 and 83, diagnosed with malignant melanoma, stepwise multiple regression analyses statistically supported hypotheses concerned with relationships among variables. Although all four variables were related to one another, only symptom distress, social dependency, and behavior-morale were significantly related to the individual's self-rating of overall quality of life. Amount and direction of life change, although not related directly to the person's own perceptual rating, were significantly correlated with each other and with symptom distress and social dependency.

To further evaluate research results in the establishment of an empirical model, subject response was analyzed for the group as a whole, for those with a poor prognosis, and for those with metastases. Although further research is recommended to support findings, results revealed differences in the percent of variance in quality of life explained by the variables in each group. In the overall group, 10 percent of the variance was explained by the variables; 26 percent was explained for persons with poor prognoses; and 22 percent of the variance was explained in subjects with metastases, with symptom distress making the greatest contribution.

The conclusions from this initial work serve to establish a beginning empirical model of quality of life for persons diagnosed with chronic, life-threatening disease. Data suggest that persons diagnosed with melanoma conduct a reappraisal of their lives with respect to what they want to do with it and how they want to live it. The investigators point out that interviews with many subjects revealed the viewpoint that such a reappraisal actually increased their quality of life in comparison with the past despite their current life circumstance. Graham and Longman (1987) caution that assessments by caregivers may not be sensitive enough to provide a true picture of the patient's quality of life given the immediate context of his or her life. To address this default, they recommend longitudinal studies with careful documentation of the meaning of the circumstances to the individual at the time of evaluation. Overall, the investigators conclude that "human beings do realign their values, making cognitive adaptations when faced with a life-threatening illness" (p. 345).

Quality of Life as an Outcome Variable (Padilla & Grant, 1985)

Padilla and Grant view quality of life as a multidimensional concept that, when measured validly and reliably, allows for a more sensitive evaluation of the individual and the intervention process. They define quality of life

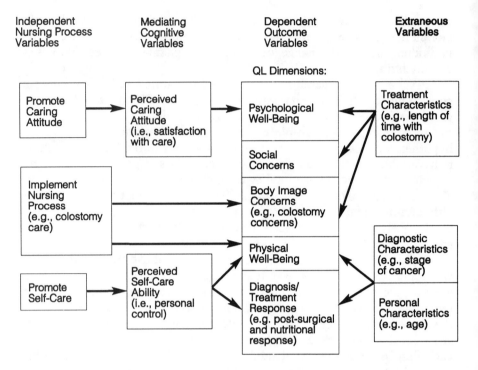

Figure 12–4   A model of the relationship between nursing process and the dimensions of quality of life (*Source:* Reprinted from Padilla, G. V., and Grant, M. M., Quality of Life as a Cancer Nursing Outcome Variable, in *Advances in Nursing Science*, Vol. 8, No. 1, p. 53, with permission of Aspen Publishers, Inc., © 1985.)

generally as "that which makes life worth living," especially as it refers to the total health care of individuals. Quality of life is viewed as a dependent variable with the potential for measuring the effect of the caring process.

Padilla and Grant's conceptual model (see Figure 12–4) rests on five quality of life dimensions that co-vary with several independent and mediating variables: (1) psychological well-being (happiness, satisfaction, fun, general quality of life, pleasure in eating and sleep); (2) social concerns (social rejection, social contact, privacy needs); (3) body image concerns (ability to adjust to and live with body deficits due to illness and medical treatment); (4) physical well-being (strength, fatigue, ability to work, health, perceived usefulness); and (5) diagnosis-treatment response (ability to have sufficient sexual activity, severity of pain, sufficient eating and nutritional activity). Internal consistency for each dimension was found to be greater than 0.80 for all factors except response to diagnosis-treatment (alpha range: 0.48 to 0.71). The social concerns factor emerged as the strongest with an alpha of 0.90.

Initial studies by the investigators revealed psychological well-being to be the most important quality of life dimension, followed by physical well-being, body image concerns, response to diagnosis-treatment, and social concerns. They conclude that quality of life is determined by cognitive processes and cite Burkhardt's (1985) work defining cognitive mediators such as perceived support, negative attitude towards illness, self-esteem, and internal control over health as most powerfully predicting the effect of variables such as pain and impairment. The meaning of illness and its limitations, not so much the actual pain and disability, determined the patient's notion of quality of life.

The Padilla-Grant model recognizes the multifactorial effects of a person's perception of his or her quality of life; and, that as an outcome variable, nursing care has an important influence over the patient's perception of his or her quality of life. In a study of 135 patients with colostomies due to colon cancer, satisfaction with nursing care was significantly correlated with psychological well-being, which impacted on social and physical well-being. Availability of and confidence in the nurse were the most relevant factors in terms of psychological well-being. In examining the overall statistical analysis of their model, it was found that as confidence in the nurse increased, the patient's sense of control over illness-wellness versus chance increased, as did the perception of their overall quality of life. Confidence in the nurse emerged as an important predictive factor in terms of the quality of life of cancer patients in this research.

Quality of Life Index (Ferrans & Powers, 1985, 1990)

Ferrans and Powers set out to construct a valid and reliable tool to measure quality of life. They viewed life satisfaction as the most important indicator of quality of life. Citing Campbell's (1976) idea that the individual's subjective assessment is more valid than objective demographic or functional indicators such as income, education, and occupation, and recognizing that overall satisfaction is colored heavily by the individual's assessment of the importance of each dimension related to satisfaction, they define quality of life as "the satisfaction of needs" (p. 17). Need, in turn, is defined as "the amount of a particular reward that a person may require" (p. 17). Thus, the Quality of Life Index (QLI) was designed to measure satisfaction with the major life domains (see Figure 12–5) as well as the unique importance each domain holds for the individual.

The Quality of Life Index consists of two sections—satisfaction and importance—scored relative to one another in the following life domains: health care, physical health and functioning, marriage, family, friends, stress, standard of living, occupation, education, leisure, future retirement, peace of mind, personal faith, life goals, personal appearance, self-acceptance, general happiness, and general satisfaction. The 32-item, six-point Likert-type scale has versions for healthy adults, kidney dialysis

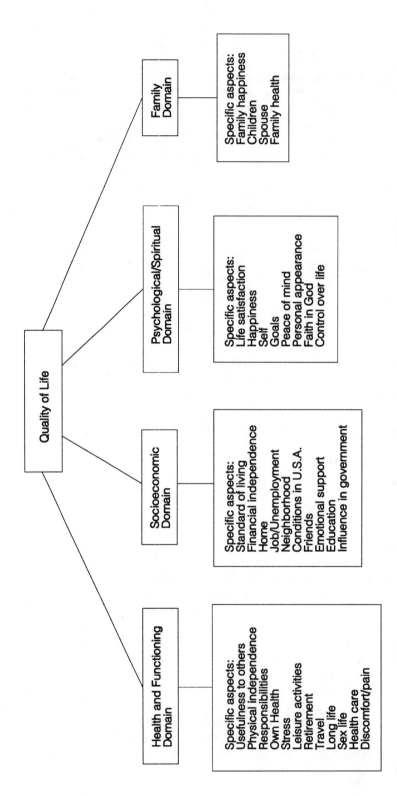

Figure 12–5   Hierarchical relationships between the global construct of quality of life, four major domains, and specific aspects of the domain (Reprinted from the *Oncology Nursing Forum* with permission from the Oncology Nursing Press, Inc. Ferrans, C. E. and Ferrell, B. R.; Development of a Quality of Life Index for Patients with Cancer. *Oncology Nursing Forum 17* (3 suppl.): 15–21, 1990.)

patients, kidney transplant patients, cardiac transplant patients, and cancer patients. The cross-tabulated scores not only reflect the person's satisfaction with a domain but its importance as well, or how much the individual values the domain. Scores are adjusted for satisfaction-importance (value) in the scoring process. Content validity, criterion-related validity, test-retest reliability, and internal consistency have been established for the QLI. Further, factor analyses found four major factors or domains: health and physical functioning, family, psychological/spiritual, and socioeconomic (see Figure 12–5). Currently, the QLI is part of the instrumentation in several major investigations throughout the country.

In summary, when the three quality of life models are compared, they are remarkably similar. Each is characterized by a set of dimensions that include psychological well-being, physical well-being, social interaction, and overall response to health and function-related life change. All three describe quality of life as being determined by a cognitive process whereby persons with chronic disease subjectively assess the meaning of an illness event and its related functional limitations in their lives and realign or reprioritize their values as a result.

All three models provide a framework for evaluation that goes well beyond the Karnofsky functional model. In contrast, each model is characterized in a slightly different fashion. Graham and Longman refer to their goal as the development of an empirical model or one that explains quality of life as a clinical phenomenon. Padilla and Grant, on the other hand, focus on intervention and how their model might provide a basis for the evaluation of nursing management aimed at promoting the highest quality of life for the patient. Ferrans and Powers contribute a psychometric model with an instrument that measures and interscores both satisfaction with the domain and its importance to the individual.

All three are more reliable and more closely approximate the patient's experience than do the previous generation of functional indicators. From these data, intervention approaches are more likely to be closely tailored to each patient's unique set of issues, problems, and resources. However, to determine how effective and useful present-day evaluation methods are, a review of the operational definition derived earlier from the Ericksonian theoretical base is in order. As such, quality of life is a personal reference for the individual's sense of integrity, especially as events change his or her life trajectory in important ways. As a developmental process, integration normally characterizes the later years of life, understood as "gaining wisdom." Erickson (1988) defines integrity as a capacity strong enough to endure loss, particularly the physical disintegration accompanying the aging process and its attendant illnesses. Integration means that a person becomes strong in "the ability to gather life experiences into a meaningful pattern" (p. 103) by acknowledging and leaning into what has accrued from living through the previous seven stages of life (see Figure 12–1).

Although the empirical-psychometric model represents a quantum leap in the ability to measure the multifactorial nature of quality of life as a construct, new understanding of adult development, brought about by increasing life-span and long-term survivorship despite life-threatening disease, has ushered in the need for health practitioners to understand the integrative process or, as Barofsky said, the judgment process. The 1980s witnessed a transition from the gross, functional approach to quantitative scales that take the psychosocial dimension into consideration. The next generation of evaluation methods should focus on the process of integration as the way the person experiences, interprets, and recreates his or her quality of living.

Applications in Practice

This section will: (1) present two case illustrations of how major change in life trajectory challenges quality of life and how life-threatening illness presents a developmental demand for integration; (2) describe the Integrated Cancer Recovery Model (Scott & Eisendrath, 1986) as a framework for clinical evaluation of quality of life; and (3) suggest four broad intervention modalities designed to assist patients and families as they interpret their quality of life and respond to their field of options.

Case Illustrations

Application of the quality of life (QL) concept in clinical practice first requires an understanding of the common QL-related clinical situations encountered in providing health care. Although quality of life as personal reference is ubiquitous, two deeply fundamental initiators provide prototypes for understanding: (1) change in life trajectory and (2) life-threatening illness as a developmental demand for integration.

Alteration in Life Trajectory.   Jane's experience illustrates how quality of life is a personal reference informing the individual's sense of integrity, especially as events change a life trajectory in important ways. Jane's initial breast cancer diagnosis occurred the same year as her husband's unexpected and sudden death, eight days following their marriage. Three years later, bone and lung metastases were discovered and treated with radiation, three intensive cycles of high-dose chemotherapy, and hormonal therapy, to no avail. Jane's condition continued to deteriorate over the next two years of her life, and she died at age 60, five years after her illness began.

The course of Jane's recovery was remarkable because it served as counterpoint to her course of illness. Recovery begins at the moment of diagnosis and continues, as a process, until the moment of death. Moreover, the two courses may diverge significantly, even when death and dying become certainties. Human beings are endowed with a remarkable capacity to survive; life is not extinquished easily, save those circumstances of overwhelming trauma and multisystem failure. The survival experience is powerfully enhanced by the level of one's quality of life regardless of its length, and the quality of life is central to the recovery process.

Jane received the news of her cancer recurrence shortly after the third anniversary of her husband's death. She reported that upon leaving the oncologist's office, she retreated to her family's cabin in the mountains where the remote isolation and beauty of the country helped to deepen the connection with her spirituality and to increase the clarity of her perspective.

The dying process was no stranger to Jane. Her father, husband, and a close friend had died in succession over the preceding years, leaving the sadness of loss and the pain of grief as familiar companions. Now, she was faced with the prospect of her own mortality and sought refuge both in the mountains and in therapy to facilitate her journey.

Initially, Jane's major question was "when." She felt hopeful with the promise of treatment, but as its rigor escalated without benefit of effect, Jane's question changed to "how." She spoke more of the quality of life, the goals to be reasonably accomplished before death, the reprioritizing of values, and the orchestration of dying in concert with her style of living and the meaning of her life.

Jane had been an interior designer, her talent and skill evident in the architecturally award-winning house in which she lived. The decor was clean, authentic, and crisp, softened by the influences of fresh flowers and proper lighting. A garden, planned by a noted landscaper with whom she had worked, became an extension of the living space through French doors in the downstairs living room and through an expanse of windows in Jane's upstairs bedroom. It was there, in the comfort of her own home, that she planned to die.

In the meantime, there was much to accomplish. The first task was to understand and harness the energy of her anger. The process of grieving the loss of her husband had been restricted due to her inability to deal with the anger she felt at having been left financially unprotected and emotionally unprepared. The experience had been grounded in her early life as an only child, when she felt unprotected by a loving but weak father from the might of a jealous, dependent, and child-like mother. She described herself as living a life of early responsibility void of a childhood. Her first marriage to an alcoholic lasted 30 years and ended in divorce. Jane's father had died of cancer several years earlier, the first patient in the newly opened community hospice, leaving her once again alone to care for her aging, demanding, critical, and increasingly demented mother. For the first time in her life, in work with her therapist, Jane began to explore these issues and to understand and channel the energy of her anger.

She consolidated her financial situation. She made a living will and invested power of attorney in her brother-in-law, ensuring that her two adult children were "protected," as she felt she had not been. She divested herself of several board memberships inherited from her wealthy husband's philanthropy, thereby strengthening her own identity. She traveled, usually with trusted, caring women friends. She visited with people she loved, carefully avoiding those for whom she felt little commitment, and allowed herself fewer visits with her mother. She prepared for her home hospice experience by hiring a live-in companion and other household staff necessary to order her space. She asked her therapist to be with her and to provide support for her children and her companion as she became increasingly unable to do so. She brought her family together with her on a memorable vacation to Santa Fe, where her last Christmas was spent. She worked with her nurse therapist toward maximizing pain control through a combined approach using pharmacologic and relaxation methods.

Jane's moments of greatest enjoyment and intimacy were when she was with friends. She had hiked the Himalayas with four women friends and she had sat together with her daughter and beloved sister-in-law engaged in lively conversation in the mountains she loved. In these instances, they would huddle together with Jane bent forward, hugging her legs while rocking slightly back and forth, having what she would describe with twinkling eyes as "giggles." These were the good times spent together in front of a fire with cigarette and glass of vodka in hand. This was quality of life for Jane.

As her days dwindled and her consciousness blurred into a morphine haze, Jane's carefully laid-out plan was enacted by her loved ones. Her daughter and companion spelled one another in her care. A night nurse was hired. Her therapist visited on a daily basis. Her son, two states away, stood ready to come to her side at a moment's notice. The goodbyes had been said, relationship "business" had been taken care of, tears of anticipatory grieving had been shed. The exhausting wait had begun.

One evening, Jane's condition took a decided turn. All whom she had wished to be present came to her bedside. Morphine had been discontinued hours before when a natural analgesia takes effect at life's end. Jane's fragile body was bathed and clothed in a white "paper narcissus" nightdress. Her hair was combed neatly. She sat propped against large white pillows with a clean, thick towel placed discretely to check incontinence. A fire glowed in the fireplace, warming the room while a window ajar allowed the flow of fresh air. Jane's favorite flowers stood in attractive arrangements throughout the softly lit room. Light strains of classical music could be heard in the background. The atmosphere was peaceful and serene and Jane was the focus.

Around her were her favorite people: The men she loved sat on either side as strong "protectors" who kept her frail body upright. Her nurse therapist sat in front of her to firmly support, gently touch, and lightly coach. Her daughter and son, her companion, her night nurse, her cat, and her daughter's dog were with her, lending their support. The therapist's husband, a friend of Jane's who was also present, scooped up the Himalayan cat, Katmandu, and stroked her until she quieted. Then he gently placed "Kat" in Jane's lap and guided her hand in stroking the soft white fur. Cool juice was offered and sipped slowly. Jane could not speak but occasionally she leaned forward, hugged her legs and rocked slightly back and forth, her gaze outward.

The gathering continued this way for three hours into the night. Then the nurse therapist suggested that it was time for Jane to rest and get a refreshing night's sleep. The night nurse made her comfortable for the night and her son and daughter camped on the floor next to her bed. Jane slept soundly through the night. The next day, Jane's son reminded her that it was the fifth anniversary of her husband's death. Soon after, Jane died peacefully.

Jane's story illustrates a human death experience carefully planned and tailored to her quality of life. Although the details reflect a woman and family with greater than average resources, the conceptual themes woven through this story of a "beautiful death" can be reconstructed as well in families of lesser means.

Jane converted a frightening change in life trajectory into an opportunity to confront death. She allowed her notion of quality of life to guide her plan for the dying experience. She balanced her hope for survival with the certainty of a death earlier than anticipated, using her strong, well-developed internal reference as the fulcrum. Her illness ran its course; her recovery was a success. Her life ended but, more importantly, her life was completed.

Illness as Developmental Demand for Integration. The capacity to integrate is considered a birthright and a strength from the moment the infant begins to determine the trustworthiness of an offered relationship. It might begin perceptually when the baby can first focus on the eyes of another and distinguish happiness from anger. It develops most heartily when the individual is free to judge with an innocent or uninitiated eye—with his or her whole being (Erickson, 1988).

Although this phase of development attains its zenith with the acquisition of "wisdom" in the later years, a serious illness provides an important opportunity to strengthen the integrative capacity. Indeed, a life-threatening illness will challenge the capacity for integration in order to assist the endurance of losses that naturally occur with the experience. Erickson

(1988) describes integration as the ability to gather life experiences into a meaningful pattern and to inventory the strengths that have accrued over the previous life cycles. More than functional, the outcome of this developmental work is affirmative.

One form of the process of illness-induced integration can best be illustrated by the story of Steve, a 41-year-old talented engineer, married to Anne for 15 years and the father of a 1-year-old son. Steve was diagnosed with lymphoma after the surgical removal of a large mass found deep in his abdomen. Pathologically documented liver metastasis led to a three-month intensive regimen of multiagent chemotherapy.

During the early phase of treatment, Steve established a multimodality support system consisting of psychotherapy, hypnosis, relaxation and imagery training, acupuncture, nutritional counseling, and T'ai Chi (a program of slow-moving exercises designed to achieve balance, control, and emotional stamina.) He tolerated treatment well with little physical distress, followed his self-care regimen faithfully, and began working on several major unresolved family issues that predated his cancer diagnosis. When the postchemotherapy pathology report revealed that cancer cells still remained in his bone marrow, Steve agreed to a bone marrow transplant.

Steve and Anne were oriented to the bone marrow transplant procedure and a team consisting of physician, primary nurse, psychiatric liaison (who had been his ongoing therapist), physical therapist, and dietician was established. The team included his wife, who worked closely with the primary nurse and psychotherapist. She continued as the family breadwinner, arranged for child care, educated other family members, fought for insurance coverage, organized platelet donors, and visited her husband on an almost daily basis.

Steve was placed in a laminar airflow room (LAF), a small enclosure with window, where the bed took up half the space, and Steve, a large man, took up the entire bed. The room was noisy with rhythmic sounds coming from the laminar airflow fan and from a continuously playing audiotape of ocean waves. He spent the weeks during the transplant mostly in altered states of consciousness due to both the hypnotic effects of several medications and his meditation practice. Steve had an autologous bone marrow transplant, receiving his own washed and frozen bone marrow instead of a matched donor's. Shortly after receiving the bone marrow, his blood counts began to rise rapidly, implying a beginning and, what turned out to be, rapid recovery.

When the oncologist, satisfied with his steady improvement, announced that he could leave LAF and go home the next day, both Steve and Anne were surprised and hesitant. Anne especially felt that Steve needed to be weaned from the depressant medications and Steve asked for more time for adjustment before leaving the hospital.

Steve's emergence from LAF was a process of rebirth. He had been in a protective environmental womb for a long time, listening to rhythms not unlike the noisy interior of the uterus itself. The fetus lives for months after hearing develops in an atmosphere where maternal heartbeat, intestinal gas movement, blood flow, and sound from outside the mother's body provide continuous stimulation. Then, a few days after making a slow, hesitant emergence from a similar environment, Steve went home. The hospital discharge planning procedure included mostly advice on taking medication and infection precaution measures. Steve went home with his medications, surgical masks for use in public places such as the supermarket, and his fear and anxiety.

A documented record of his recovery progress provided a remarkably clear picture of how the developmental demand for integration manifested itself as a fast-forward journey through the Eight Stages of the Life Cycle (Figure 12–1) in the two years following the bone marrow transplant.

Steve's early responses following hospital discharge included tearfulness and crying, remaining in bed for long periods, and eating. He communicated in many ways the need for nurturing, protection, and reassurance from his wife, mother-in-law, and female therapist, and, by telephone, from his female primary nurse at the hospital. His behavior reflected the balance of trust versus mistrust, actions that harmonized acceptance with protest in the service of survival.

Several weeks later, Steve was making trips to the supermarket (with mask on) and taking short walks with his son. His major accomplishment was the monthly 60-mile round-trip visit to his oncologist. These journeys away from home increased gradually in number, in distance, and in Steve's ability to drive himself or go alone—an indication of his attempt to balance his autonomy and doubt.

Months went by before Steve trusted himself enough to become curious about his new environment. Steve and Anne had purchased a new home in another county shortly before his transplant. He began to talk with neighbors, stopped wearing the mask, drove the car without fear of losing his way, and began to take interest in his new community. He returned, by himself, to visit and talk with his primary nurse, and one day he asked her to tell him the story of his transplant experience. This investigative behavior suggested the Stage of Purpose, when initiative is balanced with guilt; and curiosity, and inquisitiveness gain the information to go on.

Months later, Steve, a self-employed engineering contractor, began to take up his work again. Gradually, he awakened projects that had been on hold, awaiting his cancer recovery. Slowly, he began to seek new business, a venture that took more than a year posttransplant to reestablish. Steve had entered the Stage of Competence, testing his industry against inadequacy and gaining the experience necessary for his increasing control and efficiency.

More than a year passed before Steve's sense of self began to emerge. First indications were noted in the cancer support group discussions in which he and Anne took part. His self-confidence, sense of pride, and reprioritized values became increasingly apparent. Soon he began sharing his philosophy with others as well as the conflicts he had experienced in his family of origin. He went through an often painful search for his personal sense of identity, damaged in its early development, growing up in an emotionally closed family. Ironically, the illness provided Steve with the opportunity to reexamine those unresolved issues, to reprioritize beliefs and values, to choose commitments more in line with his unique capacities, and to decide who and what he would become. This important phase, identity versus role confusion, took place most actively when Steve had "held his platelets" for 1½ years, a critical time point for predicting future survival. Often the belief that one "has a future" coincides with biologic stabilization, precipitating a phase of accelerated progress in the transformation of self, and providing evidence of the biopsychosocial unity of being.

Since the Stage of Fidelity was the one most arrested for Steve, it also required his intense focus over a long stretch of time. But Anne had an agenda for her own personal recovery following Steve's illness. She desired a much faster return to normal, to the routine and the familiar she had known. She wanted, as she explained, "my Steve back." Paradoxically, she took pride in, yet resented, her role as breadwinner. She expected that shortly after his return home, Steve would begin managing the huge financial debt incurred during his treatment by paying bills, and, within a short time, by returning to work and bringing in supplemental income. In addition, Anne wanted her sex partner back. They had enjoyed a healthy sex life and had established a sense of intimacy characterized by their warm mutual affection. After 15 years of marriage, most of them spent as a couple without children, they knew each other well. She sought the counsel of the therapist who described the integration process Steve was undergoing, emphasizing the phases of industry and identity in terms of Steve's return to work, and the intimacy stage regarding his interest in and return to an active sex life. Placing the events of the recovery process, especially those that were most disconcerting to her, in an understandable framework increased her sense of hope and assisted her in modifying her expectations of Steve and reclaiming control of her own quality of life. Knowing what to expect helped Anne to focus on her own transformative process, to communicate her needs clearly, and to become responsible for her own satisfaction and happiness.

Based on the initial strength of their relationship, Steve and Anne became more patient with one another and began acting in ways that reflected their strengthened hope in the future. Testosterone injections gave a further boost to Steve's movement through the Stage of Love, or intimacy versus isolation.

Two years posttransplant, when their son was 3 years old, Steve and Anne began the Stage of Care, generativity versus stagnation, with the help of Steve's frozen sperm specimens, banked prior to his cancer treatment. Entering this stage in their lives, although it had begun earlier with the birth of their son, was dramatic evidence of the ongoing integration process. Two years after transplant, they were ready to test and exercise the "quality of caring for" in their lives by deciding to have another child—the major strength of Erickson's Stage of Care, or generativity versus stagnation. Although difficult for him, Steve began to make peace with his parents during this phase, with a strengthened ability to view them as more benevolent than he formerly believed. Concurrently, his creativity and productivity expanded.

Steve's longevity remains guarded, but his quality of life has been enhanced through the integrative process. As a result, Steve and Anne look forward to entering the Stage of Wisdom, integrity versus despair, some day, at the appropriate age—or, more accurately, to reenter the Stage of Wisdom/Integrity for a second time.

Clinical Evaluation

The Integrated Cancer Recovery Model (see Figure 12–6) developed by Scott and Eisendrath (1986) provides a clinical assessment guide that may be helpful in evaluating patients with many types of chronic illness. The

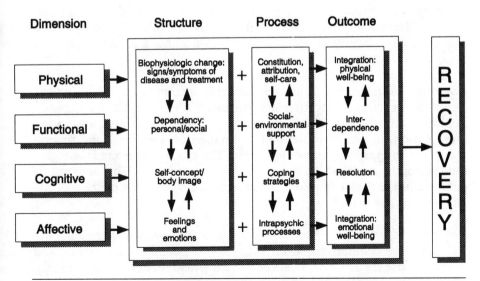

Figure 12–6 Integrated Cancer Recovery Model (*Source:* Scott & Eisendrath, 1986.)

model is useful in providing both a systematic yet open approach to assessment and diagnosis as well as a guide for intervention.

The Integrated Cancer Recovery Model is a matrix of four adjustment dimensions and three assessment parameters designed to depict a patient's total recovery progress. Although recovery, like quality of life, is holistic in nature, for assessment purposes, evaluation is systematic, requiring attention to each component. The four dimensions of human adjustment are depicted by structure, process, and outcome variables.

Physical Adjustment.   Changes in the biophysiologic balance of the body due to disease, treatment, and illness generate signs and symptoms that serve as an alerting mechanism and form the structure of human physical adjustment. The pattern of signs and symptoms provides a starting point, altered thereafter by a process composed of three major aspects: (1) inherent constitutional factors that serve to rebalance the system (e.g., natural immunity); (2) meaning ascribed or attributed to the physical experience by the patient (e.g., when a symptom is viewed as evidence of recurrence); and (3) level of self-care that subsumes compliance with medical and nursing regimens and the sense of self-esteem facilitating the process. These factors, in combination, reestablish the individual's sense of physical well-being to some degree.

Functional Adjustment.   Changes in the personal and social dependency of individuals due to disease, treatment, and illness constitute the structure of functional adjustment. The evoked process requires creation of an external support system to obtain assistance with activities of daily living and social relationships that promotes the emergence of more independent behavior. The adjustment outcome is, at best, a higher and more integrated interdependence.

Cognitive Adjustment.   The self-concept, incorporating body image, forms the structure of cognitive adjustment. With illness, the sense of self is altered and then is reintegrated by a process of cognitive absorption (information intake), assimilation (information organization), and accommodation (integration), known as coping. The process is enacted through a unique coping response utilizing a profile of strategies. The outcome is reflected in the degree of resolution determined by the effectiveness of the strategies at any time.

Affective Adjustment.   The basic feelings of anxiety, fear, anger, and joy and the more complex emotions such as guilt, conflict, depression, and grief comprise the structure of affective adjustment. In healthy individuals, these affects are closely linked to the interpretation of stimuli in the individual's internal and external environments. Feelings and emotions are mediated by a complex intrapsychic process that determines the level of awareness of the perceptions and the use of these emotional energies in reestablishing the outcome or the sense of security, mastery, and emotional well-being.

Assessment procedure based on the integrated recovery framework makes use of clear, open-ended interview questions such as: What physical changes have occurred since treatment began? Of the physical symptoms you experience, which are distressing to you? On a scale of 1 to 10, where 1 means "I feel totally comfortable" and 10 means "I feel unbearably uncomfortable," rate your overall distress. For both clinical and research purposes, standardized instruments may be employed in the assessment process. Assessment is based, as well, on careful physical examination and the analysis of laboratory results, x-ray findings, and other objective evidence.

Following the assessment intake, a thorough analysis and synthesis of data should provide a basis for diagnosis, the design of a plan for treatment, and an overall impression of the recovery status of the individual. And finally, follow-up assessment is central to the effectiveness of the evaluation process. Determining and documenting progress over time and identifying important patterns or themes of being for the individual are essential to the understanding and enhancement of his or her quality of life: physical, functional, cognitive, and emotional well-being.

Therapeutic Approaches

Any intervention assumes, a priori, a thorough assessment and the formulation of QL-related diagnoses as central to the overall health care plan, incorporating a review of pathology reports and the medical treatment plan as well, before a therapeutic approach for the patient and family is designed.

There are four principle therapeutic modalities that work toward maximizing quality of life when chronic illness imposes distressing treatments and threat to life: (1) patient education, (2) symptom management, (3) community resource assistance, and (4) counseling/psychotherapy.

Patient Education. The diagnosis a of life-threatening disease in an otherwise healthy person initiates shock, disbelief, and denial—all natural defenses that allow the news to be absorbed in manageable doses. Early on, a search for the meaning of the event in one's life is begun, and the first step in this process requires obtaining not only information about the disease and its treatment but a framework for understanding the information. A framework for understanding enables the individual to comprehend the experience as an illness, to develop a set of reasonable expectations, to set goals, and to become skilled in self-care. The education process, then, becomes a vehicle for strengthening mastery and the consequent sense of control and satisfaction.

Shortly after the shock and disbelief subside, fear and anger surface, signaling the time for education to begin. The provision of a framework for understanding by a knowledgeable person whom the patient trusts converts threat to challenge so the event is viewed as an opportunity for growth. The fearful adult fundamentally craves a framework for understanding. The angry person longs for a trustworthy coach. Knowledge gained through education becomes important in the search for the meaning of the event in one's life. Skillful teaching establishes trust, communicates respect, and paves the way to a more comfortable course of treatment.

The professional know-how of patient education employs sound principles of adult learning, the use of multisensory techniques, and a caring attitude on the part of a knowledgeable and skillful teacher. The goal is to reduce fear and anger and channel those emotional energies into constructive ways of coping.

Symptom Management.   Symptom management is an important area in quality of life maintenance and enhancement, especially when prognosis is poor, metastasis has occurred, or the person is in the advanced stage of a disease. Symptoms are concrete and, as such, provide a base upon which the clinician may initiate a solid, trusting relationship with a patient. Symptom management is an area of expert knowledge and skill requiring priority attention.

Scott and Eisendrath (in process) found between 60 and 75 distressing signs and symptoms accompanying breast cancer and its treatment in a study of 31 newly diagnosed women during the first three months following their surgery. Wellisch and associates (1983) conducted an epidemiologic study of recovery issues in 570 homebound cancer patients and found five major problem areas. Somatic side effects were most frequently reported in 30 percent of the cases, with pain being the major symptom in 13 percent of the total.

The three central goals of intervention aimed at reducing somatic distress involve provision of (1) a framework for understanding the symptoms and the somatic distress, (2) prescriptions for self-care based on the most recent research advances, and (3) follow-up support to track progress and the effectiveness of the self-care regimen.

Anticipatory guidance is key to the success of the self-care regimen. When patients fully understand the nature of a disease and its treatment prior to the experience, their sense of control is strengthened, as is their self-care agency. On this basis of trust and understanding, patient and clinician can negotiate a care contract, thus diminishing distress and maximizing quality of life.

Community Resource Assistance.   For every chronic disease, there are at least 15 to 20 specialists practicing in the field to assist the patient with some aspect of the illness. Rarely do these clinicians work as a team or consult with one another. Yet, knowledge of community resources available to patients and families, including the multitude of adjunct therapies, is paramount to recovery.

The goal is to customize a resource package for the patient based on need, the extent of disability, and the nature of the individual's quality of life. Sometimes, organizations such as the American Cancer Society, American Heart Association, the Leukemia Society, and various foundations will provide published directories of community resources. More often, the clinician must custom-design a list of helpful resources tailored to each patient's needs.

The art of this modality results in an empowerment of patients to become the "owner-manager" of their health, to acquire a "clinical coach" who will offer guidance in the formation of a team of specialists and resources and to utilize the skills and services of all team members to achieve goals for recovery. This approach helps the patient to build a reasonable set of expectations for each professional team member, as well as for family and significant others who provide support, and to accept the responsibility of becoming an active participant in the recovery process.

Counseling/Psychotherapy.   Most persons diagnosed with a life-threatening illness can benefit from individual or group supportive therapy. Not only does the event represent a crisis in its own right but it often exacerbates preexisting difficulties. Generally, many issues that have been on hold surface as the intensity of the illness strains the usually competent repertoire of coping responses. Psychotherapy, both individual and group, can assist patients to express themselves, understand themselves, examine their options, recreate their goals, gain new perspective, grieve effectively, and restore their lives.

The dominant theme in liaison therapy is loss and the consequent grieving that ensues. The work of therapy involves the recognition and identification of loss—loss of control, loss of identity, loss of relationships (Sourkes, 1982)—as the fundamental concern. Central to this work is the ability to differentiate problems from symptoms and, as such, to refocus on the loss. Frequently, in the process, symptoms will fade as the loss is fully grieved. Further, there is a need to understand and fully cooperate with the manifestations of grief as its phases are experienced: (1) shock and disbelief, (2) suffering and disorganization, and (3) reorganization. The outcome is characterized by some degree of resolution of the loss and the redirection of energies into healthy consolation activities.

A second important goal in therapy is the restitution of the self and a reintegration of body image. Siegel (1986, 1989) says that life-threatening chronic illness provides an opportunity for the "authentic self" to emerge. Perhaps this is a way to rephrase and to more easily comprehend the integrative process. Moreover, a skillful therapist who understands the gestalt of recovery can have a powerful influence over the transformation.

A third important objective in therapy is the mobilization of the social support system. Each patient can be assisted to establish a support network characterized by an amount, type, configuration, and style tailored to both present and future needs. Norbeck (Lindsey et al., 1981) defines the three major elements in social support as affection, affirmation, and aid. Helping patients to assess their needs and utilize resources effectively, to prepare for the shock of mini-isolations that are bound to occur from time to time, and to prepare for occasions that call for symbolic closure, celebration, and a new beginning (such as the end of treatment) are important to healing.

Spiegel and associates (1989) found that women with metastatic breast cancer who were randomized to weekly support group therapy lasting one year survived longer than those randomized to a control nontreatment group—a difference both statistically and clinically significant. The divergence between groups became apparent eight months after treatment was over, implying that group psychotherapy had an enduring effect. Investigators surmised that the efficacy of treatment was associated with social support and bonding among members, the opportunity to express feelings and to establish a sense of belonging, the improved mobilization of resources, greater commitment to and compliance with medical treatment, and better management of symptom distress, especially pain. Although this is the first prospective experimental study that later examined survival, other studies have documented positive outcomes in mood, adjustment, and pain, as well due to psychosocial intervention. However, more research is needed to determine the effect of psychosocial interventions that promote quality of life on the immune system and other factors augmenting survival.

In summary, the overall goals of recovery are coherent with the parameters of the recovery model and with the dimensions of intervention:

1. *Restoration* of physical comfort, function, and well-being
2. *Resumption* of normal activity and relationships
3. *Resolution* of loss and restoration of emotional well-being
4. *Reintegration* of the self, including body image and the strengthening of the ability to resolve problems

The total process enables patients and their families to improve the quality of their lives.

Conclusion

Human beings experience, interpret, and create their quality of life on every level of awareness from the moment life begins. Quality of life is coherent with the individual's biologic, developmental, and cultural demands, and becomes apparent from his or her interpretations through feelings and emotions, language and behavior.

Quality of life is dynamic in that it allows for a set of criteria guiding choice among options. Quality of living—represented by consistent themes that operate in the domains of work, relationships, and environmental organization—is uniquely different for each person.

Life-threatening illness produces a major change in life trajectory and is interpreted as a developmental demand for integration: a creative, symbolic self-formulation that enables the resolution of loss, the lessening of despair, and the strengthening of well-being. Integration normally occurs in old age, balancing the person's strengths with physical deterioration, and, in the best sense, is affirmative in nature. But serious illness, at any age, initiates the integrative process.

Integration is guided by the individual's quality of life as a criterion and as an attitude. It is characterized by a search for meaning, a consequent reinterpretation of the self, and a reestablishment of the sense of worth, wholeness, and well-being.

Life-threatening illness requires a therapeutic approach that recognizes the need for modalities to both extend life and to preserve the quality of the life extended. The overall plan calls for careful balance of medical treatment regimens with the patient's quality of life.

Self-assessment and other characterizations of a person's life communicate its quality. Although quality of life is a unique and holistic essence, its assessment requires comprehension of its multifactorial and multidimensional nature. Several reliable, valid quantitative instruments are available to measure quality of life. An Integrated Cancer Recovery Model has been proposed as a useful approach to clinical evaluation and as a base for the design of an intervention plan.

Four major modalities have been found to maximize quality of life in chronic illness: patient education, symptom management, community resource assistance, and counseling/psychotherapy. Overall, the therapeutic aims of these processes are to support recovery, potentiate healing, augment treatment outcomes, and optimize well-being throughout all phases of the living and dying experience.

References

Aristotle. (1976) *Ethics*. Harmondsworth, England: Penguin Books.

Barofsky, I. (1986) Quality of life assessment. Evaluation of the concept. In V. Ventafridda, F. S. A. M. vanDam, R. Yancik, & M. Tamburini (Eds.), *Assessment of quality of life and cancer treatment*. New York: Elsevier.

Burge, P. S., Prankerd, T. A., Richards, J. D. M., et al., (1975). Quality and quantity of survival in acute myeloid leukemia. *Lancet, 2,* 621–624.

Burkhardt, C. S. (1985). The impact of arthritis on quality of life. *Nursing Research, 34* (1), 11–16.

Calman, K. C. (1987). Definitions and dimensions of quality of life. In N. K. Aaronson & J. Beckmann (Eds.), *The quality of life of cancer patients.* New York: Raven Press.

Campbell, A. (1976). Subjective measures of well-being. *American Psychologist, 31*, 117–124.

Carlens, E., Dahlstrom, G., & Nou, E. (1970). Comparative measurements of quality of survival of lung cancer patients after diagnosis. *Scandanavian Journal of Respiratory Diseases, 51*, 268–275.

Craig, T. J., Comstock, G. W., & Geiser, P. B. (1974). The quality of survival in breast cancer: A case-control comparison. *Cancer, 33*, 1451–1457.

deGroot, A. D. (1986). An analysis of the concept of "quality of life." In V. Ventafridda, F. S. A. M. vanDam, R. Yancik, & M. Tamburini (Eds.), *Assessment of quality of life and cancer treatment.* New York: Elsevier.

Erickson, E. H. (1963). *Childhood and society.* New York: Norton

Erickson, E. H. (1968). *Identity: Youth and crisis.* New York: Norton.

Erickson, J. M. (1988). *Wisdom and the senses: The way of creativity.* New York: Norton.

Ferrans, C. E. (Suppl. 1990). Development of a Quality of Life Index for patients with cancer. *Oncology Nursing Forum, 17* (3, Suppl. to May/June 1990), 15–19.

Ferrans, C. E., & Powers, M. J. (1985). Quality of Life Index. *Advances in Nursing Science 8* (1), 45–60.

Graham, K. Y., & Longman, A. J. (1987). Quality of life and persons with melanoma: Preliminary model testing. *Cancer Nursing, 10* (6), 338–346.

Holmes, O. W. (1860). *The professor at the breakfast table.* London: Routledge.

Karnofsky, D., & Burchenal, J. (1949). Clinical evaluation of chemotherapeutic agents in cancer. In C. M. Macleod (Ed.), *Evaluation of chemotherapeutic agents.* New York: Columbia University Press.

Kaufman, S. R. (1986). *The ageless self: Sources of meaning in late life.* New York: Nalpenquin.

Lindsey, A. M., Norbeck, J. S., Carrieri, V. L., & Perry, E. (1981). Social support and health outcomes in post-mastectomy women: A review. *Cancer Nursing, 4* (5), 377–384.

Morris, T., Greer, H. S., & White, P. (1977). Psychological and social adjustment to mastectomy. *Cancer, 40*, 2381–2387.

National Center for Health Care Technology Assessment Forum. (April 21–23, 1981). *Coronary artery bypass surgery: Economic, ethical and social issues.* Washington, DC: Author.

Padilla, G. V., & Grant, M. M. (1985). Quality of life as a cancer nursing outcome variable. *Advances in Nursing Science, 8* (1), 45–60.

Roberts, M. M., Furnival, I. G., & Forrest, A. P. M. (1972). The morbidity of mastectomy. *British Journal of Surgery, 52*, 301–302.

Schipper, M., and Levitt, M. (1986). Methodological issues in psychosocial oncology with special reference to clinical trials. In V. Ventafridda, F. S. A. M. vanDam, R. Yancik, & M. Tamburini (Eds.), *Assessment of quality of life and cancer treatment*. New York: Elsevier.

Scott, D. W., & Eisendrath, S. J. (1986).Dynamics of the recovery process following diagnosis of breast cancer. *Journal of Psychosocial Oncology, 3* (4), 53–65.

Scott, D. W., & Eisendrath, S. J. (in process). Patterns of physical recovery during early phase treatment of breast cancer.

Siegel, B. S. (1986). *Love, medicine and miracles.* New York: Harper and Row.

Siegel, B. S. (1989). *Peace, love and healing.* New York: Harper and Row.

Sourkes, B. (1982). *The deepening shade: Psycholoaical aspects of life threatening illness.* Pittsburgh: University of Pittsburgh Press.

Spiegel, D., Bloom, J. R., Kraemer, H. C., & Gottheil, E. (October 14,1989). Effect of psychosocial treatment on survival of patients with metastatic breast cancer. *The Lancet,* 888–891.

Stjernsward, J., Stanley, K., and Koroltchouk, V. (1986) Quality of life in cancer patients — Goals and objectives. In V. Ventafridda, F. S. M. A. vanDam, R. Yancik, & M. Tamburini (Eds.), *Assessment of quality of life and cancer treatment.* New Yolk: Elsevier.

Ventafridda, V., vanDam, F. S. A. M., Yancik, R., & Tamburini, M. (Eds.). (1986). *Assessment of quality of life and cancer treatment.* New York: Elsevier.

Wellisch, D., Landsverk, J., Guidera, K., Pasnau, R., & Fawzy, F. (1983). Evaluation on psychosocial problems of the home-bound cancer patient. *Psychosomatic Medicine, 45,* 11–21.

World Health Organization. (1979). *Handbook for reporting results of cancer treatment.* WHO Offset Publication 48. Geneva: Author.

Yates, J. W. (1986) Quality of life assessment and health policy decisions. In V. Ventafridda, F. S. A. M. vanDam, R. Yancik, & M. Tamburini (Eds.), *Assessment of quality of life and cancer treatment.* New York: Elsevier.

Young, K. J., & Longman, A. J. (1983). Quality of life and persons with melanoma: A pilot study. *Cancer Nursing, 6* (3), 219–225.

Zubrod, C. G., Schneiderman, M., Froi, E. et al. (1960). Appraisal of methods for the study of chemotherapy of cancer in man: Comparative therapeutic trial of nitrogen mustard and triethylene theiophosphoramide. *Journal of Chronic Diseases, 11,* 7–33.

Thirteen

Past Endurance

A Construct of Pain and Suffering

Laurel Archer Copp

Laurel Archer Copp, Ph.D., is a professor at the University of North Carolina at Chapel Hill. From 1975 to 1990, she held the office of Dean of the School of Nursing. She is a Fellow in the Institute of Arts and Humanities, a Fellow of the Academy of Nursing, and was awarded an honorary degree (Doctor of Humane Letters) from Georgetown University in 1992. She is the editor of the Journal of Professional Nursing, *the official journal of the American Association of Colleges of Nursing, an organization representing over 400 colleges and universities in the United States. Her research, teaching, and lecturing on the topics of pain and suffering have extended over 17 years and represent active participation and publishing in the United States, the United Kingdom, and Sweden.*

She is presently serving as consultant to the priority panel on pain at the Center for Nursing Research. She chaired the 55th Consensus Conference on "An Integrated Approach To The Management Of Pain" at the National Institutes of Health. She also was a co-investigator in a national Research Utilization grant, facilitating current research application to the clinical setting. Copp has written over 85 articles, and written, edited, or provided chapters for half a dozen books and is currently the editor of the Journal of Professional Nursing. *Her first article, "The Spectrum of Suffering," was published in 1974, and in 1990 it was published as a classic article on the occasion of the anniversary of the* American Journal of Nursing.

When mother saw the look on my face she reassured me that she really did want my help, that she had had a good life and was ready for it to end. I believed her. The problem was that death did not oblige.... Just before Ed left she decided to stop eating, hoping to starve herself to death. She desperately wanted to die, Ed told me, weeping. But she didn't die. (Rollin, 1985)

Many persons fear death, facing the ultimate unknown with wonder and wonderings. But for the patient who yearns for death, yet is unable to die, often the confrontation is with the reality of pain and suffering. For some, the pain experience is overwhelming whether it be acute pain, chronic pain, terminal pain, or other types to be mentioned. Coexisting with pain can push an individual beyond endurance, with its inescapable fear, dread, and exhaustion.

Ironic to many, is the *inability* to die. The days and hours of pain and suffering present a prospect that ill persons fear and many well persons, including some caregivers, deny with varying degrees of success. It seems important to juxtapose the problems of those who die to those who seemingly cannot. Those who are pushed past their endurance and know suffering have taught caregivers much about their coping strategies and inner resources. Often pain has three tenses: remembered pain, experienced pain, and anticipated pain. Those who are anticipating pain say they vacillate between fearing they will die and fearing they will not.

One might assume that a small amount of noxious stimuli is hurt or even pain and that pain of great intensity over a prolonged period of time constitutes suffering. Evidently, this is not necessarily the case. Self-report of sufferers often cite quite individualistic elements that constitute suffering for them. Cassell (1991) believes that each person has a different set of needs, a different type of suffering. For some, pain exacerbates into suffering. Yet other persons reporting great pain never agree that they have had a suffering experience.

This chapter will explicate what exacerbates pain into suffering with an objective of pain and suffering prevention, where that is possible (Copp, 1990). Where not possible, one has a special obligation to assure palliation and compassion—not to do so is not only inhumane but it is negligence, raising many ethical questions (Copp, 1993).

Kinds of Pain

Most pain researchers and clinicians find it useful to refer to common terminology as explicated by the International Assocciation for the Study of Pain (1986). In addition to this pain vocabulary, however, is the vocabulary of suffering—verbal and nonverbal. In considering suffering, one must work with concepts in context, a few of which are listed here (Copp 1986).

Life Pain

We must not assume that persons in pain come to us tabula rasa. Those about whom we write and those reading these words carry burdens of life pain of varying sizes. The sources vary greatly and ebb and flow with the years. There is the pain loss through death or separation (parents, children, friends, spouses), the loss of income (and meaningful employment), the loss of relationships, and the loss of life meaning. Enter physical pain, complicated as it is, but more complex because of the life pain with which it is mingled.

Unexplained Pain

For some, the unknown reason for physical pain is greatly daunting, and untold imaginings bring untold suffering. Even the working diagnosis or the differential diagnosis provides a framework of thinking that prevents further anxiety. A person who has a headache and seeks advice, when learning he or she has cephalgia (headache), relaxes the shoulders, changes the mask of facial anxiety, and says, "What a relief! I thought I had a brain tumor."

Disease-Related Pain

There is a hierarchy of anticipated pain that sufferers carry with them. They assume that cancer brings more pain than trauma, that deep abdominal surgery hurts more than skin abrasions or burns. Often these assumptions are not based on science. But caregivers and health care professionals also hold such beliefs, though their ranking may be vastly different than those of patients and would-be patients, which, upon occasion, they also are. The purpose in mentioning this little researched phenomenon is that the very power of these assumptions seem to work, through dread, to exact suffering. And, by the mental set and associated assumptions, there evolves *permitted* and *nonpermitted* pain by caregiver and receiver alike with its accompanying nonverbal indication of formidable value judgments—from "brave lad" to "don't be a baby." Not only is there allowed pain but there are also permitted and not permitted pain behaviors pressuring and dictating to the person in pain parameters of his or her own pain experience. Perhaps the most tyrannical outcome is the self-condemnation reinforced by others, in which the sufferer further lacerates himself or herself believing that he or she has disappointed or vexed others. More effort is made to comply with staff expectations in order to "deserve" compassion.

Diagnostic Pain

The person in pain may coexist with it until he or she is driven to seek assistance, though perhaps reluctantly. Once entering into the health care system, with ongoing pain, the individual is put through evaluation, first as an outpatient and then perhaps as an inpatient. Whatever his or her status, the pain continues. Added to it is the pain of diagnosis—requiring in its strenuousness the energy and courage of a young, vibrant, healthy, energetic, and well person. So, one pain now becomes two pains as the pain of diagnostic tests (blood work, bone marrow, lumbar puncture, arterial blood, etc.) is added to the original pain. And still, there is no relief from either original or added pain until the tests are in. Hours turn into days or perhaps weeks. The sufferer must "earn" his or her care and treatment through delay—namely, for pain relief, pain reduction, or pain management.

Therapy-Associated Pain

Therapy is not easy for those who receive nor those who administer it. For the already ill person, therapy may bring new problems, such as pain, diarrhea, loss of hair, changes in body temperature, invasion of the body, vomiting, anorexia, insomnia, and all their accompanying dreads and sufferings.

As difficult as this may be for those who are recipients, there is also suffering in the person administering the therapy. Entering the room, the therapist inadvertently communicates the presence of suffering as he or she is seen synonymously with the therapy. Some patients believe a therapist brings pain or transports them to or from pain (Copp, 1974). It is not the message of compassion and comfort anyone wishes to communicate. Sensitive caregivers make every attempt to inject their humanity into the relationship by recognizing and appreciating the humanity of the patient. But when the scales of painful disease are overbalanced by painful therapy, it is hard to be on the side of the angels or even to know which side that is. It may be called "caregiver burnout" and caregivers attempt to hide or escape from it. But in the case of many caregivers, it is a oneness of suffering with the patient that cannot be escaped. It is an initiation by fire—a fire that burns giver and receiver as they suffer together.

Care-Related Pain

In striving to give care, the very care that is intended to comfort often does not. As vital as it is to require the person to move, to take nourishment, and to tolerate tubes and injections, there is pain related to that care. Even when patient and caregiver know that in the long run the care will be cardinal to improving the condition, facts the head knows do not negate the rigorousness of care. All aspects of care may not be painful, however. Assessing those care activities that seem to push the patient beyond his or her endurance is key to the constant improvement and revision of the care plan that involves pain management, palliation, and pain prevention. Required is sensitivity, timing, and the use of methods of empowering the patient.

Research-Initiated Pain

In any research protocol, the researcher is obliged to obtain informed consent. But with research associated with old diseases (cancer) and new diseases (AIDS), caregivers are moving through experimental procedures that make it more and more difficult to properly inform. This is simply because caregivers do not know the answers to the most basic patient questions: Will it hurt? Will it help? Will it cost me more? Will I have to stay in the hospital longer? In promoting participation in new clinical trials, it is disquieting to all who are involved not to be able to prevent the suffering of the unknown.

The Pain of Bringing Pain to Others

Pain compounds itself: life pain, unexplained pain, disease pain, diagnostic pain, therapy-associated pain, research protocol pain, and the pain of care. However, let us consider the pain related to the bringing of pain to others through the very nature of the illness and the consequences of that illness itself. Unfortunately, it usually cannot be helped. It is also unfortunate that most illnesses make the sufferer feel awkward, embarrassed, and ashamed. Telling someone, presenting one's body for examination, and dealing with what many call "a verdict" is a suffering experience in itself.

Only the sufferer and those he or she reveres can know how difficult it is to bring pain into the lives of others. Often it is because he or she knows of the life pain these significant others already carry. In some cases, scripts and scenarios of unfinished transactional relationships seem to hang in the air with little or no resolution. In addition, it is the guilt of believing this transferring of burden could have been avoided if one had only eaten right, acted right, taken care of oneself, seen a doctor, taken one's medicine, or accepted the advice of others.

Bringing pain to others can mean bringing pain to those who are least equipped to deal with it. The sufferer must bring pain into the family life of children, the elderly, the already exhausted persons who have had their loyalty tested rigorously. It may mean further "damaging" the parent, the beloved, the stranger drawn into the web of obligation. The patient requires privacy and cannot bear to think that loved ones will see him or her physically exhausted with little energy even for the basic necessities of life. He or she does not wish to be seen as powerless.

The pain is expressed in many forms: demands, irritation, rejection, recrimination, as well as remorse, confession, and struggling for forgiveness and fresh beginnings. For the person in pain and the significant other, it is tough love, tested and retested (Copp, 1989). The person in pain may hardly understand his or her own behavior, let alone be able to translate it and justify it to loved ones.

Because the concept of pain is complex and because suffering is a construct made up of many concepts, the definition varies with each individual. Similar to pain, these life experiences are very private. Some sufferers will share the suffering experience. For other individuals, and in some settings, the concepts seem to hold taboo power in the fact they are not spoken of by the patient, not inquired about during rounds, the subtle hints by the patient not picked up by the caregiver and imperceptible in the educational curricula of the various health professions.

Vulnerability

> Sometimes I think you have invented a tube for every body orifice... and
> when you run out of openings you invent new ones. (Unnamed patient in
> the Intensive Care Unit during an intravenous penetration)

The types of vulnerability experienced not only predate the current
condition but are exacerbated by it. These include such examples of vulnerability as potential vulnerability (crack babies); temporary vulnerability
(surgical emergency); circumstantial vulnerability (HIV exposure); episodic
vulnerability (breakthrough pain); permanent vulnerability (multiple scle-
rosis); and inevitable vulnerability (aging and death) (Copp, 1986).

Physical Stress

There are many methods of inducing physical stress, including: (1) the
inability to turn or change position; (2) constant interruptions which in
effect denies sleep, resulting in wakeless or groggy conditions; (3) experiencing the denial of basic fight-or-flight reactions (physiological and psychological); (4) circulation deficit due to a spread-eagle body position in-
duced by tubes and monitoring equipment restraints of various types; (5)
delirium and dreams; (6) subjection to speechlessness due to intubation;
and (7) the threat and actuality of negative touch. Whether or not the source
of the patient's stress is known, there are ways to empower him or her to
cope and to make available the inner resources that are perhaps dormant
but very present.

Sensory Deficit/Sensory Overload

Perhaps it seems odd to consider both sensory overload and sensory deficit
together, but knowing the difference is most complex, for they often exist
simultaneously. Careful analysis of the situation is critical for correction
purposes. For example, when a person looks at a glaring ceiling light for 24
hours, he may appear to have sensory overload, which of course he does.
But in that experience is also the deficit of those physiological and environmental conditions that produce sleep as well as sustained sleep itself.

A patient's circadian and diurnal rhythms are thrown off badly with
sustained stimuli confusing the "body clock." Other sufferings include the
constant interruptions that are round the clock. Some 50 to 80 interventions per eight-hour shift is perhaps an underestimated variable, depending
on whether the patient is at home or in a high-tech teaching hospital.

Additionally, the overtaxed sensorium must endure painful transport
from lab to x-ray to surgery. Even the kind person who transports the
patient upon discharge to the privacy of his or her own home may push the

patient beyond endurance. Energy has long since expired, and all intervention is torture. He or she begs for not one more thing—no touch, no test, no talk—merely the stillness and healing of dark nothingness. Helpful is the regime of enforced rest, employment of techniques to lend energy, and the identification of the patient's rich resources. Equally as important is knowing when to withdraw, since even well-intentioned and strongly believed "help" to a person pushed past endurance can be extension of sensory overload, resulting in exhaustion.

Stress

In addition to physical stess is the mental stress attendant to most illness. Stewart Alsop (1973), ill with "smouldering leukemia" and often hospitalized at the National Institutes of Health Clinical Center wrote:

> When I wasn't reading for escape, I spent a lot of time trying to remember quotations.... For example I kept trying to remember T. S. Eliot's "Eternal Footman." After much brain cudgeling I scribbled in my notebook:
>
> "I have seen the moment of my greatness flicker
> I have seen the eternal Footman hold my coat,
> and snicker.
> In short, I was afraid." (Alsop, 1973)

Mental stress initiates and reverberates the "why" questions. Why me? Why now? Why? They are documented in the arts, the humanities, in philosophy, and in religion (Kreeft, 1986). Mental stress includes such things as powerlessness, fear and dread, the agony of unfinished business, and the guilt of unfulfilled responsibility, which leads to much self-blame.

Strongly needed are strategies and reassurance of temporary or permanent "transfer of power and responsibility," guilt reduction, forgiveness and hope, ongoing search for meaning, and the loving gift of purpose.

The Pain Experience

There are subtle differences between pain (as stimulus, as signal, as diagnostic tool) and the *pain experience*. Though both can only be authenticated by the person, the former elucidates modern medical treatment, and the latter gives more insight into actual or potential suffering. Pain, as a symptom, is documented and assessed, and testing, diagnosis, and the treatment plan eventuates. But this common and important approach reveals little of the pain experience itself. Unfortunately, too few ask the person in pain to speak about his or her experience. This information is evidently not valued, for there is no place to chart it, and the person in pain is so intimidated by "grand rounds" and the "too busy-ness" of the staff that he or she is discouraged to describe the impact that the pain and suffering are eliciting. If the individual is reluctant to bring pain to loved ones, he or she keeps personal thoughts to himself or herself and suffers alone.

Since the suffering experience does not necessarily cease when the pain does, it is important to understand some of the aspects of the pain experience in order to help bring meaning and proportion to a profound experience—one in which he or she may have been afraid and overwhelmed, and one in which his or her world was turned upside down.

In assessing pain itself for diagnostic and treatment purposes, the standard questions of Where does it hurt? How long has it hurt? How bad does it hurt? are still asked. From the self-reports of the many persons interviewed about the pain experience, it would appear to have many dimensions, some of which include:

> The pattern of pain and its relationship to perceived time
> The meaning attributed to it
> How the pain experience is communicated (pain language and nonverbal emphases)
> The need to communicate or withhold communication about the pain experience
> Implications of the pain
> Potency, intensity, and trajectory
> What the experience is to the person having that experience
> How it is interpreted
> Methods of coping
> Energy level and choice of placement of that energy
> Retrospective view or interpretation after the pain experience
> Pain experience absorption time or the integration of the pain experience into the fabric of life along with other meaningful (positive or negative) experiences.

Pain Management

Writer Denton Welch describes his pain in ways that are unlikely to be recorded on the hospital chart, hence the rich pain language is in danger of being lost forever:

> The pain grew intense again, like some huge grizzly bear taking me between its paws. I screamed from the sheer shock of its sudden violence. But there was nothing I could do to stop myself shrieking, feeling that if I bore the agony a moment longer it would split my skin. (De-La-Noy, 1986)

Pain management is possible in nearly all cases. However, there are many barriers to the elements of pain management that are agreeable to both patient and staff. Marks and Sacher (1973) showed in their original work, which has been replicated since, that physicians underprescribe pain medication. Compounding the problem, Cohen (1980) demonstrated that of the inadequate doctors' orders, nurses administered a fraction of the pain medication that had been authorized.

The third member of the team of doctor, nurse, and patient (including family) also brings a barrier—that of unwarranted fears of addiction, no doubt an unfortunate artifact of our societal drug problem. Persons in great pain are "just saying no." Some of their reasons include fear of addiction, beliefs that if the doctor or nurse had meant for him or her to have a medication its administration would be initiated, and the fear that if the medication for pain is given now, perhaps there will not be analgesics available later. Sadly, misplaced worries about addiction on the part of staff leads to withholding, even when the sufferer is in the late terminal state. Those dying and in extremis beg for relief and are denied it, while, with a kind of bizarre irony, children can buy opiates in the schoolyard.

Major methods and strategies that address pain management, pain prevention, and paliation include (1) dispelling addiction myths held by team members, (2) reeducating oneself about the types of therapeutic drugs available and their associated actions and efficacy, (3) matching and tailoring the proper drug and the proper dosage to the proper patient, and (4) trying and retrying routes of narcotic administration until the desired effect is accomplished—oral, intravenous, subcutaneous, and so on. Initiating newer methods may take time and be resisted but once accomplished, such methods as cannula, imbedded wells for narcotics, titration of analgesia, patient administration of his or her own analgesia, and the addition to the team of the anesthesiologist and pain clinic members (if appropriate) can prevent pain and needless suffering.

As important to the techniques of pain management is commitment. This pain management commitment is to *pain alleviation,* and when and if, after a struggle to attain it, it appears unfeasible, a commitment to *pain reduction* for all.

Pain prevention is a challenge. A first bold statement toward pain management for all who needed it came in what is known as the Wisconsin Initiative (Copp, 1987). Nurses, doctors, pharmacists, members of regulatory boards, laypeople, and the governor himself insisted they would do whatever was necessary to make cancer patients comfortable. Patients who have recovered and whose pain was managed at the time do not have horror stories to tell today. For those patients who were terminal, the quality of remaining life was enhanced. They set affairs in order, they found joy in relationships, and their families will not remember them as grim lipped and pain altered. In short, patients in the many states that have similar initiatives will escape pain and suffering.

Consensus regarding pain management was established by health professionals and others participating in the fifty-fifth NIH Consensus Conference in 1985 (L. Copp, chair; Consensus Document available) (NIH, 1986). In addition to pharmacological and nonpharmacological approaches to pain management, these health professionals urged the continual search and research for methods of pain management for those experiencing acute, chronic, and terminal pain.

Pain Coping

A young woman struggling with chronic pain states:

> I feel encouraged today. I have a lot of options when my pain level begins to rise:
>
> - relaxation exercises
> - stretching
> - visualization, guided imagery
> - lying down in conjunction with relaxation activity
> - preplanning and pacing the rest of the day
> - getting absorbed in an activity
> - changing positions. (Hurst, 1990)

Research bears out the fact that pain-coping strategies tend to to be categorized in the following ways (Copp, 1985):

External Foci:

Counter pain
Muscle use and body positioning
Presence of people
Pain objects

Internal Foci:

Mental vigilant focusing (upon such things as numbers, counting, words, memorization, mental visualization of such things as routes of travel, etc.)
Mind-body separation
Spatial sensing and orienting
Tropistic yearning (for sun, water, nature, cosmos)
Dreams and fantasies

We are familiar with humor as therapy as promoted by Norman Cousins (1989), but humor is also a highly individualistic method of coping by many pain patients. A friend dying of cancer wrote:

As a lay person and as a low brow it occurs to me that not enough humor or nose thumbing has been given to the sombre hobgoblin of fear of pain. And as a low brow who would sometimes learn about life by going to vaudeville performances, I am reminded of one popular act that played for many years and brought laughter and, if you will, a more fortified courage to those members of the laughing audience when they were subsequently to face the ordeal of illness at a doctor's office.... I do not infer the cruelty of laughter drawn from the suffering but the lessening of constrictive fears and the onesideness of gloom and doom. (Kallenberg, 1985)

Mind-Body Concepts

Mind-body relationships come to us starkly as from such self-reports as the following:

Crisp orders. Quick responses. Their hands busy all about me. They were at my throat, my nose, my limbs, my back. And every touch torture. They were treating my body as if it were a thing that didn't belong to me, lifting and taping and clamping and twisting it.... Everything was confused and unreal. When I tried to touch things they moved away from me.... Sylvia! Syl! I can't find my body! (Walters & Marugg, 1954)

But since *how* the mind and body relate are the stuff from which philosophy is made, there has been profound querying through the ages, continuing today. Such a book was written by Elaine Scarry, who writes on pain, suffering, torture, and political implications. She believes:

The only state that is anomalous to pain is the imagination. While pain is a state remarkably without objects, the imagination is remarkable for being the only state that is wholly its objects. There is in imagining no activity, no "state," no experiential condition or felt occurrence separate from the objects: the only evidence that one is imagining is that imaginary objects appear in the mind. (Scarry, 1985)

Sally Gaddow (1980) writes of such mind-body relations in terms of the *lived body* (primary immediacy), *the object body* (disrupted immediacy), *harmony* (cultivated immediacy), and the *subject body* (aesthetic immediacy).

Dossey makes a strong case for mind-body unity in his work entitled *Space, Time and Medicine* (1982). He states, "I believe it is possible to show that not only does evidence for mind-body unity and a central role for human consciousness arise quite naturally from science as we know it, but there is a pervasive principle of unity that is implied in ALL human thought and perception."

Outcomes

Many who suffer do so because they know or do not know and dread the outcome of the pain experience. For some, the outcome of pain may mean birth of a much desired child. For others, the outcome of pain will be certain death. For most, the outcomes are shrouded and in the nature of the worry and speculation may come more suffering.

> What is unbearable is not to suffer but to be afraid of suffering.... But in fear is all the suffering of the world: to dread suffering is to suffer an infinite pain since one supposes it unbearable. (Evely, 1967)

For this reason the person in pain hangs on every word, glance, and interpretation by family and staff. For persons with progressive diseases, every test is waited for, dreaded, interpreted, and evaluated, hoping for a clue to the trajectory and time frame of the illness. Waiting for and watching the lab tests for a leukemic patient may take over a large part of his or her time, and when the tests dictate the perception of the type of day or week that will be experienced: good test, good day; poor tests, poor day. In general, one is waiting to live and/or waiting to die, with no way to know which. Therefore, which should one prepare for? In any case, the waiting and the wondering can produce great suffering.

> [The doctor] clearly expects the hemoglobin count to follow the other counts down into the cellar. That's what I dread most—or, to be honest, second most. (What I dread most is getting very sick and dying.) You feel so lousy when your hemoglobin is low. And how am I to cover a Presidential campaign if I can barely drag myself around. It is full spring now, the lovely Washington April. But T. S. Elliot was right. April is the cruelest month. (Alsop, 1973)

Exacerbating pain to suffering is dissonance between doctor, nurse, patient, and family as to what the tests may mean and what action should be decided upon as a result of the tests. Such suffering can be alleviated if enough time, care, and good counseling precede decisions and there is proper negotiation of treatment goals and pain management.

Time

An intubated person in intensive care later wrote her inner thoughts: "How soon would I be free to talk again? Intubation was certainly a temporary measure, but in this crisis, time seemed motionless. Temporary—tempus—time—what irrelevant concepts to one being gagged" (Carlson, 1968).

We have been trained to linear time. Therefore, the time associated with pain is disorienting for many reasons. Pain changes one's perception of time. There is little logic to it. It may not be logical but rather psychological. It indeed is related to space. The person emerges from a pain experience as psychically affected as though he has been in a space capsule or a time machine. It adds to the person's need to orient himself or herself and give reflective and retrospective insight into what has happened to him or her. Dossey (1982) states, "Health and disease, like space and time, are not part of a fixed external reality. As such they are not to be acquired, so much as they are to be felt."

There is a tyranny of time which to those in pain may be intolerable. There seems to be a kind of "outer time" made up of constant interruption by staff in which the patient is hurried, harried, and pestered. The "inner time" as described by patients (meaning literally those who wait) seems to consist of (1) waiting and dread, (2) anticipation and mental rehearsal, (3) fear-driven fantasies. But it is not only present tense. There is simultaneous (4) prospective anxiety as well as (5) retrospective search for understanding—more stitches in the fabric of suffering.

For some, the coming of twilight produces even more suffering than night. John Betjeman, the poet laureate of England, writes in his poem, symbolically titled "Five O'Clock Shadow,"* about time and terror:

> This is the time of day when we in the Men's Ward
> Think 'one more surge of the pain and I give up the fight.'
> When he who struggles for breath can struggle less strongly,
> This is the time of day which is worse than night....
>
> This is the time of day when the weight of bedclothes
> Is harder to bear than a sharp incision of steel.
> The endless anonymous croak of a cheap transistor
> Intensifies the lonely terror I feel. (Betjeman, 1971)

For others, suffering comes from the pain of waking with the knowledge of yet another long day of struggle and suffering lies ahead, knowing the depletion of energy and life force. Figes (1981) writes about it in a book in which every chapter begins with awakening: "Perhaps I am the young girl, trying to escape in dreams during the night, a body which has ceased to conform to anything I recognize as me. I think of an old doll, its members dislocated: each morning it is painfully reassembled."

Space

Space and place, though not synonymous, are related to the patient in pain. Many patients report spatial relationships with pain and describe the pain as "over there "or "I find myself above my body, looking down." Some say,

---

*Reprinted with permission of John Murray (Publishers) Ltd.

"The pain is in my leg, and its rotting smell makes me pretend it is not a part of me at all." Another patient's sharing relates the spatial dimension of pain: "The only way I can finally get relief is to go through pain and come out the other side." Still another patient said, "I know that pain is in the room."

In only few modern medical centers are the therapies (lab, x-ray, etc.) brought to the patient. In most places the body is trundled, wheeled, left, turned, manipulated, left, wheeled, and returned to "its" room. No wonder the patient feels as though he is a U.P.S. package—and no one can find a place to deliver it. Therefore time, space, place, all manipulated by literal and pharmacological mental states, induce disorientation. This disorientation may not, in some circumstances, even be seen. It may be merely heard—voices speaking about them, to them, and over them. Even worse, strange conversations between staff members about irrelevant (to the patient) experiences with shufflings, laughter, smells, and sounds communicate two things: (1) surrealistic perceptions and impressions that even in memory still do not make a whole, but only broken nonsensical pieces; and (2) the thingifying of the person—one who is not even present as the staff "works on him" as object. What is the nature of suffering and the state of the human condition in the new age of technology? It is to float in some kind of outer and inner space in which one cannot recover one's "self." It is to be treated as though one does not exist until one does, indeed, not feel to exist.

For those individuals who have a sense and spirit of place, they are bereft of the rooted associations with place and the orientation and strength gained from it. They whirl in space, cut off from the known and meaningful.

Dossey (1982) sees therapy as:

> the spacetime view of health and disease tells us that a vital part of the goal of every therapist is to help the sick person toward a reordering of his world view. We must help him realize that he is a PROCESS in space-time—not an isolated entity who is fragmented from the world of the healthy, and who is adrift in flowing time, moving slowly toward extermination.

Self-Image and Attitudes Toward Pain

How one views oneself as well as how one views pain affect the potential to suffer. Whereas we have agreed that these experiences are highly individualistic and must remain so, there seems to be some trending in certain types of individuals. There may be many types, and it is important not to categorize individuals into types. Nevertheless, for those that would help the sufferer, thinking of self-image and attitudes toward pain may prove to be helpful, especially as the sufferer can bring his or her own insight and correction (Copp, 1985).

Type I: Victim

The individual perceives pain as *all powerful* and his or her self-image is a *passive victim*. Pain is merciless, cosmic, overwhelming, and continuous. The self is perceived as fragile, helpless, dread filled, abandoned, alone, and suffering. The coping mechanisms are few and not trusted. They consist of skepticism, belief in fate, ritual, and magical thinking.

Type II: Combatant or Soldier

The individual perceives pain as *invading* and his or her self-image is a *fighter*. Pain is episodic, strong, sharp, dominating, and testing. The self is seen as fighter, coper, survivor, soldier, and confronter. The coping mechanisms used by these individuals are more trusted and available. They consist of using counterpain (setting up a second site of pain stimulus to ameliorate the original pain site) and muscle language. They have an armamentarium of coping strategies. Additionally, these individuals delegate authority and assign tasks in order to properly prepare for the invasion of pain.

Type III: Responder

The individual perceives pain as *reality* and his or her self-image is a *responder* to that reality. To these individuals, pain is testing, demanding, mysterious, hidden, and cosmic. But they see themselves in terms of confronter, endurer, sufferer, analyzer, and strategizer. The coping mechanisms are usually of internal foci and include meditating, mental focusing, and searching for meaning.

Type IV: Reactor

The individual perceives pain as *cunning* and his or her self-image is a *reactor* to all manner of that cunning. It is believed that pain is hidden, faceless, sneaky, sly, invading, and degrading. Therefore it is important for the person in pain to keep a vigil—often declining medication for pain or sleep in order to remain mentally clear and on duty. Self-image is that of watcher, waiter, monitor, and it is important to be vigilant and ready for the onset of untrustable pain. Coping mechanisms include anticipation, rehearsal, review, and looking for minute early warning signs. At best, these individuals would like to avoid the pain; at any rate, they are not risking surprises of invasion.

Type V: Consumer

The individual sees pain as *demanding* and his or her self-image is that of a *consumer* or one who buys pain management. These individuals believe high-priced health care includes pain management as a purchased service.

Therefore, they expect value for money in a literal way. Pain is believed to be intense, persistent, sharp, treacherous, ill-tempered, and strong. These people see themselves as reasonable individuals who are willing to work with the staff to achieve pain management goals. They believe themselves to be cooperators, collaborators, communicators, and contractors. They worry about being dependent but are willing to report immediately any pain symptoms or changes. Coping consists mainly of setting up contractual agreements with the staff for pain management and control. They will keep their part of the bargain and maintain staff rules to get relief. They are compliant to the point of rational understanding but set limits. If the pain management they believe they are buying is not forthcoming and the good faith between patient and staff violated, they do not suffer gladly. If the staff provides pain management service as these patients believe was agreed upon, they bond with staff and refer to them to family or friends as "my nurse, my doctor."

Meaning

Steeves and Kahn (1987) help us to see how we can encompass the goals of care by helping "to establish and maintain the conditions necessary for and helpful to experiencing meaning." In actuality, the attribution of meaning can only be done by the sufferer. Many other persons and resources are available to the sufferer in this quest, however. One suggests Old Testament, New Testament, poetry, art, music, and literature, to consider only a few (Rose, 1962), and these through significant others or/and through the individual search for meaning. For some, pain and suffering can mean life/death, mind/body integration. For others, it may mean annilhilation of the self. For many, it means an opportunity to have one's faith practiced and/or tested. Certain individuals see pain and suffering as a gift or offering, or as a sacrifice of self and mortality (Bakan, 1968). Phillips (1982) "seeks the poem in the pain," as he analyzes the poetry of R. S. Thomas. Tournier (1982) writes of creative suffering.

The search for meaning may be in silence or through the maze of voices (family members, the clergy, caregivers, etc.), all bringing their opinions and insights. The search may be solitary or in good company. The search may be short-lived or a life-long quest—but attributing meaning is to put understanding to suffering. This head-on impact with the human condition links us with suffering through the ages. But the pain of inner growth means that one *never* returns to the presuffering state with all that it may signify. "Suffering passes but the fact of having suffered never passes" (Bloy, 1961).

References

Alsop, S. (1973). *Stay of execution* (pp. 53–54, 223). Philadelphia: Lippincott.

Bakan, D. (1968). *Disease, pain, and suffering* (pp. 80, 116–128). Boston: Beacon Press.

Betjeman, J. (1971). *Collected poems* (p. 339). Boston: Houghton Mifflin.

Bloy, L. (1961). In F. J. J. Buytendijk (Ed.), *Pain* (p. 20). London: Hutchinson & Co.

Carlson, D. (1968). *The unbroken vigil* (pp. 30–34). Richmond: John Knox Press.

Cassell, E. J. (1991). *The nature of suffering and the goals of medicine.* Oxford: Oxford University Press.

Cohen, F. (1980). Postsurgical pain relief: Patient status and nurse medication choices. *Pain, 9,* 265–274.

Copp, L. A. (1974). The spectrum of suffering. *American Journal of Nursing, 74* (8), 491–495.

Copp, L. A. (1985a). Pain coping. In L. A. Copp (Ed.), *Perspectives on pain* (pp. 3–16). Edinburgh: Churchill Livingstone.

Copp, L. A. (1985b). Pain coping model and typology. *Image Journal of Nursing Scholarship, 17,* 69–71.

Copp, L. A. (1986). The nurse as advocate for vulnerable persons. *Journal of Advanced Nursing, 11,* 255–283.

Copp, L. A. (1987). Multidisciplinary pain policy model: The Wisconsin initiative. *Journal of Professional Nursing, 3* (2), 83, 125.

Copp, L. A. (1989). A nurse the patient's significant other. *Journal of Professional Nursing, 5* (2), 57–58.

Copp, L. A. (1990a). The nature and prevention of suffering (Part II). *Journal of Professional Nursing 6* (5), 247–249.

Copp, L. A. (1990b). The patient in pain: USA nursing research. In Rebecca Bergman (Ed.), *Nursing research for nursing practice* (pp. 125–144). London: Chapman and Hall.

Copp, L. A. (1990c). Treatment, torture, suffering, and compassion (Part 1). *Journal of Professional Nursing, 6* (1), 1.

Copp, L. A. (1993). An ethical responsibility for pain management. *Journal of Advanced Nursing, 18* (1), 1–3.

Cousins, N. (1989). *Head first–The biology of hope* (pp. 132–153). New York: E. P. Dutton.

De-la-Hoy. S. Y. (1986). *The making of a writer* (p. 98). London: Penguin Books.

Dossey, L. (1982). *Space, time and medicine* (pp. ix, 48). Boulder, CO: Shambhala Press.

Evely, L. (1967). *Suffering* (pp. 152–153). New York: Herder and Herder.

Figes, E. (1981). *Wakings* (p. 60). New York: Pantheon.

Gaddow, S. (1980). Body and self: A dialectic. *The Journal of Medicine and Philosophy, 5* (3), 172–185.

Hurst, B. (1990). From acute pain to chronic pain: A personal journal. *Orthopaedic Nursing, 9* (2), 41–45.

International Association for the Study of Pain. (1986). Classification of chronic pain and definition of pain terms. *Pain* Suppl. 3, S216.

Kallenberg, M. (1985). Unpublished letter to Drs. John and Laurel Copp.

Kreeft, P. (1986). *Making sense out of suffering* (pp. 57, 75, 105). Ann Arbor, MI: Servant Books.

Marks R., & Sacher, E. (1973). Undertreatment of medical in-patients with narcotics and analgesics. *Ann Internal Med, 78,* 173–181.

National Institutes of Health. (1986). Consensus Conference Development Statement. Vol. 6, No. 3. Write to: Office of Medical Applications of Research. Room 211, Bethesda, MD 20892.

Phillips, D. Z. (1982). Seeking the poem in the pain. In *Through a darkening glass* (pp. 105–190). Notre Dame, IN: Notre Dame University Press.

Rollin, B. (1985). *Last wish* (pp. 58–59). New York: Simon and Schuster.

Rose, M. (Ed.). (1962). *The problem of suffering* (pp. 1–12). London: The British Broadcasting Corporation.

Scarry, E. (1985). *The body in pain* (p. 162). New York: Oxford Press.

Steeves, R., & Kahn, D. (1987). Experience of meaning in suffering. *Image, 19* (3).

Tournier, P. (1982). *Creative suffering* (pp. 7–21). London: SCM Press.

Walters, A., & Marugg, J. (1954). *Beyond endurance* (pp. 3, 4). New York: Harper and Row.

Fourteen

Spoiled Identities

Phyllis R. Silverman

Phyllis R. Silverman, Ph.D., LICSW, is Coprincipal Investigator of the Child Bereavement Study. This study is a longitudinal prospective study of the impact of the death of a parent on school-age children. She is also a Professor at the MGH Institute of Health Professions and an Associate in Social Welfare in the Department of Psychiatry at Massachusetts General Hospital and Harvard Medical School. She developed the widow-to-widow concept and directed the research project that demonstrated its effectiveness. She has served as consultant to several task forces on bereavement and primary prevention convened by the National Institute of Mental Health; and has consulted with hospices, hospitals, and social agencies across the United States and abroad on issues of bereavement, mutual help, and prevention. She is the recipient of the 1991 Presidential medal from Brooklyn College, City University of New York, for her outstanding contributions to the fields of bereavement and social welfare. In addition to her social work degree from Smith College School for Social Work, she holds an Sc.M. in Hyg. from Harvard School of Public Health and a Ph.D. from the Florence Heller School for Advanced Studies in Social Welfare at Brandeis University. She has published extensively in professional journals and her books include Helping Each Other in Widowhood, If You Will Lift the Load I Will Lift It Too, Mutual Help Groups: A Guide for Mental Health Professionals, Mutual Help Groups: Organization and Development, Helping Women Cope with Grief, Widow-to-Widow, *and* Widower: When Men Are Left Alone.

While the Chinese see living in interesting times as a curse, Americans prefer to see living in interesting times as a challenge. One of the greatest challenges as well as a serious curse of our times is associated with Acquired Immunodeficiency Syndrome (AIDS). The challenge is not only to understand the disease but to halt its progression. The curse is the inevitability of death in those infected and the negative social climate that affects not only the individual sufferer but reaches back to diminish the social system in which we live.

With the assistance of science, we now have the opportunity not only for a longer life but for a healthier one as well. The expectation for longevity and for a quality of life has been raised as never before in recorded history. However, we are quickly learning that reason and science cannot solve all of our problems. We now face plagues not imagined before that science cannot as yet cure and for which the available treatments are barely effective. AIDS is such a plague. It brings with it other problems more insidious than the illness itself.

People with AIDS must cope not only with illness and dying but also with the fear of this disease that has stimulated irrational and hostile passions in the unafflicted. Such passion about an illness is reminiscent of the attitudes in fourteenth-century Europe with the spread of the Black Death (*Encyclopedia Britannica*, 1965). While we expect that "civilized people" have moved past this kind of irrational construction of illness, we see that it is not so. AIDS sufferers are subject not only to the vicissitudes of infection with a lethal virus but also to society's scorn. An atmosphere of suspicion seems to prevail that denies the common humanity of this group of people so that they have been treated as nonpersons: ignored and easily castaway. Goffman (1963) has described people in such a situation as having a "spoiled identity" that results from the stigmatized social role they have been assigned by the larger society. With AIDS, this process begins once tests reveal an individual is infected with HIV. This ascription affects how people see themselves, how they live, how they are treated by society, how they die, and how their loved ones will mourn their deaths. In this chapter, I examine this process of stigmatization and the meaning it has for how we respond to the lives and deaths of people suffering from AIDS. I will also look at how this same stigmatization and spoiling of identity is experienced by mourners in general in our society.

Defining Stigma

Goffman (1963) observed that people are assigned a stigmatized place in society when they have in some way violated society's taboos by becoming involved with areas of activity that are seen as forbidden. West (1985), building on the work of Goffman, defines a *stigma* as a special kind of relationship between an attribute and the stereotype that is conferred by society on the attribute in the form of images and attitudes. The stereotype is invariably negative. These images and attitudes about the attribute potentially serve to discredit not only individuals with these attributes but members of a particular social category most of whom have this attribute. Goffman observed that the impact of being stigmatized is felt when people recognize that there is a discrepancy between society's definition of who they are and their own sense of identity. In this kind of discrepant situation the individual experiences his or her identity as spoiled. As a result, people feel cut off from society and from themselves. They find themselves discredited in the face of an unaccepting world.

As we understand the way disease impacts on people or even how people respond to grief after the death of a loved one, we often focus only on their feelings about what is happening. We also need to consider how these facts and events change how people live in the world and how they see themselves in that world. We must attend to how changed circumstances bring about a shift in identity. The concept of identity, which is synonymous with our sense of self, is not something that is independent of our relationship to the world in which we live.

Berger and Luckmann (1967) describe identity as

> a person's sense of self: the self is the reflexive answer to the ongoing inescapable and quintessentially human question: "who am I?" As such it involves a "positioning" of self in reality, a symbolic placement that situates the person in the world.... We identify ourself as people of a certain type, quality, or value—we also identify ourself with others or significant objects forging a sense of belonging and attachment.

Identity involves a symbolic placement that situates the person in the world.

Goffman (1963) suggests several kinds of identity. A social identity exists without consideration of the particular individual in this role. This allows us to classify people and identify them with a group. A personal identity is the individual mark or position differentiating one person from the next. The concept of social identity may be seen as synonymous with the concept of role. The role an individual assumes in a given situation and his or her sense of identity can be the same so that, for example, a physician is a job title—it begins as a social identity and as the individual is socialized into this role it becomes a personal identity as well. I am interested in the place where these two identities merge. What leads people to adopt a social identity as their own, especially when it has negative and demeaning aspects to it? In this chapter, I do not explore the question of why we stigmatize, but the fact that it occurs.

The fact that any activity or attribute becomes taboo or forbidden is socially determined—subject to the vagaries of social construction so that it can have different meanings in different societies and in different people (Goffman, 1963; Fulton, 1965; Hughes, 1971). There is nothing intrinsic in any given activity itself that should make it forbidden or the people associated with it undesirable. The Nazis made being Jewish, homosexual, or mentally retarded undesirable qualities because, as they saw it, the existence of people with these attributes was not consistent with the Nazi concept of the ideal society. A further example can be taken from the experience of women. In some societies women must isolate themselves during their menstrual cycle since they are considered unclean and therefore can compromise the purity of others during this period (Neusner, 1980). Other societies isolate people who care for the dead and dying. They must cleanse themselves before they reenter the larger community (Rosenblatt, Walsh, & Jackson, 1976). Thus, what is stigmatized varies from society to society.

Stigmatized conditions seem to grow out of observed variations from accepted norms for what is considered, for example, beautiful or ugly, acceptable or antisocial behavior. What is being considered here is society's ability to tolerate differences or deviance. What is considered normative behavior often varies with social class, ethnic background, and historical times. At times, what are acceptable characteristics in any given individual can depend on such things as his or her age or gender. For example, similar assertive behavior in men and women has been defined in men as standing up appropriately for their rights, and in women as inappropriate aggressivity (Miller, 1986).

Given all of these considerations, Goffman (1963) concludes that what is deviant is in the eyes of the beholder and something becomes deviant simply because it has been so labeled. The person designated deviant is one to whom the label has been successfully applied; that is, the individual has to be willing to accept the label. This is where the personal and social identity come together, where personal attributes and social roles meet. Members of this category have internalized the attitudes of society around them and accept the definition of themselves propagated by the larger society. The stigmatized social identity becomes their personal identity. Since this identity is different from their original perceptions of self, their identity is now spoiled and they must seek a new one.

Particular Stigmas

Sex and death have been taboo domains in contemporary Western society (Gorer, 1965). People who are publicly identified with these domains are seen as dealing with the underside of social life in a society, be they in such disparate work as vendors of pornography or people doing the socially mandated work of burying the dead, such as funeral directors (Hughes, 1971).

AIDS has been identified as a sexually communicated or blood-borne disease primarily associated (in the minds of many) with homosexual men because of the high prevalence of those with this disease from this population. It is not only AIDS and the vicissitudes of the disease that cause a problem. Disease problems are compounded by the fact that its appearance was first noted in the gay community in the United States. Being sexually active outside marriage or a traditional heterosexual relationship is not accepted by many in the dominant American culture, the sexual revolution notwithstanding. The homophobia in our society creates a mindset about homosexuality as threatening to the very structure and values of this society. People who become ill with AIDS become associated in the larger community, regardless of the reality of their situation, with homosexuality, and what is seen as "illicit" sex. So, for example, people who have hemophilia or others who contracted AIDS through blood transfusions may be submitted to extensive questions about their sexual activities before physicians look elsewhere for the source of the disease. A contrasting stance is to make heroes of people with hemophilia who become "innocent victims" in society's eyes, while gay men are "blamed" for their illness as if the latter were any less the victims of this virus.

Death in similar fashion is not something the larger society can accept. For example, when on vacation, funeral directors are known to tell others they are salesmen of one sort or another to avoid being rejected and stigmatized, as often happens if they are truthful. Even in medicine, where death is a daily visitor, it is most often seen as an affront to the success of the medical establishment. It flies in the face of modern reason. The traditions and rituals that recognize death as part of the normal life cycle, such as funerals and other public mourning practices, are often ignored or dismissed (Silverman, 1978). We are no longer comfortable with the grief of the survivors and wish them to keep their pain circumspect and contained (Silverman, 1986; Saunders, 1989). It is not unusual for mourners, shortly after the death, to be left feeling that something is wrong with them, their sense of self no longer seems to work when their grief is pervasive, extending beyond the first weeks after the death. While they feel the need for solace and comfort from others for an extended period of time, this comfort is generally only forthcoming shortly after the death.

Some deaths, such as those that result from suicide, often lead to blaming the surviving mourners for the death (Cain & Fast, 1972). Are family members accepting this stigmatized role when they report experiencing survivor guilt? Furthermore, when mourners lose a critical part of their identity, as a parent or husband or wife, they are no longer the people they were before the death. However, their identity is spoiled further by the silence of a larger community that cannot deal with the pain or grief and the fact that people do die (Silverman, 1981).

Those infected with the human immunodeficiency virus are seen as having violated several of society's norms due to the nature of their sexual or substance use activity and because their disease may lead to death. Thus, they are involved with two taboo areas: sex and death. The facts are lost in the passion associated with the disease and persons with AIDS become pariahs in their own communities: blamed, labeled, discredited, and shunned. They are no longer the people they thought they were. Their identities, in society's eyes, are "spoiled," thereby placing them in marginal positions in contrast to their prior positions in their communities and worlds. This marginality is not the result of real deficits these individuals may experience because of their illness, but of how these persons are perceived by others.

I am reminded of a clinical situation I encountered in which a young woman, who had set herself on fire, was being treated not only for her burns but for obvious suicidal problems as well. The staff found it very difficult to care for her. They were appalled that someone could do this to herself. Not only was her identity "spoiled" because of her own behavior and how she now looked but by the staff's reactions as well. She elicited little sympathy from them, which further isolated her. She was labeled a "bad" person when she most needed the understanding of others. Rather than being comforted in her hour of adversity, she felt criticized and blamed. This phenomenon has been called blaming the victim (Ryan, 1976). While she was asked to take responsibility for what she had done to herself, she was given no comfort or support to help her do so.

Persons suffering from AIDS are hindered from dealing with their illness in a straightforward way, because in the eyes of society, and often in their own eyes as well, they are not absolved of blame. It is as if they deliberately chose to become ill like suicidal persons choose to end their lives. They are stigmatized by those around them who assume that something is wrong with them on a personal basis not simply because they are infected. The talk of quarantine is not only for the disease but for the person as well. Often the "victim" accepts this blame, assuming that the label and attributes associated with it are appropriate. They develop a sense of self that allows them to be put outside the human pale (Goffman, 1963). The person who suffers from AIDS becomes more than someone with an impaired immune system. It is as if the person with the illness has lost his or her personhood and has become the illness.

Accepting a Spoiled Identity

What is the process by which the individual realizes that this identity applies to him or to her? What does it take to acknowledge that "I am black," "I am a woman," "I have cancer," "I am the mother of a child who killed herself," "I am a homosexual," "I am a widow," "I am a birthmother," "I have AIDS"? The shift here is not that they are people who have AIDS, but that they become the AIDS, or they become the parent of a suicide, thus allowing one aspect of their social identity to become their total personal identity.

In looking at the process of stigmatization, it is necessary to consider not only who is being labeled but who is doing the labeling. We can talk about the social positions and roles of the victim and the victimizer. For example, we can ask if the AIDS epidemic would have the same meaning if it began in a white heterosexual population with power and influence rather than a homosexual or substance user population with less overt power and influence.

To understand why people accept a given role as their own, we have to consider the personal attributes of people. Personal attributes can make a critical difference in how the definition of others is accepted as one's own. For women, for example, the importance of relationships in defining themselves often forces them into situations where they are willing to adapt how they present themselves, and accept the definition of others, in order to maintain connections (Gilligan, 1982).

Another personal attribute that we cannot ignore is what is called a *fragile* or *dependent* ego. These are people who also have poor self-esteem and who may have a diagnosable mental illness, all of which makes their sense of self more vulnerable to compromise.

We must also ask what are the conditions in society, as well as the experiences of the individual, that make it easier for these two identities to merge? Some people are socialized to accept the definition of others. From the beginning, they are taught their place because they are born into a group that is considered inferior. This has been true for women throughout recorded history. When there were no options or when the voice of authority such as the church or the government supported this construction of reality, most women incorporated society's definition into their own definition of self. The legal and social system served to keep people in their "place."

We do not generally consider the health care system as an apartheid system but such dichotomous and hierarchical relationships exist. Much has been written about the elements of the doctor/patient relationship that favor the physician (Friedson, 1968). While the patient may want to be treated as a person, the doctor may want compliance.

In the name of objectivity, the health care system depersonalizes individuals. This takes place automatically with the ascription of the word *patient* to designate the individual who comes for assistance. *Patient* is defined in the dictionary as "a person or thing that undergoes action." A patient is someone who is acted on. Accepting the stigmatized role may be necessary if the individuals involved seek or need acceptance from the sector of society that may be conferring the stigmatized identity. In the case of AIDS, infected people require the care of agencies, professionals, and a special mobilization of the scientific and health care communities of the world.

Goffman (1963) relates the techniques that people adopt to accommodate to this setting without challenging the system. They may try telling their story in the short time allocated as competently as possible. The patient may strive to make a good impression, to document his or her social value, and to monitor his own behavior so that he or she behaves in a more acceptable way. These techniques imply an acceptance of the definition of self held by the dominant system. The system's control of access to necessary resources influences the nature of power and control in the relationship.

A position of dependency and a sense of social vulnerability increase the likelihood of acceptance of a definition of self suggested by those in a superordinate position. For example, birthmothers, who were unmarried and without any economic resources, were counseled by agencies who controlled their access to resources to surrender their unborn children for adoption. These birthmothers understood from the agencies' response that they did not have the qualities to be a good mother and their sense of self as mother was spoiled (Silverman, 1981). In similar fashion, widows who mourn their spouse for an extended period of time are criticized for not getting on with their lives. Nonmourners are uncomfortable with their pain, with the association, with death, and turn from these women, leaving them with the feeling that something is wrong with them. Their sense of self is spoiled or compromised as a result (Silverman, 1981).

People with AIDS are also at a place in their lives when they feel extremely vulnerable. They, too, are dependent on the health system and often on the welfare system as well. While some are now challenging the correctness of the larger system, putting aside their fear of rejection, others cannot put aside this fear. The vulnerability I am referring to here is that associated with this dependency and with the changing situation in which the individual's accustomed sense of identity no longer applies or is threatened. Their reality is such that they cannot continue as before; a world has crumbled. Their sense of self, of identity, simply does not work and what they know about who they are is no longer applicable. This is the true meaning of a spoiled identity. In response to this spoiling, a fundamental shift in identity, in the way people live their lives, is required.

What are the choices for a new identity? When we talk about spousal death in the case of women, the shift is from wife to widow. When we talk of people with AIDS, the shift is from a healthy person to one who has AIDS. There is little honor attached to either of these roles regardless of the apparent difference between them. The more stigma is attached to a role, to who you will become as a result of the change, the greater the difficulty there is in accepting the new identity (Lopata, 1979).

Lopata describes widowhood as a period of temporary identity transformation. Before the transformation can take place, the new widow must first accept the fact that she is widowed. Widowhood is not a desirable role in a world built around married couples that does not value single women, in a world that says that to be someone a woman must be married (Lopata, 1979; Silverman, 1986). It is often very difficult for a woman in these circumstances to acknowledge that she is indeed a widow. For some women, the role of wife was so pervasive that they had no other sense of who they were in relationship to themselves and to others. When one's entire sense of self is invested in the role to be given up, a sense of personal integrity and continuity is lost. It may be easier to maintain the spoiled identity.

What happens when it is not the individual who feels that his or her entire sense of self is at stake but when society insists that the stigmatized role is now the only identity available to the individual? For example, once the ascription of dying person is assigned to someone, society often insists that this becomes his or her total role (Lofland, 1978). Persons with HIV infection, who are newly diagnosed, find themselves in a stigmatized situation, and all other identities seem to fall by the wayside as far as society is concerned. There is a lack of congruity between society's definition and the infected person's sense of who he or she still is.

Lofland (1978) notes that people live a long time in the role of the dying person, a role which has no function and no status in this society. Would the shift in identity be enhanced if the world was so constructed that people were accustomed to knowing all of the selves that can make up their identity? The more complex the construction, the less likely people are to allow a single role to define who they are.

For persons with AIDS, society has provided few options for finding a model for maintaining their identity that can be modified to include the fact that they have AIDS. When their former identity is spoiled, is the only one available an equally spoiled one? Even prior to the time they are terminal, persons with HIV infection are forced into the category of "patient with AIDS." There is often a tension in most individuals as they face the need to relinquish their old sense of self and develop a new one. When the only role they see available to them is a stigmatized role, the tension is compounded (Silverman, 1986).

Impact on the Grieving Process

Grief is often seen as an illness from which one recovers with appropriate treatment. The expectation of such treatment is that it will, at the least, relieve the mourner's pain and, at the most, remove it entirely. Implicit, too, is that grief ends and that people will pick up their lives and carry on as before. The affective and psychological aspects of grief are emphasized in this approach; so that the crying, sadness, pining, feeling alone, and feeling cheated by the loss come into focus as the primary issues to be attended to. The need to accept the reality of the loss is emphasized, as is the expectation that grief can be "resolved" and that life goes on as before. This approach ignores the identity shift described above and does not recognize

the fundamental change that the death introduces to the life of the mourner. Dealing with this change is an integral part of any bereavement process.
It is impossible to divorce the mourning process from the nature of the
death, from who is lost and from the place that person had in the life of the
mourner. Grieving, then, is a social process, more than simply dealing with
feelings. It may better be characterized as a critical period of transition. The
transition ends when the individual has developed a new sense of self and
assumed a new role in society, when the grief that is experienced no longer
controls the mourner but is controlled by the mourner, and when the
mourner is comforted by memories of the deceased (Silverman, 1986).

The context in which one lives will impact on how any transition is
negotiated. What happens when the dominant theme in that context is the
experience of social isolation and stigma? In the case of widowhood, the
stigma may follow the death and emerge from the social isolation they
experience. In the case of AIDS, the stigma begins with the onset of the
illness and carries through, leaving the survivors equally isolated without
legitimation of their mourning. While many people fear that they will be
contaminated by associating with death in any way, when a person dies of
AIDS the guilt and shame they may feel is the legacy they leave for their
survivors. One way of avoiding this stigma is to lie about the cause of
death. A necessary part of bereavement is to remember the deceased, to find
a way of carrying within oneself a representation of who it was that died.
These memories can provide comfort and solace (Klass, 1988). The AIDS
quilt was one attempt by friends and family of people who died of AIDS to
break through this silence and not only legitimate their loss but memorial-
ize those who died.

We need to look at ways of dealing with this tension between the needs
of the dying and those who mourn them and the way the larger society
reacts. People cannot silently accept nonpersonhood, but must instead find
the supportive environment that will allow them to develop a new voice
(Silverman, 1986).

Damage Control and Prevention

One way a person can maintain control over his or her personal identity is
through information management (Goffman, 1963). Goffman notes that
this can be done in several ways. Where possible, avoid the situation.
Sometimes people lie about what is happening. We talk of people "passing" by saying "not me" and denying the situation. If the stigma is not
readily apparent, this can involve the decision to not tell others about their
condition. Goffman talks about people using disidentifiers so that an otherwise coherent presentation of self is not discredited. There are signs that
convey social information. People become hazy about what happened so

that if you ask bereaved children what their father does, they have learned that when they say "he is dead," people pull back. To avoid being left with the feeling that "I did something wrong," children learn not to identify themselves as bereaved or as orphans.

The family of a person with AIDS can avoid or conceal what is occurring by repackaging it. They can move to redefine the outer reality by retreating from the community where truth must be known. They can selectively disclose what is happening, avowing normality (i.e., "nothing is wrong; she is just feeling a bit under the weather"). They can choose to say their child is living in a geographically distant community, making visits very difficult, or they can blame the disease on a blood transfusion, ignoring the way the disease may have in fact been transmitted. They can attribute the death to an accident or a disease of unknown origin.

While internally the inevitable trajectory of AIDS is always with the infected person, he or she may choose to "pass" as well. The person can do this by not sharing the fact that he or she is ill, by talking of having a cold, and often by simply putting off a confrontation with the reality of what is ailing him or her. We can talk of denial but this avoidance may be quite functional in allowing the individual to carry on with a intact identity (Silverman, 1986). The unwillingness to accept a new or a spoiled identity may reflect resilience and emotional health.

People learn to fight back. Goffman (1963) describes "huddling together" as one method that is effective. In self-help organizations, infected individuals, widowed people, and former alcoholics can feel normal among others like themselves (Katz & Bender, 1990; Silverman, 1978). This coming together and the strength people gain from common concern and activity is largely responsible for the changes we see in what is called a stigma and how those who have been stigmatized react. The mothers of children who committed suicide joined together in Compassionate Friends, for example, where they can find others who have had a similar experience. They feel less isolated and less alone, and in this context can acknowledge what happened to the child and what they have to live with. They can change the social construction of suicide so that those touched by it are no longer victimized but are understood and the recipients of solace and support.

People with AIDS have begun to organize, to develop services, to encourage research, to be there for each other in their hours of need, to tell their story in their own voices. They talk of living with a serious illness, thus focusing on life rather than death. In so doing, they are redefining their situation by destigmatizing the social identity assigned to the person with AIDS as well as affirming their personal identities and taking charge of who they are. Help from the larger community was forthcoming as persons with AIDS began to reject the stigmatized self and act affirmatively in their own behalf.

Conclusion

In adding the dimensions of stigma and spoiled identity to our understanding of dying and bereavement, I hope that practitioners will make a shift in how they view these phenomena and the help they offer. We are not simply dealing with affect—that is, how those who are dying or bereaved feel about what is happening. We are dealing with a dynamic process involving larger social values and shifting roles and identities. Any loss involves not only the loss of a person but the loss of a place in the larger society and a loss of the sense of self. Intervention is not simply in the hands of the professional but must emerge from a collaboration between those who are involved personally and on the larger societal level as well.

References

Berger, P. L., & Luckmann, T. (1967). *The social construction of reality.* New York: Doubleday Anchor.

Black death. (1965). *Encyclopedia Brittanica, 3,* 742. Chicago: William Benton.

Cain, A., & Fast, I. (1972). The legacy of suicide: Observations in the pathogenic impact of suicide upon marital partners. In A. Cain (Ed.), *Survivors of suicide.* Springfield, IL: Charles C Thomas.

Freidson, E. (1968). The impurity of professional authority. In H. S. Becker, et al., *Institutions and the person: Essays presented to Everett C. Hughes.* Chicago: Aldine.

Fulton, R. (1965). *Death and identity.* New York: Wiley & Sons.

Gilligan, C. (1982). *In a different voice: Psychological theory and women's development.* Cambridge, MA: Harvard University Press.

Goffman, E. (1963). *Stigma.* Englewood Cliffs, NJ: Prentice Hall.

Gorer, G. (1965). *Death, grief and mourning.* London: Cresset Press.

Hughes, E. C. (1971). *The sociological eye: Selected papers.* Chicago: Aldine, Atherton.

Katz, A. H., & Bender, E. I. (1990). *Helping one another: Self-help groups in a changing world.* Oakland, CA: Third Party Publishing.

Klass, D. (1988). *Parental grief: Solace and resolution.* New York: Springer.

Lofland, L. H. (1978). *The craft of dying.* Beverly Hills, CA: Sage.

Lopata, H. (1979). *Women as widows: Support systems.* New York: Elsevier.

Miller, J. B. (1986). *Toward a new psychology of women* (2nd ed.). Boston: Beacon Press.

Neusner, J. (1980). *A history of the Mishnaic law of women.* Leiden, Netherlands: E. J. Brill.

Rosenblatt, P. C., Walsh, R. P., & Jackson, D. A. (1976). *Grief and mourning in cross-cultural perspective.* HRAF Press.

Ryan, W. (1976). *Blaming the victim.* New York: Random House.

Saunders, C. M. (1989). *Grief: The mourning after dealing with adult bereavement.* New York: Wiley & Sons.

Silverman, P. R. (1978). *Mutual help: A guide for mental health workers.* NIMH, DHEW Publication No. ADM 78-646. Washington, DC: U.S. Government Printing Office.

Silverman, P. R. (1981). *Helping women cope with grief.* Beverly Hills, CA: Sage.

Silverman, P. R. (1986). *Widow to widow.* New York: Springer.

West, P. (1985). Becoming disabled: Perspectives on the labelling approach. In U. E. Gerhardt & M. E. J. Wadsworth (Eds.), *Stress and stigma: Explanation and evidence in the sociology of crime and illness* (pp. 104–128). New York: St. Martin's Press.

Fifteen

Complications in Mourning Traumatic Death

Therese A. Rando

Therese A. Rando is a clinical psychologist in private practice in Warwick, Rhode Island. She is the Clinical Director of Therese A. Rando Associates, Ltd., a multidisciplinary team providing psychotherapy, training, and consultation in the area of mental health, specializing in loss and grief, traumatic stress, and the psychosocial care of the chronically and terminally ill. She is the founder and Executive Director of the Institute for the Study and Treatment of Loss, which was established in 1991 to provide advanced training, supervision, and consultation to professional working with the dying and the bereaved. Since 1970, she has consulted, conducted research, provided therapy, written, and lectured internationally in areas related to grief and death. Rando holds a Ph.D. in Clinical Psychology from the University of Rhode Island and has received advanced training in psychotherapy and in medical consultation-liaison psychiatry at Case Western Reserve University Medical School and University Hospitals of Cleveland. A former consultant to the U.S. Department of Health and Human Services' Hospice Education Program for Nurses, she developed its program for training hospice nurses to cope with loss, grief, and terminal illness. Her research interests focus on the operations and course of mourning, the experience of bereaved parents, and the emotional reactions of rescue workers.

Rando has written over 45 articles and chapters pertaining to the clinical aspects of thanatology. She is the author of Treatment of Complicated Mourning, How To Go On Living When Someone You Love Dies, *and* Grief, Dying, and Death: Clinical Interventions for Caregivers; *and she is the editor of* Loss and Anticipatory Grief *and* Parental Loss of a Child. *Rando is the media resource expert in dying, death, and loss for the American Psychological Association. She has appeared on many television shows and has been interviewed by and quoted in many national magazines and newspapers.*

For her accomplishments in the field of thanatology, Rando was the recipient of the Association for Death Education and Counseling's 1987 award for Outstanding Contribution to the Study of Death, Dying, and Bereavement and a 1990 grantee of its lifetime certification as Certified Death Educator.

When the death of a loved one occurs under traumatic circumstances, the survivor's mourning is predisposed to be complicated by his or her reactions to the specific event. In such situations, the caregiver must be skilled at intervening in the ensuing posttraumatic stress reactions to the event as well as in the bereavement over the loss itself, and must comprehend the interplay among both processes. Unfortunately, however, posttraumatic elements of bereavement too often are neglected totally or are insufficiently appreciated. Posttraumatic stress is treated just like other loss-related elements of bereavement, usually to the mourner's detriment.

Relatively little has been written in the thanatological literature about the clinical combination of posttraumatic stress and mourning. It is true that in recent years there has been increasingly strong interest evidenced in those types of deaths that inherently lead to a mixture of both (i.e., accidental deaths, disaster deaths, suicides, and homicides). However, with the exception of the works of a few writers (most notably, Amick-McMullan, Kilpatrick, Veronen, & Smith, 1989; Lindy, Green, Grace, & Titchener, 1983; Raphael, 1986; Redmond, 1989; and Rynearson, 1987), the interest on the parts of those in the bereavement aspects, thus overlooking the posttraumatic aspects. This incomplete perspective not only has left a serious gap in the treatment literature but has contributed to the persistence of treatable complications in mourning traumatic deaths.

The purposes of this chapter are to identify and discuss those issues that generally complicate mourning after traumatic death and to delineate relevant concerns in the conceptualization and treatment of mourning complicated by posttraumatic stress. While an in-depth examination of the perspectives, guidelines, and interventions for the treatment of complicated mourning in general or complicated mourning secondary to traumatic death is prohibited here due to space constraints, it is found in my work, *The Treatment of Complicated Mourning* (Rando, 1993), to which the reader is referred for the specifics of the interventions mentioned here.

The Increasing Prevalence of Complicated Mourning

Despite many changes, today's mourner still must contend with most of the same issues, experiences, and processes as did the mourner of previous times. There still is the agonizing experience of separation pain and the often unanswerable question of "Why?" There continues to be a struggle to find expression and closure for uncomfortable psychological reactions, accompanied by anxiety about who and what one is and will become as intense and unexpected emotions are encountered. Confusion, disorganization, and depression are the results when the old world is shattered by the death of the loved one. There remains resistance to relinquishing old ties to the deceased and to forming new ones more appropriate to the present reality. Attempts to avoid changing the old ways of thinking about and being in the world keep being made. Despite all of this, ultimately, in healthy mourning, there is a yielding to these demands and resultant alterations are made in relationship to the deceased, the external world, and the self and the self's assumptive world. Appropriate reinvestment stays a critically important goal.

However, while the actual experiences of mourning and its demands have not changed very significantly over time, what has changed is the potential for problems with them. In today's world, the typical mourner sustains a greater probability of being compromised in his or her mourning as a consequence of a number of sociocultural and technological trends (i.e., there is a greater chance that a bereaved individual may develop complicated mourning). Elsewhere, I have identified and discussed factors resulting from such trends that contribute to the increasing prevalence of complicated mourning in Western society (Rando, 1993). These include (1) the types of deaths occurring today, (2) the characteristics of the personal relationships severed by today's deaths, (3) the personality and resources of today's mourner, (4) present-day limitations of the mental health profession regarding bereavement, and (5) contemporary problems in the field of thanatology. Because of these developments, today's caregiver can expect to see an increasingly greater number of bereaved persons with complicated mourning.

Complicated Mourning

In order to appreciate how traumatic death specifically predisposes to complicated mourning, it first is necessary to understand that phenomenon. *Complicated mourning* is a term describing the state, wherein given the amount of time since the death, there is some compromise, distortion, or failure of one or more of the six R processes of mourning. The six R processes of mourning (Rando, 1993) necessary for healthy accommodation of any loss are:

1. Recognize the loss.
   Acknowledge the death.
   Understand the death.
2. React to the separation.
   Experience the pain.
   Feel, identify, accept, and give some form of expression to all the psychological reactions to the loss.
   Identify and mourn secondary losses.
3. Recollect and reexperience the deceased and the relationship.
   Review and remember realistically.
   Revive and reexperience the feelings.

4. Relinquish the old attachments to the deceased and the old assumptive world.
5. Readjust to move adaptively into the new world without forgetting the old.
   Revise the assumptive world.
   Develop a new relationship with the deceased.
   Adopt new ways of being in the world.
   Form a new identity.
6. Reinvest.

In all forms of complicated mourning, there are attempts to do two things: (1) to deny, repress, or avoid aspects of the loss, its pain, and the full realization of its implications for the mourner; and (2) to hold onto and avoid relinquishing the lost loved one (Rando, 1993). These attempts are what underlie the complications in the R processes of mourning.

Complicated mourning may take any one or combination of four forms (Rando, 1993). Complicated mourning *symptoms* refer to any psychological, behavioral, social, or physical symptoms that reveal some dimension of compromise, distortion, or failure of one or more of the six R processes of mourning. They are of insufficient number, intensity, and duration, or of different type, than are required to meet the criteria for any of the other three forms of complicated mourning.

Seven complicated mourning *syndromes* have been identified. These may occur as syndromes independent of or concurrent with each other. (Also, various elements of the different syndromes may intermingle with each other to form diverse constellations of complicated mourning symptoms.) The seven syndromes include the three syndromes with problems in expression (i.e., absent mourning, delayed mourning, and inhibited mourning); the syndromes with skewed aspects (i.e., distorted mourning of the extremely angry or guilty types, conflicted mourning, and uninanticipated mourning); and the syndrome with a problem with closure (i.e., chronic mourning).

The third form that complicated mourning may take is of a *diagnosable mental or physical disorder*. This would include any DSM-III-R diagnostic mental disorder (American Psychiatric Association, 1987) or any physical disorder. Finally, a fourth form of complicated mourning is *death*. This may be consciously chosen death (i.e., suicide); death that is immediately secondary to complicated mourning reactions (e.g., automobile crash consequent to driving at excessive speed); or death that stems from the long-term consequences of complicated mourning reactions (e.g., cirrhosis of the liver caused by alcoholism). The latter two types of death may or may not be subintentioned on the part of the mourner.

There are seven generic high-risk factors for complicated mourning (Rando, 1993). These are factors associated with either the specific death or with relevant antecedent or consequent variables which would tend to predispose any mourner to complications. These high-risk factors include:

Factors Associated with the Specific Death

Sudden, unanticipated death (especially when it is traumatic, violent, mutilating, or random)
Death from an overly lengthy illness
Loss of a child
The mourner's perception of the death as preventable

Antecedent and Subsequent Variables

A premorbid relationship with the deceased that was markedly (1) angry or ambivalent or (2) dependent
Prior or concurrent mourner liabilities of (1) unaccommodated losses and/ or stresses or (2) mental health problems
The mourner's perceived lack of social support

To the extent that any bereaved individual is characterized by one or more of these factors, that individual is said to be at risk for the development of complications in one or more of the six R processes of mourning, and hence at risk for complicated mourning.

Traumatic Death

While it is understood that virtually any death may be perceived by the survivor as personally traumatic, the focus of the remainder of this chapter is exclusively on death that transpires under circumstances that are *objectively* traumatic. These are to be differentiated from internal subjective experiences engendering feelings of trauma (eg., a feeling of helplessness or powerlessness, the perception of untimeliness in the deceased's death, etc.), which are not the topic of discussion here. Factors that make a specific death circumstance traumatic include (1) suddenness and lack of anticipation, (2) violence, mutilation, and destruction, (3) preventability, and/or randomness, (4) multiple deaths, or (5) the mourner's personal encounter with death, where there is either a significant threat to his or her own survival or a massive and/or shocking confrontation with the death and mutilation of others (Rando, 1993). In each of these situations, the external circumstances are such as to engender the disordered psychic and/ or behavioral state resulting from mental or emotional stress or physical injury that is known as "trauma" (adapted from Merriam-Webster Dictionary, 1987). Refining this further, the use of the concept of trauma henceforth in this chapter shall represent "an emotional state of discomfort and stress resulting from memories of an extraordinary, catastrophic experience

Specific
Circumstances of the Death

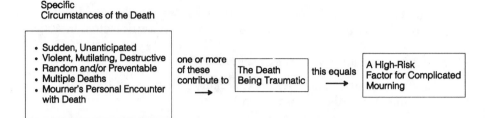

Figure 15–1.   Diagram for the relationship between the elements comprising traumatic death and complicated mourning

which shattered the survivor's sense of invulnerability to harm" (Figley, 1985, p. xviii) (see Figure 15–1).

Sudden, Unanticipated Death

Across approxmately 1,380 cultures studied, a sudden, unanticipated death is considered "bad news," stimulates concern about whether the loved one suffered before death, and initiates rituals to build the deceased back into the group in some form (Platt, 1991). It is a determining factor in at least three of the complicated mourning syndromes (i.e., distorted mourning of the extremely angry type, chronic mourning, and the unanticipated mourning syndrome), although it certainly often plays a part in the others as well.

Suddenness and lack of anticipation influence the mourner's internal world and coping abilities so adversely that a subjective trauma is created regardless of whether the actual external circumstances are traumatic. Raphael (1983) has termed this the "shock effect" of sudden death. With no time to gradually anticipate and prepare for the loss, the full and total confrontation of it all at once is overpowering. The mourner's coping abilities are assaulted by the sudden and dramatic knowledge of the death, and the adaptive capacities are completely overwhelmed. The sequelae of sudden, unanticipated loss of a loved one tend to leave the mourner stunned, feeling out of control and confused, unable to grasp the full implications of a loss that is perceived as inexplicable, unbelievable, and incomprehensible. The mourner becomes bewildered, anxious, insecure, self-reproachful, depressed, and despairing. He or she is in shock emotionally and physiologically, and it persists for an extended time. This further interferes with the mourner's ability to grasp what has occurred and exacerbates the intensity and duration of the acute grief symptomatology. Often the mourner engages in the avoidance of others and social withdrawal.

Although the person mourning a sudden, unanticipated death has the same six R processes of mourning to complete as does any other mourner, the devastated adaptive capacities secondary to the shock of this type of loss tend to compromise their completion. The additional intellectual confusion and emotional intensity wrought by this type of death handicaps the person. In essence, the shock effect overwhelms the ego and its resources, which then become taken up with trying to master the helplessness and other flooding affects, the intrusion of associated traumatic memories, and the resulting sense of personal threat and vulnerability—all of which interfere with the mourning that is required (Raphael, 1983).

Specifically, there are 11 issues inherent in sudden, unanticipated death that particularly complicate mourning (Rando, 1993). These include:

- The capacity to cope is diminished as the shock effects of the death overwhelm the ego at the same time new stressors are added (e.g., heightened personal threat and vulnerability).
- The assumptive world is violently shattered without warning and the violated assumptions (e.g., the world as orderly, predictable, and meaningful; the self as invulnerable; etc.) cause intense reactions of fear, anxiety, vulnerability, and loss of control.
- The loss does not make sense, and cannot be understood or absorbed.
- There is no chance to say good-bye and finish unfinished business with the deceased, which causes problems due to the lack of closure.
- Symptoms of acute grief and of physical and emotional shock persist for a prolonged period of time.
- The mourner obsessively reconstructs events in an effort both to comprehend the death and to prepare for it in retrospect.
- The mourner experiences a profound loss of security and confidence in the world which affects all areas of life and increases many kinds of anxiety.
- The loss cuts across experiences in the relationship and tends to highlight what was happening at the time of the death, often causing these last-minute situations to be out of proportion with the rest of the relationship and predisposing to problems with realistic recollection and guilt.
- The death tends to leave mourners with relatively more intense emotional reactions, such as greater anger, ambivalence, guilt, helplessness, death anxiety, vulnerability, confusion, disorganization, and obsession with the deceased along with strong needs to make meaning of the death and to determine blame and affix responsibility for it.
- The death tends to be followed by a number of major secondary losses (Rando, 1984) because of the consequences of lack of anticipation (e.g., loss of home because of lack of financial planning).
- The death can provoke posttraumatic stress responses (e.g., repeated intrusion of traumatic memories, numbing of general responsiveness, increased physiological arousal).

If circumstances are such that there has been no body viewing to confirm the death, the mourner is at additional risk for complications. So, too, if there are legal inquiries and/or processes, these can complicate the mourning by forcing the need for intentional repression and/or presenting the mourner with circumstances causing secondary victimization (Redmond, 1989).

Suddenness and lack of anticipation are nonspecific variables that can be found in all forms of death. They are inherent aspects of a number of high-risk deaths (e.g., accidents, disasters, suicides, and homicides) and tend to occur concurrently with other factors known to contribute to complicated mourning, most especially the other four sets of circumstances associated specifically with traumatic death.

Violence, Mutilation, and Destruction

Deaths involving violence, mutilation, and destruction are particularly traumatic because of the massively frightening feelings they engender in the survivors: terror, shock, helplessness and powerlessness, vulnerability, threat, anxiety, fear, violation, hyperarousal, and victimization. Ultimately, they typically lead to significant anger, guilt, self-blame, and shattered assumptions. Such deaths are particularly problematic to mourn for a number of reasons which, because of their frequent association with suddenness and lack of anticipation, must be added to the complications already delineated above. These deaths breach the mourner's senses of invulnerability, security, predictability, and control, viciously violating the mourner's assumptive world and bringing all the types of adverse consequences such violations cause. Other problems stem from the fact that violence is highly associated with the development of posttraumatic stress (Rynearson, 1987), which includes among its many sequelae posttraumatic imagery that can be particularly overwhelming and recalcitrant. Additionally, because of personal attachment and identification, survivors of these types of death are compelled to work through an internalized fantasy of grotesque dying that not only increases their own fears but additionally complicates their mourning by presenting them with the task of assimilating the violence and, in cases of homicide, assimilating as well the transgression implicit in this type of death (Rynearson, 1988).

A major problem is that violence, mutilation, and destruction stir the mourner's previous aggressive thoughts or fantasies regarding the deceased, often bringing guilt as a result and linking the death with these prior thoughts (Rapheal, 1983). The violence itself can cause aroused hostility in the mourner, which can contribute conflict within the conscience and lead to guilt or shame (Horowitz, 1986). Raphael (1983) has observed that violence, mutilation, and destruction fulfill the most primitive destructive fantasies and reawaken the most basic death anxiety and fears of annihilation, leaving those affected called upon to master these additional stresses along with their mourning. As well, she notes that the mourner must confront the general destructiveness of humankind and/or nature.

All of this leaves the bereaved having to contend with and work through the heightened senses of personal vulnerability and threat and the violated assumptive worlds that are left. Such deaths inevitably conjure up for the survivors images of what suffering they imagine the deceased felt at death, and this adds enormously to their distress and increases their guilt for not being present and/or able to alleviate that suffering. In homicide, and presumably in other scenarios as well, bodily mutilation appears to result in stronger identification with the deceased and in the survivor's losing more control of his or her personal life and environment (Redmond, 1989).

Preventability and/or Randomness

The death that is preventable and/or random presents the survivor with distinct complications of the mourning processes. Often polar opposites, each characteristic brings its own specific problems to the mourner.

The mourner's perception of the preventability of the death often is an underappreciated factor in that individual's response. The perception of death as *preventable* appears to increase the duration and severity of grief and mourning (Bugen, 1979). This is viewed as a death that did not have to occur. It could have been avoided; it was not inevitable. Anger is intensified. The perception of preventability propels mourners to spend great time and effort searching for the cause and/or reason for the death, to affix responsibility by determining who or what is to blame, and to mete out punishment if possible. It prompts attempts to find some meaning in the death and the striving to regain a sense of control. The violations of the mourner's assumptive world make it difficult to make any sense out of the event. The fact that this was a death that did not have to occur is obsessively ruminated on by the mourner, who struggles to comprehend how and why such an avoidable happenstance transpired and to manage the outrage and frustration it engenders. The unfairness and injustice in this being a death that did not have to happen boggles the mind, begs for explanation, and intensifies the emotions

The volition (as an act of willful, intentional killing or irresponsible negligence leading to death) and the violation (as an unprovoked, transgressive, exploitative act) of preventable deaths lead to two major compensatory psychological responses seen after these types of traumatic deaths (Rynearson, 1987). The volition, as previously observed, leads to compulsive inquiry to establish the locus of responsibility and purpose of the death; while the violation leads to the psychological reaction of victimization, including such aspects as shame, self-blame, subjugation, morbid hatred, paradoxical gratitude, defilement, sexual inhibition, resignation, second injury, and socioeconomic status downward drift (Ochberg, 1988).

Truly *random* events are especially terrifying because they are unpredictable and therefore uncontrollable: Individuals cannot protect themselves from them. Therefore, a common tendency on the parts of mourners and those who have been victimized by random events is to assume blame for them. It is relatively easier to cope with an event's being one's own responsibility—and thus potentially being within one's own control—than it is to contend with the fact that it was a genuinely random event. The assumption of blame is the price paid to maintain the needed perception that the world is not random and unpredictable, but orderly and dependable. This is similar to the psychological dynamics behind the phenomenon of "blaming the victim." In both cases, there is an attempt to take the event out of the realm of a random occurrence against which one cannot protect oneself and make it manageable by identifying elements the survivor can control or avoid in the future to forestall a recurrence.

Caregivers must be mindful that the most important point here is that it is the mourner's perception of the death's preventability or randomness that is the issue, not the objective consensus of others.

Multiple Deaths

With the increased number of traumatic, unnatural deaths occurring in contemporary society (Rando, 1993), there are greater chances for an individual to be confronted with the loss of two or more loved ones in the same event or to experience a number of losses occurring sequentially within a relatively brief period of time. Each of these circumstances can give rise to what has been termed *bereavement overload* (Kastenbaum, 1969). As applied to the topic of mourning traumatic deaths, the focus here is on simultaneous multiple deaths, such as might occur in a common accident, a natural disaster, or a murder-suicide scenario.

Essentially, simultaneous multiple deaths confront the mourner with the high-risk factor of concurrent crisis when it comes to mourning each deceased individual. Mourning for a given loved one is compromised by the concurrent crisis of the ongoing, stalled, or delayed mourning for the other loved ones. A vicious cycle often exists: The death of person A cannot be worked on in the fashion ideally desired because of the emotional press of, unfinished business from, and remaining reactions to the deaths of persons B and C; each of these deaths, in turn, cannot be worked through because of incomplete mourning and stress associated with the death of person A.

There are eight types of dilemmas in mourning multiple deaths, each of which call for specific treatment interventions (Rando, 1993). These dilemmas are found in the following specific areas: (1) the approach to be taken in mourning multiple deaths, (2) prioritization of the loved ones to be mourned, (3) differentiation among the loved ones, (4) loss of social support, (5) conflicts inherent in multiple deaths, (6) the overwhelming nature of the situation, (7) compromise of the six R processes of mourning, and (8) survivor guilt.

The Mourner's Personal Encounter with Death

Posttraumatic reactions are quite common following an individual's personal encounter with death in which he or she experiences a significant threat to survival or subsequent to a massive and/or shocking confrontation with the death and mutilation of others. Both scenarios bring about intense psychological reactions. Raphael (1986) notes that it should be expected that there always will be some feelings about survival when one has faced death and lived, especially if others have died. She observes that many people are psychologically traumatized by such experiences despite the support of others and their own efforts to master it. This is particularly the case when the stress and death confrontation is sudden, shocking, intense, and massive. Further, Raphael has found that cardinal reactions to trauma (i.e., intrusive repetitious images and avoidance) are always common in those experiences where there is personal threat to the self, an intense shock effect, and where the individual is rendered helpless. Issues of what one did or did not do to survive become critically important considerations.

In a personal encounter with death wherein one experiences a *significant threat to survival*, the traumatic stimulus of the event can overwhelm the ego and cause posttraumatic reactions. Examples of such events might include a mourner's surviving an automobile crash that kills other passengers or being rescued from a brutal assault right before the assailant attempts murder. The direct exposure to the threat of one's own death brings fear, terror, anxiety, heightened arousal, helplessness, a sense of abandonment, increased vulnerability, and the yearning for relief and rescue (Raphael, 1986). As with other trauma, the need often exists to relive and reexperience the event, as well as to defend against it by avoiding it or shutting it out. This undergirds the stress response syndrome (Horowitz, 1986), which is the process believed to underlie all dimensions and variations of posttraumatic stress disorder.

In situations involving the *massive and/or shocking confrontation with the death and mutilation of others*, the mourner loses a loved one in circumstances that expose him or her to intense terror, sudden helplessness, and frightening perceptions. Examples of such scenarios include mutilating airplane crashes or devastating disasters. For purposes of this discussion, included herein also are situations in which the exposure to the death and mutilation of others is on a smaller scale but still quite shocking (e.g., finding the blue and bloated body of a loved one hanging in a garage after a successful suicide attempt or having to identify the burned and mutilated body of one's kidnapped child). In both types of cases, the mourner must contend with a variety of stimuli stemming from severe injuries to other human beings. These may involve all the senses, not just vision (e.g., the smell of burnt flesh or the screams of wounded friends). The sights, the sounds, the smells—and all the other sensory images of death—become emblazoned in the mourner's mind and fuel the traumatic impact of the event. They produce reactive phenomena (e.g., nightmares, flashbacks, intrusive images, memories triggered off by situations and stimulus cues similar to the original experience) that require integration (Raphael, 1986). Such phenomena complicate the mourning that must be undertaken.

Sequelae of Traumatic Death

The *stress response syndrome,* as identified and described by Horowitz (1985), is accepted herein as the process underlying posttraumatic reactions. Briefly, the process commences with an initial outcry in response to a stressful event. A phase of denial and numbing is usually witnessed in reaction to the initial realization that a traumatic event has occurred. After this initial phase, the individual is confronted with phases of intrusive repetitions of traumatic memory, thought, feeling, or behavior which alternate repeatedly with the denial and numbing. Such alternation of phases constitutes a way of the mourner modulating the emotional reactions to the event by containing them within tolerable, paced doses. The processes of reliving and reexperiencing aspects of the trauma and inversely attempting to shut them out continues until the traumatic event is worked through by being integrated cognitively and emotionally, and the individual develops appropriate adaptational responses. The press for repetition of the trauma ceases because cognitive completion with affective release has been achieved and the distress stimulating it is terminated.

The stress response syndrome catalyzed by a traumatic death can produce a number of sequelae in the mourner which coexist in different degrees with bereavement reactions. These may be found in one of two forms: (1) posttraumatic stress symptomatology overlays the mourning much like a blanket and requires full-scale intervention first in order to get to the mourning underneath which is completely shut out, or (2) posttraumatic stress elements are interspersed with the mourning and intervention requires paying relatively more attention to them initially, but not overlooking those aspects of mourning that are available to be treated simultaneously. The information below is presented as if the former case were at hand (i.e., the posttraumatic stress symptomatology is preventing the mourning). To the extent that a given clinical situation departs from this, the information must be extrapolated to accommodate the treatment needs.

Posttraumatic stress symptoms may or may not meet the criteria for a full-blown posttraumatic stress disorder (PTSD) as delineated in the *Diagnostic and Statistical Manual of Mental Disorders, Third Edition, Revised*

(DSM-III-R; American Psychiatric Association, 1987). According to the criteria, the type of stressor prompting the disorder must be "a psychologically distressing event that is outside the range of usual human experience... [and which] would be markedly distressing to almost anyone, and is usually experienced with intense fear, terror, and helplessness" (p. 247). Four types of situations are potential stressors: (1) serious threat to one's life or physical integrity, (2) serious threat or harm to one's loved ones, (3) sudden destruction of one's home or community, and (4) seeing another person who has recently been, or is being, seriously injured or killed as the result of an accident or physical violence. Thus, deaths caused by accidents, disasters, war, suicide, and homicide, as well as the death of a child—which is specifically in the DSM-III-R—readily qualify as traumatic stressors. These deaths, more so than others, tend to embody the five previously identified risk factors associated with traumatic death and predispose towards PTSD and its three categories of symptoms (i.e., reexperience of the traumatic event, avoidance of stimuli associated with the traumatic event or numbing of general responsiveness, and increased physiological arousal).

As synthesized from Rando (1993), the most common generic posttraumatic stress sequelae complicating mourning—regardless of whether they reach the criteria for formal diagnosis of PTSD—include: (1) anxiety, (2) reactions to the helplessness and powerlessness that usually constitute the central features of a traumatic experience, (3) survivor guilt, (4) one or dimensions of psychic numbing, (5) repetitious reactions to the trauma (e.g., intrusions of posttraumatic imagery), (6) violated assumptive world, (7) the need to formulate meaning in the trauma, and (8) personality disturbances. These are the general posttraumatic issues the caregiver will have to focus on in the posttraumatic stress portions of the treatment.

For some traumatized individuals, reactions will be minimal or relatively short lived due to personal factors, a lower degree of exposure to the traumatic event, or therapeutic support from others. However, for many others, posttraumatic reactions can become entrenched and evolve into full-blown PTSD. Factors associated with more severe reactions to trauma have been identified by Raphael (1986) and include: (1) the shock effects of sudden, unexpected trauma, which leave the ego no time to protect itself; (2) the severity of the threat to life; (3) the degree to which the individual feels helpless and powerless in the face of the trauma; and (4) the intensity, degree, proximity, and duration of exposure to shocking stimuli, violence, death, destruction, mutilation, and grotesque imagery. Preexisting vulnerability from earlier trauma plays a part as well.

However, it must not be assumed that a person who has developed a mental disorder subsequent to a traumatic event is a person who was more impaired at the time of exposure (Horowitz, 1985). Psychological trauma is the type of experience that can produce posttraumatic symptomatology in almost anyone, regardless of pretrauma characteristics. Unless there is clear evidence that there was preexisting psychopathology that has influenced the posttraumatic reactions over and above the normal responses to trauma, the caregiver must avoid interpretations of psychopathology. Especially in cases of unnatural dying (i.e., accidents, suicides, and homicides) which involve varying degrees of violence, volition, and violation, it is imperative that posttraumatic stress, compulsive inquiry, and victimization be understood as the psychologic consequences of overwhelming affect and defensive collapse, not as the reflections of unconscious conflict (Rynearson, 1987).

Treatment Concerns

As noted at the beginning of this chapter, when the death of a loved one occurs under traumatic circumstances, the survivor's mourning is predisposed to be complicated by his or her reactions to the specific event. This does not mean that complications inevitably occur, only that they are likely to do so. While there are a number of possible forms of complicated mourning that can develop, posttraumatic stress of some dimension typically is a consequence of traumatic death. As one form of complicated mourning, it may occur collaterally with any of the other forms of complicated mourning.

This requires that the caregiver be skilled at intervening in posttraumatic stress reactions as well as skilled at intervention in bereavement. After addressing the posttraumatic elements, the treatment of mourning complicated by posttraumatic stress then necessarily builds in two areas of components as found in Rando (1993). Intervention for the generic issues of complicated mourning *must* be added to the specific interventions for: (1) the type of death involved (i.e., accident, disaster, war, suicide, homicide), and (2) any other high-risk factors the death entails (e.g., guilt, anger, dependency, lack of social support, etc.).

Treatment of Mourning Complicated by Posttraumatic Stress

Problems in treating mourning complicated by posttraumatic stress tend to fall into two main categories: (1) problems stemming from the inadequate appreciation and treatment of the posttraumatic stress and (2) problems resulting from the insufficient understanding of the nature, dynamics, and treatment of complicated mouring. Regarding the former, many caregivers focus exclusively on the loss and bereavement aspects of the traumatic death and do not attend appropriately to the sequelae identified above as stemming from the traumatic circumstances. Hence, the point of concentration tends exclusively to be on the loss per se and not on the overwhelmed individual who has sustained it. In their desire to arrive quickly at the heart of the loss-related issues, caregivers frequently overlook, minimize, purposefully avoid, or attempt to rush through the trauma-related ones. In such scenarios, several nontherapeutic results are known to occur. The mourner may flee treatment, be retraumatized, develop additional symptomatology and/or defenses, or become engaged in a power struggle with the caregiver.

Problems with complicated mourning may cluster around a number of issues too numerous to mention here (see Rando, 1993). Suffice it to say that insufficient attention is paid to the *reasons* for why mourning becomes complicated to begin with and the *working through* of the resistances to the necessary six R processes of mourning which must occur if mourning is to be uncomplicated. By definition, in the situation of traumatic death, one of the complications is the effect of the posttraumatic stress on the mourner (e.g., impaired adaptive capacities after the sudden and unanticipated loss), which combines with the complications posed by the additional issues created by such circumstances (e.g., the increased guilt stimulated by the violence and mutilation). Therefore, traumatic death results in complicated mourning because of (1) its adverse impact on the mourner himself or herself and (2) the additional issues that the mourner is forced to confront as a consequence of it.

In treating mourning complicated by posttraumatic stress, the caregiver must integrate intervention directed at ameliorating the effects of the trauma with intervention focused on promotion of healthy mourning. However, if the posttraumatic stress overlays the mourning, the order of intervention is not arbitrary: Working through of the effects of the trauma and the defenses erected to protect against them must take place first (Lindy et al., 1983). Failure to do so leaves the mourner unable to progress with mourning as the self remains anxious and overwhelmed, fragmented and dissociated to varying degrees, victimized by repetitive trauma-related intrusions, fixated on particular concerns, and without full and conscious access to the ego functions.

Generic Treatment of Posttraumatic Stress

This section examines generic psychotherapeutic goals for intervention in posttraumatic stress. These must be embraced by the caregiver working with the mourner traumatized by the circumstances of a loved one's death, and must be incorporated with intervention for mourning. Depending on the degree of severity of the posttraumatic symptomatology, these interventions must be implemented prior to work on mourning the loss or integrated with such work as necessary to treat specific aspects of the mourner's bereavement.

A review of approaches designed to treat PTSD and its variants indicates that the broad goals are to empower the individual and liberate him or her from the traumatic effects of the traumatic event. Issues of grief and mourning are consistently mentioned as inherent aspects of healthy adaptation to traumatic stress, and an examination of the following strategies for treatment of posttraumatic stress in general reveals their similarities to the R processes of mourning. As abstracted from Rando (1993), the caregiver attempts to assist the person with posttraumatic stress to achieve the following:

- Bring into consciousness the traumatic experience; repeatedly reviewing, reconstructing, reexperiencing, and abreacting the experience until it is robbed of its potency.
- Identify, dose, express, work through, and master the affects of the traumatic encounter (e.g., helplessness, shock, horror, terror, anxiety, anger, guilt).
- Integrate conscious and dissociated memories, affects, thoughts, images, behaviors, and somatic sensations from the traumatic experience.
- Mourn relevant physical and psychosocial losses.
- Discourage maladaptive processes and therapeutically address the defenses and behaviors used to cope both with the trauma itself and the mechanisms employed to deal with it.
- Acquire and develop new skills and behaviors and/or retrieve overwhelmed ones to promote healthy living in the world after the trauma.
- Counter the helplessness and powerlessness with experiences supporting mastery; a sense of personal worth and value; connectedness to others; coping ability; release of feelings in small doses; undertaking of action to give testimony, help others, or minimize the effects of similar traumatic experiences; and the avoidance of further victimization.
- Develop a perspective on what happened, by who, to whom, why, and what one was and was not able to do and control within the traumatic experience; recognizing and coming to terms with the helplessness of the trauma.
- Accept full responsibility for one's behaviors as is appropriate and ultimately relinquish inappropriate assumption of responsibility and guilt after therapeutically addressing survivor guilt.
- Create meaning out of the traumatic experience.

- Integrate the aspects of the trauma and its meaning into the assumptive world; placing the event in psychic continuity within the totality of one's past, present, and future.
- Form a new identity reflecting one's survival of the traumatic experience and the integration of the extraordinary into one's life.
- Reinvest in love, work, and play; reconnecting with others and reassuring the continued flow of life and development halted by the traumatic experience.

These goals specific to posttraumatic stress are facilitated by 11 therapeutic processes that the caregiver must integrate with interventions that either facilitate uncomplicated mourning or work through complicated mourning. Interventions which work through complicated mourning are discussed in Rando (1993) and not repeated here. Those that pertain specifically to posttraumatic stress are addressed there as well, but are also delineated below in summary:

1. Establish a trusting relationship.
2. Provide psychoeducational and normalizing information about posttraumatic stress and trauma, loss, grief, and mourning.
3. Focus interventions not only on the cardinal symptoms of posttraumatic stress, but also on (a) the defenses erected against the symptoms (e.g., distancing or distortion), (b) the behaviors used to control the symptoms (e.g., acting out or self-medication through drug abuse), and (c) the skills required to implement alternative responses to the symptoms and promote healthy posttraumatic existence (e.g., assertiveness or problem solving).
4. Intervene in denial and numbing reactions.
5. Intervene in intrusive and repetitive reactions.
6. Assist in the recall of the trauma.
7. Enable appropriate acceptance of the helplessness and powerlessness during the trauma.
8. Work to understand, transform, and, as appropriate, transcend survivor guilt.
9. Assist in the management of anxiety associated with traumatic memories.
10. Enable the individual to recollect and reintegrate traumatic memories into a new identity while adapting to, reconnecting to, and reinvesting in a revised assumptive and external world; facilitating healthy reintegration, rebuilding, and reconnecting.
11. Provide access to proper medical and psychopharmacological treatment as necessary.

A Caveat for Caregivers

Treating those mourning traumatic deaths is often enormously stressful for caregivers. We are susceptible to our own posttraumatic stress reactions secondary to this work and are vulnerable to countertransference phenomena and a number of therapeutic errors in working with this population. The reader is referred to Rando (1993) for full discussion of the personal and professional pitfalls and promises of providing care to the traumatized mourner.

Summary

Today's deaths are increasingly more likely to result from circumstances that are traumatic in nature. Reactions to death in these circumstances tend to complicate the normal processes of grief and mourning. Consequently, caregivers must be prepared to address both the posttraumatic elements of the bereavement, as well as its loss-related elements. Failure to understand the dynamics and complications of posttraumatic stress seriously hampers the caregiver in his or her attempts to uncomplicate the mourning and enable the mourner to achieve healthy accommodation to the loss, reintegration after it, and the resumption of appropriate investment and growth.

References

American Psychiatric Association. (1987). *Diagnostic and statistical manual of mental disorders, third edition, revised.* Washington, DC: Author.

Amick-McMullan, A., Kilpatrick, D., Veronen, L., & Smith, S. (1989). Family survivors of homicide victims: Theoretical perspectives and an exploratory study. *Journal of Traumatic Stress, 2,* 21–35.

Bugen, L. (1979). Human grief: A model for prediction and intervention. In L. Bugen (Ed.), *Death and dying: Theory, research, practice.* Dubuque, IA: William C. Brown.

Figley, C. (1985). Introduction. In C. Figley (Ed.), *Trauma and its wake: The study and treatment of post-traumatic stress disorder.* New York: Brunner/Mazel.

Horowitz, M. (1985). Disasters and psychological responses to stress. *Psychiatric Annals, 15,* 161–167.

Horowitz, M.(1986). *Stress response syndromes* (2nd ed.). Northvale, NJ: Jason Aronson.

Kastenbaum, R. (1969). Death and bereavement in later life. In A. H. Kutscher (Ed.), *Death and bereavement.* Springfield, IL. Charles C Thomas.

Lindy, J., Green, B., Grace, M., & Titchener, J. (1983). Psychotherapy with survivors of the Beverly Hills Supper Club fire. *American Journal of Psychotherapy, 37,* 593–610.

Merriam-Webster Inc. (1987). *Webster's ninth new collegiate dictionary.* Springfield, MA: Author.

Ochberg, F. (1988). Post-traumatic therapy and victims of violence. In F. Ochberg (Ed.), *Post-traumatic therapy and victims of violence.* New York: Brunner/ Mazel.

Platt, L. (1991, April 25). Workshop on "Interventions for Complicated Grief: Helping the Survivors of Sudden and Violent Death" Presented at the 13th annual conference of the Association for Death Education and Counseling, Duluth, MN.

Rando, T. (1984). *Grief, dying and death: Clinical interventions for caregivers.* Champaign, IL: Research Press.

Rando, T. (1993). *Treatment of complicated mourning.* Champaign, IL: Research Press.

Raphael, B. (1983). *The anatomy of bereavement.* New York: Basic Books.

Raphael, B. (1986). *When disaster strikes: How individuals and communities cope with catastrophe.* New York: Basic Books.

Redmond, L. (1989). *Surviving: When someone you love was murdered.* Clearwater, FL: Psychological Consultation and Education Services.

Rynearson, E. (1987). Psychological adjustment to unnatural dying. In S. Zisook (Ed.), *Biopsychosocial aspects of bereavement.* Washington, DC: American Psychiatric Press.

Rynearson, E. (1988). The homicide of a child. In F. Ochberg (Ed.), *Post-traumatic therapy and victims of violence.* New York: Brunner/Mazel.

Sixteen

Suicide
Understanding Those
Considering Premature Exits

Judith M. Stillion

Judith M. Stillion is a Professor of Psychology at Western Carolina University in Cullowhee, North Carolina. She is currently serving as Associate Vice Chancellor for Academic Affairs and University Planner at the University. She received her bachelor's degree in education from the University of Southern Maine, her master's degree in counseling from the University of New Mexico, and her Ph.D. from the University of Alabama in psychology.

She is the author of nearly 50 articles and chapters dealing with attitudes toward suicide, children and death, the nuclear threat, and sex differences in death and dying. In 1984, she edited a special issue of Death Education *on the subject of suicide. Her research on sex differences in suicide attitudes received national attention when it was presented at the American Psychological Association Convention in 1984. Her first book,* Death and the Sexes: An Examination of Differential Longevity, Attitudes, Behaviors and Coping Skills, *was published in 1985. Her second book, coauthored by Eugene McDowell and Jacque May, appeared in 1989. Entitled* Suicide Across the Lifespan: Premature Exits, *it is already into its second printing.*

Stillion has been active in the development of the field of death and dying. A charter member of the Association for Death Education and Counseling, she served as its Vice President from 1985 to 1987, as President from 1987 to 1989, and has completed six years on the Board as Immediate Past President. She has lifetime certification as a Death Educator from the Association of Death Education and Counseling. She has also served as an Associate Editor of Death Studies for over a decade. In demand as a speaker, she has made major addresses at two of the King's College Conferences in London, Ontario, as well as nearly 100 presentations at other national, regional, state, and local meetings.

Introduction

Suicide is arguably the most complex and the least understood of all human behaviors, although it has been documented throughout history. The Old Testament of the Bible, for example, describes the suicide of Samson, which is thought to have occurred around 1000 B.C. This suicide seems to be the final self-inflicted punishment for failing to stand strong in his faith. The New Testament describes a similar suicide—that of Judas Iscariot, who killed himself in an attempt to atone for his betrayal of Jesus of Nazareth. While a few noted suicides such as the death of Socrates (399 B.C.) and Seneca (65 A.D.) came about as a result of pressure from their societies to atone for perceived crimes against the state, most suicides recorded in early history seem to involve the themes of regret and atonement (Stillion, McDowell, & May, 1989).

As years passed, under the influence of the Catholic Church, suicidal behavior came to be regarded as sinful. Around 400 A.D., St. Augustine taught that suicide was a sin because it violated the sixth commandment ("Thou shalt not kill") and it usurped the power over life and death that belonged only to God. Three Councils of the Roman Catholic Church held in the sixth century built on Augustine's pronouncements, establishing specific punishments for suicides. Thus began more than a 1,000 years of persecution of suicide as a sin—one for which many believed there could be no atonement or forgiveness. Punishments were directed toward both those who committed suicide and their families. For example, the bodies of suicide victims could not be buried in consecrated ground. It was not unusual for bodies of suicide victims to be dragged behind carts or buried at crossroads with stakes in their hearts (Farberow, 1975). Family members of suicides in some cultures could not inherit estates and, in some sects, could not enter religious orders. By 1670, suicide began to be viewed as a crime against the state and secular laws were passed describing suicide as a triple crime: murder, high treason, and heresy. Even as late as 1860, there is an account of a man who was resuscitated after having cut his throat in a suicide attempt, only to be hanged for attempting suicide (Alvarez, 1970).

In the mid-eighteenth century, a French physician, Merian, published the first medical treatise that held that suicide resulted from emotional illness, thus ushering in the modern era which views suicide from a mental health perspective (1763). In 1838, another influential physician, Esquirol, wrote a widely read chapter that described suicide as a symptom of mental (1965). By the end of the nineteenth century, this view, which was gaining acceptance, was helped along by the now classical work of Durkheim, *Le Suicide* (1897), which postulated that suicide occurred as a result of the pain individuals experienced from not fitting well within their societies.

In the early part of the twentieth century, Freud began theorizing about the roots of human behavior. Freud described suicidal behavior in *Mourning and Melancholia* (1917) as a result of intrapsychic conflict He suggested that much of the pain experienced by suicidal people resulted from unresolved struggles among the id, ego, and superego of the personality. Later, he suggested that suicidal behavior might also result from anger or aggression turned inward. Durkheim and Freud's work, taken together, ushered in modern study of suicide in the social and behavioral sciences.

Neither the sociological nor the psychological approaches used throughout the twentieth century have been able to capture the complexity of suicidal behavior. Recent biological discoveries (e.g., Asberg & Traskman, 1976, 1981) have added a new dimension to the understanding of suicide as have studies into the thought patterns (e.g., Beck, Rush, Shaw, & Emery, 1979) and the environmental circumstances of suicidal people (e.g., Maris, 1981). Perhaps equally important, our growing insight concerning the predictable changes that occur across the life-span has added to our understanding of suicide.

In spite of all these developments, suicidal behavior remains one of the least understood of all human behaviors. Those considering, attempting, or completing suicide are still viewed negatively by most people. Attitudes toward suicidal people range from pity and compassion to impatience with or contempt for the weakness or mental instability of the suicidal person. Current approaches to dealing with suicidal people include ignoring them, treating them as sinners or criminals, counseling with them in a variety of ways designed to influence their behavior, treating them with drugs, institutionalizing them against their wills, and helping them to commit suicide.

In order to make sense of this confused situation as well as to attempt to organize the growing body of literature about suicide, researchers and practitioners need a model that will organize the interactions of the various causal aspects of suicide, shed light on the act of suicide as carried out by people of different ages and still allow for the individual differences seen in suicidal behavior.

The Suicide Trajectory: A Model

Such a model has been introduced into the literature and appears in Figure 16–1. Called the suicide trajectory model, it asserts that much of the burgeoning literature attempting to explain suicidal behavior can be categorized into four major risk factor categories: biological, psychological cognitive, and environmental (Stillion, McDowell, & May, 1989).

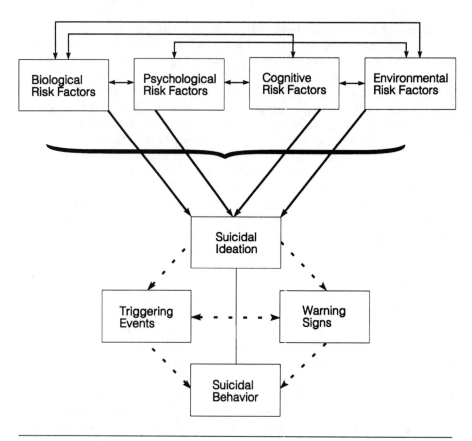

Figure 16–1   The suicide trajectory (*Source:* Stillion, J. M., McDowell, E. E., & May, J. H. (1989). *Suicide Across the Life Span—Premature Exits* (p. 240). Hemisphere Publishing Corporation, Washington, D.C.)

These risk factors may influence each other, as shown by the interconnecting arrows. As we move through life, we encounter situations and events that add their weight to each risk factor category. When the combined weight of these risk factors reaches the point where coping skills are threatened with collapse, suicidal ideation is born. Once present, suicidal ideation seems to feed on itself. It may be exhibited in warning signs and may also be intensified by triggering events. In the final analysis, however, when the suicide attempt is made, it occurs because of the contributions of the four risk categories. Understanding any individual suicidal patient requires probing into and exposing the life experiences of patients in each of these risk factor categories. Understanding suicidal risk in general requires a knowledge of the ways in which these risk factors contribute to suicide across the life-span as well as ways in which predictable life events may increase suicidal risk at various stages across the life cycle.

Commonalities in Risk Factors Across the Life-Span

Biological Risk Factors

Evidence of a biological base or substrata to suicidal behavior is accumulating from three separate types of research: research on brain functioning at the cellular level, research into possible genetic bases of suicidal behavior, and research into behaviors associated with being male or female. Much of this research has been carried out with depressed patients who may or may not have reached the point of being suicidal. While nondepressed people may take their lives, the great majority of suicidal people report depression as a major symptom. One psychiatrist has estimated that "direct suicide claims the lives of at least 15% of depressed patients" (Gold, 1986, p. 205). Therefore, it is reasonable to review what is known about the biological basis of depression in order to shed light on suicide.

A growing body of research indicates that neurotransmitters in the brains of depressed people may play a role in depression and, indirectly, in suicide (Asberg & Traskman, 1981; Banki & Arato, 1983; Schildkraut, 1965). Although research is continuing on a number of such chemicals as acetylcholine and norepinephrine, the most provocative research for students of suicide has been conducted on serotonin. Serotonin is a substance that has been implicated in the regulation of emotion. A deficiency of serotonin has been found in the brains of some people who have committed suicide (Asberg, Traskman, & Thoren, 1976). In addition, one of the main metabolic products of serotonin (5-HIAA) has been shown to be correlated both with depression and with the seriousness of suicide attempts. Among a group of patients hospitalized for a suicide attempt, those who had lower levels of 5-HIAA during hospitalization were 10 times more likely to have died from suicide a year later than were those who had higher levels (Asberg, Traskman, & Thoren, 1976). This research, while clearly in its early stages, has lent credibility to drug approaches for treating suicidal people.

A second line of research into the biological basis of suicide has attempted to tease out possible genetic components by studying monozygotic twins and suicide across generations in the same family. In a review of this research, Blumenthal and Kupfer (1986) cited three intriguing findings. First, they reviewed data that showed that half of a sample of psychiatric inpatients who had a family history of suicide had attempted suicide themselves. They then reviewed a study that reported 10 cases of identical twins who committed suicide compared to no recorded cases of fraternal twins in which both had committed suicide. Finally, they reviewed a study of 57 adoptees who had committed suicide. Among their biological relatives, 12 (4.5 percent) had also committed suicide while no adopting relatives had committed suicide. Among a matched group of 57 adoptees who did not commit suicide, only two (0.7 percent) of their biological relatives and none of their adoptive relatives had committed suicide. Later work, reported by Gold (1986), showed a familiar pattern in suicide among the Amish, who have strict religious taboos against suicide. Researchers found a total of 26 suicides across the last century in a Pennsylvania Amish group. Of these, 73 percent occurred within four families. The researchers have suggested that since other Amish families experiencing mood disorders did not have suicides, their findings might provide some support for the inheritability of suicide. While this line of research is, by its very nature, indirect, it does indicate some support for a genetic component in suicidal behavior.

The third area of research into biological bases of suicide began with the observation that, in all developed countries where suicide statistics are kept, males complete suicide more often than do females. Table 16–1 shows comparative figures for male and female suicide across cultures, while Table 16–2 shows sex differences in suicide across time in the United States. Both of these indicate that male deaths by suicide are three to five times more common than are female deaths by suicide.

Whenever a behavior shows consistent sex differences across cultures and across time, there is reason to suspect that biology may play a role in establishing a threshold or susceptibility for that behavior. A cursory examination of the literature on sex differences will find support for the idea that the differences in suicide rates by sex may be related to other accepted sex differences. Human males, as well as the males of other species, display higher levels of aggression at earlier ages than do females (Unger, 1979; Maccoby & Jacklin, 1974; Hoyenga & Hoyenga, 1979; Money & Ehrhardt, 1972; Goy & Resko, 1972; Svare & Gandelman, 1975; Mitchell, 1979). If suicide can be viewed as aggression turned inward, it would follow that male suicides would outnumber those of females. Since the Y chromosome inherited from the father defines maleness, this line of research has been interpreted as indirect support for a genetic component in suicidal behavior.

Perhaps the most important insight in the area of biology as it relates to suicide can be gleaned from Akiskal and McKinney's work on depressive disorders (1973). These authors maintain that there is always a biological component to true depression. Whether the individual inherits a genetic tendency toward depression or not, when there is sufficient environmental, psychological, and/or cognitive reasons, the resulting stress comes to be expressed biologically, changing the chemistry of the brain and adding a physical component, which they call the "final, common pathway" to

Table 16–1   Suicide rates for selected countries, by sex and age group*

Sex and Age	United States 1984	Australia 1985	Austria 1986	Canada 1985	Denmark¹ 1985	France 1986	Italy 1983	Japan 1986	Netherlands 1985	Poland 1986	Sweden¹ 1985	United Kingdom² 1985	West Germany 1986
Total	12.4	11.8	26.7	12.8	26.9	21.8	7.3	21.1	11.2	13.8	17.2	8.8	17.0
MALE													
TOTAL³	19.7	18.2	42.1	20.5	35.1	33.1	11.0	27.8	14.6	22.0	25.0	12.1	26.6
15–24 yrs. old	20.5	24.0	31.0	25.2	17.0	17.0	5.2	14.1	10.6	17.5	14.3	8.2	17.7
25–34 yrs. old	24.9	26.6	48.6	27.0	38.7	35.2	8.4	25.1	17.6	29.3	32.0	15.3	25.3
35–44 yrs. old	22.6	22.5	53.3	24.7	38.5	36.5	9.1	31.6	16.1	33.5	29.0	16.3	28.5
45–54 yrs. old	23.7	21.5	54.2	26.4	56.6	45.4	14.8	51.0	20.0	36.7	39.3	17.1	35.6
55–64 yrs. old	27.2	22.0	52.5	26.5	55.3	48.0	18.4	44.8	21.0	35.9	32.7	18.1	36.7
65–74 yrs. old	33.5	24.8	72.8	28.5	57.7	61.4	29.7	43.9	26.1	30.6	36.2	16.9	44.7
75 yrs. old and over	49.1	27.4	106.5	28.4	83.4	120.5	47.9	78.8	41.0	29.3	45.3	22.3	72.8
FEMALE													
TOTAL³	5.4	5.1	15.8	5.4	20.6	12.7	4.3	14.9	8.1	4.4	11.5	5.7	12.0
15–24 yrs. old	4.4	4.9	9.7	4.0	8.1	4.7	1.3	8.0	3.1	2.7	7.6	1.8	5.3
25–34 yrs. old	6.1	4.7	14.3	6.6	14.3	10.6	3.3	11.6	9.3	5.3	13.2	4.4	9.1
35–44 yrs. old	7.7	6.1	18.5	8.0	28.6	14.6	3.7	12.8	9.9	5.8	15.5	5.4	10.5
45–54 yrs. old	9.2	8.7	20.2	9.0	34.0	17.7	5.6	18.4	12.5	8.4	14.8	9.2	14.8
55–64 yrs. old	8.5	8.3	18.9	8.0	41.5	20.8	8.3	20.2	14.6	7.6	13.8	10.5	16.5
65–74 yrs. old	7.3	7.6	29.0	7.8	34.1	26.8	10.1	33.0	15.5	6.6	20.1	11.9	23.6
75 yrs. old and over	6.0	9.7	31.5	5.3	24.6	27.5	11.0	59.1	10.8	5.5	14.0	10.1	24.8

*Rate per 100,000 population. Includes deaths resulting indirectly from self-inflicted injuries. Except as noted, deaths classified according to the ninth revision of the *International Classification of Diseases* (I.C.D.); see text, section 2
¹Based on the eighth revision of the I.C.D.   ²England and Wales only.   ³Includes other age groups not shown separately.
Source: US Bureau of the Census, *Statistical Abstract of the United Sates: 1990* (110th Ed.), Washington, DC, 1990.

Table 16-2 Suicide rates, by sex, race, and age group: 1970 to 1986

Age	Total¹ 1970	Total¹ 1980	Total¹ 1986	Male White 1970	Male White 1980	Male White 1986	Male Black 1970	Male Black 1980	Male Black 1986	Female White 1970	Female White 1980	Female White 1986	Female Black 1970	Female Black 1980	Female Black 1986
All Ages²	11.6	11.9	12.8	18.0	19.9	22.3	8.0	10.3	11.1	7.1	5.9	5.9	2.6	2.2	2.3
10–14 years old	.6	.8	1.5	1.1	1.4	2.4	.3	.5	1.5	.3	.3	.7	.4	.1	.4
15–19 years old	5.9	8.5	10.2	9.4	15.0	18.2	4.7	5.6	7.1	2.9	3.3	4.1	2.9	1.6	2.1
20–24 years old	12.2	16.1	15.8	19.3	27.8	28.4	18.7	20.0	16.0	5.7	5.9	5.3	4.9	3.1	2.4
25–34 years old	14.1	16.0	15.7	19.9	25.6	26.4	19.2	21.8	21.3	9.0	7.5	6.2	5.7	4.1	3.8
35–44 years old	16.9	15.4	15.2	23.3	23.5	23.9	12.6	15.6	17.5	13.0	9.1	8.3	3.7	4.6	2.8
45–54 years old	20.0	15.9	16.4	29.5	24.2	26.3	13.8	12.0	12.8	13.5	10.2	9.6	3.7	2.8	3.2
55–64 years old	21.4	15.9	17.0	35.0	25.8	28.7	10.6	11.7	9.9	12.3	9.1	9.0	2.0	2.3	4.2
65 years and over	20.8	17.8	21.5	41.1	37.5	45.6	8.7	11.4	16.2	8.5	6.5	7.5	2.6	1.4	2.4
65–74 years old	20.8	16.9	19.7	38.7	32.5	37.6	8.7	11.1	16.1	9.6	7.0	7.7	2.9	1.7	2.8
75–85 years old	21.2	19.1	25.2	45.5	45.5	58.9	8.9	10.5	16.0	7.2	5.7	8.0	1.7	1.4	2.6
85 years and over	19.0	19.2	20.8	45.8	52.8	66.3	8.7	18.9	17.9	5.8	5.8	5.0	2.8	-	-

- Represents or rounds to zero. ¹Includes other races not shown separately. ²Includes other age groups not shown separately.
Source: US Bureau of the Census, Statistical Abstract of the United States: 1990 (110th Ed.), Washington, DC, 1990.

depressive and suicidal behavior. One young college student described his dramatic recovery from a serious depression in the following manner, "I knew the minute that the drugs took hold. It was as though someone turned the lights on in a darkened room. My life's situation hadn't changed. I still was hopelessly behind in my courses and my social life was "caput" but it didn't seem so grim anymore. I could handle it again. Nothing had changed and yet everything had changed." While not all improvements are as spectacular as this, the success of drugs to counteract the biological bases of depression mandates that therapists learn about drugs used to combat depression and work closely with physicians in monitoring the effects of drugs as an adjunct to therapy.

Psychological Risk Factors

Psychological risk factors form the second category to be explored with suicidal patients. In this instance, we include within the psychological category such elements as mood, feelings of helplessness and hopelessness, poor self-concept and low self-esteem, poorly developed ego defense mechanisms and coping strategies, and existential questions concerning the meaning in life.

Inherent in a diagnosis of depression are the elements of poor self-concept and low self-esteem. Individuals who see themselves positively and value themselves highly are rarely depressed. However, recent research seems to support the idea that hopelessness outweighs depression, poor self-concept, and low self-esteem as the major psychological factor leading to suicide (Wetzel, 1976; Goldney, 1981; Kazdin, French, Unis, Esveldt-Dawson, & Sherick, 1983).

Suicidal people have also reached the limit of their coping strategies. The ego defense mechanisms they have learned to use have not been effective and have left them with overwhelming feelings of hopelessness and helplessness. People working with suicidal persons should be willing to explore types of defense mechanisms used in the past and reasons they are no longer effective. They may also have to teach new coping strategies directly.

Finally, depressed and suicidal persons generally struggle at some level with existential issues, questioning the meaning of life. "From the existential perspective under the *best* conditions life is short, painful, fickle, often lonely, and anxiety generating" (Maris, 1981, pp. xviii–xix). Suicidal people often view living as an empty exercise. One suicidal woman expressed it this way, "I don't think I'll ever feel better. But even if I do, what's the use? It's all illusion anyway. All those people thinking that their little lives mean something. They'll all be dead in 100 years. In 200, nobody will even remember that they lived. What's it all about anyway?" Caregivers need to be prepared to face and deal with such nihilism in some suicidal people with whom they work.

Cognitive Risk Factors

The category of cognitive risk factors is one which is assuming growing importance as we come to realize the power our thoughts and words have to maintain or change mental states. This category can best be viewed as consisting of three major parts.

The first is the cognitive level that a person has attained. From a Piagetian point of view, we attain our understandings of the world slowly, passing through stages that include sensori-motor, pre-operational, concrete operational, and formal operation (Piaget & Inhelder, 1969). Understanding where a child or adolescent is in each of these stages is important in assessing their suicide risk as well as in deciding strategies for treatment.

A second component of the cognitive risk factor lies in the messages we tell ourselves about ourselves and the way we fit into the larger world. Meichenbaum (1985) has identified these messages as "self-talk." He maintains that poor adjustment is maintained by negative self-talk and that positive self-talk can promote better adjustment.

The third and most important category of cognitions influencing depression and suicide has been elaborated by Beck and his colleagues (Beck, Rush, Shaw, & Emery, 1979). They have shown that depressed people develop rigidity of thought. Typically, they engage in three types of thinking that may predispose them to developing suicidal ideation. These include overgeneralization, selective abstraction, and inexact labeling. Overgeneralization is the tendency to view the world pessimistically and to pile negatives upon negatives. Selective abstraction is the tendency to focus on the negative and ignore or deemphasize the positives in one's life. Inexact labeling occurs when an individual places a negative label on himself or herself and reacts to the label rather than to the situation at hand. An example of all three types of thinking can be seen in the following case. A young, male college student tried to commit suicide by taking an overdose of pills mixed with alcohol. He left a note explaining his reasons for taking his life, which read:

TO WHOM IT MAY CONCERN
Jason Kelvin Joyner
(July 16, 1968–April 30, 1989)

Why?!—Because my life has been nothing but misery and sorrow for 20¾ years! Going backwards: I thought Susan loved me, but I suppose not."I love you Jason" was only a lie. I base my happiness on relationships with girls—when I'm going steady, I'm happy. When a girl dumps me (which is *always* the case) I'm terribly depressed. In fact, over the last 3 years I've been in love at least 4 times seriously, but only to have my heart shattered—like so many icicles falling from a roof. But I've tried to go out with at least 30–40 girls in the last few years—none of them *ever* fell in love with me. My fate was: "to love, but not be loved."

My mother threw me out of the house in March. I guess she must really hate me; she doesn't even write me letters. I think she always hated me.

In high school, and even before that, nobody liked me. They all made fun of me and no girl would ever go to the proms with me.

I haven't anything to live for. Hope? Five years ago I wanted to end my life—I've been hoping for 5 years. Susan was just the straw that broke the camel's back. I simply cannot take it anymore! I only wanted someone to love; someone who would love me back as much as I loved her.

Yeah, I had pretty good grades, but the way my luck runs, I wouldn't have gotten a job anyway. I got fired over the summer cause the boss said, "Jason you don't have any common sense." Gee, that really made my day.

I walk down the streets of Madison and people call out of dorm windows: "Hey Asshole!" What did I do to them? I don't even know them?

I've been pretty miserable lately (since 1979), so I think I will change the scenery. What's the big deal? I was gonna die in 40 or 50 years anyway. (Maybe sooner: when George decides to push the button in Washington, D.C.!)

Good bye Susan, Sean, Wendy, Joe, Mr. Montgomery, Dr. Johnson, Jack and everyone else who made my life a little more bearable while it lasted.

Jason Kelvin Joyner
April 30, 1989

PS. You might want to print this in the campus newspaper. It would make excellent reading.*

There is no doubt that Jason was serious in his suicide attempt. He took over 50 pills of different types, washing them down with bourbon, on a Friday night after his roommate had left for the weekend. Only quick action by a Resident Assistant saved this student's life. He was taken to a hospital, his stomach was pumped, and he was admitted for psychological examination. On his way from the emergency room to his hospital room, he remarked angrily to the nurse, "Boy, am I a loser! I even mess up when I try to take myself out."

Examination of this suicide attempt from a cognitive perspective is instructive. Jason's entire note is a classic example of overgeneralization. A specific example of overgeneralization is "When a girl dumps me (which is *always* the case), I'm terribly depressed." However the note goes on to pile negative upon negative by discussing his mother's treatment of him, his boss's negative remark prior to firing him, and the fact that even strangers call him names.

---

*Stillion, J. M., McDowell, E. E., & May, J. H. (1989). *Suicide Across the Life Span—Premature Exits* (pp. 86–87). Hemisphere Publishing Corporation, Washington, DC.

Selective abstraction is also seen in the note. One specific example of selective abstraction is in the paragraph about his mother. Clearly, he has chosen to ignore or forget any positive caring that occurred across his childhood and to focus on recent events and the lack of letters to conclude, "I think she always hated me." A second example can be seen as he deemphasizes the positive factor of good grades and chooses to link it to a negative outcome.

Jason's remark to the nurse on his way to the hospital room is a classic example of inexact labeling. The young man has clearly forgotten that he has been a good student, that he has coped with life's hardships to this point in time, as well as any other victories, large or small, he has attained across his 22 years. All those are gone, replaced with a label that invokes utmost disgust and anger, "Loser." (As an aside, males seem to view suicide attempts more negatively than do females [White & Stillion, 1988].)

One last point about the cognitive state of many suicidal people can be seen in Jason's note. In this short note, there are no less than 45 references to Jason by name or to "me," "my," or "I." The cognitive set of the suicidal individual is self-absorption, a form of renewed egocentrism which is so extreme that there is no room for humor or objectivity. Such narrowness is the fertile soil in which suicide ideation flourishes.

Environmental Risk Factors

The final category of risk factors is called environmental. Much research exists to show that environmental factors do influence suicidal behavior. Negative family experiences have been shown to be correlated with suicidal thoughts and behavior (Bock & Webber, 1972; Garfinkel, Froese, & Hood, 1982; Pfeffer, 1986). In the example above, Jason refers to feeling unloved by his mother as a factor that influenced his decision to commit suicide. Among suicidal children, abuse and neglect are common as is the existence of a turbulent parental relationship. Among suicidal adolescents, parental discord and disorganization in the home are often present. Suicidal adults are much more likely to be living in a discordant home or to be single, divorced, or widowed than to be happily married (Stephens, 1985). Across the life-span, then, we have evidence that poor home environments are important elements feeding into suicide.

A second environmental factor associated with suicide is the occurrence of negative life events. In Jason's case, the negative life events of being turned down for dates to the proms, of being fired from his summer job, and of being "kicked out" of his home all have added to his pessimistic view of the world, his negative self-image, and ultimately to his suicide attempt.

Loss is a third environmental event that affects the inclination toward suicide. Loss of any kind—whether a relationship, a job, prestige, or a loved one through death—triggers a depressive reaction in nonsuicidal people. For those already considering suicide, such losses, particularly if they come close together, may be the final blows in destroying their weakened or fragmented coping techniques.

A final environmental factor that is related to suicide behavior is the easy access to instruments of self-destruction. In Jason's case, he had put together a lethal mixture of across-the-counter medications, the remains of several old prescriptions, and washed it down with alcohol. In many suicides, it is the easy availability of firearms that makes a suicide attempt easy—and fatal. One authority has gone so far as to point out that the rise in suicide during the last three decades can be accounted for almost entirely by the rise in deaths caused by handguns (Hudgens, 1983).

Suicide Ideation

All four of the risk categories discussed above work together to increase an individual's likelihood of attempting suicide. In order to make such an attempt, however, in all but the most impulsive suicides, there is a period of suicidal ideation. In Jason's case, the period was 5 years according to his note. He first considered suicide 5 years before, although he claims to have been feeling miserable for 10 years.

After the attempt, he admitted thinking through his suicide plans. The day after Susan broke up with him, he went to the drugstore and purchased "lots of junk—whatever was the cheapest and had a warning on it that it would make you drowsy or one that warned it shouldn't be taken with alcohol." He had a few pain killers left from an ankle injury a few months before as well as a few sleeping pills prescribed by the college doctor who was treating him for anxiety. He purchased a pint of bourbon, although he generally drank nothing but a beer or two. He even planned the timing of his suicide attempt. He would wait until his roommate had left and the fellows in the adjoining rooms had gone out for the evening.

Once he had made the plan in his head, it seemed right. He even admitted to feeling "such relief that it felt like happiness." This feeling of "being right" is typical of suicidal ideation in its advanced stages. While Jason waited for Friday to come, he rehearsed his planned actions again and again in his mind. If something happened to upset him, he had only to think, "Well, by Friday, it will all be over," and he could regain peace of mind. In Jason's case, the semi-euphoric feeling lasted even as he put on his favorite record, propped himself on the bed, and slowly ingested the lethal mixture of alcohol and pills.

For some, suicidal ideation almost takes on a compulsive quality. One middle-aged suicidal woman confessed that she "couldn't shake" her suicidal thoughts. They intruded again and again as she went about her everyday tasks, finally taking on the clarity of a vision of a place where she could commit suicide by driving over a cliff. The period during which suicidal ideation is forming may vary in length from a few minutes to a few years, but it is an intensely important period in the final definition of the suicidal act. The contemplation of the prospective suicide builds on itself until suicide is seen as "the solution to the problem of life—of having to eat, to breathe, to work, to get up each morning, to shave, to move about, to go to school, to cope with other humans, to experience pain, anxiety, and so on" (Maris, 1989, p. 450). Even when suicidal ideation is well advanced, however, some ambivalence generally remains (Shneidman, 1985). Although the decision to commit suicide may have been reached and the details of the suicide plan may be complete, caregivers may call up ambivalence with questions, such as "What would it take for you to change your mind? What specifics in your life would have to change for you to choose to go on living? Under what circumstances can you see a future for yourself?" Such questions may move suicidal persons back from the brink as their essential ambivalence is reengendered and they are forced to consider possible alternatives for the present and the future.

Triggering Events and Warning Signs

Also shown on the model in Figure 16–1 are rectangles depicting triggering events and warning signs. These rectangles are connected to the rest of the model by dotted lines because they are not always evident in a suicide attempt. Triggering events can best be conceived of as "last straw" phenomenon. The events need not necessarily be the worst losses or most dramatic events in a person's life. The crucial element in a triggering event is that it occurs *after* suicidal ideation has begun. Susan's breaking off with Jason was a triggering event. Jason had broken up with other girls before. However, this particular break-up occurred after suicidal ideation was well developed. Warning signs may or may not be exhibited by suicidal people. Indeed, his suicide ideation was so complete that he prided himself that no one or could interfere with his plan. However, there are some warning signs that are fairly common across all ages of suicide. These include verbal threats of suicide, self-injurious behaviors, and closure behaviors such as unexpected calls and visits intended as a final good-bye. Warning signs generally become visible following a triggering event or after the decision for death is finalized.

Suicide Across the Life-Span

We have already seen that suicide is not a unitary act; that is, all people committing suicide do not do it for the same or in the same way. To add to the complexity of the situation, as we have seen, there are different rates of suicide in different countries, and between men and women in the same country. At least as important as cultural and sex-related differences are the age differences evident in suicidal behavior. A reexamination of Table 16–2 in the column marked *1986 (Total)* will attest to the fact that the suicide statistics vary far more widely across age groups than across the reported time periods. Similarly, when reexamined, Table 16–1 shows clearly that differences among the age groups are at least as great as those among cultures, with the possible exception of males aged 75 and over.

As we become more aware of the predictable life stages which most people in the United States will experience, we can examine those stages for developmental events or typical experiences that may lead to added susceptibility to suicide for people of different ages. Such an examination may help caregivers become aware of the questions to ask and areas to probe with suicidal people of different ages. (For a more complete discussion, refer to Stillion, McDowell, & May, 1989.)

Biological Considerations by Age

During childhood, impulsivity seems to be one biological factor that might predispose toward suicide. Childhood suicide is often, though not always, highly impulsive (Pfeffer, 1986). Children, who have a tendency to act first rather than to reflect on the consequences of their action, may try to alleviate their emotional pain by running into traffic or jumping from a high place. Caregivers working with suicidal children need to be aware that children's tendencies toward impulsivity may make them choose highly lethal methods and act out their impulses on the spur of the moment. Therefore, it is important to keep at-risk children in "suicide-proof" environments.

At adolescence, puberty occurs with its many hormonal changes. Physically, young adolescents experience a growth spurt and bodily changes that cause them to have to readjust to their changing body on an almost daily basis. The hormonal changes no doubt spark some of the psychological and cognitive changes that make adolescence such an extremely painful period for many youngsters. Effective therapists will be aware of the many biological changes occurring at this time in life and will not hesitate to explore issues of sexuality and body image as they may contribute to impulses.

During early adulthood, humans generally experience their peak in biological well-being. However, for young women and middle-aged women, there are two biological conditions that may feed suicidal tendencies. The first, pre-menstrual syndrome (PMS), has only recently begun to be realized as a real entity. Rooted in the hormonal changes that occur across the menstrual cycle, PMS can cause women to feel depressed and/or anxious, to experience low self-esteem, and even to feel hopeless about their abilities to cope during the pre-menstrual phase of their cycle. The second condition, also related to a changing hormonal state, is post-partum depression or the "baby blues." Long recognized as a condition that may occur after childbirth, post-partum depression can be mild or severe and may last only a few months or as long as a year after giving birth. The painful feelings of depression, hopelessness, and low self-esteem may cause susceptible women to consider suicide.

In middle age, menopause—another biological change—occurs. Once again, particularly in women who have experienced post-partum depression or earlier suicidal urges, females may find themselves confronting a biologically influenced suicidal crisis. Males also face a "change of life" period. Called the climacteric, it is marked by decreasing testosterone. While not as apparent or dramatic as the female menopause, the climacteric can result in reduced feelings of virility and may lead to depression, especially in males who are experiencing stress in other risk factor categories. Both sexes begin to note the biological changes associated with aging, such as wrinkles, graying of hair, and decline in their physical abilities and attractiveness. These unremitting biological changes may feed into feelings of decreased self-esteem, increased anxiety, and result in more negative self-concepts.

In old age, the physical decline begun in the earlier stage begins to accelerate. Elderly people begin to develop chronic diseases with accompanying pain and inability to function. They may also develop an organic brain disorder such as Alzheimer's disease. The anxiety and depression rooted in these biological changes may become potent factors influencing suicidal behavior in old age. Caregivers need to remember that commitment to living may lessen as elderly people develop biologically based problems. Exploring ways to improve the quality of life with the elderly may enable them to reject suicide and renew their commitment to life.

Psychological Considerations by Age

Childhood is a time for developing positive feelings of competence. Erikson (1959) hypothesized that healthy children between the ages of 5 and 12 must build on already positive levels of trust, autonomy, and initiative to develop a strong sense of industry. Children who have been raised in such a way that they develop a world view of mistrust, shame, and doubt about themselves, and a sense of guilt will have much more difficulty exploring the many types of activities in which they may develop competence. Erikson believed that such children will develop a basic life stance of inferiority, which will result in poor self-concepts and low self-esteem as well as hinder their future growth in adolescence. This sense of inferiority may become so extreme that the child views himself or herself as unworthy or "expendable." If this occurs, suicidal ideation is a next natural step. Caregivers working with children who evidence feelings of inferiority may need to encourage children to attempt new activities in which they can succeed and support them in their attempts. Competence is a powerful antidote to feelings of inferiority (White, 1959).

If we regard the period of adolescence as spanning the years between 15 and 24, we must acknowledge two major psychological conflicts, again suggested by Erikson. First, adolescents must deal with the question of who they are. Young people who have developed a positive sense of industry and real competence in one or more areas have less trouble with this stage than do those who have major feelings of inferiority. Whatever the base, however, adolescents must struggle with both present and future identity problems. Much of the angst of adolescence, recognized since G. Stanley Hall's writings in the early part of the twentieth century (1904), stems from wrestling with the questions, "Who am I?" and "Who do I want to be?" Such questions, coupled with the biological changes discussed earlier, may so overwhelm susceptible adolescents that they feel helpless to answer them and develop a sense of hopelessness about their current and future identities and roles in life. In short, they may give up on themselves. Once again, helpful caregivers who are aware of the identity issues with which depressed adolescents are coping may help to sharpen their thinking and may be able to relieve some of the pain involved by helping them explore their vocational strengths and preferences, as well as by listening, supporting, and encouraging their movements toward self-definition.

Beginning in late adolescence and continuing throughout early adulthood, Erikson suggests the main struggle is to establish a sense of intimacy with at least one other human being. A true sense of intimacy will result in positive mental health as two people plan and grow together, each invested in the well-being of the other. The opposite pole of intimacy is isolation. Young adults who fail to develop at least a modicum of intimacy find themselves in a state of psychological isolation that may easily lead to depression and accompanying lowered self-esteem. Interested professionals working with young adults should probe their sense of psychological intimacy with others. Group therapy and/or growth groups can be powerful tools to help suicidal young adults explore new ways of being with other people and attain skills necessary to help them develop a positive sense of intimacy.

In middle adulthood, occurring concurrently with the biological decline in physical abilities and attractiveness, many people experience a sense of increased inferiority (Levinson, Darrow, Klein, Levinson, & McKee, 1978). They "take stock" of their progress in life to date and many find that they must give up some of their youthful dreams. As they begin to realize that they will never attain the presidency of the company, or have a baby, or become a successful rock singer, or attain their most secret dream of success, they become more susceptible to feelings of stagnation. Erikson theorized that healthy adults are generative, contributing to their society in meaningful ways. Suicidal adults in their middle years may no longer believe in their abilities to make meaningful contributions. They may be bored with their current roles, regretful of "roads not taken," and overwhelmed with the feeling that it is too late to begin anew. Thoughtful caregivers will take time to explore such feelings because psychological stagnation is the mirror image of depression.

Among the elderly, psychological issues include increased feelings of loneliness, passivity, and despair. Once again, Erikson shed light on the psychological poles of this stage by pointing out that healthy people at this stage experience a sense of ego integrity—of having lived their lives in a meaningful and positive manner. He characterized unhealthy elderly as experiencing "despair and disgust"—overwhelming feelings that their lives have been wasted and that nothing has any meaning. Such people are at a very high risk for developing depression and acting on it. Helping professionals dealing with suicidal elderly people may want to master reminiscence therapy. This approach, in the hands of a skilled therapist, allows elderly people to reexperience their lives and the decisions that they have made to reexamine the conditions under which they made those decisions and to attempt to find meaningful patterns and values in their life experiences.

Cognitive Considerations by Age

Children younger than age 9 or 10 have immature conceptions of death (Nagy, 1948; Swain,1979; Wass & Corr 1984; Wass & Stillion, 1988). Young children do not realize that death is final and irreversible. Because of this, there is reason to believe that many, especially younger children, do not fully realize the implications of their suicidal behavior. They often expect to "wake up" and rejoin their grieving families after a brief time. A second cognitive factor affecting child suicide is the rigidity associated with concrete operational thinking, which characterizes the mental processes of children between the ages of 6 and 11. Children in concrete operations view the world in black and white, here and now, concrete terms. They are very poor abstract and hypothetical thinkers and are unable to consider multiple outcomes in a problem situation, including the possibility that things might get better. Caregivers working with them may need to find ways to lead them to deeper understandings of the finality of death as well as to develop ways to express their current pain. They may also have to use didactic methods to lead the children to consider alternative futures. Traditional play therapy and art therapy approaches work well when practiced by a skilled listener.

In adolescence, cognitive abilities take a giant leap forward as the young person becomes capable of using formal operational thought. Such thinking permits adolescents to envision different ways of being and to struggle with deep, philosophical questions for the first time. However, it may also lead to overly idealistic expectations (e.g., of a world where perfect justice prevails) and result in disillusionment. Adolescents, perhaps because of their newfound philosophic abilities, seem to experience renewed egocentrism (e.g., "No one has ever felt like I do now. No one understands me"). They tend to see themselves on center stage and may develop extreme self-consciousness as they feel they must continuously perform before an imaginary audience (Elkind & Bowen, 1979). Such a perception may account, at least in part, for the high dependence on peer opinion during this stage. Because they feel they are the center of a drama, their peers become important to their sense of self-esteem. Effective caregivers need to remember that adolescence is the period in life when suicide by peers or by famous people may lead to copy-cat or cluster suicides. Many of the intervention approaches in high schools have been initiated because of that recognition. Many adolescents also develop an illusion of invulnerability that permits them to experiment with dangerous behaviors such as taking drugs and driving while intoxicated. These behaviors, though not overtly suicidal in themselves, may lead to subintentioned death or, at the very least, may reduce adolescent ability to develop a positive sense of identity and increase identity diffusion, resulting in lower self-esteem and laying the groundwork for depression.

During young adulthood, many people experience a cognitive reevaluation of life choices. Described as "Catch-30" by Sheehy (1976) and documented by adult development researchers (e.g., Gould, 1978), this reevaluation seems to occur in recognition of the fact that one has undeniably entered adulthood and is responsible for the decisions and directions of his or her own life. For some young adults, this reevaluation involves setting new goals and directions. For others, it involves ending relationships, leaving secure jobs, or cutting ties with parents or mentors. Such decisions always involve loss and its accompanying emotions of anxiety, depression, and regret. Caregivers working with young adults need to help them understand that even the clearest, most positive, cognitive decisions for life changes carry with them an emotional cost.

Sometime during middle age, a major cognitive change occurs with regard to time. According to adult development texts, middle-aged people begin to reckon time, not from birth but time left in which to accomplish their goals (e.g., Santrock, 1985). Such a shift in their sense of time may lead to yet another major evaluation of their past life experiences; this one directed toward setting priorities for the time remaining. It is not unusual to find depressed middle-aged people compulsively reviewing their past decisions, filled with regret for roads not taken, and verbalizing a sense of hopelessness because they feel that it is too late to begin anew making healthier choices. Faced with this situation, caregivers may need to reframe the issue. For example, a 40-year-old depressed client who had left nursing school to be married at age 20 told her counselor that she would always regret not becoming a nurse. The counselor, knowing that the woman's children were now in college, asked her why she did not return to nursing school now. The client replied that the training would take 3 years and she would be 43 years old before she got her degree. "Yes," the counselor responded, "but in 3 years, you will be 43 with or without the degree. The choice is yours." The client went back to school, earned her B.S. in nursing, and came back to thank the counselor for reframing the issue for her. Middle-aged people cannot remake or unmake their youthful decisions, but they can move forward, grounded in their own life's experience and using current time wisely, to attain the goals they value.

Cognitive shifts in the elderly include declines in rate of learning and retrieval from memory of previously learned material. While gerontologists disagree about the rate of such declines and point out that rates of decline can be dramatically slowed by involvement in life and learning, many agree that learning and memory abilities do decline after age 65. This, coupled with the growing cognitive acceptance of death as a natural, and not necessarily negative, part of life, may lead elderly people to consider suicide as a possible alternative. Indeed, much of the argument about "rational suicide" comes from and is directed toward the elderly, particularly those who are terminally ill. Proponents of rational suicide argue that suicide may be justifiable under certain conditions. A 76-year-old Dutch suicidologist is cited by Maris as saying that suicide among terminally ill people is justifiable when "(1) it is a free decision, (2) if the physical or mental condition is painful and irreversible, (3) the wish to suicide is persistent over time, (4) the suicide minimizes hurt to others, (5) the suicide helper is a qualified professional, and (6) helping decisions are group professional decisions" (Maris, 1989). Clearly, caregivers working with suicidal people in this age group need to have thought through their values with regard to quality-of-life issues.

Environmental Considerations by Age

For children, the environmental factors influencing suicidal inclination the most heavily are naturally centered in the family. Perhaps the most difficult situation for children, aside from outright abuse and neglect, is to experience confusion over role definitions, a situation that often occurs when there is drinking or drug abuse by parents. Children find themselves coping with adult responsibilities beyond their years—putting a parent to bed, attempting to prepare meals for a "sick" parent, in effect, becoming a parent to their own parents as well as to younger siblings. The strain and anger children experience in this type of situation, coupled with their helplessness to change the situation, may promote suicidal behavior in an attempt to escape. Outside of the home environment, repeated failure experiences in school may also predispose a child to depression by feeding into a growing sense of inferiority rather than a healthy concept of industry.

In adolescence, while the quality of family life is still important, events and experiences outside the home take on relatively greater importance. Peers become especially important, and loss of peer approval can be devastating to adolescent self-concepts. In addition, many adolescents begin experimenting with alcohol and/or drugs during this period. Such experimentation, when combined with the dramatic hormonal changes, may exacerbate the turbulence of this period of life. If addiction occurs, the adolescent's emerging identity is further compromised by feelings of being out of control and helpless in the face of his or her cravings. Caregivers working with adolescents need to probe personal habits in the area of substance abuse and routinely point out that many of these substances are depressants that will exacerbate suicidal feelings.

In young adulthood, marital problems, especially for women, and occupational problems, especially for men, are often involved in suicidal depressions. Women with young children in the home, especially if they have few outside contacts and little support from a husband or boyfriend, seem at high risk for depression (Brown & Harris, 1978). Men who experience unemployment or downward occupational mobility experience higher levels of depression (Breed, 1963; Maris, 1981; Powell 1958). A third factor influencing depression in both sexes is mobility, although women may be affected more strongly than men (Hull, 1979). Although people of every age may move, young adults move more often than those of other ages. The dislocation and inevitable loss of relationships and sense of place associated with moving can be powerful negative environmental factors. Finally, a new factor influencing the suicide rate among young adults is a positive test for AIDS. AIDS affects people of all ages but is presently most prevalent among young adults in the United States. One study has shown that the suicide rate among people who tested HIV positive was 66 times higher than the suicide rate for the general population (Marzuk, Tierney, Tardiff, Gross, Morgan, Hsu, & Mann, 1988). Clearly, the existence of AIDS is becoming an environmental factor that must be taken into account as caregivers attempt to work with potential suicide victims.

In middle adulthood, many normative losses occur. Most middle-aged adults experience the deaths of their parents as well as some of their friends and other family members. The "empty nest" or "child-free home" becomes a reality, necessitating a redefinition of the parenting role. Middle-aged adults may find themselves participating in fewer social activities as they become free of child-related obligations such as P.T.A., school plays and recitals, and so on. Coupled with the psychological shift toward interiority and accompanied by the cognitive change in time perspective, middle-aged adults may find themselves becoming increasingly ego-absorbed. This is also the age period in which alcoholism begins to influence suicide rates drastically. The person who was a social drinker during adolescence and young adulthood may find himself or herself an alcoholic in middle age.

The risk of suicide among alcoholics has been estimated to be 58 to 85 times greater than that for nonalcoholics (Roy & Linnoila, 1986). The rate of suicide for alcoholics has been estimated to be around 170 per 100,000 population (Miles, 1977). The typical alcoholic suicide can be described as a middle-aged male between 45 and 55 years old who is currently drinking and has been abusing alcohol for two or more decades (Barraclough, 1987). Clearly, alcohol is an environmental factor that enhances the likelihood of suicide and therefore must be addressed by caregivers, especially those working with middle-aged males.

Some environmental factors feeding into suicide among the elderly include the normative events of loss of a spouse, retirement and its accompanying relative inactivity, and experiencing society's negative attitudes toward the elderly. Although these are normative events (i.e., they are to be expected given the current state of medicine and cultural attitudes), they are powerful experiences affecting the well-being and self-concepts of elderly people. Not only do each of these experiences have substantial negative effects of their own but, taken together with other losses, they constitute a pattern of "cumulative loss" that is inevitable in old age. The elderly must continuously face losses as friends die, as they succumb to chronic illnesses, as they move to smaller quarters or nursing homes, and so on. In old age, these losses may occur in such rapid succession that the elderly cannot work through one loss before they must face the next. Feelings of hopelessness and helplessness are easily understood in the face of cumulative loss. Loneliness and isolation are also powerful factors feeding into elderly suicide (Darbonne, 1969; Miller, 1979) as is the lack of financial security. Caregivers should be aware that double suicides, occurring as a result of suicide pacts, are most common among the elderly. Euthanasia, both active and passive, becomes an issue that elderly people may want to discuss with caregivers. It is important to realize that in old age, there is less warning about suicide, fewer attempts compared to completions, and the highest lethality level of all age groups. Simply put, elderly persons do not *talk* about suicide; they *do* it (see Table 16–1). Thus, in working with this age group the challenge may become one of spotting indirect signs of impending suicide such as putting one's affairs in order and of working to keep the comfort/discomfort balance on the side of a decision for life.

Summary

Suicidal behavior is as old as the human experience. Across history it has been regarded as sinful, a crime against society, and as evidence of mental illness. Currently, in the United States, elements of all three views remain, adding to the burden of attempted suicides and that of the families of completed suicides.

Suicide is one of the most complex human behaviors to understand. Suicide rates differ across countries, between sexes, and among different age groups in the same culture. Exploring four categories of risk factors that contribute to suicide (biological, psychological, cognitive, and environmental) may help to illuminate the behavior of any potential suicide. Combining those risk factors with understanding the particular developmental stages or normative events occurring at various ages may lead to even greater insight.

The model of the trajectory presented in this chapter (Figure 16–1) may help caregivers to organize their work with prospective suicides. Models are neither good or bad, right or wrong in themselves. If they provide useful guidance to people struggling to understand a given phenomenon, then they are worthwhile. By systematically exploring the four categories of risk factors and paying special attention to the age and developmental stage of the person, helping professionals may develop a more thorough understanding of the suicidal person. Probing suicidal ideation and scanning for warning signs or triggering events typical for people of that age may enable professionals to predict more accurately who is at risk for suicide. In these ways, the model may serve as a finer screen for sifting and examining information from troubled people of different ages and may increase our understanding of those who are considering making premature exits from the stage of life.

References

Akiskal, H. S., & McKinney, W. T. (1973). Depressive disorders: Toward a unified hypothesis. *Science, 218,* 20–29.

Alvarez, A. (1970). *The savage god: A study of suicide.* New York: Random House.

Asberg, M., & Traskman, L. (1981). Studies of CSF 5-HIAA in depression and suicidal behavior. *Experiments in Medical Biology, 133,* 739–752.

Asberg, M., Traskman, L., & Thoren, P. (1976). 5-HIAA in the cerebrospinal fluid: A biochemical suicide predictor. *Archives of General Psychiatry, 33,* 1193–1197.

Banki, C. M., & Arato, M (1983). Amine metabolites, neuroendocrine findings, and personality dimension as correlates of suicidal behavior. *Psychiatry Research, 10,* 253–261.

Barraclough, B. (1987). *Suicide: Clinical and epidemiological studies.* London: Croom Helm.

Beck, A. T., Rush, A., Shaw, B., & Emery, G. (1979). *Cognitive therapy of depression.* New York: Guilford Press.

Blumenthal, S. J., & Kupfer, D. J. (1986). Generalizable treatment strategies for suicidal behavior. In J. J. Mann & M. Stanley (Eds.), *Psychobiology of suicidal behavior* (pp. 327–340). New York: New York Academy of Sciences.

Bock, E. W., & Webber, I. L. (1972). Social status and relational systems of elderly suicides: A reexamination of the Henry-Short Thesis. *Suicide and Life-Threatening Behavior, 2,* 145–159.

Breed, W. (1963). Occupational mobility and suicide among white males. *American Sociological Review, 28,* 179–188.

Brown, G. W., & Harris, T. (1978). *Social origins of depression.* London: Tavistock.

Darbonne, A. R. (1969). Suicide and age: A suicide note analysis. *Journal of Consulting and Clinical Psychology, 33,* 46–50.

Durkheim, E. (1951). *Suicide.* (J. A. Spaulding & G. Simpson, trans.). Glencoe, IL: Free Press. (Original work published in 1897.)

Elkind, D., & Bowen, R. (1979). Imaginary audience behavior in children and adolescents. *Developmental Psychology, 15,* 38–44.

Erikson, E. H. (1959). *Identity and the life cycle.* New York: International Universities Press.

Esquirol, E. (1965). *Mental maladies: A treatise is on insanity.* New York: Hafner Publishing Co. (Original work published in 1838.)

Farberow, N. (Ed.) (1975). *Suicide in different cultures.* Baltimore, MD: University Park Press.

Freud, S. (1961). *Mourning and melancholia.* In J. Strachey (ed. and trans.) *The standard edition of the complete psychological works of Sigmund Freud* (Vol. 14, pp. 243–258). London: Hogarth Press. (Original work published 1917.)

Garfinkel, B. D., Froese, A., & Hood, J. (1982). Suicide attempts in children and adolescents. *American Journal of Psychiatry, 139,* 1257–1261.

Gold, M. S. (1986). *Good news about depression.* New York: Bantam Books.

Goldney, R. D. (1981). Attempted suicide in young women: Correlate of lethality. *British Journal of Psychiatry, 139,* 382–390.

Gould, R. L. (1978). *Transformations: Growth and change in adult life.* New York: Simon & Schuster.

Goy, R. W., & Resko, J. A. (1972). Gonadal hormones and behavior of normal and pseudohermaphrodetic non-human female primates. In E. Astwood (Ed.), *Recent progress in hormone research.* New York: Academic Press.

Hall, G. S. (1904). *Adolescence.* New York: Appleton.

Hoyenga, K. B., & Hoyenga, K. T. (1979). *The question of sex differences.* Boston: Little, Brown.

Hudgens, R. W. (1983). Preventing suicide. *New England Journal of Medicine, 308,* 897–898.

Hull, D. (1979). Migration, adaptation, and illness: A review. *Social Science and Medicine, 13A,* 25–36.

Kazdin, A. E., French, N. H., Unis, A. S., Esveldt-Dawson, K., & Sherick, R. B. (1983). Helplessness, depression, and suicidal intent among psychiatrically disturbed inpatient children. *Journal of Consulting and Clinical Psychology, 51,* 504–510.

Levinson, D. J., Darrow, D., Klein, E., Levinson, M., & McKee, B. (1978). *The seasons of a man's life*. New York: Knopf.

Maccoby, E. E., & Jacklin, C. M. (1974). *The psychology of sex differences*. Stanford, CA: Stanford University Press.

Maris, R. W. (1981). *Pathways to suicide: A survey of self-destructive behaviors*. Baltimore: John Hopkins University Press.

Maris, R. W. (1989). Suicide intervention: The existential and biomedical perspectives. In D. Jacobs & H. N. Brown (Eds.), *Suicide: Understanding and responding*. Madison, C/T: International Universities Press.

Marzuk, P. M., Tierney, H., Tardieff, K., Gross, E. M., Morgan, E. B., Hsu, M., & Mann, J. J. (1988). Increased risk of suicide in persons with AIDS. *Journal of the American Medical Association, 259*, 1333–1337.

Meichenbaum, D. (1985). *Stress innoculation training*. Elmsford, NY: Pergamon.

Merian, J. (1763). Sur la crainte de la mort, sur le mepris de la mort, sur le suicide, memoire (about the fear of death, about contempt for death, about suicide, recollection). In *Histoire de l'Academie Royale des Sciences et Belles—Lettres de Berlin* [Vol. 19].

Miles, C. (1977). Conditions predisposing to suicide: A review. *Journal of Nervous and Mental Disease, 164*, 231–246.

Miller, M. (1979). *Suicide after sixty: The final alternative*. New York: Springer.

Mitchell, G. (1979). *Sex differences in non-human primates*. New York: Van Nostrand Reinhold.

Money, J., & Ehrhardt, A. (1972). *Man and woman, boy and girl*. Baltimore: Johns Hopkins University Press.

Nagy, M. (1948). The child's theories concerning death. *Journal of Genetic Psychology, 73*, 3–27.

Pfeffer, C. R. (1986). *The suicidal child*. New York: Guilford Press.

Piaget, J., & Inhelder, B. (1969). *The psychology of the child*. New York: Basic Books.

Powell, E. H. (1958). Occupation, status, and suicide. Toward a redefinition of anomie. *American Sociological Review, 23*, 131–139.

Roy, A., & Linnoila, M. (1986). Alcoholism and suicide. In R. Maris (Ed.), *Biology of suicide* (pp. 162–191). New York: Guilford Press.

Santrock, J. W. (1985). *Adult development and aging*. Dubuque, IA: William C. Brown.

Schildkraut, J. J. (1965). The catecholamine hypothesis of affective disorders: A review of supporting evidence. *American Journal of Psychiatry, 122*, 509–522.

Sheehy, G. (1976). *Passages: Predictable crises of adult life*. New York: Dutton.

Shneidman, E. S. (1985). *Definition of suicide*. New York: Wiley.

Stephens, J. B. (1985). Suicidal women and their relationships with husbands, boyfriends, and lovers. *Suicide and Life-Threatening Behavior, 15*, 77–89.

Stillion, J. M., McDowell, E. E., & May, M. J. (1989). *Suicide across the life span: Premature exits.* New York: Hemisphere.

Svare, B. & Gandelman, R. (1975). Aggressive behavior of juvenile mice: Influence of androgen and olfactory stimuli. *Developmental Psychobiology, 8,* 405–415.

Swain, H. L. (1979). Childhood views of death. *Death Education, 2,* 341–358.

Unger (1979). *Female and male psychological perspectives.* New York: Harper and Row.

Wass, H., & Corr, C. (1984). *Childhood and death.* Washington, DC: Hemisphere.

Wass, H., & Stillion, J. M. (1988). Death in the lives of children and adolescents. In H. Wass, F. M. Berardo, & R. A. Neimeyer (Eds.), *Dying: Facing the facts* (pp. 201–208). Washington, DC: Hemisphere.

Wetzel, R. D. (1976). Hopelessness, depression, and suicide intent. *Archives of General Psychiatry, 33,* 1069–1073.

White, J., & Stillion, J. M. (1988). Sex differences in attitudes toward suicide: Do males stigmatize males? *Psychology of Women Quarterly, 12,* 357–366.

White, R. (1959). Motivation reconsidered: The concept of competence. *Psychological Review, 66,* 297–333.

Seventeen

Religious Approaches to Dying

David Head

David Head is a Church of England parish priest. Since 1989, he has divided his time between his parish and chaplaincy at Trinity Hospice in South London, which has cared exclusively for the terminally ill since 1891. He has been curate in a parish in Surbiton, South London and in Marylebone Parish, London, where a church, healing and pastoral center, and medical practice involving a number of complementary therapies work side by side in a church building. He has also been an assistant chaplain at St. Christopher's Hospice, South London.

Religion, The Religious Person, Religious Viewpoints

Religion

Define *religion* at your peril. There will always be people to disagree. Your definition will already be descriptive of your values. Leszek Kolakowski (1982, p. 9) writes, "Any definition of religion has to be arbitrary to a certain extent." However, for the sake of this chapter, a *religion* is a system of beliefs, rituals, and behavior that interprets a human's total environment and defines that human's proper conduct towards it.

This chapter will only focus on theist and transcendental systems of belief, ritual, and behavior (Becker, 1973, p. 7). Communism, market capitalism, sex, money, and football may also be described as a person's "religion," being the central object of value and formative of behavior, but they don't go down on hospital forms, nor do they focus on or have much of interest to say about death.

Religions are, broadly, groups of people involved in social orders, having belief systems and behavior in common, with a common goal or focus. Many nursing handbooks talk about spiritual care rather than religious care. There is a difference. Though a strict religionist and an atheist will agree that spirituality and religion are inseparable, and that spirituality is a part of religion, those who are more liberal will allow the spirit to be part of every human being, whatever their religious standing, and will accept that they have a spiritual life, however unlived, and spiritual needs that may not coincide with religious answers. Ruth Stoll (1989, p. 11) writes, "Spirituality is a dimension within every person—religious, atheist, or humanist." It is this latter viewpoint that is most common in nursing manuals: that spiritual search of the person is a drive toward both openness and belonging, toward love and meaning, without these being necessarily found through the medium or disciplines of a religion.

Religions offer much to those enquiring spiritually; the results of other people's religious experience, writings to examine, disciplines to explore, social groups and support, beliefs and morals to live by. That is, religions offer either a framework or a system. As with spirituality, there is a difficulty in marking the dividing line between religion and culture. They overlap heavily in rituals and taboos and many cultural taboos will have the weight of religion behind them if they are clearly integrated.

A Multiplicity of Religions

There are many thousands of religious groupings in the world (Turner, 1984, p. 449). In the United States alone, there are over 900 Christian groupings and over 600 other religious groupings (Melton, 1984, p. 459). Detailing religious attitudes must therefore be very specific or done in broad sweeps.

The complexities and richness of a religion are more apparent from the inside. Simple approximations to the core beliefs of a religion do not give the same understanding as living it. A cursory glance may make oriental religion attractive to the Western mind, but generally within the limits of Western individualism. Ideas of rebirth or reincarnation are attractive to those who wish to negate the idea of their own death, but the mathematics of reincarnation, the attendant disciplines of the religions, and the cessation of consciousness between lives are seldom taken into account (Hick, 1985).

With respect to death, religions generally offer an approach to timelessness; either the entry into an eternity, or a timeless (or extremely long) cycle of existences, or occasionally the advance into a timeless nothingness/everythingness. Religions that are historically centered—often round the life of their prophet, such as Judaism, Christianity, or Islam—refer frequently to specific times in the historical past to offer religious guidelines for present living yet offer a future chronological timelessness.

Religions that speak of cycles of birth and rebirth are in themselves timeless approaches to history, and admit of an infinitesimally slow human development. However, not everybody holds to the tenets of orthodox belief of their declared religious affiliations. Individual death attitudes may vary widely from the official doctrines.

The Self-Definition of the Religious Person

Following the trends of the cultures in which it is situated, religion is experiencing movement as well toward reaction as toward customization and democratization. Religious affiliation is becoming increasingly a field with the expectation of choice, rather than of discovery or conversion. Those who were brought up strongly within a tradition tend to remain within it; but there are many others. The choice of a religion may possibly be influenced by personality type (Brown, 1988, p. 9), but it is also influenced by social relationships and opportunity.

In contrast to the growing element of choice is a growing fundamentalism in the world. The tendency of fundamentalist religion is of intense group loyalty, a nonhistorical understanding of the world and their religion, and a sense of alienation. Fundamentalists not only need an enemy, whether it is Satan or the permissive society, but also tend to see themselves as a minority (Barr, 1977). Their tendency is also to see those who disagree with them as not really religious—nominal rather than true believers. This attitude may have an effect on caregivers.

The intensity of an individual's adherence to a religion varies, and studies have shown that those with the greatest death anxiety with relation to their religious standing are the peripherally committed. The uninterested and the heavily committed suffer less anxiety (Lemming & Dickinson, 1990). How religious people are can only be judged by their own admission. Any criteria for assessing objectively a person's religious beliefs or behavior will be dominated by the attitude of the researcher. A person is not necessarily less religious for not believing in life after death; this may be part of that person's deeply held belief system. Many professing Anglicans do not believe in it, yet are more committed to Christianity than others who do.

A Provisional System of Approaches to Religion

This disintegration of objective certainty about religious beliefs and behaviors is extremely helpful in a clinical setting. It forces the caregiver to beware of unwarranted assumptions and to ask questions.

Michael and Norrisey (1984) examined the different ways of praying already existing in the Christian tradition with relation to people who used the Myers Briggs type indicator, and had found a strong correlation between personality types and preferred methods of prayer. In practice, however, the customary prayer pattern of a Christian will frequently depend on the education or personality type of a teacher, which may explain an unfulfilling prayer life. Knowing a person's preferences can be of value in providing appropriate religious and spiritual care. It may be posited that the freer the individual is to explore inside a religious system, the more relevant personality type becomes.

Before this information can be brought into play, there are more basic descriptions of religious systems that can be of help. If people's religious affiliations are primarily formative of their religious beliefs, attitudes, and behaviors, then we may posit various religious types, expressive of a range of attitudes to a number of religious concepts. These types will describe both religions and people. The types chosen here are not new; they are all descriptions that have been applied to religion or branches of religion from time to time.

If approaches to religion are primarily learned responses, the following generalizations are what we may broadly expect to happen. Both religious systems and individuals may have dominant approaches to their religion— termed here either fundamentalist, liberal, social, or mystical. These are frequently, but not always, two opposing ends of two scales: the fundamentalist and liberal scale being one of intellectual openness, the social and mystical of openness to the immanent and transcendent. Such types of religious system will be described as having different sources of authoritative cognition, different extents of authority, different goals, and presenting or offering different things to their adherents. A fundamentalist type of religion will be described as having as a source of authority revelation, often in a book; expecting its area of authority to be total; presenting demands to its worshippers; having salvation as a goal; and offering itself as the single answer. A liberal religious type will be described as giving primacy to reason, will see its authority as relative, will present opportunities to its adherents, and will have the goal of their development. A social religious type will find authority in the tradition or in consensus, will seek adequate authority, will present functions and rituals, and will have as a goal the relationship of its adherents with human and divine persons. A mystical religious type will have cognition itself as authoritative, either intuitive or experiential, will have authority over the person, will present techniques, and will have the goal of union or annihilation. A liberal approach will be less culturally conforming than a social approach.

Individuals within their religious systems may approach their religion in each of these ways. Also, individuals and systems may have more than one approach: They may be fundamentalist social, fundamentalist mystic, liberal social, liberal mystic, or others, and the separate elements of these approaches will be present. Sacramentalism, for example, can be seen as a mystical social approach. Individuals may move from one approach to another.

The value of these labels lies in their offering an "approach" model, rather than simply the beliefs and rituals of specific named religions, such as Hinduism, Buddhism, and so on, and their larger and tinier denominations and sects. A person's religious approach is usually but not always formed by the approach of his or her learned religious system. It should be taken in conjunction with the formal belief systems and with the intensity of adherence, as well, in certain cases, as personality type, in order to assess the religious needs and possible religious problems of a person either dying or involved with a death.

How Religion Approaches Dying and Death

There are numbers of questions about death to which religious systems generally provide answers: death anxiety, awareness of death, the meaning of death, and regulations surrounding the death event. Individuals' expectations of what a religious system is able to offer of direction or support in the face of death will vary with approach and intensity of adherence.

Religious systems will approach death and the fact of death in a number of ways: openly and positively encouraging its integration and embrace, and as often attempting to control it or enabling its avoidance. Religious systems may offer explanations of the existence of death or of why it is the way it is, generally or specifically. Religious systems may be used by individuals in any of these ways to fulfill these functions for them.

The ways in which religious systems approach death may be adopted at any time and in any order. The strain on people facing thousands of deaths, as in the Holocaust, will be reflected in a strain on the resources and doctrines of a religious system. Yet all systems must be able to give general and individual responses.

Religion the Explainer

Death arouses great curiosity as well as fear; the bodies of the dead may provoke a numinous awe in their watchers. As the person changes from a living being to remains and a being defined by a religious system, observers are involved in a process of questioning. Unknown things are happening to the life that was. Questions of the meaning and purpose of life are joined by questions of what happens next. Religious systems seek to give answers to the major mysteries of human existence.

No religious system can avoid the charge that at some point believers make an act of faith or accept beliefs, and that therefore however internally logical the systems may be and however reasonable, they cannot ultimately be proven. Much has been made recently of the experiences of people clinically but not finally dead. Experiences of out-of-the body states where otherwise unknowable details are later recounted suggest the existence of a "me" that is not entirely bound by physical consciousness (Moody, 1975). Such experiences may have been achieved or partly achieved also as part of religious rites, such as in Native–American sweat lodges, and may have been included in religious attitudes to the remaining life of the dead.

Near-death experiences have also included the awareness of peace, arriving in a place of light, being met by loved ones or a religious figure, and the awareness that there was a state beyond final death. Other experiences reported are considerably bleaker, and include Dantesque images of hell (Rawlings, 1978). These experiences may be the culturally formed images of a brain deprived of oxygen (Hick, 1985), they may be the results of half-hidden expectations, or they may be in other ways more significant; the question is open. If anything, they add another part of human experience upon which religious approaches can be brought to bear: liberals speaking peace (Moody, 1975), fundamentalists urging repentance (Rawlings, 1978), mystics bewailing the lost unity that restoration of life entails (Nouwen, 1990). These experiences are not yet conclusive proof of anything and do not yet significantly underwrite the explanations offered by any religious system.

Religious explanations of what happens after death are common, main-ly because the idea of continued existence after death is common to most cultures. Some affirm the complete annihilation of the self, though many primal religions that had no optimism for the afterlife still had a shadowy grey existence in indeterminacy for the souls of the dead, which were somehow not completely blotted out. Then there are varieties of heavens and hells in historically centered religious systems, and of progressions in cyclical religious systems. However, all religious answers are the result of revelation or speculation, and explain only so far as a person is content to believe.

Religious systems have to provide individuals with a means of explain-ing their own death, if they have time to prepare for it or think about it beforehand, and the death of others, especially sudden deaths and early deaths. The more that an active purpose is believed to control human life, the more the purpose and reason for this particular death is sought. Active and passive fatalism are found in all approaches to religion, and the desire for explanations and meaning are present also in varying degrees of adher-ence. Some individual deaths are bound up with moral attitudes and therefore encourage a religious explanation. There have been a rash of responses to the AIDS epidemic that speak of divine judgment, in ways that are congruent with social and fundamentalist approaches. Mass deaths, such as millions starving in disasters, may be seen by liberals as an event by which those who do nothing to help should come under judgment.

Religion Embracing Death

Religious systems may encourage adherents to embrace death. Some systems that tend to the fundamentalist and mystical are more likely to encourage this both emotionally and practically (e.g., sallekhana; see below). Some liberal and social approaches tend to be more "this-worldly," and to value human life on earth with all its attendant enjoyments and relationships more highly. Yet all see the value of a positive attitude toward death, and often count some things more valuable than life, such as the refusal to deny faith or betray beliefs.

Descriptions of the emotional embracing of death vary from resignation to submission to acceptance. These may sound passive, but aggressively wanting to die is generally observed to be counterproductive to its stated aim; and prayers to die are frequently covert prayers to avoid the realities of dying and death. Satisfaction with religious meanings encourages a timely embracing of death.

Religious meanings of death include promises of an afterlife, by which a faithful adherent is promised not only continuity of self-hood and consciousness thereof but also happiness, cycles of rebirth, by which adherents are assured of the transitory nature of the state of death, and entry into an unknown mystery that is congruent to human experience. For the religious adherent, all meanings surrounding death may be comforting. The meanings that life itself has appropriated and how far a life has been fully lived within an accepted outlook will encourage the acceptance of death. Courage to live is often seen as the precursor to the courage to die.

In a religious system individuals are already given personal validation by their inclusion into a social system. For some, their relationship with the structures of authority within the system may be masochistic in encouraging self-hatred in adherents, yet religious systems fundamentally approve of their correct and faithful adherents. The individual learns to adapt to the system and occasionally submerge. Concepts abound in religious systems of little deaths, deaths to self, or self-denial. Christian baptism is a ritual death and rebirth into a religious system. Already the adherent has experienced death technically and has been repeatedly coached in the practices and techniques of self-transcendence.

Practically, religious systems have encouraged their adherents to embrace death, as a willed acceptance or even activity. When death becomes a vehicle to the afterlife, martyrdom and self-sacrifice gain appeal. Fundamentalists and mystics are generally most open to these, having already achieved larger degrees of obliteration of the self, the former by repression and the latter by the expansion of boundaries and dropping of barriers. Martyrdoms in missionary religious systems are generally to do with the proclamation of or conflicts over the faith. In Jainism, however, where immortality is seen as being achieved after numerous rebirths through rigid asceticism, holy people will perform sallekhana (a ritual death by fasting) simply as a holy practice and not from contentiousness (Folkert, 1984, p. 266). Suicide bombings sometimes have overtones of religious martyrdom, and sometimes the death of others may be seen as a holy necessity.

Religion Integrating Death

Death is integrated as a concept into religious belief systems, and also the religious belief systems integrate death and life. Thus, religious systems maintain awareness of death, include it in its rituals in the community, and affirm it as part of life.

By practicing their religion, people frequently come across death as a concept. Well people are encouraged to envisage their own death (Shah, 1967). Sometimes this is a missionary ploy, sometimes a spiritual exercise. The value of the practice for adherents, though, is the integration, and therefore relativization, of death into the religious system.

Death is also integrated into religious life by the performance of rituals in community. Frequently those who are minimal adherents of a religious system will use its rituals in death or bereavement because they are available. Military remembrance rituals are generally more civic than religious, and provide a framework for those who have seen too much to remember without having to say too much. Familial and domestic remembrance rituals are often aided and formed by the surrounding religious culture, and present satisfying acts to perform about the inexplicable. The rituals themselves offer a chance for individuals to integrate the meaning of the death in their lives, either in preparation or bereavement (Ainsworth-Smith & Speck, 1982, p. 39).

It is perhaps in religious systems with more mystical approaches that death is integrated comfortably with life by being seen clearly as a part of it. Death is not the antithesis of life, but a part and function within it. Hindu samsara (the endless cycle of birth and rebirth) includes death as a mere stage of onward movement (Hinnells, 1984).

Religion to Control Death

Religious systems that see death as the defeat of life frequently attempt to overturn this with dogmas of the defeat of death. The promise within the system is that, for adherents, death has lost its power. By right belief, by good living, or by acquiring merit, an individual may expect to be delivered from the finality of death, in historically based religions. These promises are the more important the more dire the possibilities of the afterlife mentioned in the system and especially with fundamentalist and some social approaches.

As well as claiming knowledge of the power over death itself, religious systems may demand authority concerning the death event, so that death is no longer a part of life but a part of religion. This is again natural to the more authoritarian approaches. So religion owns death, and has the right to say who may or may not die. President Bush was typical of the "religious right" when he declared he would favor legislation to ban abortion and would support capital punishment, both preventing killing and encouraging killing. Jehovah's Witnesses provoke ethical conflict by asserting their right on religious grounds to refuse life-saving treatment for their children. Despite the glorification of martyrdom, suicide from despair is condemned widely, as the perpetrator is not allowing the higher powers the right to end life. Debates about euthanasia also raise the question of the ownership of death. For the individual, the religious ownership of death absolves him or her of responsibility in a death.

"Most of the major world religions read certain passages of their sacred writings to the dying so that they may be an inspiration to them in their last hours" (Ainsworth-Smith & Speck, 1982, p. 73). The concentration on the disposition of the person at the exact moment of death, which again is general, is focused on the next life. The classic Christian idea that "a tree lies where it falls," and beyond death there is no possibility of further change, generally antithetical to liberals, was tempered over the ages, and has also become more equivocal with the occasional necessity to switch off life-support machines. But the activity of religionists at a death bed is to reinforce the dying person within their religious system, and exert the system's claim to authority over this individual death. They not only comfort the dying person but, by their implicit acceptance of the words, comfort the surrounding adherents for whom the patient is dying safely within the authority of the system.

With all approaches, the minister/priest/holy man or woman is a person of power, representative of a system and approach. Christian clergy have sometimes been seen as "the angel of death" (Ainsworth-Smith & Speck, 1982, p. 8), the person who talks about death, breaks the bad news, and comes to console the dying, rather than having a ministry to everybody. To be singled out by a minister is either a sign of favor or danger. Yet ministers deal in and talk of powerful meanings that can comfort. In being seen as an expert on death, a minister is the recipient of the feelings of anxiety of the patient. The control of death anxiety for individuals may be assisted by turning religious people into death professionals.

Religious Ways of Avoiding Death

Religious systems have encouraged the avoidance of death, both practically, which is probably laudable, and emotionally, which is probably less so. Liberal and social approaches have generally encouraged health within this life, with fundamentalists seeing it as a matter of providence and mystics seeing the question as a distraction. Many religious laws include primitive health regulations. Not only were medieval monks the main source of medical help in their cultures but from its beginnings Judaism had codes of diet and purity that were highly beneficial to the health of the society as a whole. Untimely death served little purpose to the society.

The main way in the modern age, where health care is predominantly secular, for religious systems to be involved in the desire to avoid death is in the putative provision of miracles. Divine intervention or religious techniques may be seen to triumph over symptoms of illness or even the illnesses themselves. Circumstantial evidence abounds from most religions. One would certainly expect prayer to have an occasional therapeutic effect; what differs, according to the religious approach, is the agency which is believed to have brought about the healing. For fundamentalists, the agency is the transcendent empowered by the faith of the adherent; for mystics, the transcendent empowered by the self-abandonment of the adherent; for liberals, the transcendent allied with the unlocking of latent powers within the person; for those with a social approach, the restoration of the relationship of the personal with the transcendent. The therapeutic effect of prayer may, though, be an expression of the focused determination on healing of the subject without reference to the transcendent.

Miracles mess up dying. The hope for a miracle may continue long after an illness has been accepted as terminal, and is often only the expression of denial rather than anything springing from faith. The numerous reports of miracles encourage it. The tenacity with which this hope is clung to has very little truly religious in it. Yet a miracle affords a very satisfactory temporary practical avoidance of death.

Emotionally, religious systems can be used to avoid both the awareness of death and its attendant anxiety. Confidence in hidden meaning and in an afterlife can still anxiety, and enforced silences within religious systems (such as Shinto) as well as religious professionals using very generalized prayers can still awareness. Involvement with religious systems can form a valid distraction from the meaning of symptoms or circumstances. Because the death, putative or actual, may be placed firmly in the religious realm, it can be seen as something that needs to be seen on the religious rather than emotional level, and therefore sanitized.

"Religion" approaches dying and death along the lines of personal needs: the need for explanation, the need to affirm one's death and be involved in it, as well as the need to control it and avoid it. It functions thus because, however much authority a religious system is given by its adherents, it is essentially a human construct in response to the transcendent and inexplicable.

Helping a Religious Person to Approach Death

The key concepts for caregivers in the provision of religious care are respect, continuity, and appropriateness. The relative value and interpretation given to each of these by the caregiver will depend largely on his or her own religious approach. Hence, a liberal approach would respect the dying person's previous decisions, and provide continuing religious care of the same sort as far as it was physically appropriate. A fundamentalist approach would subordinate continuity with past beliefs to a course of action appropriate to the imminence of death and respect of a person's perceived inner needs. A social approach would—intentionally—or unintentionally—tend to be more interactive; and a mystical approach more distant, either resigned or accepting. The caregiver must be aware of his or her own religious approach, the approach of the dying person, and the ethos of the situation, whether family, home, hospice, hospital, or other institution. These need to be taken into account when deciding on any religious course of action. The dying person is facing losses, both gradual and terminal, and religion may be among the areas of loss.

Facing the Possible Loss of Religion

Religion itself may be the focus of anxiety for a dying person. Dying may cause people to question long-held feelings, beliefs, and meanings. Christians may find themselves railing at God, Muslims unresigned, Buddhists terrified. The theoretical systems they have grown up with or into may be no consolation or use; and the possibility they might be losing their faith may be terrifying to those who believe that their disposition at the moment of death is vital to their life beyond.

People sometimes seek in religion an explanation of their personal tragedy. This may involve questions about sins committed, taboos broken, faith lost, or the inscrutable purposes of some higher intelligence or law. Delving in religious guilt may end in experiencing the loss of support of one's religion, or feelings of being cast aside or judged by it. Unless the fears and guilt feelings are adequately questioned and dealt with, the religious system may seem to turn into an implacable enemy.

In practical ways also, elements of religion are lost to a dying person. Treatment may conflict with religious and cultural taboos, and individuals may find themselves increasingly unable to function in their previous religious way. A taboo such as the Jehovah's Witness ban on blood transfusion is a potentially fatal conflict. Religions that ban alcohol may demand strict observance, so that it is not administered internally in any way or as part of any product. For a proper Muslim fast, nothing should enter the body at any point. A Buddhist, in order not to let the last moment of life have a clouded consciousness, may refuse pain-killing drugs. Practitioners at these points are faced with ethical questions of the authority to act; occasionally, practitioners may cross the boundaries of these and other taboos.

Dying people face the loss of their ability to participate in observances freely; for some of them, this may be a source of religious anxiety. Maintaining a cycle of prayer, fasting, worship, and rising early may all become increasingly physically difficult. Attendance at special places of worship becomes impossible: for, say, a Sikh, with a strongly social side to the religion, the inability to attend the gurdwara may be distressing. Correctly performed ritual, often central to a social approach, may be increasingly lost to dying people.

Thus, religion sometimes finds itself as an indicator charting the decline of health, among more obvious physical disabilities. There are permitted changes in observance, such as the Islamic exemption of the seriously ill from prayer, and the truncation of Christian rituals of communion and confession to the bare essentials, and sometimes less. Changes in religious practice that aim to be appropriate to a person's impending death, such as anointing the sick, may declare categorically to someone who has not wished to know their state. Maintaining a pretense of ignorance may deprive a person and any relatives of the religious comforts of preparation. Some religious systems, such as Orthodox Judaism or Shinto, would maintain the value of life and of hope, to the extent of encouraging prevarication about the prognosis; hope and face demand that the dying person should not know. Those with a social approach are the most likely to experience this kind of conflict.

Maintaining the Religious Environment

Many health care institutions and providers have a liberal ethos, partly because of conviction, partly because it is where the lines of truce have been drawn, and partly because they offer a service for which they are paid. For them, continuity is important in religious care, especially where other continuity, such as home living, has been lost. Those with other approaches may be proportionately less motivated to meet accurately a person's declared needs.

In dealing with people of other faiths, there are many key issues in death care as far as practical caring, nursing, and attitudes and nominal beliefs are concerned. These are well laid out in part or in full in a number of books (see For Further Reading) which, unless the practitioner has a compendious memory, should be kept to hand. Knowing the names of religious books, people, and places, and the theistic position of a religious system, as well as expectations of diet, behavior, and ritual—all these are incalculably helpful in establishing rapport with a dying person; they indicate a positive, not a laissez-faire, sympathy. The practitioner's knowledge is permission for patients to be fully themselves; it enables the patients or patients' families to explain what is needed in their context with some hope of being understood. They may be nonreligious, or have elements borrowed from other religions, or belong to an obscure sect, so listening is important. A liberal approach will encourage a person to define his or her stance, and not to be more or less religious than he or she is.

A practitioner may have to involve relevant others in care, especially at home. He or she may have to refer to someone more competent—to a religious leader already involved or locally based, or to one more sympathetic to the basic approach of the dying person. The family also is likely to be involved in the same religious system and approach, and may be the best maintainers of a religious environment; praying with, providing reading and encouragement, enabling observances to be kept, supervising diet. Islamics, for example, are the natural religious carers, and may have specific religious duties such as the washing and laying out of the dead. Practitioners may not be of the right gender to work effectively, if a man expects to speak for his sick wife and does not value a woman's opinion, or if cross-gender nursing offends notions of modesty. The practitioner will seldom have to arrange for others involved in death rituals, such as Jewish watchers, employed after a death, or wailers, these normally being arranged by the family.

Caregiver needs and attitudes may conflict with religious systems and approaches, especially with those that advocate practices and cultural standards that the caregiver sees as damaging. A caregiver may even have fears about religion in general, but will tend, even from a nonreligious base, to find one religious approach easier than others; but any fears need to be recognized, because they will cause conflict on some level otherwise. Different religious approaches within the same system are perhaps the most problematical. A fundamentalist Christian may well consider an Orthodox Jew misguided but moral, yet liberal Christians as ready to pervert the truth. A fundamentalist woman claiming physical healing from God because of her faith, up to two days before her death, was supported by members of her church praying in tongues round her bedside, yet caused distress to her atheist husband and a liberal chaplain alike by her desperate and angry refusal to prepare herself. Perhaps it is easier to deal with alien responses when the world religion is different and alien. There comes a point where religious approaches and beliefs, as well as practices, cut across what the practitioners may believe to be therapeutic. Practitioners are left with ethical dilemmas arising from this conflict, especially if their belief in orthodox medicine as against other ways of treating a patient, including the religious, has a certainty that borders on a kind of fundamentalism.

The Possibility of Renewed Interest in Religion Round Death

A possible danger of a liberal approach is that the respect for a person's religion and positive desire to ensure its continuity may stifle the accurate hearing of the person's desire for change that may be positive and appropriate, once their position has initially been understood. In the same way that religion may be lost in the course of a final illness, or elements of it, so it may also be found. Those facing serious operations often ask spiritual and religious questions; these may well not be invitations to instruction, but responding to life-issues and attempting to use a known framework to make some sense of a specific incident. It is appropriate to check which is happening. This point is the most tempting for a caregiver with a proselytizing religious system, and any caregiver may use it as a chance to explain his or her own system. By overeagerness at this point, those who wish to proselytize do themselves a disservice, except possibly in closing the person's mind to any other kind of religious comfort as well.

Renewed interest in religion may be a response to fear of death, though many refuse the available comforts of religion through fear of being thought hypocritical, and scorn to turn to God—or whatever—when there is no possibility of living a religious life. It is more likely that in the light of other losses, a patient can reestablish contact with a known former "me." There is a continuity of personal meaning in the relationship with the religion, even after a break of years; however, the contact that is reestablished is often tentative.

Religious rituals offer a person the chance to participate in religious behavior without specifying the extent of his or her belief. Familiar rituals may symbolize a former life of faith; unfamiliar rituals may indicate a half-glimpsed half-hoped-for nexus of meanings. The extent of the commitment to these is only of interest to one of a fundamentalist approach.

Proselytization, actively seeking to convert, becomes more urgent to some fundamentalists with the approach of death. Some religious organizations cynically target old people's homes for proselytization, encouraging those actuarially near death to leave legacies. Those near death may find themselves suddenly the focus of other people's religious activity. Not proselytizing is generally a premise of most hospice care.

The Value of Religious Approaches in the Death Setting

Critics such as Becker (1973, pp. 198–207) suggest that religious systems avoid the reality of the human predicament by reducing complexity and chaos to a manageable absurdity. They are, however, some of the ways in which interim sense can be made of our world, enough to stave off madness.

Religious systems offer meanings in the face of the incomprehensible, and meanings that are not the individual's desperate attempt to coordinate experience but that are sanctioned by being involved in the experience of others. These meanings offer continuity of theory as well as a wide framework often integrated into cultural and psychological life. These meanings do have an observable effect in reducing terror and death anxiety. The practice of religion and involvement within it are also beneficial, as long as the primacy remains with the patient, not the practitioner. Acute stress can be relieved by prayer, or even by other religious acts, within every religious approach.

Religious systems offer symbolic languages for experiencing the event. Many religious language systems include much metaphor and become paradigms of expressions of personal awareness surrounding death. The possibility of asking religious questions as either a half-way stage toward or metaphor for personal feelings gives people a chance to take their time with expressions of awareness, or to continue to talk in a soothing code, until openness is appropriate or bearable.

Lifton (1973) has written of five modes of the sense of immortality: the biological, continuity of family, tribe, or humanity; the theological; personal influence; the continuity of nature; and experiential transcendence. The sense of immortality is not limited to the religious, and the nonreligious approach to immortality will be indicative of the personal approach to religion; for instance, those with a social approach to religion are likely to emerge (if at all) from a biological nonreligious view and posit a peopled afterlife. Those who as agnostics hold personal influence and achievements on the one hand and nature as the other (i.e., individual and global creativity) to be the most satisfactory image will find themselves most at ease with a liberal approach. Religious systems cannot promise immortality without fail. Yet experiential transcendence, a psychic losing oneself to the point of the disappearance of death, is possible in religious systems and one of the by-products of mystical technique. The theological immortality of the religious triumph over death, the only immortality satisfying to fundamentalists and available to all, is the least accessible to those outside a system.

There is value in human terms in having meanings and rituals that alleviate distress, symbolic language, and one of a number of senses of immortality, all of which religious systems provide. Although religious systems may sadly be used to blanket emotions and perceptions of reality, they are also disciplines through which openness and understanding may be found.

References

Ainsworth-Smith, I., & Speck, P. (1982). *Letting go: Caring for the dying and bereaved.* London: SPCK.

Barr, J. (1977). *Fundamentalism.* London: SCM Press.

Becker, E. (1973). *The denial of death.* New York: Free Press.

Brown, L. (1988). *The psychology of religion—An introduction.* London: SPCK.

Hick, J. (1985). *Death and eternal life.* London: Macmillan.

Hinnells, J. R. (Ed.). (1984). *The Penguin dictionary of religions.* London: Penguin.

Kolakowski, L. (1982). *Religion.* Fontana.

Leming, M. R., & Dickinson, G. E. (1990). *Understanding dying, death, and bereavement.* Fort Worth, TX: Holt, Rinehart and Winston.

Lifton, R. J. (1973). The sense of immortality: On death and the continuity of life. *American Journal of Psychoanalysis, 33,* 3–15.

Melton, J. G. (1984). Modern alternative religions in the west. In J. R. Hinnells (Ed.), *A handbook of living religions.* New York: Viking Penguin.

Michael, C. P., & Norrisey, M. C. (1984). *Prayer and temperament: Different prayer forms for different personality types.* Charlottesville: The Open Door.

Moody, R. A., Jr. (1975). *Life after life.* Covington, GA: Mockingbird.

Nouwen, H. J. M. (1990). *Beyond the mirror.* London: Fount.

Rawlings, M. (1978). *Beyond death's door....* Nashville: Thomas Nelson.

Shah, I. (1967). *Tales of the dervishes.* London: Jonathan Cape.

Stoll, R. I. (1989). The essence of spirituality. In V. B. Carson (Ed.), *Spiritual dimensions of nursing practice.* Philadelphia: W. B. Saunders.

Turner, H. W. (1984). New religious movements in primal societies. In J. R. Hinnells (Ed.), *A handbook of living religions.* New York: Viking Penguin.

For Further Reading

Campbell, A. V. (Ed.). (1987). *A dictionary of pastoral care.* London: SPCK.

Carson, V. B. (Ed.). (1989). *Spiritual dimensions of nursing practice.* Philadelphia: W. B. Saunders.

Feifel, H. (Ed.). (1977). *New meanings of death.* New York: McGraw-Hill.

Happold, F. C. (1963). *Mysticism: A study and an anthology.* London: Penguin.

Hinnells, J. R. (Ed.). (1984). *A handbook of living religions.* New York: Viking Penguin.

Hoban, R. (1983). *Pilgermann.* London: Jonathan Cape.

McGilloway, O., & Myco, F. (1985). *Nursing and spiritual care.* London: Harper and Row.

Neuberger, J. (1987). *Caring for dying people of different faiths.* London: Austen Cornish.

Report of the Archibishops' Commission on Christian Doctrine. (1971). *Prayer and the departed.* London: SPCK.

Sampson, C. (1982). *The neglected ethic: Religious and cultural factors in the care of patients.* London: McGraw-Hill.

Part Three

Other Ways of Knowing

Eighteen

Past the Smart of Feeling
Some Images of Grief
in Literature, Pop Culture, and the Arts

Sandra L. Bertman

Sandra L. Bertman, Ph.D., is Professor of Humanities in Medicine at the University of Massachusetts Medical School and Graduate School of Nursing, and Director of the Program in Medical Humanities for the Medical Center. The hallmark of her teaching is the use of visual and literary arts to instruct and support professionals working with illness, loss, and grief. The Program also provides outreach workshops for patients, families, school systems, and community groups. Bertman has lectured nationally for 20 years and has won numerous awards, including the Dame Cicely Saunders Award from the American Journal of Hospice Care *for her innovative training techniques, a UPI award for a radio program on bereavement, and the 1991 Outstanding Death Educator Award from the National Association for Death Education and Counseling. Author of* Facing Death: Images, Insights and Interventions, *she is currently developing programs on the language of grief and the art of consolation, the changing images of AIDS, and the cross-cultural experience of aging, illness, and death.*

It's hard not to laugh at a dead man. (Webb, 1971)

He's dead
the old bastard—(Williams, 1966)

These rather shocking contemporary expressions of grief seem to belie the well-known, almost archetypical reactions to death and dying that are so much a part of our culture today. What of these more conventional demonstrations of the bereaved, the ones with which we feel more comfortable, even in our relative discomfort: the tears, the numbed silence, the faints and swoons, the wailing and keening? This chapter presents a critical interpretation of several images of grief from the literary and visual arts in an effort to explore the universal experience that underlies these traditional and not-so-traditional expressions, to examine the truth that lies past the smart of feeling.

Emotional Explosives

A letter attributed to Montaigne describes a father's reaction to viewing a son's dead body: "He only without framing word, or closing his eyes... stood still upright, till the vehemence of his sad sorrow, having suppressed and choked his vital spirits, fell'd him starke dead to the ground" (Parkes, 1972).

Greek objects dating back to the early fifth century are covered with funeral art. Mourners are represented striking their heads, tearing out their hair, beating their breasts, and scratching their cheeks until they bleed (see Figure 18–1).

Figure 18–1. Greek classic mourning gestures: Attic red-figured loutrophoros, fifth century. Athens NM 1170, P. of Bologna 228, ARV.2 512.13, courtesy of the National Museum, Athens.

Spenser's description of a grief-stricken woman in *The Faerie Queen* remarkably echoes these depicted Greek gestures:

> She willfully her sorrow did augment
> And offered hope of comfort did despise;
> Her golden locks most cruelly she rent,
> And scratched her face with ghastly detriment.*
> (Spenser, 1589/1968, p. 245)

Reactions, Albeit Tongue-in-Cheek

Through the wonderfully ingenuous observations of Huck Finn, Twain brilliantly satarizes the dress, gestures, and utterances detailed in "mourning pictures"—painted or embroidered tributes to the dead, often wrought by school girls, that were fashionable in the nineteenth century. Huck, though fascinated by several of these pictures, painted by a now deceased young lady, admits they give him the "fan-tods":

> One was a woman in a slim black dress, belted small under the armpits, with bulges like a cabbage in the middle of the sleeves, and a large black scoop-shovel bonnet with a black veil, and white slim ankles crossed about with black tape, and very wee black slippers, like a chisel, and she was leaning pensive on a tombstone on her right elbow, under a weeping willow and underneath the picture it said, "Shall I Never See Thee More Alas.". . .
> Another one was a young lady with her hair all combed up straight to the top of her head, and knotted there in front of a comb like a chair-back, and she was crying into a handkerchief and had a dead bird laying on its back in her other hand with its heels up, and underneath the picture it said, "I Shall Never Hear Thy Sweet Chirrup More Alas!"(Twain, 1967, p. 12)

The ultimate mockery of mourning ritual is Twain's guide to demeanor in his piece entitled "At the Funeral." In this delicious passage, the traditional, extravagant gestures of grief have been tailored to a strictly defined guise of restraint, decorum, and even studied detachment. The sanitization of ritual and behavior is explicit in Twain's language. The deceased is referred to as "the person in whose honor the entertainment is given." Mourners are instructed how to react to the flowers ("if (their) odor. . . is too oppressive for your comfort, remember that they were not brought there for you, and that the person for whom they were brought suffers no

---

* Spenser, E. (1968). "The Faerie Queen," in *Edmund Spencer's Poetry.* New York: W. W. Norton. (First published in 1589.) Reprinted with permission.

inconvenience from their presence."); the casket ("if the handles are plated, it is best to seem not to observe it"); and the eulogy ("if these statistics should seem to fail to tally with the facts, in places, do not judge your neighbor, or press your foot upon his toes, or manifest, by any other sign your awareness that taffy is being distributed").

For Twain, form rather than feeling reaches its acme in governing the degree of acceptable outburst:

> where a blood relation sobs, an intimate friend should choke up, a distant acquaintance should sigh, a stranger should merely fumble sympathetically with his handkerchief. Where the occasion is military, the emotions should be graded according to the military rank, the highest officer present taking precedence in emotional violence, and the rest modifying their feelings according to their position in the service. (Twain, 1938, p. 152)

A Place for Convention

Twain's intention in advising restraint with respect to funeral behavior is satiric. Amy Vanderbilt's is deadly serious. In her guide to gracious living, she advocates restraint in written condolences to the degree of avoiding the words *death, sadness,* or *died*. In such expressions of sympathy, she insists, "It is quite possible to write the kind of letter that will give a moment of courage and a strong feeling of sympathy without mentioning death or sadness at all" (Vanderbilt, 1967, p. 127). This utilitarian approach, although well-meaning, is misguided; it deprives both the comforter and the bereaved of the vital healing that comes from acknowledging these "unmentionables."

Traditional grieving practices, such as those depicted on Greek funerary art, were, for the most part, anything but spontaneous. The Greek *goos*, or sentimental laments, were part of an elaborate funeral ceremony and sung by women according to their degree of intimacy with the deceased or by professional *exarches*, magician-priest-poet types who were hired by the family for this purpose. These loud wailings were stylized and artificial in tone, but apparently helped to facilitate the grieving process for the bereaved, much as a wake, in which the dead body is viewed, does today. Moslem Kirghis of the Altai Valley in central Asia perform a similar ritual. Their laments present a repetoire of bereavement gestures that are not unlike those satarized by Twain:

> Two women knelt facing the wall; their voices rose and fell in continuous shrieks of lament, the wail required by custom for the death of a near relative. A relation of the younger woman had recently died; the older woman was merely sociably accompanying the lament. After half an

hour of monotonous wailing, the women suddenly ceased, took off the lofty headdresses and more cumbersome garments, and busied themselves with housework as if nothing had happened. There were no tears in their eyes or sorrow on their faces. (Strong, 1931, pp. 229–231)

Concessions to convention often place limitations on the length as well as the manner of expressing grief. In Shakespeare's *Hamlet*, the protagonist, a bereaved son, is berated for his unabashed and prolonged public display of grief over the death of his father. Claudius calls Hamlet's sorrow "obsequious," "obstinate," and "impious"; in short, "unmanly grief" (Shakespeare, 1974, p. 1144). The criticism stems less from having the feelings than for demonstrating them. "Manly grief," as it were, is portrayed by the woman protagonist in Amy Lowell's poem "Patterns." Set in the eighteenth century (frequently referred to as the Age of Reason), the lady presents a "stiff upper lip" in reaction to the notification of her lover's death. Her true reaction is betrayed only to the reader:

"Madam, we regret to inform you that Lord Hartwell
Died in action Thursday se'nnight."
As I read it in the white, morning sunlight,
The letters squirmed like snakes.
"Any answer, Madam," said my footman.
"No," I told him.
"See that the messenger takes some refreshment."(Lowell, 1940, p. 301)

The poem is a protest against patterns: the inescapable patterns of nature and the contrived societal patterns of dress, attitude, and manner. Ironically, the man who should "loose" the lady from the patterns which she so detests has, by his death, forced her to conform in the cruellest way. She can express no grief. Helpless, bereft of purpose in the world, she must carry on as though everything were normal.

In a month, here, underneath this lime
We would have broke the pattern;
He as Colonel, I as Lady...
The man who should loose me is dead,
Fighting with the Duke in Flanders,
In a pattern called a war.
Christ! What are patterns for? (Lowell, 1940, p. 301)

The Raw Expression of Grief

The epigrams that appear at the beginning of this chapter openly flout both conventional, "civilized" social mourning and the unrestrained, stylized gestures of antiquity. The poems from which they are drawn implicitly express impassioned, self-indulgent grief. Defying the propriety prescribed in Vanderbilt's etiquette, they also fly in the face of Twain's first mandate, which is absolutely *not* to criticize the deceased. Without regard for manners, modesty, or euphemism, the first epigram suggests laughing at the dead man; the second dares to curse him.

The overtones of vulgarity and disrespect are reinforced by the imagery of both poems. In neither case is any attempt made to remove the corpse from view or to disguise the image of death—no elaborate dress or flattering cosmetics, no concealment in a closed casket. In the Williams poem, attention and anger are directed at the *rigor mortis* of death: The dead body's silent stiffness is ironically compared with the agility, concentration, and balance of an acrobat.

> Put his head on
> One chair and his
> Feet on another and
> He'll lie there—
> Like an acrobat—* (Williams, 1966)

Without nostalgia or artifice, Williams bitterly addresses his anger at the heartless, betraying act of dying "committed" by the subject of his poem. Once a man and now nothing, Williams's subject has become illegitimate, a "bastard," a "godforsaken curio": inanimate, devoid of breath, unable to feel joy or pain. Williams finds this "nothing" insufferable and rails against it.

Webb's poem, like Williams's, forces us to face the harsh realities of death. It reminisces over the erotic moments, the dreams, emotions, and anxieties that made the dead man of his poem a unique individual. Depicting him "in bed/For the last time"—in the place associated with warmth, intimate human contact, and procreation—the poem details the dead man's decline from potency to ultimate incontinence ("A wet circle/By his penis") to underscore the bitter indignity of death.

> It's hard not to laugh
> At a dead man—
>
> A man in bed
> For the last time,
> A wet circle
> By his penis;
> His doves
> And mice gone—

---

* William Carlos Williams, *Collected Poems 1909–1939, Vol. I.* Copright 1938 by New Directions Pub. Corp. Reprinted with permission.

Harder to lie next to him,
So foolish and laughable
To cry shamelessly on his neck,
To kiss his eyes and lips;
Hardest is to step out the door
Into the sun. (Webb, 1971)

A series of remarkable sketches and paintings by contemporary Australian artist Davida Allen, in which she records her father's illness and death, provides a sort of visual roadmap for the trajectory of grief. In the first illustrations of the series, Allen sketches her father before his death, imagining him in his coffin (Figure 18–2). After his death, her preoccupation persists, only now she includes a portrait of herself grieving as part of the visual detail (Figure 18–3). Other sketches in the series include showing herself pregnant and then caught literally between the image of her dead father and the fetus growing inside her, and the addition of the words," My father is dead I weep for him" (Figure 18–4). The figure of the father remains an acknowledged presence: dead yet symbolically alive, a memory to be drawn upon for strength and renewal. One of the most moving sketches is Figure 18–5, in which her newborn daughter joins hands with her father through the boundary of the coffin. The result is a "life work" emerging from images of death, a permanent memorial to the dead person and proof positive that although "death ends a life, it does not end a relationship" (Anderson, 1970, p. 113).

Both the Williams and Webb poems and the Allen paintings express the intense emotions of grief. They also give voice to the traumatic, terrifying, and disorienting aspects of death. They are particularly eloquent in the way that they detail the antithetical desire to maintain a permanent bond with the dead and the urge to break free. Webb (1971) puts it metaphorically when he writes, "Hardest is to step out the door/Into the sun."

The works portray particularly well the unmentionables so casually comfortable for Mel Lazarus's "Momma," the comic strip character who continually berates her dead husband for leaving her with the mess of their children's lives while he plays blissfully on his harp (Lazarus, 1977). They voice raw, unadulterated anger toward the deceased, and yet, at least for Allen, they demonstrate how acceptance and even a measure of comfort can be achieved. Painful though it may be—for the bereaved artist as well as for the reader or viewer—recalling fond memories, remembering special qualities and idiosyncrasies (the "doves and mice" of Webb's deceased), acknowledging the emptiness and loneliness, railing against the inability of the dead one to offer comfort—all are aspects of accepting "the sad incompetence of death"(Cooke).

For these artists and their predecessors, exposing this distress through art is part of the work of grief. It is labor that is at once painful and healing, traumatic and cathartic. Tears—silent or histrionic—and gestures—consid-

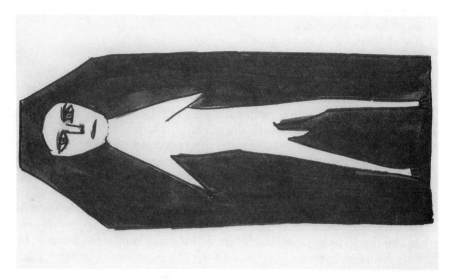

Figure 18–2

Figure 18–3

Figures 18–2 through 18–5   Davida Allen's sketches, "Death of My Father," 1983.
Courtesy Ray Hughes Gallery, Australia.

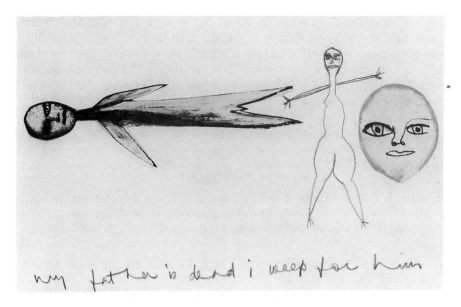

Figure 18–4

Figure 18–5

erate or irreverent—provide an outlet for painful feelings. Shakespeare encourages us to "Give sorrow words; the grief that does not speak/Whispers the o'er-fraught heart and bids it break" (1974, p. 1334). Literature and the arts, too, can give sorrow words (Bertman, 1991). They expose, ennoble, even transform the smart of feeling by awakening in us a wonderfully full, fresh, and intimate sense of it.

References

Anderson, R. (1970). *I Never Sang for My Father*. New York: New American Library.

Bertman, S. (1991). "Facing Death: Images, Insights, and Interventions." In *A Handbook for Educators, Healthcare Professionals, and Counselors*. Washington, DC: Hemisphere Publishing.

Cooke, "The Curse." Source unknown.

Lazarus, M. (1977). "Momma," in *The Boston Globe*. See especially May 21, September 3, and December 2.

Lowell, A. (1940). "Patterns," in *The Pocket Book of Verse—Great English and American Poems*. New York: Pocket Books.

Montaigne, M., (1533–1592). (1978). Description of the Death of John, King of Hungaria quoted in Parkes, C. M., "The Broken Heart," in R. Fulton, E. Markusen, G. Owen, & J. Scheiber (Eds.), *Death and Dying: Challenge and Change* (p. 238). Reading, MA: Addison-Wesley.

Shakespeare, W. (1974) "Hamlet, Prince of Denmark," in *The Riverside Shakespeare*. Boston: Houghton Mifflin.

Shakespeare, W. (1974). "Macbeth," in *The Riverside Shakespeare*. Boston: Houghton Mifflin.

Spenser, E. (1968). "The Faerie Queen," in *Edmund Spencer's Poetry*. New York: W. W. Norton & Company, First published, 1589.

Strong, A. (1931). *The Road to the Grey Pamir*. New York: Little, Brown.

Twain, M. (1938). "At the Funeral," in *Letters from Earth*. New York: Fawcett Book Group.

Twain, M. (1967). *The Adventures of Huckleberry Finn*. Indianapolis: Bobbs-Merrill.

Vanderbilt, A. (1967). *The Complete Book of Etiquette*. New York: Doubleday & Co.

Webb, I. (1991). "Poem." Unpublished; part of the Bertman Collection.

Williams, W. C. (1966). "Death," in *Poems by William Carlos Williams*. New York: New Directions, p. 78.

Nineteen

Creativity and the Close of Life

Sally Bailey

Sally Bailey is Director of Support Services/Arts at The Connecticut Hospice where she has designed and implemented a model program in the arts for patients, families, and staff. She holds a BA degree in Speech from the University of Michigan and studied Theology at the University of Edinburgh and New York Theological Seminary from which she graduated with a master's degree in Professional Studies in Pastoral Counseling. She trained in Clinical Pastoral Education at Bellevue Hospital in New York City. In addition to an extensive background in music, she is an ordained minister in the Christian Church (Disciples of Christ). As a member of the International Work Group on Death, Dying and Bereavement, she participated in the Spiritual Care work group which developed the document "Assumptions and Principles of Spiritual Care" and she serves as co-chair of the Arts work group. She is a founding board member of the Society of Healthcare Arts Administrators. Her essay "The Arts as an Avenue to the Spirit" appeared in the November/December 1987 issue of New Catholic World Magazine *and she is coauthor of* Creativity and the Close of Life *published by The Connecticut Hospice in 1990.*

Introduction

On experiencing her first autumn in New England when the trees are at their height of color, a visitor to my home commented, "The leaves are the most beautiful just before they fall." That observation led me to reflect on my years of working with the dying and members of their families in chaplaincy training at Bellevue Hospital in New York City and through the Arts Program at The Connecticut Hospice. These settings have given me the opportunity to see people's creativity at the close of life—their beauty "just before they fall."

A number of involvements with dying people at Bellevue Hospital helped form and inform my understanding of the role and need for the arts and creative expression in peoples' lives, particularly at the time of dying. What concerned me most was the fragmentation I saw in the lives of people about me. I wondered: How does one become whole? How does one achieve balance? I became more acutely aware of these questions when I saw people who appeared to be cut off from their spiritual roots in facing the crises of aging, dying, and death. I saw people who were detached from a strong religious faith—religious people, paralyzed by fears, with hearts that appeared "frozen." I pondered how the Gospel could become real to them— how lives could become unlocked so the Creator might enter. I thought about how more persons could be set free to pray and praise, to mourn and celebrate life, to give thanks in every circumstance. I saw that traditional forms of ministry do not reach all people. I was concerned that so many of the patients appeared to lack the spiritual energy to move through the crises before them.

However, I also saw that the most alive patients were those in touch with their own creativity. Three patients—a poet and two painters—were pivotal in aiding my understanding that if one is in touch with one's creative center, the spirit is energized to move one forward on the journey of life. These three artists were pouring forth their rage, fear, and anger; some of it coming out on canvas, some through words. In the process, new creations came forth. Only one of the patients was I able to follow through, and that was the poet. In time, she, who had raged against her "lot" and against those who cared for her, moved out into transcendence with a spirit of compassion for those about her—and then quietly died. Her spirit had been enlivened through her creativity. She lived as she was dying—and she died while she was living!

Since those days at Bellevue, I have been with hundreds of dying people who were enlivened through their engagement with an art form—either by actively participating in hands-on arts projects in a variety of media, or by passive involvement in viewing works of art or listening/responding to the performing arts, especially music. The following text will illustrate some of the experiences that reflect the role and need for the arts and creative expression in peoples lives, particularly at the time of dying.

The arts have been a part of the interdisciplinary program of care at The Connecticut Hospice since 1979, when the Board of Directors adopted a philosophy statement on the arts as follows: "Hospice affirms life and focuses on the quality of life. To this end, Hospice embraces and views the Arts as an important and essential component of care. Hospice believes that the Arts can enhance the personal living and working environments of patients, families, and caregivers."

Recognizing that the arts are an essential component of hospice care is further reflected in the fact that the arts were mandated in the licensure document in the State of Connecticut Public Health Code in 1980. One of the implications of this law is that the arts are recognized as indispensable to the quality of life and are considered in the same light as other services (medicine, nursing, pharmacy, social work, pastoral care, dietary) benefiting patients and families.

In the intervening years, we have grown to see that it is imperative that the arts have a place in all health care settings, and particularly, hospice programs as well as in our personal lives. The arts help to keep our imaginations alive and maintain our connection to the earth and the created order of the universe. For this is what the arts are all about: They are reflections and expressions of our engagement with our environment, with our surroundings, with our "grass roots." The arts and creativity connect us to the energy and breath of life; that is, the spirit. When we are cut off from the breath of life, we die both literally and figuratively. By staying in touch with our creativity, our imaginations are heightened to be alive to what confronts us, be it a life-threatening illness or the tremendous problems of injustice in our world.

In many ways it is difficult to write or speak about the arts because one can really only understand the arts by experiencing them in every facet of one's being. However, for the purposes of this chapter it might be helpful to broadly and simply define the arts as the creative manifestations of a person's response to one's surroundings through a variety of media (i.e., words, music, movement, film, paint, wood, stone, glass, metal, cloth, yarn, plants, etc.).

A creative artistic person works in a particular medium to make order out of what she or he may be experiencing. For, as Simone Weil (1952, p. 9) has stated: "The first of the soul's needs, the one which touches most nearly its eternal destiny, is order." Order is a conduit for truth. Therefore, one might say that the arts function to make truth more real to us, particularly the ineffable truths of life.

You may ask, "What do the arts do?" The arts serve as regenerators of body, mind, emotions, and spirit. The whole person is touched when one engages with an art form. The arts enable people to find meaning for their lives, to become reconnected to their spiritual roots, to the source of life, to overcome the fragmentation in their lives. Engaging in the arts or creative process can enable people to become a more whole person.

How is a person regenerated in body, mind, emotions, and spirit when engaging with the arts? One way to illustrate engaging with the environment and the act of creation is portrayed in Figure 19–1. We receive images and sounds from the environment through the senses of our body. The images are processed through our emotions, spirit, and mind and become inspirations/ideas that move through the body and are given form in other images and sounds. Thus, through the creative process, connections to each dimension of one's self are made. All parts of one's being are regenerated. We respond to the images and sounds in a variety of ways, depending on the meanings the images and/or sounds may have for us.

The arts are catalytic to the "unthawing" of our emotions and spirit that become frozen when we are fragmented. Many people fear becoming "unthawed" because they fear losing control of their emotions. They per-

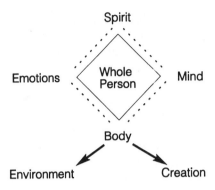

Figure 19-1

ceive showing their grief and tears to be a sign of weakness. Likewise, they fear engaging with the pain and suffering in their lives that they repress. However, experience has taught me that only when people have fully mourned and grieved their previous losses in life are they then able to fully celebrate life. Therefore, the integration of the arts in health care programs that affirm life and focus on the quality of life is fundamental. The arts enable people to mourn, to grieve, and thus to celebrate life.

As a result of these years of experience, there are hundreds of stories that could be told about the patients and families with whom the arts staff at The Connecticut Hospice have worked that illustrate the impact of the arts on grief and enabling people to celebrate life—in the midst of dying. Three of them are presented here as exemplars (see Bailey, 1987, 1990a, 1990b).

One of the most dramatic stories is about an older woman patient who was enabled to grieve while participating in an arts happening that occurred on the morning of Good Friday. It also reflects how an interdisciplinary team of caregivers worked in supporting a patient. Along with other patients, families, and several staff members, the patient came to the Commons—a large room for group events—to listen to music and watch the creation of a visual piece of art by a gifted Japanese artist who had spent several weeks at the hospice introducing rock gardens and brush painting to the patients and families.

The Japanese brush painter used a bed sheet for the canvas and stretched it across one end of the Commons. Unseen by the people present, he stood behind the canvas and began to paint to the music of a flutist and pianist who played several contemplative pieces by Bach. Gradually there emerged what appeared to be a circle of dancers. Soon, however, the figures were filled in and the image of the crown of thorns formed on the canvas. Simultaneously the music was taking the patient to the depths of her own soul and she began yelling loudly, "Get me out of here. I am sick of this death and dying." And then she burst into tears and wept.

A nurse gently wheeled her back to her room where she wept much of the day. Heretofore, the patient had not dealt with the reality of her dying nor made decisions in regard to some of her prized possessions. The artist, nursing, and pastoral care staff visited the patient intermittently through the day, allowing her to grieve about her own dying. These events enabled her to begin to make the decisions she needed to make and to move through the actual day of her death with gentleness and peace.

The second story is about a dentist who frequently spent his mornings on the patio sketching. He loved music and also wrote poetry. He was eager to try other media available to him. Just two days before his death he wrote a poem full of life to accompany the stencilled wall hanging of a bright red cardinal that he had crafted as a gift for his family.

The third story vividly illustrates a patient who vacillated between grieving and celebrating life throughout the several months that the arts staff worked with her while she was a patient on the home care and inpatient program. She was a young mother who regretted that she had never developed her innate gifts of writing, music, and drawing. She also had many spiritual issues, old regrets and memories for which she sought forgiveness and she struggled to forgive the people who had wounded her. Times of sharing music often were intermingled with reading passages from Scripture which she requested, and intercessory prayers.

This patient had a very strong need to leave her children "something to remember her by" and when her physical and emotional strengths allowed her, she busily worked on needlework, batik, and stencilling projects. After she was introduced to metalsmithing, she designed and crafted pieces of silver jewelry for her children, the final piece being a gold ring with an eagle etched on the crest to inspire her adolescent son as he grew to manhood. She struggled in tangible ways to help her fragmented family know how much she loved them. Thus, at her funeral I chose to sing "All I Ask of You Is to Remember Me as Loving You" (Norbet, 1972), a song that seemed to reflect her journey. Intermingled in her life were tears of sadness and tears of joy—and through it, new creations were born.

When people become "thawed out," or unblocked, as some would describe it, one can observe that they are then enabled to reconnect in a whole new way. They seem to discover that they are alive only when they are putting something back into the world, when they are being cocreators with the Creator of the universe. They find new meaning for their lives, new hope, and a sense of continuity as they are being creative and giving birth to something new—even as they are dying. They find they are no longer just persons who have to be cared for, but that they now are persons who are caring for others through their creative expressions.

Through the Arts Program at The Connecticut Hospice it has been illustrated that when people engage in an arts experience they can be assisted as they mourn, grieve, celebrate life, overcome fragmentation, and find a sense of meaning in their lives. Many become noticeably strengthened or reconnected to their spiritual roots. They enjoy the physical, mental, emotional, and spiritual expression and communication that an engagement with the arts can bring. They have the opportunity, in some cases for the first time, to discover a new creative vehicle or fulfill a lifelong wish through creative expression.

However, in the lives of persons who are confined either at home or in an institution because of illness, the opportunity to experience the arts is diminished if not entirely removed. This deprivation is often accentuated when a person is dying. It is surely felt in the life of the one who is dying, but it can be felt no less in the lives of those who are giving care. To help overcome the deprivation, caregivers need to assess what gives meaning and engenders the creative spirit in patients. Another story illustrates this.

A woman patient in her mid-eighties was being cared for by her 87-year-old sister in the home they had shared together all their lives. She was a retired secretary who, for over a year following her surgery, had stopped playing the piano that she always enjoyed, having accompanied singers and playing regularly in a band. She loved the times the musicians had come to her home, but now there was silence. When she became a hospice home care patient, her nurse asked if someone would go out to the sisters' home and play the piano for them. The nurse was concerned that the patient seemed depressed and "sat all day doing nothing."

The day was set, and on entering the sisters' home one could see that they were not only waiting for a concert but had brought out all the music books and pieces that had been meticulously catalogued and carefully packed up to give to the musician to take to hospice. The patient thought her playing days were over. Some time was spent reminiscing together about all the people she had played for and identifying her favorite pieces. The two sisters chose several they wished to hear played from their collection.

Meeting the patient, feeling the strength in her hands when they were shaken, and observing the agileness in her fingers suggested that she might be persuaded to try to play the piano again. This was proposed to her, while acknowledging that there had been a lapse in time in the musician's life when she did not play regularly so she knew some of the fears and stiffness in fingers the patient might experience, so not to be discouraged. Her joy of playing could come back with practice.

Together they chose a piece in which the musician was quite sure the patient could be successful. And she was. She had tried to play the piano a time or two before, but could not and, thus, could scarcely believe she was playing that day. In no way would the boxes of music that the patient had offered to give that day be taken back to hospice. She knew she would be playing again!—and again!

A person's spirituality is linked to his or her creativity and self-expression. Music was the avenue to the patient's spirit and for as long as life lasted, the sisters shared music together.

At the time of an illness or crisis, many patients and family members are isolated from their families and communities. Engaging in an arts experience can serve to create a sense of integration and community that bridges cultural, religious, and racial divisions. To illustrate, consider the words of another home care patient:

> I needed something to keep me going. I had to have hope, something to keep my mind going, to take life as a challenge and not just as a bitter remedy to exist, but to be able to live. I don't want to wake up in the morning, but each day I say: You woke me up, now you carry me along, dear God. You find what will pick me up to live. My experience has been that through the arts program I've been able to live. Although my skills are limited now, I've been given new ways of doing things that "pick me up." Bohdanna (needlework artist) has taken me where I am. She is honest and helps me work with my present physical circumstances.
>
> Through the arts program all classes of people are brought together regardless of education or financial status, or whether they're patients, family, or staff. They have the opportunity to develop their creativity, to be a person first, a "title," a "role" second. The arts bring people together. Even my neighbor who was afraid to visit me for several years because I have cancer finally came this week and we worked on projects together and picked up right where we left off as if no time had ever passed. This happened through the arts projects I have been doing and she was interested in them too.

When first meeting this patient, one could see how discouraged she was. Because she was dying, her family presumed she no longer needed her needlework, her paints, her organ—which they had packed away in the attic. In the weeks of being privileged to work with her, members of her family began to participate in the arts projects as well as join in family sing-a-longs. She loved flowers and her garden but could not go outside. By moving a couple pieces of furniture, she soon was able to wheel herself to the window and watch her garden grow.

These examples are mentioned briefly because caregivers also need to focus on the patient's environment to see what is in it as well as what might be missing from it or could be added to bring life and beauty to the patient's space.

In many respects, although a homebound patient has the comfort of dying in familiar surroundings, many times these persons are among the most deprived in regard to aspects of community as well as environment. Consider the times you have gone into homes and visited a dying patient surrounded by wilted flowers and dying plants. Yes, it is true that often people desire to keep the last flowers given to them to remember a beloved person in their life. But visitors and caregivers can brighten a patient's bedside with even one fresh flower. How simple a task to discover a person's favorite color and flower—and then surprise him or her with it on the next visit.

Gardening volunteers drawn from local garden clubs can often assist with repotting or pruning plants. For those with no plants, small dish gardens and/or terrariums can be constructed with patients and, in addition to being a source of beauty, can serve to be something for which patients can care. Regarding a patient's own yard or garden, gardening volunteers and scout troops can often help clean-up and plant. Gifts from nature, flowers, plants, seashells, and rocks continue to be among the universal comforters and harbingers of beauty for people. They love to reminisce about their special trips to the woods, sea, mountains, or desert. Again, the environment can be enhanced with pictures of their favorite places.

In the home care setting, we enter the patient's and family's environment. Even though we are guests in their homes, we can gently add grace to their space when needed. In the inpatient setting, we have the responsibility to create a space that is comforting and welcoming for the patients and families. The arts can enhance and enrich the personal living and working environments of patients, families, and caregivers. This can be achieved through the careful placing of works of art and rotating art exhibits, musical and dramatic performances and other "arts happenings," programmed for both patients, visitors, and staff to enjoy together. These, along with artfully arranged flowers and plants inside and out-of-doors and well-tended and landscaped grounds, can contribute greatly to the sights and sounds of a health care environment.

I believe that the hospice movement with its attention to establishing a pleasing and comforting environment for dying people has contributed to the consciousness being raised among other health care providers that aesthetics do matter. Aesthetics contribute to creating a healing environment. In recent years it is been particularly exciting to see old hospitals being renovated and new hospitals being built that reflect grace and beauty.

Before concluding this chapter, a comment needs to be made as to the role of artists in the health care setting, as they are the members of the team who facilitate much of what can happen through the arts. In addition to giving attention to the aesthetics of the environment, artists who are well trained and competent in their particular medium of expression, as well as sensitive and compassionate in relating to persons who are dying, make a unique contribution in enabling people in the grief/celebration process.

In a hospice team all caregivers—particularly those working in pastoral care, social work, or bereavement—have similar goals to enable a patient or family member to grieve and celebrate life. However, perhaps it is the artist's own experience of constantly engaging with the environment—with the negative and positive aspects of life—that is the foundation for all creation, that prepares the artist to be a special guide to those who are searching for meaning in their lives. For the artist in a health care team is a teacher who enables people to enter the pain and suffering, as well as the ecstasy of life and to create something new out of it.

Hospice care ministers to the whole person—body, mind, emotions, and spirit. Through our work in the Arts Program, we have seen that creativity and the arts have an impact on all these facets of human personality. The whole person is touched when one engages with an art form. Engaging in the arts or creative process enables people to find meaning for their lives, to become reconnected to their spiritual roots, to the source of life, to overcome the fragmentation in their lives. Thus, especially at a time of dying, the arts are of utmost importance to enable persons to live more fully as they are dying and to inspire those who care for them "to keep on keeping on."

References

Bailey, S. (1987, November/December). The arts as an avenue to the spirit. *New Catholic World Magazine*.

Bailey, S. (1990a). *Creativity and the close of life*. The Connecticut Hospice.

Bailey, S. (1990b, November). *Caring*.

Norbet, G. (1972). *All I ask of you*. Weston, VT: The Benedictine Foundation of the State of Vermont.

State of Connecticut Public Health Code. (1980). 184, sec. 19.13.D4b, Chapter 4.

Weil, S. (1952). *A Need for roots*. London: Routledge and Paul.

Twenty

Integration

Jody Glittenberg

A product of the Dust Bowl Days of the 1930s in eastern Colorado, Jody Glittenberg learned early the capacity for survival. As the winds blew the family farm away, her parents and six brothers and sisters trekked to the West Coast, living in a tent and on a day-to-day existence as did others depicted in Stein-beck's Grapes of Wrath. *She discovered that survival depended on social support, family, and friends. These lessons of adaptation and coping are still found in her work as a psychiatric clinical nurse specialist and a cultural anthropologist.*

Glittenberg has worked as a missionary nurse, re-searcher, teacher, and consultant in many developing and developed countries around the world, including Australia, Bolivia, Brazil, the Congo, Cameroon, Gua-temala, Papua New Guinea, and the Philippines. She is best known for her cross-cultural, longitudinal National Science Foundation study of Guatemala's adaptation to the 1976 nat-ural disaster. Her other important work has been in developing a model of community study and participation in primary health care known as Project GENESIS, a new begin-ning, which still is used as a model, now for over a decade, in community health nursing. Glittenberg also is known for her leadership role in establishing the first World Health Or-ganization collaborating center for international nursing at the University of Illinois, Chi-cago. She currently is Professor and Chair of the Division of Mental Health, College of Nursing, Univerity of Arizona, Tucson.

Three of her co-authored books have received the American Journal of Nursing Book of the Year Award: Out of Uniform and Into Trouble, *(1972),* Out of Uniform and Into Trouble... Still *(1982), and* The Biocultural Basis of Health, *(1978, 1987).*

As a professional psychiatric nurse, I know that grief is an emotion experienced by all people at some time during their lives, for we all have losses. This experience varies from individual to individual. Some people hang on to grief and, as we say, "they don't get through the grieving process." As professionals, we know there are ways of facilitating grieving as a learning, expanding, healing process. Primarily we deal with assisting people to integrate the loss, with all of its meanings, into their ongoing lives. This process of adaptation is described in my reflections on my own mother's death and the way I went about *integrating* this loss into my life.

The withered face upon the pillow was but a whisper of the being I had called Mom for over 55 years. The wisps of snow-white hair fell in waves on each side of her high, proud forehead. Lips that once had laughed and kissed and spoken of joys now writhed in pain as the growing tumors raced toward their final destiny. Her hands, now long and bony, were but a shadow of the soft and loving ones I'd known. Her eyes, once the color of the skies with twinkling lights, were now dull and lost in the glaze of the final stage of dying. She who had danced the nights away and felt the serenity of soft, loving moments now was in complete surrender as the exploding cancer cells marched on. Her voice—so clear and sweet—still retained its messages of love for each one she saw; no words of regret or pity were to be heard, but always, "It will be all right—I've had a good life; now it's time to go home." But, oh the pain for those who were to be left behind; the wish for the impossible—the weight of reality kept pushing in.

My grief was overwhelming: At times I could hardly breathe. Through the long and lonely nights and days I sailed those waves of grief, reliving each memory of the woman who had been the center of my life and was now leaving my world. I searched for something—some place to go—to soothe my aching heart.

As a professional nurse I'd counseled and calmed many bereaving survivors during these past decades, yet the knowledge of the stages of death and the dying process proved so empty, so comfortless. How I tried to be strong and courageous! I needed to be a pillar of strength for my five brothers and sisters and all my kin, for I was the *nurse*. They asked so many questions—the questions asked of professionals every day: Why does she shake? What are they giving her now? Why can't they control the pain? How long will she last? My nurse-self left and my daughter-self cried out in pain and loneliness. And as the days and nights went on, the mystery of the dance of life and death eluded all. My eyes longed for sleep, my limbs ached, and my soul felt weary, redundant, useless, empty. How could I deal with this pain-filled heart—how could I transform this loss into gain? Where could I go? What could I do?

At last the answer came: I could shape her "going world" from the one she was leaving behind. So I left her side in the hospital room and went to the small place she called home. And here I scoured and scrubbed and did the tasks of emptying—and letting go.

At first I found the usual things, the things left for all to see when a crisis steps in unannounced. The half-filled food cartons, the unmade bed, the trash to be taken out, the wash about to be done. I straightened and threw out the obvious but then I found a new awareness taking shape—the things she'd left behind. At first I saw little; but gradually, as the day wore on, I saw that these, too, left messages of her being—of her specialness.

I found empty spools of thread that once held rainbows of colors for mending or making miracles with artistic scraps of cloth. I found buttons strung on elastic for some child's play. The frugal past came swooping in as

I recalled her stories of being an immigrant girl from Denmark who was too "green" to speak "American." The family had arrived with their carton of belongings and dreams of an abundant life. Those were lean years, she'd tell, as her father, educated for teaching literature and loving the arts, now wrestled with the chores of breaking sod and building fences on the dry land of South Dakota. "They weren't successful," she'd say, "except in growing a family of 14 and a pioneer spirit."

The life was tough, but she was tougher. That's how she made her way to Colorado while still a young teenager. She told the tale often of how she met our Dad, her Fred. "He was a handsome young farmer with kind, brown eyes," laughingly she recalled. She worked as a waitress in a small cafe, and he seemed to find it necessary to eat there often. Soon there were buggy rides and stolen kisses. How she would laugh as she recalled, "We loved to dance and, oh, my Fred could sing!" Yes, I shut my eyes and heard my Dad's voice—a strong baritone that could match any for miles around. Then he'd pick up a mouth harp, a banjo, or play the piano—a natural talent. And in this dream state, I'd see them dance and hear the fiddle jump; the beat was strong and steady as round and round they'd go.

Those years of challenge had set into a pattern of saving—old mayonnaise jars, pins and thread, a garter snap, a pantyhose to mend. Stacks of Cool Whip cartons sat awaiting bits of leftovers for a tasty snack, a stew to make, a cat to feed—always to meet some need.

Then I saw the recipes cut carefully for some special dinner—a birthday to be rejoiced in, a surprise of the moment, now yellowed with time. What thought went into clipping, what plans for creative feasts yet to be done! I remembered strangers stopping at our home, but never "strangers" long as they sat with the eight of us dining on what was the major meal of the day. Oh, she could cook—some said the best in the county—and never just an ordinary thing but a feast to fit a queen or king. I could see her sweating brow as she pushed and kneaded the weekly bread, or spread the cinnamon rolls with the thickest brown sugar and real butter. Then she'd hurry to bake a pie for neighbor or friend. The old cookstove demanded coal and wood and, most of all, her special "knowing" when something was just done. I could see her face, so hurried, at the end of the day as she rushed to fix and comb her hair and add a bit of rouge and lipstick and change her apron—for her Fred was coming home!

And in a box of photos, now grown golden with time, was a picture of a beautiful, glowing girl with curly blond hair in flapper knickers and a saucy, impish smile. Her cocky stance and sparkling smile said, "Get on with life!" and so she did. I found photos of days of survival and of triumph—the babies —then growing teenagers—then new brides and grooms— then more babies. At last the room was filled with the joy of all her 22 grandbabies and 23 greatgrandbabies, too. I shuddered at the wonder of it all.

I looked about to see how these treasures spoke: There were no outer things of glitter or of gold; there were no jewels. I didn't need to check. I saw such simple things—a little pin, a single earring—nothing more. Her jewel box was empty, but next to it I saw the treasured book she always kept close by, *Mother Teresa*, her ideal. It spoke of my Mom's faith and attitude of sharing. I could hear her gentle voice, "I don't need anything; give it to the children—or some needy soul." For it was to her, the giver, that people came, the old and young, for her careful, gentle loving advice and support. Her arms were meant for hugging, her hands for kind caresses; *these* were her jewels, her special treasures. They were the gifts she gave away so freely.

The place was taking shape; my job was almost done. Then at the bottom of her dresser, I saw a box marked "Love Letters." My hand trembled as I opened it. I saw the yellowed envelopes—the first ones addressed to Mr. Fred Kropp and then below, the other half—those addressed to Mrs. Fred Kropp. How could it be, I wondered, although they were never often apart, each had saved the other's letters written so long ago. Those letters, as I read, told the story of a circle of hardships, illnesses, losses, disappointments, but also the job of living fully, of being together, and of the beauty of an unending love and faithfulness.

Lower still—in the corner of the drawer—I saw a simple black box, and as I opened it, I cried, for I remembered that day in 1960 when Dad had surprised our Mom with a new wedding ring. The first one, a simple gold band, had long ago worn thin and was lost as she worked one day. There hadn't been extra money to replace it during the Great Depression for we had lost our farm in the Dust Bowl and had to join the *Grapes of Wrath* migrants trekking our way to the West Coast. But times change; 25 years later, there was extra money. Dad took me one day, near Christmas, to help him pick out just the right wedding ring as a surprise for Mom. As he placed it on her finger, on Christmas Eve, he said, "You see it has six hearts with six diamonds—one for each child we have." Mom wore that ring with six hearts every day; then when Dad died, we didn't see it on her hand any more. We wondered what had happened to it. Now the mystery was solved; she'd prepared it in a special place—with the love letters—for the time she, too, would be gone. I closed the box and looked around.

Like a sculptor whose work is done, I saw what had emerged. Through the shaping of her "going world," I found my grief had changed from overwhelming pain to acceptance of a journey I had shared with a very special person—my Mom. What was left behind was not an empty cocoon, not a shell of a spirit nor a shadow, but the Fullness of a Being who had Been.

And so I left that space Mom had called home. Returning to the hospital room I could feel the joy that this shaping had done. For I saw emerging a newer being; the clay was being transformed. Mom was transcending. I felt serene, knowing that I, too, was part of that process—her past, present, and future—and that we are, indeed, an integrated One.

A Daughter,
Jody

Twenty-One

Olga's New Year

Myra Bluebond-Langner

Myra Bluebond-Langner is Professor of Anthropology at Rutgers University, in Camden, New Jersey.
Among her publications are: The Private Worlds of Dying Children *(1978, 1980);* "Research in Thanatology" *(Special issue of* Omega, *Spring, 1988);* "The Impact of AIDS Education on College Students AIDS Related Knowledge, Attitudes and Behaviour" *(with Ted Goertzel in* Journal of American College Health, *September 1991);* "Living with Cystic Fibrosis: The Well Siblings Perspective" *(in* Medical Anthropology Quarterly, *June 1991); and* "Children's Knowledge of Cancer and Its Treatment: The Impact of an Oncology Camp Experience" *(with Dale Perkel and Ted Goertzel in* Journal of Pediatrics, *February 1990).*

Bluebond-Langner is the recipient of several grants and fellowships from the National Science Foundation, the National Endowment for the Humanities, the Department of Higher Education of New Jersey, the Howard Foundation, and, most recently, the American Council of Learned Societies.

In 1990, Bluebond-Langner received the Warren I. Sussman Award for Excellence in Teaching. In 1987, she received the Margaret Mead Award from the American Anthropological Association and the Society for Applied Anthropology.

Interested as I am in how families handle illness and death, when my own grandmother died I paid more than passing attention to how I and others reacted. I kept detailed notes about the experience. And even as the years passed, whenever the subject came up I made note of it. However, when I sat down to write, I felt I needed more than my own recollections, my own notes. I decided to formally interview all of the family members. I asked each person to tell me what he or she remembered from the night Olga became ill through to her death and funeral, as well as other memories that they had of her. The interviews were then transcribed verbatim from the tapes. The names of institutions and nonfamily members have been changed.

In the original account that I wrote, Olga's death and all of the events surrounding it are a vehicle for exploring the complex family dynamics, individual reactions and feelings that crystalize and become starkly apparent in the terminal phases of a family member's illness, death, and funeral. Given the constraints of space, the editors streamlined the original and have focused attention on the aspects of the account most appropriate to the purposes of this volume.

Coming out of the hospital delivery room, Myra decided the first call would be to Grandpa Marty.

"Hello, Grandpa. It's Myra."

" Hiya, My. "[short for Myra]

"Rachel Olga was born this morning."

"Rachel Olga?" There was a pause and then he said flatly, "That's nice." His voice picked up clarity and definition as he said, "Why not Olga? Just Olga?"

"I couldn't, Grandpa, I just couldn't," Myra added, an the verge of tears.

"You couldn't! How could you put a stranger's name in front of Grandma's?"

"It's not a stranger's name. Rachel was one of the four matriarchs of the Jewish people. It's not like I put the name of another person or relative, or anybody else we knew, in front of Grandma's."

"I see," came the stiffened, choked reply.

"But Grandpa, I couldn't. I just couldn't put Grandma's name first."

"Well, I can't say I'm not disappointed."

"And hurt?"

"Well, take care, dear. My best to Richard."

"Will you come to the hospital?"

"I'll have to see when Mother can bring me."

"Okay."

"Bye, dear." Martin hung up.

As Myra slowly hung up the receiver, her thoughts drifted back to that Rosh Hashannah dinner. She remembered it all so clearly. The words, the feelings, the look on people's faces. It was as if it was all happening now for the first time.

Claire, Myra's mother, was rushing around the kitchen in her cobbler's apron, while Mahlon, Myra's dad, offered his brother-in-law, Harold, and his two sons-in-laws, Richard and Jack, cold drinks.

Everyone turned at the sound of one rap on the back door. The big white costume jewelry ring made a sound all its own on the glass. There was Olga, Claire's mother, her white hair catching the last rays of sunlight. Her teeth shown between her bright red lips that matched her nail polish. One would expect her to be wearing strong perfume to go with the look, and if she had not been coming to Mahlon and Claire's, she would have put on a dab or two. Olga liked perfume. She like dressing up, "looking her best" as she would say. But Mahlon claimed perfume bothered him. "Gives me a headache," he would say. Olga took note of these things. They were important to her. "You know," she would often say to Myra and her sister Judy, "I love my children [her children included her sons-in-law] and I wouldn't do anything to hurt them. Your father is someone to be respected." For Olga, this extended to foregoing perfume.

Marty, Olga's husband, was right behind her with the brown shopping bag that everyone knew contained the herring jar. "Happy New Year, darlings," crooned Olga as she kissed everyone.

"Muttle," Olga instructed Marty, "give Claire the herring. She'll put it in the refrigerator." Olga turned to Mahlon, "It's not quite ready yet, dear. It needs to stand a few more days before you eat it."

"Thanks, Mom," said Mahlon as he took her handbag and Marty's coat and hat.

"Okay. Dinner's ready. Everyone come in and sit down," announced Claire.

"Where do you want us to sit, dear?" Olga asked Claire.

"Anywhere you like, just leave this seat here for me, so I can get up to serve."

Mahlon, craning his neck over the table asked, "Does everyone have wine?"

After choruses of "Yes, thank you," from various places at the table, he welcomed everyone to his home. He raised his cup, quickly recited the blessing over the wine, and added in English, "May we all be here again next year."

With the last 'awmain' of the traditional holiday blessings said, the family dove into the gefilte fish. "Would anyone like to try some fish soup?"

"How about the roe?"

"I don't know if my fish is as good this year," searched Reba over the crowd of chewing faces.

"Nana, you say that every year," said Myra.

"Reba, it's good, like always," replied Marty.

"Very good," said Louise, Olga's youngest daughter, swallowing her last forkful.

"Really? Reba asked. "Well you know every year Dave used to take me to get the fish and… " her voice trailed off as she wiped away a tear. Mahlon reached over to his mother and patted her hand. Dave, Reba's husband, had been dead for over a year now, but the holidays were still difficult and family gatherings continued to evoke tears.

"Clairey, what a delicious dinner," beamed Mahlon as Claire and Judy finished clearing the table.

"Thank you, dear," said Claire, proud of her performance. Claire had very definite ideas about how such dinners should proceed and could not tolerate anything getting in the way of her expectations.

As others echoed Mahlon's sentiments, Olga quietly excused herself from the table and went and sat down in the living room. She looked somewhat uncomtfortable as she called, "Marty, come here. I don't feel well. Come with me."

Marty helped Olga to the bathroom. Claire could hear her mother throwing up. "Why is she spoiling everything? Is she really sick? Don't get sick, please not tonight. Don't get sick. Mother, you can't get sick," thought Claire as Marty led Olga back to the sofa.

"Marty, dear, please unloosen my bra. Thanks dear. It makes it easier for me to breathe. You go back now. I don't want to spoil Claire's dinner."

Marty returned to the table.

"Is everything all right?" someone asked.

"Yeah, fine. Mother's stomach is just a little upset," replied Marty. His face conveyed more worry than an upset stomach would engender.

"Dad, do you want some tea?" offered Claire.

"Yes, dear. Yes, please," answered Marty, his mind obviously somewhere else. Claire poured the tea and then got up from the table and went over to join Olga on the couch. Soon, others were getting up, stretching, standing around, or taking more comfortable seats in the living room. Olga and Claire went into the den.

"Mahlon!" yelled Claire.

Mahlon quickly got up from the table and headed for the den. Myra and Judy followed. Olga was sitting on the loveseat with the yellow mixing bowl between her legs, looking pale and disoriented.

Myra tried phoning Sue, her sister-in-law, who was a nurse. Judy went into the dining room, walked over to Louise and said, "Grandma fainted."

"Oh, my God," cried Louise in obvious fear.

"Mother," said Myra looking up from the phone, "Sue said it could be an insulin reaction. Did she have any today?"

"I don't know."

Marty was in the room, and explained that Olga had had her insulin. In fact, Dr. Cohen had changed her dosage just that morning.

"Sue, she did," said Myra turning back to the phone. "What should we look for?" As Sue spoke, Myra jotted down the signs. "Okay..., Uh-huh..., Yes..., We'll call him."

Myra, hanging up the phone, said, "Mother, we should call Cohen."

"It's the holiday," Claire answered.

"I know that, Mother, but he is her doctor."

"It's probably just an upset stomach," repeated Reba, hovering at the doorway.

"Mother, we really better call. You don't know what it is. None of us are doctors. It might be the insulin. In any case, he'll tell us what to do."

"I hate to bother him."

Claire finally relented. "Okay, I'll call him."

She went to the phone to call Dr. Cohen as Louise bent down and knelt at her mother's knees.

"Well, what did he say?" asked Myra impatiently, when Claire returned.

"He said," said Claire drawing a deep breath, trying to hide her concern behind a mask of feigned calm, "that Mother probably just overate, not to worry, just to watch her and make her comfortable."

"Did you ask him about the insulin?" questioned Myra.

"No."

"Why not?"

"I don't know," said Claire on the verge of tears. "I just didn't. He seemed angry that we disturbed his dinner."

In a restrained voice, Claire announced, "Mother and Daddy will sleep here." Then, with the air of the older sister in charge, Claire continued, "Louise, you go home with Harold."

"Will you be okay, ma?" asked Judy.

"Sure, dear. You take Nana Reba home. Grandma'll be just fine."

Everyone slowly filed out of the den, gathered their things, and left.

Marty sat on the loveseat next to Olga, while Claire began getting sheets down out of the linen closet for her parents to sleep on.

"Need some help?" Mahlon asked Claire as he approached the linen closet.

"No, dear, everything's just fine," Claire answered in that sweet, crackling, yet calm voice that she often used when she was afraid, worried, or didn't want to talk about something.

"It's better that they stay here," thought Claire as she made up the bed.

Marty and Claire helped Olga into the bedroom and carefully sat her down on the edge of the bed. Marty remained at Olga's side while Claire went into her bedroom to get her mother some pajamas.

"Marty, I have to go to the bathroom," said Olga. Marty gently helped her up and into the bathroom. When they came back into the bedroom, Claire helped her mother into Claire's mint-green nylon pajamas. Then Claire left her parents alone in the bedroom.

"I need my mirror and lipstick," called Olga.

"What do you want that for?" asked Marty looking confused.

"I want to look nice."

"But you always look beautiful to me," he said, more like a courting lover than a husband of over 50 years.

"No, I need more lipstick and a mirror." Her voice grew more and more agitated, as did her behavior. No sooner would Marty make her comfortable than she would call to him to take her to the bathroom. He would take her. Finally, after the sixth trip, he yelled, "Olga, it's enough already. You don't have to go. You just want...." Marty lowered his voice and pleaded, "Please, dear, you'll wake Mahlon and Claire."

Claire, who wasn't asleep anyway—she couldn't sleep—decided to bring the television into her parents' room.

"Daddy, maybe this will help," said Claire, tuning in Johnny Carson's show.

"Thanks, dear," said Marty.

Claire glanced over at her mother and went back to her room to sleep. Through a fog of fatigue, she heard her father hollering, "Olga, get back into bed. Stop getting out of bed." Then there was a crash.

Mahlon and Claire ran into the bedroom. "What happened?" asked Mahlon, looking at the TV on the floor.

"Mother knocked it over," said Marty. He looked shaken and scared. "Is it broken?" he asked.

"No, see," said Claire assuringly as if she were talking to a child. She turned it on to prove to him it wasn't broken, but the worry didn't leave his face.

Claire went out of the room and brought back the rocking chair. "Maybe Mother would be more comfortable sitting up."

They helped Olga into the chair. She seemed to be muttering to herself.

"Daddy, she'll relax and then we'll put her back in bed."

"You go back to sleep, dear. I can take care of her," he said.

Claire went back to bed with Mahlon and slept fitfully, roused off and on by Marty's plaintive calls, "Olga, dear, please."

The alarm went off and Mahlon got up to get dressed for services. It was the first day of Rosh Hashannah, when Jews, no matter how unobservant they are during the year, manage to find their way to some synagogue.

"Mahlon," she called from the bed. He turned around. "I don't think I should go. Someone should stay here with my father. You understand."

Claire got out of bed and went across the hall, passing the room where her parents slept on the way to the kitchen. All seemed quiet.

In a few minutes, Marty joined his daughter in the kitchen. "Dear, I think I should call Dr. Cohen and find out if I need to give mother her medication."

"What medication?" asked Claire.

"Well, there's the insulin and her pills," he replied.

"Okay. I'll call." Claire went out to the den and called while Marty stared blankly out the kitchen window.

"Daddy," Claire called from the entrance to the kitchen, "Cohen said not to give her a needle—just watch her."

The morning wore on. Olga wouldn't eat. She just kept asking to go to the bathroom. Sometimes Claire would take her; sometimes Marty. Sometimes they would try to talk her out of it.

When Louise arrived, Claire was in the kitchen making broth. She was concerned that her mother hadn't eaten anything.

Louise walked into the bedroom, "Mom, how are ya feelin'," she sang as she kissed her mother hello.

"Weezie, I don't feel so good."

Holding her hand and sitting down on the bed across from the rocker, Louise asked, "Any better than last night?"

"No. I feel worse." she replied weakly.

Olga's fear was reflected in Louise's face. Louise knew what was really troubling her mother. Olga was afraid she was dying. Once when Myra was telling her Aunt Louise about the course she taught in death and dying, Louise had said, "Maybe you could help Grandma. You know she is very scared about dying."

"Really? Did she ever talk to you about it?" Myra had asked her aunt.

"Yeah," her aunt recalled.

"What did she say she feared? Pain?"

"No, she said she just feared the thought of dying and not—never living again. Just her life being cut short. Of her...her leaving altogether. She doesn't want to die. It scares her. Whenever she gets sick, I can see it in her eyes. It's always in the back of her mind that she's going to die."

Olga had just dozed off in the rocking chair when Claire came in with some broth.

"Claire, do you think we should call Cohen?" Louise asked.

"I already called him. He said just to make her comfortable and watch her."

The women stood silently by as their mother became more and more incoherent. The afternoon wore on. There were more trips to the bathroom.

Olga dozed. Marty stayed in the room with her. Louise and Claire sat in the kitchen, their hands wrapped around their coffee mugs, neither drinking nor speaking. Louise broke the silence, "Maybe we should put mother in the hospital?"

"No. Let's wait and see. Cohen said it was probably a virus."

The sun was setting. It had been 24 hours since that little white ring had tapped on the door. The color now gone from her face, Olga faded in and out of consciousness. Her remarks seemed increasingly restricted to requests to go to the bathroom and questions about different family members' whereabouts.

"Claire, let's call Cohen again," urged Louise. "She doesn't seem any better."

"Yeah, maybe there's something else we can do?"

"Maybe she belongs in the hospital."

"Maybe," said Claire as she wearily walked to the phone and called Dr. Cohen. Louise followed her sister and stood next to her as Claire spoke to the doctor.

"He said if we could get along for the next 48 hours, we would be better off having her home. He doesn't want to send her to the hospital. He said, 'Knowing your mother, she would be better off at home where she could get more tender loving care.' I'll keep her here with me. "

"And Daddy?"

"We'll see."

Louise left and Claire sat in the living room trying to decide what to do about her father. Her thoughts went round and round. "If he goes home, he'll get some sleep. But what if something happens? He loves her with an intensity that most men don't love women. I shouldn't make the decision. He should."

"Claire, dear," said Marty, suddenly standing beside her chair. "The car insurance is due."

"When?"

"I have to mail the payment in today."

Claire seized the opportunity. She didn't like the way Olga was looking and she also knew how Marty was afraid the insurance would be canceled if he didn't pay on time. "Then why don't you go home, pay the insurance, and rest up. I'll call you if I need you."

Marty was both apprehensive and relieved. He was tired, but he didn't want to leave Olga. On the other hand, if the insurance was canceled, what would he do? He was already in an assigned risk group.

Marty collected his hat and coat. "I'll bring a fresh change for mother in the morning."

"Fine."

They kissed each other good-bye at the front door. "Drive carefully," she called as he went down the walk. Claire went back to her seat by the fireplace and waited for Mahlon to come home. Olga slept fitfully in the spare room. Claire checked on her frequently.

Mahlon returned home from services. They ate in silence, except for brief polite exchanges about Olga's condition, the course of the day, and services.

Claire cleared the table and washed the dishes. Mahlon went into the den and picked up the newspaper. After a few pages, he was asleep.

"Mahlon," said Claire, passing his chair on her way to check her mother, "Go to bed."

"Uh-huh," he answered and nodded. He soon lifted himself out of the chair and went into his bedroom and got ready for bed. Claire, too, changed clothes as Mahlon drifted off.

Olga slowly awakened. Claire went in to her, helped her to the bathroom, wiped her hands and face, straightened the bed, and again put her back in bed. No sooner was Olga back in bed than a repeat of the night before began. This time, however, it was Claire, not Marty, getting in and out of bed to help Olga to the bathroom and to fix the covers she was constantly throwing off. And it was Claire, not Marty, who at one point hollered, "Why don't you stay in bed already!"

Louise arrived at 9:20 A.M., just as Claire was getting off the phone with Dr. Cohen.

"How's mother?" asked Louise.

"Not good," said Claire stifling a cry. "I just spoke to Cohen."

"And?"

"He said he'd come right over after he made rounds. Louise, I'm just so tired."

"I know. I'll take over now."

"I've never felt so physically exhausted."

"You go to bed and get some sleep."

The two sisters made their way out of the den, Claire to her bedroom, Louise to Olga's room.

"Weezie," Olga called.

"Yeah, Ma," said Louise taking her hand and sitting down. The phone rang.

"I'll get it," Louise called as she got up, left the bedroom and went to pick up the phone in the den.

"Hello."

"Hello, Aunt Louise. It's Myra. How's Grandma?"

"Oh, Myra. I'm so scared. She's not any better. She looks worse to me. She's so out of it."

Before Myra could ask another question, Louise was crying.

"Okay, take it easy, Aunt Louise. I'll come right over."

"Come over, My."

"Okay. Is Grandpa there?"

"No, he went home last night to get some things for grandma."

"Okay, I'll be there as soon as I can."

Louise answered the door. "Thank God you're here, darling." Myra and her aunt embraced and went into the bedroom. Olga sat staring straight ahead, expressionless, motionless. Suddenly, the wide-eyed statue spoke, as if calling out from a trance.

"I have to go to the bathroom," called Olga.

"This is what it's been like all morning," said Louise.

"Okay, Mother," chorused Louise and Claire as they helped lift her out of the chair and to the bathroom. Myra followed. With Olga perched an the toilet seat, the two daughters took several steps backward and Myra moved up to sit on the edge of the bath tub right next to her grandmother.

"Why hasn't Myra called?" said Olga angrily.

Claire was so shocked by the question that before Myra could answer, Claire simply said, "She did."

"Oh. Well, why didn't she come yesterday?" demanded Olga. Again Claire responded, "She had to lead Children's Services at the synagogue."

"Well, why isn't she here now?" Olga was agitated.

"Grandma, I am here, now." Myra quickly answered for herself at last. She stretched out her arm and rested her hand on her grandmother's thigh.

Olga stared alternately at the wall and at her daughters, as if looking through them. Olga never turned in Myra's direction. Myra wasn't sure if her grandmother was angry and this was just her way of showing it, or if in fact she had lost some awareness of the world around her. If she was angry, it was in a way Myra had never seen. If it was a loss of awareness, Myra wasn't quite ready to accept it; for at some level Myra knew where that would lead.

"Where's Richard?"

"He's at school, Grandma."

"That's good, dear," her voice becoming calm, gentle, and lucid again.

"Let's take her back," said Claire. Her daughters held her around her waist and sat her in the rocker.

Olga rocked and rocked. "Claire, eat your jello." Olga paused. "Thank you, dear."

The women all looked at one another. It was clear Olga was not talking to them.

"I don't like my coffee out of a mug," she replied as Claire put the cup of tea to her lips. "When I come over here, I want my coffee in a china cup, with a saucer."

"Of all things" said Louise.

Claire sat down. Olga rocked and stared vacantly.

"Mama, Mama," Olga called, her voice suddenly young again.

"Do you think she is calling for her mother?" Louise asked.

"Maybe," said Claire.

"Wasn't grandma very young when her mother died?" Myra asked.

"Oh, yes. You're named for her."

"I remember Grandma bragging all the time about what a brilliant woman her mother was. How many languages her mother spoke and how compassionate a woman she was and how you, Myra, were just like her."

"Tante, Tante," Olga called.

"That's what she called her stepmother," Claire explained. "Tante Letza. She was a very kind, gentle woman that made them very, very happy and I know that Grandma always regretted that she never called her mother or mama, but that she only called her Tante. Tante, of course means 'aunt,' and her name was Letza."

"I'm named for her," said Louise.

"Abe! Abe!" called Olga.

"That must be her brother. He died when Grandma was rather young," said Myra, as if deciphering a code.

"I have to finish that dress," Olga remarked.

"Always busy doing something—knitting, sewing or embroidering. Always handy. Always doing something," said Louise. Olga's declaration inspired recollections easily shared among the three women.

"I remember as a child sometimes resenting the fact that when I came home from school the house wasn't as orderly or as tidy as I would have wanted it to be," said Claire. "But I could hear her up in her sewing room with that sewing machine going away a mile a minute, deeply engrossed in making or sewing something.

"She was the one that everyone in the family came to whenever they had troubles," added Claire.

"I know," said Myra. "She was the only one who understood when Dick and I were seeing each other and wanted to get married."

"That's right," replied Claire. "It was because of Grandma and her understanding and her talking with me and with Daddy a great deal that we came to see... Well, she just kept saying, 'They love each other. You must accept it. You have to understand.'"

Olga stopped rocking. Her body became very still.

"Maybe she'll sleep now," said Myra.

The three helped Olga back to the bed and laid her down. They stood in the doorway to her room.

"What do you think we should do?" asked Louise.

"I can't take another night like last night," said Claire.

"We could take shifts," suggested Louise.

"I think we should call Cohen. She doesn't seem to be getting any better," said Myra.

"Well, she's resting now. Maybe when she gets up, she'll feel better." said Claire.

"Mommy, I really think we should call or something."

"No! I don't want to put her in the hospital. Cohen said it was nothing more than a butcher shop. She would do better here, if we could just wait."

"Well, maybe we could get a nurse to come to help out," suggested Myra.

"She's gonna get better. She always gets better. She's not that sick. She's gonna come out of it," said Claire, more to convince herself than those around her.

"I'll go call him," said Myra as she walked out to the den to phone him. Louise and Claire remained with Olga, staring at her.

"Mom, all I could get was the answering service," said Myra.

"Okay, dear. We'll try later."

And they did try, several times, to no avail, in between what seemed to be endless discussions of the pros and cons of hospitalization, getting a nurse, and Olga's condition.

Finally, Myra asked, "Mother, do you think we should call an ambulance?"

"Oh, I don't know. What do you think?

" It's up to you."

"Maybe," said Louise.

"Yes, maybe," said Claire. "She does seem to be breathing differently. "

"Okay, I'll call." Myra went out, called, and came right back. "I called. and..."

"When will they be here?" Claire interrupted.

"Soon, I guess. You and Aunt Louise go get something to eat. You haven't eaten all day and it's already past lunch time. I'll stay here with Grandma."

"She's resting," said Louise.

Claire nodded and the two sisters filed out of the room like obedient zombies.

Myra sat on the edge of her grandmother's bed. She searched her grandmother's face for the look she remembered.

The sun seemed to be trying to force its way through the window shades, drawing attention to Olga's perfectly polished nails. For as long as Myra could remember, Olga had worn the same dark red nail polish. It matched her lipstick. Myra wondered if Judy had polished them (Olga loved it when Judy polished her nails) or whether she had had a manicure when she went to the beauty parlor.

Olga didn't go to the beauty parlor often—just when she needed a rinse to keep her grey hair grey, not yellow. Although, many times it came out blue. Whenever Olga talked about dying her hair like Nana Reba did, Myra and Judy would say, "No. Grandmas are supposed to have grey hair." Then Olga would smile and hug them both.

Myra's eyes moved down over Olga's body. Her mother's thin filmy green pajamas clung to Olga's sagging breasts, usually supported by what Olga called a "good garment."

Then came the sounds. Myra knew what they meant. How often she had heard them when she was doing her research on dying children. She kept going over in her mind, "Should I call them now or wait until it's over? Do they want to be here or would they rather not? Here I am, supposedly an expert an this dying stuff, and I don't know what to do. But God, she's my grandma, my Grandma Olga."

Suddenly, Myra found herself standing in the doorway, calling, "Mother, Aunt Louise, could you come here a minute."

The two came running. As they knelt by Olga's bed, Myra walked toward the bed and bent down between her mother and her aunt.

"Mommy, Mommy—Myra, that's my mommy," sobbed Louise.

Myra put her arm around her aunt as they both turned and looked at Claire. Claire was bent over her mother's face, breathing into her mouth and calling in a sweet sing-song voice, as if she were trying to coax a child off a high ledge she had chosen to walk along. "Come on, that's a girl. Good girl." Then, with greater command, she urged her, "Come on, Mother.

That's it, Olga." Then, finally, almost angrily, she pleaded, "Breathe! Come on, breathe! Breathe for me."

Claire stopped for a moment and Louise tried. Myra looked at them in amazement, thinking, "What kind of artificial respiration is that? Certainly not any offered in any Red Cross course. Besides, she's dead. Grandma's dead. Grandma's dead."

"Mother," said Myra putting her arm around her, "Stop it. Stop it. There is nothing more you can do."

Claire stopped, momentarily gained control of herself and said to Myra, "Okay. What do we do now? Can we say a prayer or something?"

"Yes," said Myra. Almost reflexively she began, "Shema, y'Israel Adonoy Eloheynoo, Adonoi Echad. Hear O Israel the Lord our God, The Lord is One. Amen." Her mother and aunt joined in where they could.

"What do we do now, Myra?" her aunt asked.

"I don't know. The doctor still hasn't called back," Myra answered.

"Oh, my God," Claire exclaimed, "What about Daddy? He'll be here soon with mother's things."

Just then the phone rang. This time no one bothered to go into the den to answer. Myra picked it up immediately, right there in the bedroom where Olga had just died.

"Hello."

"Hello, this is Dr. Cohen. Is…"

"You're a little late. She's dead. My grandma's dead. Why didn't you call back sooner?"

"Your line was busy."

"We were trying to reach you and the ambulance. Didn't your service tell you?"

"Well, if it was so bad, why didn't you just call an ambulance?"

"I told you we did. It still hasn't come. I don't know why."

Hearing no response, Myra continued. "What should we do about Grandpa? He does have a heart condition you know."

"Marty's tough. He can take it."

"If he gets upset, should we give him something?" Myra asked dryly.

"He knows which pills to take."

"The nitros under his tongue."

"Yes."

"Do you want to talk to my mother?" Without waiting for a response, Myra handed the phone to her mother. Claire held her tears in check as she talked. "Thank you, doctor. Yes, we know we did everything possible for her… Yes, she was very comfortable with her loved ones around… Yes, she would have wanted it this way."

Meanwhile, Louise kept sobbing, "My mommy, Myra. My mommy's dead." Myra kept her arm around her aunt.

"What about Grandpa?" Myra asked. "He'll be here soon."

"I don't know," said Claire. "Let me think. Myra, you go call Daddy."

Louise and Claire stood in the bedroom, their back to Olga, and cried, while Myra went into her parents' bedroom to call her father.

When Myra walked back in the room, the two sisters were facing her, their backs still turned to their mother.

"Daddy said we should call Stern's Funeral Home."

"Okay. My, you call," urged Claire.

Myra obeyed. When she hung up, she explained to her aunt and mother what she already knew—that the funeral home could not take Olga, or anyone else for that matter, from a house without a release signed by a physician. The funeral director explained that since Olga had been under a doctor's care, there was no need for her to be taken to the hospital to be pronounced if Dr. Cohen would come and fill out the necessary papers.

"Okay. I'll call." This time, Claire was able to get through to him immediately.

"Dr. Cohen said that we should call Stern's and tell them that Mother was under his care and that he'd stop by on the way home."

"Okay. I'll go do that," said Myra.

When she came back, her aunt and mother were no longer in the bedroom. They had gone into the living room and were discussing what to do about Marty.

As they went round and round, Myra stood unnoticed in the doorway, trying to decide whether she should first go and clean her grandmother up, comb her hair, straighten up a bit, as the nurses often did with the dying children, or go in and tell her mother and aunt what else the funeral director had said.

But before any of them came to any decisions, Mahlon walked in. As Mahlon walked toward the sofa, Claire stood up. He embraced her and Myra and Louise in turn as they walked over to him.

"What do we do about Daddy?" asked Claire.

"You haven't told him?" asked Mahlon.

"No, we were waiting for you," Claire replied.

"What do you want to do, dear?"

" I don't know. "

"Okay, I'll go over to Dad's and tell him," said Mahlon. "Myra, did you call Stern's?"

"Yes. They'll be here soon," Myra replied.

"What if Daddy wants to see mother?" asked Louise.

"Tell them to wait. I'll call you from Dad's," Mahlon replied.

"I'll go with Daddy," Myra volunteered.

Myra followed Mahlon out to the car. On the way, she told her father what happened that day.

Myra stood behind her father as he knocked an the door. Marty opened the door, stared for a moment, sensing something amiss but quickly dismissing it. He simply said, "I was just getting ready to leave."

Myra and Mahlon followed Marty in.

"Dad, sit down," Mahlon gently commanded.

Marty obediently sat down. Mahlon pulled over an ottoman next to the arm of the chair and addressed his father-in-law, "Dad, Mom passed away."

Marty bent closer to his son-in-law. "What? I can't hear you."

"Mom died."

"My sweetie! My sweetie!" He alternately called and sobbed. Mahlon waited for a moment and then asked. "Dad, do you want to go back to the house and see her?"

"No!"

"Grandpa, are you sure?"

"My sweetie. My sweetie," he cried.

"Daddy?" Myra asked.

"Call Mother and tell her Grandpa doesn't want to go back to the house to see Grandma."

"Dad, do you want to go back to the house?" asked Mahlon.

"No. Not just yet, Mahlon."

"Okay. Myra, tell your mother that she and Louise should come here."

"Dad. Can I get you anything?" asked Mahlon.

He shook his head no. "How I loved her. Oh, Olga. Why Olga? You were such a good woman. My sweetie." The refrain stopped and started, punctuated by sobs.

"There's a picture of her on the refrigerator," Marty said. The crying seemed to be stopping.

"I know. I saw it, Grandpa." Myra got up and got the picture.

"That was taken just a few weeks ago, at the Algiers [a hotel at the shore]. She had such a good time." He paused. The crying began anew. "Olga, what will I do without you?"

Mahlon and Myra just listened, both deep in their own thoughts and memories of Olga and Marty.

The sisters let themselves into the apartment and went over and embraced their father. Harold followed shortly behind, dressed in his work clothes. He quickly embraced his wife, Louise, then Claire, Myra, and his father-in-law.

"Mahlon, we have to make arrangements," said Claire.

"Okay."

"Daddy, do you want to go with us?" Claire asked.

Marty blankly shook his head and wiped his nose with his handkerchief.

"Louise, you take Daddy back to our house. We'll meet you there. Myra, are you coming with Daddy and me?" Claire directed.

"Uh-huh," Myra said, without thinking, following her parents out the door as she kissed her aunt and grandpa good-bye.

They all sat in a row—Harold, Mahlon, Claire, and Myra—facing the funeral director, across a huge expanse of desk. As the funeral director explained what they would need and what they would have to do, Claire thought to herself, "I'm going to be very brave and go and pick out myself what's necessary."

"Now, if you will follow me," said the funeral director, rising from his chair.

Claire turned to Mahlon. "Honey, you go."

"But I thought... " started Mahlon.

"We can go look and then come back and discuss it all with you before any final decision is made," said the funeral director firmly but gently, ushering the men out.

"Thank you," said Claire.

Claire sat there transfixed with her daughter beside her, as the men filed out.

"I can't believe it," Claire cried. "Myra, I just can't believe it."

After a few moments, Claire began to speak, "Dr. Cohen came in the front door, and I let him in and he looked at me and he said, 'I made a mistake, didn't I? I made a mistake.' He was sincerely upset. He told us it was better this way. She wouldn't have... Even if she went to the hospital, all they could have done was prolong her life. She would have been a vegetable."

Claire sobbed quietly. "I left her in the room. I left her in the room." Her speaking voice slowly returned. "I was sitting in the living room on the sofa, the same place where she was sitting. Why I chose that place, I don't know. And when the funeral home came in..." Claire once again began to cry as she spoke. "They asked me where she was and they had this big black sack with a zipper an it. And all I could think of was when I was a child my mother used to say you had to have the headboard on the bed facing a certain wall so in case you died, you wouldn't go head first. Or was it feet first? I still can't remember exactly which way grandma said. I didn't want to remember, but that kept flashing through my mind, how she used to say to me as a child, and then when I grew up as a young woman, and then when I set up housekeeping, that the bed had to be in a certain position in a room so in case a person passed away, they should be carried out of the bedroom the proper way."

Claire slowly became calm again. "And I didn't watch them put her in that black...." The calm was like a lull before a storm, for all of a sudden, from depths Myra couldn't fathom, came waves and waves of wails. "Oh, my God," Claire shouted, "Oh my God. Like a sack of potatoes, like 10 pounds of potatoes, a whole life being dragged out of her."

Claire quieted and began anew, telling a story. "Claire Quarry came in, my next door neighbor a very religious Catholic lady. She knocked on the door and said that she saw, I don't know what she called it, a hearse or whatever it was. 'Was everything all right?' And I said, 'No, my mother passed away.' And she said, 'Please, can I go and see my friend once more?' And I couldn't go with her. And she went in and she said some prayers, Catholic prayers, for which I was very appreciative and very grateful because she loved my mother.

"My mother was never a very religious woman. But to me, religion is not something that is practiced in a synagogue. Religion is love in the heart, a respect and love for God, and bringing up children in the Jewish tradition, the way we were, but not radically so. So I want for her what Jewish people have, a plain pine box, and with the Jewish star because I know she's going to heaven. I know it's a fantasy, but she is going to live in heaven now, with God. She's with her father and mother and her brother whom she loved very much. "

Claire wiped her eyes and continued to stare straight ahead. Myra reached out her hand and moved closer to her mother, but Claire did not move. She continued to stare straight ahead as she had since the funeral director had left.

Mahlon, Harold, and the funeral director filed back in and took their original seats. Mahlon put his hand on top of Claire's.

"Claire, dear, you can have whatever you want," said Mahlon.

Claire turned to Mahlon and asked, "What do you mean?"

"There are basically two kinds," explained Mahlon, "Metal, like Dad had, or wood."

"What's the difference in price?" Claire asked looking at the funeral director.

"That doesn't matter," said Mahlon. "It's whatever you want."

"Here are some pictures," said the funeral director leaning over his desk to show Claire.

"Okay," said the funeral director, withdrawing the pictures of metal coffins and spreading out the pictures of wooden ones.

Myra, knowing what her mother said she wanted and seeing only very fancy cherry, mahogany, and walnut caskets in the photos, asked, "Do you have shoulder caskets?" referring to the less expensive and traditional casket.

"How do you know about shoulder caskets?" asked the funeral director almost accusatorily.

"I teach about it."

"I see," said the funeral director. "Well, they're more expensive, all hand done. Pine. Very traditional."

"That one is fine," said Claire pointing to the picture of the highly polished cherry coffin with the star of David.

"Claire, are you sure that's what you want?" asked Mahlon.

"Um-huh," nodded Claire.

"You can have whatever you want," said Mahlon.

"I know, dear. Thank you. I like the wood. It's not as cold as the metal."

"It's cherry wood," added the funeral director.

Mahlon looked at Claire one last time and leaned forward. "We'll take that one," he said.

Everyone leaned back.

"Fine," said the funeral director, "The cherry one with the Jewish star. Now what about limousines?"

The making of the funeral arrangements continued much like any other domestic business transaction—buying a refrigerator, a stove, or a washing machine. Mahlon spoke with the salesman and turned to Claire for final approval. The salesman continued writing while Claire nodded. Harold and Myra listened without saying anything.

It was decided that there would be one limousine for Marty; his children—Louise, Claire, and Alvin; Olga's sister, Marion, and her daughter Lenore; and Marty's two sons-in-law, Harold and Mahlon. Everyone else would use their own cars. Olga's body would be dressed simply in a shroud, no viewing. Her son, Alvin, since he hadn't seen her, would go in and identify her before the coffin was closed. The funeral director explained that the law required identification. The shiva stools, prayerbooks, shiva candle, extra chairs, and coat rack would all be delivered on Thursday. They would wait until Friday for the funeral since they couldn't reach the rabbi until after sundown. After all, it was the second day of Rosh Hashannah. Besides, they still hadn't heard from Alvin.

The negotiations completed, they all stood up. Mahlon fumbled for his checkbook.

"That's all right. We'll send you a statement."

"Hank, we'll see you back at the house?" said Mahlon as they walked across the parking lot to their cars.

Myra and Claire got out of the car and started up the front path to the house.

"Dr. Cohen must be here," said Claire spotting his Mercedes.

"A little late, isn't he?" Myra retorted.

Claire opened the door and in her perfect hostess manner said, "Hello, Dr. Cohen. No, don't get up."

In the electric silence that followed, everyone found seats and then Dr. Cohen stood up.

"Claire, your dad seems to be taking it quite well. I left some Valium here, if he needs it. He should take some."

Claire nodded.

Dr. Cohen addressed Claire, "Would you want some?"

"No, no thank you. This is something I have to face up to. It's part of life," Claire replied.

"Well, if you need anything, don't hesitate to call me," Dr. Cohen said as he started to make his way to the door.

Dr. Cohen looked at Claire, "I'm truly sorry. I never thought."

Mahlon went to the door with Dr. Cohen. "Thanks for coming."

Claire immediately started taking charge. "We'll sit shiva here," Claire announced.

The family nodded in agreement.

"We'll have fish platters. We'll get them from Kappies Deli. Is that okay, Mahlon?"

"Sure. If that's what you want, that's what we'll have."

"Yes," Claire said clearly, "Fish is for death. Meat is for birth."

The doorbell rang and Myra got up to answer it as the discussion about what to serve, who to call, whether or not to cover the mirrors, 'what Grandma would have wanted' continued.

"Hi."

Myra hugged Dick. "Grandma died." After another hug she said, "I better go call my sister."

"Okay." Dick went into the living room to see everyone and Myra went into her parents' bedroom to call Judy. As she closed the door, she felt somewhat anxious but didn't know why.

"Hello. "

"Hello, Judy. It's Myra."

"What's up?"

"Grandma died."

"Oh, my God! When? What happened?"

"This afternoon..."

"Why didn't you call me?"

"I did, earlier, but there was no answer. You must have been at work or something."

"I don't believe you."

"Judy, I tried."

" I don't believe it."

"I'm sorry. I guess I just forgot."

"Yeah, I know. Okay, I'll call Jack and we'll come down."

"Fine. Look Judy, please..."

"Bye."

Before Myra could say bye, Judy hung up.

"Why didn't I call her?" thought Myra, putting down the receiver. "I really didn't mean to leave her out. I just didn't think of it. But why? She probably would have called later after dinner. After all, Mother did say Judy called yesterday and I'm sure Mother told her everything was fine. Nobody's straight with each other about illness in this family. Everyone denies it all to themselves anyway, so how can they say anything different to each other? Anyway, they wouldn't want to upset anyone, especially 'the girls'—'little Myra and Judy.'"

Myra went and joined the family for dinner. Claire had everyone mobilized. Each person knew what she or he had to do and whom to call.

"Did you reach your sister?" Dick asked.

"Yes, I did," Myra nodded. "She'll be down soon with Jack."

"I better go call Steven and Teri," said Louise, excusing herself from the table. Harold followed Louise out to speak to their children.

"Someone should try Alvin again," Claire called after her sister. "I wonder if he got any of our messages?" she said as much to herself as anyone.

"I think Judy's mad at me."

"Why?" asked Mahlon.

"Because I didn't call," Myra replied.

"Well,..." Claire began.

Myra wasn't listening. "But I couldn't help it. I didn't mean not to. Things just got... and, I don't know."

"When she gets here, I'm sure you girls can work it out," said Mahlon.

Myra finished eating. Mahlon and Claire started clearing the table. Grandpa wandered into the living room. He stood in the middle of the room for a few moments and then went out the front door. He stood by himself on the front step, as if expecting someone.

It wasn't long before Judy and Jack arrived.

Claire quickly assigned jobs for the evening. On the surface, one would think a last-minute wedding or family reunion was being organized. Everyone was busy making lists, calling family and friends, discussing what to wear, where people would sleep, what to serve, and on and on. The air was almost festive.

Finally, Mahlon said, "I think we should all get a good night's sleep. There'll be enough time tomorrow."

Everyone agreed.

"Besides, some of us have to go to work," said Harold. "Ready, Louise?"

"Yes, dear," said Louise. "Claire, what about getting a dress?"

"Well, we can go tomorrow in the morning," said Claire.

"Okay, but wait a minute. Teri's due in," said Louise.

"Fine. You go get Teri and then come meet me here. How's that?"

"Yeah, she can help me," said Judy.

"You're staying?" asked Claire.

"Yeah, I'll stay overnight."

"That's beautiful, darling," crooned Claire. "What about Jack?"

"He has to go back. He's in the middle of a trial."

"Will you be here for dinner, dear?" Claire asked her son-in-law.

"I don't know. It depends when I finish with the trial. But I'll be here later to get Judy. She'll need to change and all for Friday."

"That's great. And what about you two," asked Claire turning to Myra and Richard.

"I have a lot to do. It's the first day of Hebrew School. I have to be there," said Myra.

"That's fine, dear. I understand. Now what about dinner?"

"Yeah, sure. We'll come for dinner," said Myra looking over to Dick.

"Now let me think. What should I have? Oh, I can worry about that tomorrow," said Claire.

"How about if I just pick up some fried chicken from Gino's on my way back," asked Harold.

"Fine. Great. Thanks. That'll make things much easier. Then we'll be ready when the rabbi comes."

"He's definitely coming tomorrow night?" asked Louise.

"Yes, to talk about mother," Claire answered.

"For the eulogy," added Myra.

"Oh right, right. I see. What about Daddy?" asked Louise, looking over to her father who hadn't said much all evening.

"Daddy'll stay here with me. Now, is everyone taken care of?" Claire asked.

As if on cue, the family nodded and got up to leave.

Thursday began as Wednesday had ended, with everyone making the necessary preparations for the funeral and shiva. Judy made more calls to friends and caterers. Claire was concerned that people would come right around dinner time and there wouldn't be enough food. Everyone reassured her that no one expected to be served, but she felt some might, since they were coming from out of town. Teri and Judy went to the airport to pick up Marion, Olga's youngest sister. Louise and Claire went to Gimbels, a store they didn't tend to patronize, to buy black dresses.

By dinner time, everyone was once again assembled in Claire's kitchen, eating fried chicken. Talk was light; everyone wanted to finish before the rabbi came. Each took his or her own plate away and did whatever last-minute chores Claire had assigned and then collected in the living room to await the rabbi.

Claire and Mahlon welcomed the rabbi into their home and introduced everyone. Each introduction was followed by appropriate nods, handshakes, and sweet smiles, and on the rabbi's part, expressions of "I'm sorry."

The formalities over, the rabbi sat down and carefully wrote down everyone's name and their relation to Olga.

"Now, in preparing a eulogy, I like to have some idea of what everyone thought about the..."

Before the rabbi could finish, Louise, who rarely was the first in a group to speak, began. "I loved Mother very dearly, as we all did, but I felt extremely close to Mother. I felt like she was my friend, my best friend, and that I was always able to tell her my most intimate secrets and confide in her with every little thing, and she was always there to help.

"I just felt there were times when she was very, very close with me. When I first got married and they were always running to my house. They were always over. And she was always there to help me. Do you know what I mean?"

"That's beautiful," said the rabbi, as he jotted down what Louise said. Others echoed his words and embellished on what Louise had said.

"Now, as to a minyon, will you have enough men every night?"

"Yes, Rabbi, I think so," said Claire. "Let's see. There's Mahlon, Harold, Richard."

Before Claire could finish, Olga's sister, Marion, who hadn't talked much since she stepped off the plane, spoke up rather prissily. "Excuse me, Rabbi, but Richard's not Jewish."

"I didn't know that," said the rabbi looking askance.

"Rabbi, our son-in-law was not born Jewish," explained Claire.

"Did he convert?" questioned the rabbi.

"No, not exactly, but he practices what we practice," said Claire.

"And more," Judy quickly added. "He even knows Hebrew."

"He identifies as a Jew," said Myra.

"That doesn't mean anything, I'm afraid. Unless he's been formally converted, I cannot count him."

"He's more Jewish than any of us," shouted Judy.

"That's not the same as being formally converted," answered the rabbi.

"What difference does that make? What about what he does? What he feels in his heart? Doesn't that...?"

"Judy, please," said Claire. "Rabbi, what do you mean you won't count him?"

"I cannot say there is a minyon and do a service if he is one of the ten. He is certainly welcome to be there, but there must be ten other Jewish men."

"Well, we'll manage, "said Claire quickly looking over to her daughters with that familiar, "Leave it to me, I'll take care of it," look in her eyes.

"I can't believe it," Judy whispered to Myra, so all could hear.

"What do you expect?" Myra replied.

Claire again looked at her daughters, who this time seemed to hear her eyes say, as she had said to them so many times when they were growing up, "Please, let's not have any fights."

Calm relatively restored, the rabbi asked, "Now what about the pallbearers?"

"I guess it will be Steven, Jack, Richard, and..."

"I'm sorry," the rabbi broke in, "but I would prefer that the pallbearers be Jewish."

"Now, look, just who do you think you are?" burst Judy.

"Let me explain..."

"No! You let me explain," Judy countered. "My grandmother loved Richard very, very, much. He's part of our family and what's more..."

The rabbi spoke before Judy could catch her breath. "If you want me to do the service, you'll have to respect my beliefs. I'm the rabbi."

"So what?" Judy retorted and she stomped out of the room. Myra ran after her. The screaming and yelling and what she soon realized must be crying rang in Myra's ears.

Myra found Judy standing in the backyard, by the garden that Dick had planted. Most of the plants were dead, gone to seed. With the bristles on it from the dead thistle plants, the garden looked like an untended cemetery plot.

"Why are you standing here?" asked Myra embracing her sister.

"I just couldn't stand it in there any more.... That bitch. Why did she have to say anything?" Judy implored.

"Yeah, and all the times Dick schlepped her when we were in Chicago."

"How could she say such things?" Judy spoke clearly between blows on a dirty tissue.

"And there's Mother and Daddy just taking it. Why didn't they say anything?" Judy spoke with anger and amazement.

"Well, you know. The rabbi's the big authority, and you know the be all and end all."

"Girls," said Mahlon.

"Where did you come from?" asked Myra. Neither of the girls had seen him.

"Look, why don't you come back in?"

"No. We want to stay out here," they chorused.

"It's cold." It was the same voice that had always told Myra and Judy to take a jacket on a summer night and to wear their boots when rain was forecast.

"We'll come in when we're ready."

"Okay, but ..." Mahlon waited and then turned and went in.

The two girls stood and looked up at the sky. It was getting cold. They decided to go in. Mahlon met them at the door.

"Come on in here with me," said Mahlon leading them into the bedroom filled with their old bedroom furniture, where Olga had died. They all sat down, Mahlon on one bed, the girls on the other.

"Now, girls, please try..."

"No, Daddy," said Myra. And the fight was on. Sometimes Mahlon, Myra, and Judy even used the same phrases, albeit for different reasons. The noise grew louder and louder. Judy stopped yelling and buried her head in her hands and cried, "Oh, my God, I'm losing my father. I'm losing my sister. They're never going to talk to each other. She'll never come back here again."

Mahlon and Myra continued shouting at each other. The only phrase Judy was able to distinguish through all the noise was, "You're hurting me! You're hurting me." Both spoke in tandem. By the time Judy picked her head out of her hands, she saw her father crying and holding Myra in his arms, her head against his chest.

"My," he whispered for no one else to hear, "I would never hurt you. You are my firstborn."

Seeing them hugging, Judy came over, too. All three hugged. Soon Mahlon got up. "I have to go see how your mother is."

As Mahlon got up to open the door and leave, they could all hear Marty reprimanding his sister-in-law, Marion. "Look, Marion. You just shut up. Olga loved Richard. When she needed a fan, no one would come and put it up. No one had time. But Richard came. So you just better..."

Then turning to the rabbi, he said, "Now, Rabbi..."

"Daddy, please. This isn't good for..." said Claire.

"Claire, dear," said Mahlon, putting his arm around her. I think the rabbi probably would like to go now."

"Yes. Thank you," said the rabbi, rising to leave.

"We appreciate your coming," said Claire, following him to the door.

"I'm sorry, but I have my beliefs."

"Yes, Rabbi. We understand. We don't blame you," said Claire.

"I'll see you tomorrow."

By 9:30 on Friday morning everyone was dressed and waiting in Claire and Mahlon's living room. Claire gave everyone last-minute instructions and directions. As she left with the others going in the limousine, she kissed the mezzuzah on the door. Myra and Judy made one last check around the house; coffee urn set up, bathroom neat, stove off, and water in the bottle near the door for when they would get back from the cemetery. And then they, too, left with their husbands for the funeral home.

They all waited in the little room next to the chapel for Alvin and Marion to come back in.

"Maybe I should go in and take one last look," said Louise quietly, half to herself.

"No. Just remember her as she was, when she was living," said Claire motherly to her sister.

"Okay," said the funeral director. "If you'll all just follow me, I'll show you to your seats."

When the service began, Claire stared rigidly ahead. She seemed unable to look at anyone, least of all her father.

Louise looked all around. "Mother, they're all—all here," she thought. "The whole family's here, and 'the Corsages' too." ['The Corsages' was the name a group of Olga's friends gave themselves.] I'm sure Daddy doesn't care. He never did like 'the Corsages.' Once they all came into money, they didn't have time for you and Daddy and after all you did for them!"

Louise was suddenly jolted back from her reveries. "Did I hear right," she whispered to Harold. "He, he, that rabbi just gave my children to my sister. Steven and Teri are mine."

"I don't believe it," Myra whispered to Judy. "He's got it all mixed up."

"How could he? He's got notes." Judy replied.

"I know. Listen. Aunt Louise's feelings about Grandma were just attributed to Mother."

"Other people seem to be noticing, too," whispered Jack.

The buzzing in the chapel grew louder and louder. Nothing the rabbi said or did seemed to stop it. Perhaps it was because he didn't change, he just droned on. He totally ignored what was happening.

No one could stop talking about what had happened. No one could understand it. In their cars on the way to the cemetery, people asked each other, "Why was the rabbi so mixed up?" "He didn't even mention Louise." "I thought he was the family rabbi." "Didn't he have notes?"

As the family assembled around the grave, the rabbi began the traditional recitation of the 'Kaddish' [mourner's prayer]. "Y's gadol. V yis Kaddash." By the time he reached the phrase, "And she will live on in the works she has performed on earth," the only other sound was the buzz of a fly.

"Olga," Claire thought as she listened to the fly. "It's Olga. Olga's here as a fly." Claire picked up the trowel and tossed the dirt over the coffin.

Myra finally drifted off to sleep, the first since Rachel had been born. The rest was brief, not more than 20 minutes. With the dream that awakened her still fresh in her mind, she conversed out loud with her grandmother about the dream she had had.

"Grandma," she began with a mischievous grin. "Okay. You can stop waking me now. You have a namesake—Rachel Olga is asleep in the bassinet over there. Now please let me have some sleep. Don't you get tired too, not to mention cold. I saw you walking around by the seashore in those thin green pajamas.... Yes, I know you come in sometimes, but you try to go into the house on Pentridge Street. That house is cold, too. It has been deserted by the people you sold it to. It was sold at a Sheriff's sale.... Grandpa's waiting for you at the apartment in Lynnwood Gardens. He watches out the kitchen window.... Yes, Grandma, Dick took the fan out of the window at the end of the summer, like he always does.... Grandma, you know your peds and shower cap are right where you left them. Grandpa won't let anyone move them.... Dinner's at my house again this year.... Yes, ever since you died, Rosh Hashannah dinner has been at my house.... I use the table cloth you made me—really. By the way, Grandma, how will you be coming this year—as a ladybug or as a fly?"

Twenty-Two

Letting Go
Mourning a Fallen Soldier

Patricia Z. Fischer

Patricia Z. Fischer received a BA in Biological Sciences from Stanford University (1957), an MA in Zoology from the University of California at Berkeley (1960), and a Dr. P.H. in public health (1972) from the University of North Carolina at Chapel Hill. She immediately took a faculty position in the Department of Health Policy and Administration at the University of North Carolina School of Public Health, where she has taught ever since. Her teaching specially is in interpersonal skills, conflict resolution, and cross-cultural communication.

Her son, Gregory Barry, was born in New Haven, Connecticut, in 1961.

Summer, 1989

Yesterday for the seventh time we went down together to the cemetery to remember Gregory. Seven years ago he was killed in Lebanon. I have not seen him in seven years. I wonder, how can that be? Seven years, already? Seven years since that terrible morning when the rabbi came to tell me he was dead? No. Yes. Seven years.

I write in Israel, from the kibbutz. There is some irony in the fact that I sit in Yaniv's room; Yaniv is a soldier in training who was only a boy of 11 when Gregory died. A large ashtray holds pencils, safety pins, small change, and eleven bullets. On the wall are pictures: several pretty, sexy women; a small boy clutching a cross-eyed cat around the neck; a black man emerging from a rest room that has a sign over the door saying White Men Only; and a peculiar picture of a human skeleton with a long tail, sitting on an iceberg. It is a picture Gregory would have appreciated. Personally, I don't understand it.

Gregory Chase Barry, my firstborn son, went to Israel after high school. He lived and worked on Kibbutz Gazit, fell in love with the kibbutz, with a woman, and with Israel. He took a Hebrew name and called himself Gid'on. "Gid'on (Greg) Barry" is chiseled in Hebrew on the headstone of his grave. He lived for three years in Israel before he fell in battle, aged 20, in that dreadful, useless war. He was very happy here. Two years after he was killed the Army gave me a letter from him that was found among his belongings. It was written the day before he went to Lebanon, four days before his death. His last words to me were, "I want you all to come here. I don't want to leave this country, not in life and not in death." The letter was not signed; he had stopped writing in the middle.

As I write, I find I must remind myself that this article is about me, not about him. Right after he was killed I had the same problem; it took about six weeks to realize that something terrible had happened to me, not just to him. This article is about my own journey since he died. After seven years I find I am still in transit, so perhaps there is no end to it.

We did not learn of his death until six days after he fell. I was in the United States in North Carolina, where I live. All during the spring of 1982 the news from Israel was bad. In his letters Gregory said that he was doing border patrol; he did not tell me that he had been transferred to a fighting unit. I rather stubbornly refused to worry about him. But after the storm broke and Israeli forces entered the neighboring country to the north, I was afraid. As the week progressed, I felt worse and worse. He fell on the third day of the war, on a Wednesday. I was not informed about it for six days, but during that time I think that I knew at some subconscious level what had happened. As the days went by I could not work; I refused social invitations; I sat at home and did needlework for hours.

I was in my office on the following Tuesday when the rabbi knocked on my door. It did not enter my consciousness why he was there; it crossed my mind that since I work across the street from the hospital perhaps he was coming to encourage me to visit someone who was sick. Without any warning he told me very simply that my son had been killed. I screamed my denial at him. I shrieked. I howled. I tried to stop, but I couldn't. I wailed, as women before me have wailed over their dead soldier sons until the message could no longer be denied. After the screaming I was numb, like a block of ice. To this day it strikes terror in me to remember that morning.

I stayed frozen for several weeks. I did not let in the full reality of what had happened. In my rational mind I knew, but emotionally I was quite numb. Jewish tradition has excellent mourning customs; after someone dies, the bereaved sit at home for seven days while family, friends, and neighbors gather there to comfort them. Streams of people came to our house bringing food and comfort. I was never alone during the first week. The most terrible time was at night. For a month I invited my best friends to sleep with me in my bed so that I would not have to wake up in the dark and be alone with my thoughts. Human contact provided a protective shield against the yawning abyss of despair that threatened to swallow me alive.

I had always thought that if one of my children were to die, I would either lose my mind or commit suicide or first one and then the other. I knew quite soon after Gregory's death that neither of these things would happen. I remember exactly when I realized that I would survive. On the day we learned of his death, I flew to Israel with my youngest son and my brother, and the next day we buried his body on the kibbutz with military honors. We walked to the cemetery, the three of us leading the long procession of people from the kibbutz, slowly, slowly following behind the jeep that carried his coffin guarded by six young soldiers who could not look at me. An unbidden thought came to me: "Well, I know you have to let go of your children, but this is ridiculous!" It was a joke, a small joke I made to myself in the midst of my grief, and at that moment I knew that I would continue to live. How, I did not know, but I knew then that I was still myself. Several days later, home again in the United States, I remarked to a friend, somewhat surprising myself as I said it, that Gregory had been killed, not I. Although I truly would have welcomed having died in his stead, I realized that I was still living, and I was glad.

Immediately after Gregory was killed, and for several weeks thereafter, I could not really cry. For me, this was quite unusual. In the first place, I cry easily; secondly, for many years I have been a teacher of Re-Evaluation Counseling, a peer counseling method that encourages crying and the expression of other emotions in healing and personal growth. I was no stranger to crying, and yet I could not cry in any sustained fashion. It was as though crying would open the gate to despair; in crying, I would have to really feel the pain of what had happened. I was terrified that I would not be able to stop. So, although sometimes tears would spring to my eyes and I could briefly let go a little, it was a matter of months before I could allow myself to cry to the depths of my feelings.

I did not really cry until I returned to Israel. Before Gregory was killed I had arranged a sabbatical year here, to begin in October. He died in June; I continued with my plans, although friends and family warned me that I was crazy to leave home in the midst of my grief. Close friends met me at the airport. As we drove through Haifa on the way to their house, following along a route that Gregory and I had walked when I had visited the previous summer, I began to cry, to really cry, to cry to the depths of my being. I remembered walking with him in the warm sunshine of the summer before, he so proud, showing me his city, his favorite places, his land. With these memories, I finally allowed the tears to freely flow.

I had to cry in order to remember him. There was no way around it, I think; with the thought of him the tears would well up, whether I wanted them or not. After he died I was afraid that I would gradually not be able to remember him, and therefore that I would lose him completely. So I set about very deliberately to remember him in as much detail as I could. Soon after I arrived in Israel, I located a woman who knew Re-Evaluation Counseling and we set up regular counseling sessions to listen to one another. We met for two hours at least once a week and often more frequently to take turns being counselor and client. When it was my turn to be the client I would spend my time simply remembering him—Gregory as a baby, as a toddler, as a fourth-grader. Trips we had taken, medical emergencies, birthdays, his clothes, things he said, embarrassing moments. I cried throughout this process as I tried to remember it all. I cried over unfinished business— cross words, unforgiven insults, disappointments that could never be reconciled. I cried tears of regret for the future that would not be, for the anticipated pleasures that were now as dust. I cried tears of anger and frustration, anger at God and anger at Gregory; how could he have done such a thing? I cried for his life that was cut off before its time, and my grief knew no bounds. I cried for myself, for my own loss, for the shredded fabric of my life. I cried because more than anything in the world, I wanted him back.

Grief that is not discharged through crying sits around all the time, waiting for an opportunity to be heard. The slightest thing would remind me of Gregory—a song on the radio, the tilt of a curly head, a tall soldier in uniform, a child in a striped T-shirt. Unaccountably the grief would surface in the middle of an otherwise quite enjoyable day, because small things were always there to remind me. I found, however, that the more I cried, the better I felt when I was not actively grieving. I learned Hebrew, made friends, taught at the University, and coped with life in a foreign country. I think, in retrospect, that I appeared to be quite strong even to the Israelis, although I "broke down" often and allowed myself to "fall apart" regularly. By the end of the first year I knew that things were better; the grief no longer smacked me from behind, taking me by surprise when I did not expect it. It was there, to be sure, but I had more control over it.

I decided that recovery would mean that I would be able to remember Gregory's childhood as easily as I remember the childhood of my other two sons. I wanted to be able to remember all kinds of details with pleasure and delight, without being overcome with grief all over again. I wish that others, too, would take on this task. Even now, after seven years, it is often difficult to speak about him with people who knew him well if they have not shed their own tears. They become grief-striken all over again and clearly would prefer not to think about him. Am I then to not mention him, in deference to others' difficult feelings about him? But if I cannot mention him, I cannot talk about him; how unfair! How unfair to me, and how unfair to him! The fact that he died cannot take on more importance than the fact that he lived. He was a large part of our lives for 20 years and I want all of us, his family and his friends, to be able to reminisce about him without feeling overcome with grief.

I was committed to the grieving process, however long it might take; I did not tell myself that I should be completely over it by the end of the first year, or even the second, or the third. I found, in fact, that even after a number of years, there was some reluctance to recover, to be fully happy, to live a joyous life. It was as if to be fully happy would be to betray him in some way. An important step in the grieving process seems to be letting go of grief itself. I clung to my mourning as a way of remembering how much I loved him, as a way of continuing to hold him close to me.

How could I possibly reconcile being happy with the fact that he was dead? I think of it now as though a limb had been amputated. The loss is with me and will be with me forever. At the same time, is an amputee never to be happy again because she has lost a leg? Certainly not. Amputees are encouraged to live the same full lives that whole-bodied people live. The same should be true for mourners, even mourners of dead sons. It is no betrayal to the dead to let go of our grief. It is, in fact, what my son would expect and want. He would not want me to weep forever over his grave and my loss. Rather, I think he would want me to remember him with joy and to be happy in my life.

"They wasted him," said my ex-husband in anguish, during one of our rare telephone conversations. My first response was flat denial. How could he say such a thing? And anyway, how could he possibly understand? He is not a Jew, he has no connection with Israel; how could he be expected to understand what Israel means to Jews all over the world when most Jews themselves have little understanding? How could he be expected to understand the fire in Gregory's eyes when he talked about Israel? Once Gregory and I rode a bus from his kibbutz to a nearby town. As we looked out the window at the spectacular view of rolling hills covered with wheat fields and olive trees, he told me that he had never loved anything more than he loved Israel. He spoke of a time when he was five, when he was at a neighbor's house and his father unexpectedly came in and Gregory hugged him hard around the knees. "I remember how I felt," he said. "That's how much I love Israel."

They wasted him. The sentence banged around in my head with its many layers of meaning, not for days or weeks, but for years. Since Biblical times the term *waste* has meant to ruin, to destroy; in the American slang of the 80s, to waste someone means to kill him. Then they surely wasted him, for they sent him into battle in the midst of a raging war.

They spent him carelessly, without regard for the value of his currency. Israel is a tiny, beleaguered country whose greatest need is human resources. One day there came this fine young man of sunny disposition, strong and bright and full of zeal, eager to contribute whatever he could to build the country, and what did they do? They sent him into battle and they killed him at the age of 20—before he could marry and produce gorgeous children who would also contribute, before he knew what he would do as a worker, before he could inspire and lead others with his unfettered optimism and his natural talent for organizing people to do things. Indeed, they wasted him.

And if they recognized his value? Then they wasted him; they squandered all his value on a worthless cause. Gregory was killed on June 9, 1982, on the third day of the Israeli invasion of Lebanon. The people of Israel were divided, even in the early days, about the justification for Operation Sh'lom HaGalil. I could not bear to think about the war at all. I shut my mind to it, I refused to read about it, to talk about it. I would not let people discuss it in my presence. If he had died for no good cause? If the invasion were not justified? Worse than that, if the war that subsequently developed were unjust? How could I bear it? The war wore on. The Israelis rained bombs on Beirut and tens of thousands of Arab children and adults were killed or maimed. The American news media and the American government decried the carnage: 200 Israeli soldiers died; 300; 400. In the end, more than 600 Israeli soldiers gave their lives. And I was supposed to agree that the war was not justified? I was supposed to concede that he had given his life for nothing worth having? I could not. In fact, I searched for justification. I read right-wing opinions. I sought out Israelis who would tell me why the war was necessary.

Many years before, when Gregory was a toddler, I had stood week after week in silent vigils to protest the war in Vietnam. Now I had to come to terms with the fact that my own son had died in a war. People said, by way of trying to comfort me, "Well, at least he wasn't killed in a senseless traffic accident; at least he died for a good cause." Did he? I searched for credible reasons to believe that he had not died in vain. In the end, I could find none. The Lebanese war served no valid purpose that I can understand. They wasted the lives of more than 600 Israeli soldiers and many thousands of innocent Lebanese citizens. Among the dead was my firstborn son.

Making peace with how he had died was a central issue in my grieving. I could only come to terms with it by finally accepting a few simple truths about war itself. I understand now that all wars are waged in the name of ideology: to make the world safe for democracy; to ensure that the Holocaust may never happen again; in the name of liberty and freedom, against creeping communism. Entire populations can be mobilized by means of convincing rhetoric. Mistrust of the enemy makes negotiation seem unfeasible; generations of tradition make war appear to be a reasonable course of action. Soldiers who fall in battle are honored as heroes in ceremonies that convince the next generation of small boys that to fight is heroic and to die in battle is the most heroic of all. Military obligation is seen as an honor in Israel, an inevitable part of living here; it would be heresy and foolishness to speak otherwise. I can see now how Gregory got caught up in such a mentality, even as the firstborn son of a mother who would not allow her children to point cap-pistols at one another. It is a bitter truth that he was attracted to the army and its mystique in spite of all my beat efforts to teach him otherwise. He sought status as a fighting soldier because his friends were fighting soldiers, and he went into battle with pride. He believed completely in the justice of the cause; he was convinced of the critical importance of Israel to the future survival of the Jewish people, and he believed that the security of Israel's northern border was at stake in June of 1982. From all reports, he enjoyed being a soldier. He had the difficult job of carrying a large automatic weapon that required strength and judgment to operate, and he was killed as he covered the medic who went to rescue his wounded commander. I am very proud of him. He did what he had to do, according to his own inner vision. He was a willing participant, caught up in the rhetoric of military power, heroism, and love of his country. The war was a decision of his government, and his participation in it was by his choice.

As I look back on the last seven years, 1 see that it has been a long process of letting go. From the moment when I made that little joke to myself on the way to burying him until today, I have been involved in the long and often painful process of separation, of disengagement from him. First was the physical separation, as we buried his body forever. Then a seemingly endless period of weeping as I remembered him and worked my way through the many facets of mourning. Remembering him in as much detail as possible was a way of keeping him close; at the same time, it was the route to letting go of grief. Finally, I could even let go of my illusions that he died for a noble cause and that his death was not a waste. Mourning was coming to terms with reality.

There was yet one more dimension of letting go to accomplish, which took all these seven years to work through and to understand. It was symbolized for me by the yellow blanket I wrapped him in when he was just born. After he died I thought of the yellow blanket often. Oh, if only I at least could have been with him when he died, to wrap him in the yellow blanket, to comfort him, to be with him. The fact that he died without me was intolerable. Terrible questions: Was it painful? Did he die immediately, without knowing what had happened, or did he bleed to death, lying in the hot sun, knowing? What did he think about then? Had he in some way sought death? Could I have prevented it?

These questions were endless and asking them brought up the most terrible feelings of all. Even after I recovered to the point that I really felt quite myself again, these dreadful questions haunted me. I would not let myself think about them; I felt overpowered by them. I believed that they could send me back to the edge of the abyss. I wanted to be rid of them, but I could not see how.

In fact, the questions provided me with yet another means of holding him close to me. I can ask them forever, because there are no answers. I will never know, can never know, what the final moments of his life were like. It was *his* death, just as it was *his* life. I was very slow to understand this. I shall spend the rest of my life honoring him, and I will always regret that his life was so short, but I have had to fully accept the fact that it was his life. He led it as he wished. He did not want to die, but he chose how he lived. To let go is to recognize this, to stop hanging on to every detail, to loosen my grip, to stop obsessing about questions that have no answers, to let him have his own death, without me. To open my hands, to let go, to allow him to go.

This is also the job of parents of living children, and indeed, one of the most difficult lessons of parenthood. It seems, when our children are young, that we as parents have tremendous control over what happens to them, and that we are responsible for their happiness, their adjustment to the vicissitudes of life, their choices, their fortunes, and their misfortunes. At some point we know they will be in charge, but at what point we are not sure. When are the happiness and well-being of our children no longer our responsibility? We see mother cats push their kittens away; mother birds teach their nestlings to fly and then abandon them. At what point do human parents release their children into the world to sink or swim? Ever?

And if the child dies? It seems so unfair, so impossible to leave him behind. How could I abandon him, even if he is dead? Especially since he is dead! I swore to take him with me, to keep him by me, to remember everything, to make sure that others remember too. The teachings of Judaism, in fact, require that we remember, for it is through memory that the dead continue to live. I took on this responsibility in the same way that I had taken on the responsibility for his dental care, for his learning manners, for his participation in after-school sports. Remembering became my job. Through it I could keep him forever, or so it seemed. But those dreadful unanswerable questions haunted me in the middle of the night, unbidden, without warning. Did he suffer? What were his last thoughts? Did he know he was dying? Did he think of me?

It was finally through work with an Israeli social worker schooled in counseling bereaved parents that I was confronted with the interpretation that hanging on to these questions was a way of hanging on to him. These questions were my refusal to let him have his own death. I was not there to protest it, nor to comfort him, nor to protect him, nor to wrap him in the yellow blanket. That was the reality, and my continuing to torture myself was a way of denying it. It was a way of continuing to believe that I could have been in charge, or should have been in charge, or might have been in charge of his life. But he had been living his own life for years before he died, whether I was willing to accept that fact or not.

I remember him well, but he is gone forever. Never again will I see that curly head, that broad smile, that cocky walk he would assume on occasion. Never again will he hug me in his big bear hug, will we talk until the small hours of the morning, will we smoke a cigarette together, will we share confidences. He is gone. He had a very rich life, I believe; he did what he wanted to do. He flourished as a young man, experienced many things, was a good friend to many men, and enjoyed friendship and intimacy with women. He lived fully. His life was short.

To let go, to let him go, to bid him farewell—this process has two separate aspects, like the two aspects of a coin. On one side, the focus is mine. To let go means to open my hands, to relax my grip, to have confidence in the fact that he is ever a part of me and I do not have to work to assure that this will be true. I do not have to clutch each memory, to wind my arms tightly around the idea of him, to guard against losing him. I can relax and turn my attention to other things; I can fully engage in a life without him. That is my side of letting go.

On the other side of the coin the perspective is his. To let him go is to allow him to leave me, to see only his back as he walks away from me to his own life, to his own fate. To let him go is to accept the fact that he was responsible for himself, for his joy and his sorrow, for his failures and his success. To let him go is to accept with a whole heart that it was his life as he chose to live it and that in the end, it was his death. To let him go is to never again consider those dreadful unanswerable questions, because I know that the answers belong only to him. I will never know what he thought as he died, or if he died suddenly or if his life force leaked slowly from him. Only he knows. And so it should be, and so it must be. It is thus for all of us. Each of us is, in the end, unique and apart and with a life of our own, no matter how closely we are connected to our parents or our spouses or our children or our friends. He was he and I am I.

It has been a long time since he died. I have moved on. I believe that I have done well; I miss him, but I am not haunted by his death. I can speak of him freely with delight and humor; his memory enriches my life. Because he is dead, I am not so afraid of my own death. I believe that his spirit is alive. It is in the wind that ruffles the leaves of our beech tree in North Carolina and sighs through the pines in Israel, even as it fills the universe and beyond.

Twenty-Three

Sundays for Ruth

Ruth Harvey

Ruth Harvey began her years as a volunteer at the Capital District Psychiatric Center, Albany, New York. Two years later, she entered the Albany Medical Center's Burn Unit to serve as a volunteer for more than four years. The past eleven years, she has been a volunteer at St. Peter's Hospice, Albany, New York. Harvey is dedicated to its work and the concept of hospice care for the terminally ill.

Weekdays are workdays. Sundays are my days. I chose to spend my Sundays as a hospice volunteer. I'd like to share with you some experiences I had with the guests at the Inn at St. Peter's Hospice.

The first experience and guest I would like to tell you about is Jonah. I think he had a wonderful name. Jonah was African American, perhaps in his late sixties. He was with us for many weeks. Jonah had serious breathing problems. It frightened him a great deal.

When I would come in on Sundays, my first order of business became collecting his coins, taking the elevator, and purchasing his Sunday paper. The funny papers were on the front of the Sunday paper he chose to read. One morning when I handed the paper to him, I commented about "Peanuts," the comic strip. This led to talk about peanut butter. We laughed—snacking was one of our common interests. As peanut butter is quite dry, I suggested to Jonah that I get him some kind of liquid. We explored all of the possibilities I could think of in the refrigerator, and each time he, childlike, shook his head, "No." Finally I said, "Jonah, I don't have a clue to what you want. Is it a glass of wine?" It was 10:30 in the morning and his face lit up. He laughed. I checked at the nursing station and that seemed OK with his primary nurse. Throughout the day, Jonah drank perhaps a half dozen tiny cups of wine and had a delightful time. He really couldn't deal with the peanut butter very easily.

Late in the day, when I was getting ready to leave, I went in to say goodnight to Jonah. (It's always been my practice to never say "goodbye" to a patient, unless they indicate that they won't actually be there in another seven days). Jonah's habit was always to get up from his chair. He chose to be in a sitting position most of the time because of the threat of breathing difficulties. He always had a robe and slippers on; he was very fussy about his attire. When I said, "Goodnight, Jonah," he wanted to escort me to the door. This had become the usual pattern for us. Since his breathing was difficult this particular day, I suggested he not try that. But, nevertheless, he insisted. The next morning, he was leaving by ambulance for New York City. He was very worried about the trip. He had come to love the people who were his caregivers at the Inn. He really preferred to stay with us until he died. In spite of this, there were government regulations and so Jonah had to be transferred to the city. We shared the ambivalence he had about the trip, and the fact that he was very frightened. Sometime during the day, he had discovered that I took the bus each Sunday to the Inn, and had made arrangements to have the exact coins for my bus trip home. Haltingly, he took me to the door. We embraced. He reached into his robe pocket and said, "Miz Ruth, you hep me today, you hep me." He put the coins in my hand, and I left.

I thought about that a great deal on my return trip home because one of the many lessons I have learned from our patients is that some people who are terminally ill still have the ability to think and act in the interest and out of love for others. And that was one of the great characteristics I learned about Jonah the many weeks he was with us. To end Jonah's story, early the next morning, when they went to his room to prepare him for the trip to New York, they found he had died in the night.

There's often another dimension to our caring for people in the Inn, especially for those of us who are white, when we have African-American patients. During his stay, Jonah had shared several things, mostly by innuendo. I think there were certain things that were resolved through a lifetime of living in a ghetto in New York, and through unusual circumstances, when he found himself in upstate New York. He was surrounded by white people, no family, and white caregivers. For those of us who have very little touching with African-American people, I think we all, at least Jonah and I, resolved something that was very important. I feel he decided it was all right to die with white caregivers.

In the early years after we opened the Inn, we had a patient with metastatic breast cancer who had had a colostomy about 20 years ago. She came from a rural area. She and her husband had been married a long time. The reason I mention this particular patient is because the circumstances were curious to me and to others. When Alice was at the Inn, I would irrigate her colostomy on Sundays. These were the days when our patients would stay with us for weeks or months. Alice was one of these first patients. One Sunday, when I was irrigating her colostomy, she discussed with me the fact that she was very sensitive about her colostomy and all the inherent problems, in spite of the many years. I tried to ease her embarrassment, discussing the fact that one day, if I had a colostomy and the roles were reversed, she would take care of me. We laughed and that settled the issue.

But she went on to explain the agony that her colostomy had created for her in her life with her husband. She revealed that he never knew that she had had the colostomy. When I related this to her primary nurse, we explored the question further. Alice's circumstances were curious and seem to illustrate our uneasiness with our bodies, especially when illness makes our discomfort with ourselves more emotionally and physicially acute. What happened between Alice and her husband is, of course, a private issue. When we are caring for patients in our hurried ways, we need to remember that these kinds of personal discomforts become a very important part of their lives, especially toward the end.

Another patient that we had several years ago was very interesting and lots of fun. She showed us another side of life, and perhaps another side of ourselves. Joan was a prostitute. She was perhaps a half-dozen years younger than I. One of the first things I would do on Sunday mornings was to give Joan a bed bath. She was no longer capable of being transferred to the whirlpool bath. She was very frank, very open, and had a very good sense of humor. We started discussing who we both were as women and our ages. She said, "Oh, you're only a few years older than I am. Some day you might be here." I said, "Joan, that's true." She asked me what I had done and then I revealed that I knew that she had been a prostitute most of her life. I asked if she would like to talk about that. She replied that she would.

I asked, "Joan, what was it like?" She answered, "I loved what I did." And I said, "Explore that with me a bit." "I was an abused child in a home where most members of the family were abused. I decided that if I survived, I was going to become a holder. I had never been held." Because of her background, the only thing that seemed open to her was to become a prostitute. Joan went on to explain that she didn't take just any man from the street, but that she had had many men who had come to her for years on a regular basis. She said, "I was a very good holder." Joan craved holding and she saw that there were many men, especially the ones who came over the years, who were also in need of holding.

Obviously there was much more to this sharing than I will reveal here. You can fill in all the gaps. Between the lines there was much laughter, and she had a very free and easy way about her body. It was deteriorating terribly. She knew that and laughed about her teeth falling out. I finished her bath and the last few minutes of our conversation were with me sitting in a chair holding her hand and her looking at me. She became the stroker, and I became the passive patient. It was a very interesting morning.

The next patient I will go to is Luigi. Luigi was an Italian. The morning I arrived at the Inn, the nurses and I sat down to discuss the patients and their needs. The nurses indicated that they had a new admission during the week and that he was in desperate need of a whirlpool bath. He had, however, steadfastly refused. My task was to convince Luigi that he should have his whirlpool bath. Approaching Luigi, I told of all the benefits of a whirlpool bath. He said, "Don't discuss it I with me because they've tried to convince me all week and I don't want one." So I said, "Well, Luigi, that's fine, you don't need to have a whirlpool bath. But I'll be here most of the day and if you change your mind, just ring the bell and I will discuss it with you." I went on to explain the logistics and the easy transition from bed, to chair, to whirlpool.

Later in the day, he called me and said, "I think I'll have one of those things." So we made the transition and I took him to the whirlpool. He was very frightened, but I lowered him into the water very slowly and hung on. Once he was in the water I activated the pool. He relaxed and I suggested that he really needed a shampoo. I got soap in his eyes, he complained, and then we laughed. The next problem was that he didn't want to get out. Finally we got him out of the whirlpool, dried, powdered, and creamed. I shaved him, cut his toenails, and delivered him to his now clean bed. And as much as he hated to admit it, he said, "Well, it wasn't too bad, but I don't think I want another one." Of course, he had a twinkle in his eye and I knew this was his way of hanging on to what he thought had been his original decision.

Luigi was with us some weeks, and each morning it became the routine that when I entered the Inn, I was to give him his weekend whirlpool. After several weeks, I stepped off the elevator and the nurses said, "Luigi wants to see you as soon as you arrive." Going into his room, I said, "Good morning, Luigi, what's the deal today?" "Ruth," he said, "You gave me my first whirlpool, and I want you to be the one to give me my last." I said, "You think this is going to be your last?" "Yes, I do," he answered. So I said, "Well, that will be my privilege."

We went down to the whirlpool. He was having more and more difficulty moving, but was making a real effort to have this last whirlpool. Pushing him as far back as I could, with his feet just slightly extended over the tub because he was no longer capable of raising his legs, he said, "Don't lower me into the tub." "Well, Luigi, what is your plan?" I asked, as I gazed up and saw him peering down. He says, "Now, I want you to take a look at me. I want you to take a good look. Don't you think this is the God-damnedest wreck you ever saw?" "Well, Luigi," I answered, "It's pretty bad, but to tell you the truth, I've seen worse." Paralyzed on one side, he grabbed a bunch of his hair with his good hand, and of course, it responded. He said, "Now look at this. This arm doesn't work, these fingers don't work. I can't piss, I can't shit. And take a look at this," he said, as he wiggles this tiny little organ that has now shrunk to perhaps the size of the fifth finger on his hand. Well, we were both laughing uproariously, he most of all.

While passing through the hall, one of the nurses heard us and opened the door a crack to see Luigi hovering high in the air over the whirlpool. Knowing that we had left for the bath some minutes before, she asked, "What are you guys doing in there? We can hear you all the way down the hall!" Luigi responded, "Now, Ruth and I are just having a few good laughs. If you want to come in and join us, fine, otherwise close the door." "Well," she asked, "are you going to have a bath or not?" "When we're good and ready!" Luigi answered as the nurse left the room. Still laughing, the tears rolled down our faces. The tears, as you know, were for several reasons. I lowered Luigi into his last whirlpool. He asked me to give him a shampoo for the few hairs still left on his head, and I did an extra powder, and an extra cream job that day. I took him back to his bed and he fell into a very sound sleep. He said later that sharing many of the fears he had and just simply saying, "Isn't this the God-damnedest wreck," was a kind of comic relief. He had a very insular Italian family and it was denial all the way for them.

The last experience I will share is about a man who was some years older than I. He'd was a retired police officer from New York City and he had stomach cancer. In the beginning, that's all we really knew about him. He was tall, and it was easy to see that he had been extraordinarily handsome. He had a tall, handsome wife and three equally handsome sons. His story gradually unfolded as the weeks passed. Our patient had joined the police force when he was a very young man.

One Sunday when I came in, the nurses asked that the first thing I do was go and sit with him. He'd had a very difficult night. When I entered the room—we knew each other by this time—I said, "Tom, you've had a rough night. I'm going to sit with you a while. Very soon, he had to be assisted to his bathroom. His throwing up was extraordinarily difficult, and, when it was finally over, he was in a very weakened condition. I led him back to the chair, indicating that I wanted to sit with him until he was somewhat stabilized. "Yes," he replied, "I'd like that." "Tom, it's lousy to feel sick," I began. He said, "Ruth, it's not so bad. I'm bowing out a little bit earlier than I would like to have, but it's OK. I've had a wonderful marriage. I've lived long enough to see my three sons grown. They're over those difficult years, and you can imagine that with my work, I know the dangers on the street." He revealed to me that he'd had a job that he loved, truly loved. He never mentioned the fact that he had been highly decorated (but I'm sure that he knew that we knew). It was only important to him in that he had performed his job and that he loved people.

Within the year that Tom died, I took a bus to New York City. As I pursued my way uptown, I realized that there was some kind of activity, but I did not know it was the St. Patrick's Day parade. Of course, I have heard, like most others, that New York is a very bustling place on this day, but I certainly had no idea that it would actually be difficult to cross the avenue throughout the day! About 5:30 P.M., when I was leaving the east side of the city to catch my bus home, attempting to cross Fifth Avenue to get back to Forty-Third Street, I found it virtually impossible to move west. The streets were cordoned off. (The *New York Times* reported the next day that there had been in excess of 2,000 police on duty because there had been an incident in Ireland the previous week.) The time I was attempting to move westward was also the time when there was much traffic because the offices were closing.

In the distance, as I was standing at the cordoned-off corner, I saw a police officer with much gold braid, and obviously a much older man. I kind of sidled over to where he was and started a conversation. I told him that I was from upstate, attempting to go to Sixth Avenue and Forty-Third Street to catch my bus and asked how long it would be before I could cross the street. I also indicated that it was the first time I had been in New York during a St. Patrick's Day parade. We laughed because I could not believe that a parade could last from 10:00 A.M. until 5:30 P.M. It was still going full force. Seeing his gold braid, and talking with him for some minutes, I said, "You know, I work as a volunteer in a hospice in upstate New York and I'm reminded that some time ago, we had one of your men as a patient. He was a very interesting man, with a very interesting family."

The police officer asked, "Well, what was his name?" Neither one of us thought there was any possibility the men would have known each other. Telling him, he said, "Of course I knew him. Did you know that Tom was one of the most highly decorated men on the force?" I answered, "Yes." He proceeded to ask me what I knew of his last days. I told him and added that I had met his family. He was very touched, saying he had known Tom very well. Then he said, "Stay here." He went to the middle of the street and talked to one of the men who was directing traffic. He did not stop the parade for me, I must add, but he made a kind of "hole," let us say. He beckoned me to the middle of the street and took my hand. When we got to the other side, there were two spectators, one of whom said to the other, "I wonder who the hell she is!" Stepping on the curb, we wound our way through the crowd. "Come on," he said, "Come around the corner with me." Going around the corner, and out of the maddening crowd, he put his arms around me, and said, "Thanks a lot for taking care of Tom."

That hug reminded me that if we enter life with those who wish to hold us, our need to be held as we exit is as great if not greater. For now, I'll hold on to Sundays for Ruth.

Twenty-Four

A Diary of Dying and Living

Barbara Mims

Barbara Mims received her bachelor's degree from the University of Colorado and is currently enrolled in the Graduate School of Social Work at Portland State University, Portland, Oregon, where she will receive her M.S.W. degree in 1993. She served as a volunteer for various hospice programs in both Montana and Oregon for 10 years prior to taking the job as the initial Administrator and Director of Social Services for Hospice House, which was the first free-standing, inpatient hospice in Oregon. Since leaving Hospice House, she has continued to work with people with HIV disease on a volunteer basis. Currently she is Coordinator of the Homemaker Program for Jewish Family and Child Services in Portland.

Mims has been a practitioner of Therapeutic Touch, as taught by Dora Kunz and Delores Krieger, Ph.D., RN, for seven years and is interested in integrating the use of Therapeutic Touch, guided imagery and visualization, and other nontraditional healing methods with more traditional psychotherapy. Her primary area of interest is the connection between the body and the mind and in working with people with both chronic and life-threatening illnesses.

January 15

"And he writes music and plays the piano. He was the Song Fest chairman for his fraternity at the University. He loves drama, draws, and designs clothes. He was a model for Coke, Brittania, and *Seventeen* magazine. He's very creative."

"How old is he?"

"Twenty-seven."

I hung up the phone feeling my stomach turn over. Another one. I had just the day before sat at a service at the church where the first AIDS patient at hospice had been the organist. As I viewed the magnificent organ and heard its music, tears overwhelmed me as I pictured the patient who lay dying, no longer able to remember how to play that organ, body and soul suffering in a way I had never seen. This man was also very creative, the winner of a national prize in the playing of the carillon. Tapes of his music filled his room, and I could make no sense of this disease called AIDS.

The several months of inservices had done little to prepare me. I had an understanding of the various opportunistic infections AIDS patients were susceptible to, but was yet unable to see how difficult the nausea, vomiting, diarrhea, pain, and anxiety would be to control. I had worked through most of my fears for my personal safety. I wondered and hoped that I could meet these patients with compassion, not allowing the hysteria surrounding AIDS to affect my work. I was no stranger to death and it had always reaffirmed my faith in life, and deepened its reality, but this was something new.

January 18

I watched the 27-year-old AIDS patient, bundled in a comforter, stocking cap pulled down over his head, very tall and lean, being wheeled down the hall by his parents. They looked young. As I went into his room to meet them, there was almost an air of festivity, with pictures and balloons and flowers. I thought that these people should be decorating a dorm room at college, not a room in a hospice where their son would die. Shawn was polite. I was struck by his eyes—blue and deep.

January 19

I talked to Shawn today. I asked him what he needed from us and he said, "Just the cheery attitude that keeps coming in this room, and something for the pain." He folded his hands over his chest and went on. "I've done what they call responsible dying. I've written my will and my memorial service. I've prepared my family for grief and now I'm ready to die. I don't plan to be here very long—a week or two at the most. I don't want any phone calls or any visitors except my family. No one outside my family knows that I have AIDS or that I'm dying, and that's the way I want it. I've never been a 'boo-hoo' type person and I don't plan to start now."

He showed me a self-portrait he had done, very different than the way he looks now, and he talked a little about his music and his family. He wanted to keep his family protected, protected from people knowing he has AIDS, and protected from any more pain. I liked him.

January 21

I had a long conversation with Shawn today. I felt like I broke every rule I've ever learned. My own need to work through my struggle about AIDS just overtook my usual professionalism. I said, "I just can't figure it out."

"Figure what out?"

"What you're doing here. You're 27 years old and I'm having a really hard time with it. And why do you have to be dying when you're only 27? I just can't make any sense of AIDS."

He began to share with me what sense he had made of it. He talked openly and easily, and it helped.

"Nothing but good has come from this."

"Good," I said, "you call this good?" I really didn't believe I was talking like this to a patient!

"I've learned to give and receive love because of this in a way I never knew before. And that's really what life's about, isn't it? And I've brought my family closer together."

"But what about anger? Aren't you angry?" I felt my own anger come up, my own anger at what this disease was doing to people, and I shared that with him. And it was Shawn who helped me with my anger, with his very real belief that "nothing but good has come from this."

Shawn talked about how he had gone through incredible anger when he was first diagnosed, but that finally he had been able to move through it when he realized that the possibilities he had imagined for his life were just that, that he really had no guarantee that the possibilities would have ever become reality. He had graduated from college and had wanted to get a master's degree and become a teacher. Then he said he imagined teaching in Alaska, being married to someone who was also a teacher. He had hoped to make enough money there to be able to come back to the States eventually and be able to concentrate on his music. He pictured a family. I could understand what he was saying, and shared with him how difficult it had been for me when my life hadn't turned out how I'd pictured it, when I hadn't gotten married and lived "happily ever after," but had ended up divorced with two children to raise by myself. And how that had been like a death for me.

As I got up to leave the room he said, "Thank you. I feel like I've grown from this conversation."

"Thank you. I've grown too. It was a gift."

January 22

As I left the house this morning, I came back to get a piece of amethyst crystal to take to Shawn to thank him. I figured as long as I was breaking the rules, I might as well really break them. I had never taken a crystal to a patient. The amethyst seemed right because of its spiritual nature, and I had read somewhere that it could help a person in his or her transition out of the body. I really wanted him to know how grateful I was for our talk yesterday. I keep thinking of Steven Levine saying, "Working with the dying is all work on yourself. If you think it is anything else, you shouldn't be doing it."

I thought about how all relationships are such a dance of risk—the dance of "here's who I am" and the fear of rejection, and I felt that as I handed the crystal to Shawn.

"I just wanted to thank you for yesterday, it meant a lot to me."
He held it very tightly and said, "I love it. It's beautiful."
"It's supposed to help with the dying process."

January 23

I stopped by to say hello to Shawn today but he wanted to be alone. He said he had received a very emotional letter from his brother and was trying to get himself together before his parents came so they wouldn't be upset.

January 24

A nurse reported that she had talked to Shawn last evening because she felt he was withdrawn and sad. He took offense at her being concerned and stated she was the third person to approach him. He also told her he really didn't want to talk with the nurses about how he is feeling. He said that he will continue to talk with his family and that he enjoyed talking with Pat and me about his spiritual needs.

My sense is that he needs a lot of space to continue to process internally, and I feel like I need to honor that too.

February 1

I really miss talking with Shawn, but I still feel like it would be my need more than his that would take me into the room, as he is still indicating that he wants privacy.

February 4

Today it suddenly seemed all right to go see Shawn, and it was. As I stuck my head in the door, he said, "Oh, hi, I want to play my music for you." And he played a tape of incredibly heart-felt music. He said he was so weak at the time he recorded it, he had to be propped up with pillows to play the piano. It was very powerful music. Spiritual music really. And then he showed me a portfolio of his modeling pictures. He wanted his niece to be able to say, "This was my uncle." I was really amazed at the pictures. He was a very, very handsome young man. And it was hard to see this emaciated person with a purple lesion on the end of his nose in the beautiful body shown in the pictures.

Then we just kind of picked up the conversation at the point where we had ended the last talk. He talked more about his dying and had told the nurses that he wanted to be alone when he died. Maggie had explained to him that they would come in and give him Atropine, which would help his breathing, but that they would respect his wish to be alone. Shawn began to talk about his feeling that he didn't have much time left and that he was beginning to be afraid. He talked more about the dying, and all of a sudden he kind of looked out of the corner of his eye at me and said, "I wouldn't mind if you were there." It was his turn to take a risk.

"I'd be really honored to be there, Shawn." I told him that I already had put my name on his chart to be called if he went into the active dying phase. I had never done that before, because I didn't want to be called in the night, but I had done it because it seemed important to me to know when he was dying, even if he didn't want anyone there.

We began to talk about what he wanted and he said, "I just want to keep moving toward the light." And I told him I could keep talking him toward the light. "I want to be a part of loving energy when I die because I think what AIDS has taught me is how to give and receive love."

"I'm sure you will be. I have no doubt about it."

I told him that I would keep talking to him, and that even if he could not respond, he would be able to hear what was being said. I asked if he wanted his music playing and he said no because he felt that it would keep him too much on this planet and he wouldn't be able to let go, and that was why he was afraid to have his parents there. He began to talk about the energy it had been taking him to stay "OK" for his parents when they came every night.

"But if I ask them to be there when I die, I'll have to tell them that I'm afraid."

"Why wouldn't you be afraid?"

"Well, I guess I think I should be able to conquer it."

"What if someone told you tomorrow that you were going to have to get on a space ship all by yourself, and take off into space? How would you feel?"

"Scared."

"So what's the difference with dying? You're doing something you've not done, and you don't know where you're going. Why shouldn't you be scared?"

"Is everybody scared?"

"I think so."

"Maybe if you are able to tell your parents that you are afraid, they will be able to tell you that they are afraid too. And then maybe all of you won't have to put so much energy into pretending that you're not afraid."

I told Shawn that I did Therapeutic Touch, and explained that it was a healing technique that worked with the energy field of the body.

"It seems to help people relax and when I've done it with people who are actively dying, it does seem to help the fear and anxiety. There's no reason we couldn't even start to work with it now, and see if it helps."

"I think Rosie did that one day, but it didn't do much for the pain. But I'll try it. What do you think about Rosie being there too?"

"I think she's a good choice."

February 5

Last night Shawn told his parents that he was scared and he was also able to tell them that he wanted them there. Both his parents cried and he said it was the first time that he had seen his dad cry in his life. Apparently they had not all cried together about his AIDS and his death.

"Did you cry?"

"No, I wanted to, but it just wouldn't come out."

"Have you ever cried about AIDS?"

"When I used to drive the hour back and forth to work. I would cry then. It was the music that would get me and then I would cry."

Shawn said he had shared with his parents that I was going to do Therapeutic Touch with him and was really quite thrilled at their response.

"They didn't seem to think it was too weird. They were open to it. They didn't think it was 'too Shirley MacLaine.'"

"Do you have any images you want to work with?"

"I just want to make my mind like a beautiful clear lake."

"Imagine that you are walking through the woods, along a path, and come out to a very beautiful clearing. As you walk through the clearing, you see a deep, still clear lake. Go over and sit by that lake, feeling the sun in your face, hearing the birds, feeling the wind. When anything comes up to disturb that lake, any ripples, anything, just let it go. Imagine at the end of the lake there is a river that it feeds into, and any disturbance that comes up on the lake, you can just let go down the river. Keep that lake clear and calm and still. When any tension comes up in your mind, just let it go down that river. When fear comes, when anger, when pain, let them all go. See if you can just see them bubbling down the lake, out and down the river. And feel the peace of that lake throughout your whole body. Imagine that your mind is as clear and still as that lake. When thoughts arise that disturb your lake, let them go. Just breathe them out down your arms, feeling deeper and deeper the relaxation of that clear lake. Just be with the lake, be with its peace. Feel the warmth of the sun spreading throughout your entire body, and know that the light and warmth of the sun bring in healing energy. Your mind is calm and still like the lake. Breathe the fear out. Let it go. Imagine that your arms are the river that come out of the lake. Every ripple that comes up, every negative thought, just let them go, all the way down your arms. Feel the river rushing down your arms, cleaning, allowing you to let go. Breathing deeper and deeper. Feel the wholeness and completeness as you sit watching the lake, feeling the sun, smelling the woods and the water, filled with relaxation and peace."

"That was good. I feel incredibly relaxed. But I couldn't get it all the way down my arms. It got stuck at my wrists."

"We'll try again tomorrow. You can't expect to let it all go in one time."

February 9

Shawn is beginning to talk more about his sadness about dying. He has had several episodes of shortness of breath. We talked about feeling the sadness and sharing that with his family. He is really frustrated because he can't cry, and wants to be able to do that. He seemed to need reassurance that I really would be there be there when he dies, and I told him they could call me day or night and I would come in.

"I am so afraid of panicking and losing control and having other people see that. It makes me feel very vulnerable."

"It seems to me that the more you are able to process your fear now, the more control you will have of the dying."

"I don't want my body to be taken out of this room right after I die."

"How long do you want to be here?"

"Eight hours, I think."

"I'll write it in your chart."

"OK, I'm ready for Therapeutic Touch."

"What do you want to work on today?"

"How about the crying? I'd really like to cry."

I pulled a piece of rose quartz crystal out of my pocket and put it on his heart center for the session. I explained that it was a stone that seemed to help gently loosen the deep emotional wounds in the heart and that I had found it comforting as sadness came up for me.

I worked with moving the rose quartz energy down into his heart space and ended with a visualization to help him feel less vulnerable.

Shawn's experience of the rose quartz was that it felt like champagne with pink and little gold bubbles and that afterwards his entire chest felt very very open.

February 11

Shawn asked Rosie to be with him when he is dying. He began to talk about his memorial service because he feels like it is the last thing he intellectually has to hang on to. He said that the minister is working on it, but that he would feel better if he knew it was done. He has put incredible details into it and knows exactly what he wants: 27 white roses. He has written and recorded his own requiem.

He has begun to visualize the moment of death, and verbalized that he has a fear of choking to death. I told him that my experience was that usually the moment of death was a very gentle, peaceful moment, and that there may be periods where there is fear or anxiety, but that the actual moment is very gentle.

"I guess it's just that I am a real television kid. I've had 27 years of watching television, and watching violent death over and over. I can't let that idea of a gentle death in. I have to let go of a lot of conditioning there."

"Maybe we ought to try to work with an image of dying that might replace the violent images. What about seeing the moment of death as the moment when a butterfly leaves a cocoon?"

"I like that."

"What color butterfly?"

"'Yellow."

"Take a deep breath in, and on the exhale, let go with a sigh. Each time you breathe in, imagine peace and relaxation coming in to you, and each time you breathe out, release any holding and tension. Release down your arms, past your wrists and out.

"Now focus on the area in the center of your chest and begin to breathe into your heart, breathing in peace and a soft golden light. See that light at your heart center, shining deep inside you and now beginning to radiate further out. Picture threads coming from that center of light, and imagine that you are spinning a golden cocoon around your entire body with those threads, spinning out from your heart, slowly surrounding your whole body, keeping it safe and warm and protected. Breathe deeper, with each breath in allowing more light energy to radiate out from your heart, until the cocoon is filled with light and you feel relaxed and peaceful. Imagine that at the center of your heart there is a yellow butterfly, being held in that cocoon, growing until it is ready to fly. And now imagine that dying will be as if that butterfly will slowly and gently begin to work its way out of the cocoon, held in its light, safe and secure. See that butterfly moving from your heart up the cocoon until it can release itself through the top of your head. Breathe and let go of any fear or tension. See that butterfly fly free, being all that it is, moving toward the light. Feel its peace and joy in being free. See its beauty and grace. Now come back to focus on your heart area, and feel the light and warmth that is there. Know that you are safe. You are totally surrounded by light, held by light."

February 15

Shawn has more complaints of pain, and they keep increasing the morphine, so he's groggier. We continue to work on releasing and relaxing instead of tightening around the pain.

February 16

I had a very deep session with Shawn. More fears keep coming up. He was concerned that he might not have left his body when he was being cremated and it scared him. I reminded him that it was on his chart that his body would be left at hospice for eight hours and that once he was out of his body, he wouldn't be experiencing any physical pain.

"It sounds good, but it's hard for me to accept."

We talked about whether he wanted to lower the dose of morphine so that he would feel more because he was so concerned about his inability to cry. He decided that if it was going to come it would come, but that he didn't want to go down on the morphine.

February 17

Shawn wondered about where he would go after he died, and I told him about the experience with the hawk at my dad's burial.

"There was this hawk that slowly circled around as the burial was going on. I noticed it because it just stayed there, almost like it was watching. Then as we began to walk out of the cemetery, up the hill the hawk followed us and stayed with us until we reached the cars. Then it circled one move time and just flew away over the horizon. It sounds strange, but I really felt like somehow my dad had hitched a ride on that hawk."

"Wow."

"I think I'll go in the car with my parents. But I think at the memorial service, I'll be in the flowers."

He grabbed my hand and said, "You'll be there won't you to keep talking me toward the light."

"Yes."

"I hope they remember to call you."

I don't know how I am going to tell him that I'm going on vacation. I found out today that Rosie is going to be gone the same time I am. I really do believe that if he needs me to be there, I will be there.

February 18

Shawn was real restless and distracted. His body has so little flesh left on it. Sometimes he will put his hands up to the sides of his face and feel his cheekbones in disbelief and say, "I really am just wasting away. That's why they call it the wasting disease. There's nothing left."

Talked with Dr. Walker today, because the nurses were becoming concerned about continuing to increase the dose of morphine, which didn't seem to be touching Shawn's complaints of pain. He and I wondered whether they ought to look at giving Shawn a medication for anxiety, which seemed to me more the problem than the physical pain at this point.

February 19

Shawn was calmer today. He said that he had a really nice talk with his dad the night before and that he had been real open about his fears of a violent, out-of-control death.

"I think I just have to give up watching television. It is all violence."

I had brought in *Emanuel's Book* because of the imagery about death, which was light—things like, "death is like taking off a tight shoe." I read to him a bit: "If death could be seen as a beautiful clear lake, refreshing and bouyant, then when a consciousness moves towards its exit from a body, there would be that delightful plunge and it would simply swim away." But Shawn couldn't concentrate; he was agitated and fearful and restless.

Before I went back in the afternoon, I found the reason for his fear. The nurses were talking about putting him on a PCA pump so that he could administer his own doses of medication, giving him the control of the amount and the timing. The staff was frustrated that so much of their energy was focused on giving the morphine and incrementing it when there was breakthrough pain, and felt as if they were not able to give much attention to any of his other needs. And there was also the feeling of discomfort that Shawn was choosing to "numb out" his feelings with the morphine.

In the afternoon we talked about the pump, and Shawn was able to express his concern that the nurses wouldn't come in the room if they didn't have to give him the medication.

I have begun to take little steps in anticipating the loss his death will be for me. I asked to make a tape of his music, and asked if I could have the picture of him that is over his sink after he was gone. Every day when I wash my hands I look up at that picture.

"Why do you want that picture particularly?"

"I guess because I look at it everyday—plus it has your smile in it. And that smile always reminds me of the real spark of your spirit."

"Yeah, I see that. Would you move it over to the other side of the mirror so I can see it better? I'll tell my parents that you want it."

February 20

I know that I have to tell Shawn early next week about my vacation to give him some time to adjust and work through it. It's going to be hard to get the words out of my mouth.

He's still very concerned about the PCA pump. He has complained more of "hallucinations"/bad dreams. He generally has more fear—fear of being alone and fear of dying.

"TV keeps doing it to me. Last night I saw things about drugs and drunk driving and nuclear war. I worry about my family. I worry about my brother and sisters. You know, sometimes I really feel a little guilty that I'm going to get peace, and everyone here will be left to struggle with the worldly dilemmas. But at least I'll be able to be a guardian angel for my family."

We began Therapeutic Touch and I started with the clear lake imagery.

"Imagine walking through the woods until you can see your clear lake, peaceful and calm."

One eye opened. "I can't get the lake, Bobbie, it's too filled with litter!" We both laughed, and I decided to stay with his image.

"OK, Shawn, let's work with getting that litter out of the lake. Imagine that you have got a garbage bag and that you can walk into the lake and begin to pick up the pieces of litter and put them into the bag. Keep walking through the lake calmly and gently pick up all of the litter. When it's all in the bag, walk over to the river and watch all of the litter move away down the river, knowing that you don't need to hold on to it anymore."

February 22

Shawn is having his morphine held today because of the hallucinations. More and more, the frustration of not dying bothers him.

"I'm tired of the pain and I'm tired of the waiting. I wish there was just an easy way to get it over with."

February 23

I told Shawn today that I was going on vacation.

"This is a blow. You know that, don't you?"

We talked a lot about what he wanted to do as far as the Therapeutic Touch when I was gone.

"You can do Therapeutic Touch at a distance, Shawn. I don't have to be in the room with you, and I would be willing to sit down at 11:00, at our regular time, and send you the energy.

"That's too weird, Bobbie, too 'Shirley MacLaine!' I think I'd rather have a surrogate."

"How about Pat? I've talked with her and she's willing to learn, and we can work together this next week."

"It won't be the same but I guess I'll try it."

And we talked too about whether he would die when I'm gone.

"What's your feeling, Shawn? You know how much I want to be with you, but you also need to know, that if you decide the time has come and you need to go, I understand that."

"I don't think I'll die while you're gone."

February 24

I went in to see Shawn today and he was reaching out more than he ever has.

"I really need to talk with you. I had a horrible night last night. My dad was here and I just started to get real anxious. Finally I asked Pat to come in and she put on the Halpern tape and massaged my feet, and I started to do Therapeutic Touch on myself."

"Did it help?"

"A little. I almost had them call you. Would you have come in?"

"Of course, because I know you would never ask that unless you really needed it."

"My dad helped. He held my hand and told me he loved me."

February 25

Shawn has made the decision not to go on the PCA pump, and they have started a medication for anxiety. He seems calmer and continues to talk about wanting to get it over with. He is uncomfortable and bored; his color seems more grey and he is weaker. He is still smoking a good deal. He often falls asleep in midsentence, and then just wakes up and completes the sentence.

February 26

I have taught Pat the basics of Therapeutic Touch and feel that she will be good with Shawn because they already have a relationship. I plan to continue the 11:00 session with Shawn until I leave.

His spirits are better. He watches videos on TV, and has many people who come and smoke with him. I continue to struggle with mixed emotions about going on vacation because I know that it will be very hard if he does die when I'm gone.

"You know, it's harder for me than it was in the beginning to promise to talk you toward the light. I know I can still do it, but there's much more of a personal connection now, and the loss will be a personal one."

"You kind of like to hide back here, don't you?"

I laughed, "Yes, I really look forward to 11:00. It's the peaceful part of my day. I like it in here."

February 27

Shawn and I had a good session. He's more peaceful. I keep working with visualizations that will give him a sense of participation and control so that the sessions are really his.

February 29

Tomorrow is my last day before I go to Hawaii. It is going to be so difficult to say goodbye.

I met Shawn's minister today, the one who is going to do his memorial service. Shawn introduced her as his friend, Carol, and it took a while to put the pieces together. She's an unlikely looking minister, quite young. Shawn told her I was the one who was doing the Therapeutic Touch and she said, "Oh, I know about that. I took a class in seminary in Berkeley." And we all laughed, but it seemed to make Shawn feel good that she knew what it was. Carol and I walked out together and shared our mutual delight with Shawn and she gave a wonderful description of trying to write the memorial—Shawn smoking out in the garage at home, stocking cap pulled down over his head, wanting to hear each word she was going to say. She said she finally had to tell him that she couldn't write it completely until he dies, that it was a creative process for her, and he seemed to understand that, being as creative as he is. It made me happy that someone with as much life and spirit as she had would be shaping that service for Shawn.

It was as hard to have the last talk with Shawn as I thought it would be. He reached for my hand and held it tightly, which was unlike him, and said, "Don't worry about me."

"I won't worry about you, but I will miss you. Very much."

He said that he would miss me also, and a single tear rolled down his cheek. It was the first time I had seen him cry.

"Would it be all right with you if I just kind of mentally popped in once in a while to see how you're doing?"

"It's pretty 'Shirley MacLaine,' but its OK."

"Do you want me to bring you anything from Hawaii?"

"No. Just yourself."

As I looked back into the room on my way out the door, Shawn smiled his wry grin and I said, "Just don't forget the yellow butterfly," and he said, "I won't, but I'll be here." I ran into Maggie coming down the hall and she held me for a long time while I cried the tears of sadness that I might come back to an empty room and this might have been goodbye.

March 10

I went to hospice today. I hoped so much that Shawn would be there. The first person I saw was Ginny who said, "I'm so glad you're back. Shawn's been waiting for you. He almost died on Monday, but he came out of it." She said he was weaker and they had had to put him in respiratory isolation, so that he could no longer go outside his room in a wheelchair, and everyone going in had to wear a mask.

He was sleepy and pretty groggy from the medications, but finally woke up with his usual greeting, "Hi, how are you doing?"

"Good, how are you doing?"

"I almost died."

"I heard. I'm glad you waited."

"So am I."

I gave him the ceramic yellow butterfly I had found in Hawaii. I remember debating in the store about buying it, wondering whether he would like it. Shawn put it around his neck and kept patting it and saying, "It's so pretty. It makes me feel so good."

"It really does remind me of your essence—the part of you that won't die. That's why I bought it."

He talked about the week that Pat had worked with him and the sessions had been good and that Christ had come into his life.

"What does that mean to you, Shawn?"

"I guess that he will help me with this. And somehow I think that God cries with us. I never thought that before."

March 11

Shawn was much more alert than usual and expressing tremendous frustration and anger that he has not died yet. He could feel his own survival instinct pulling against the part of him that just wanted it all over.

"I'm still afraid that I can't let go. Can we work on that some more?"

As I did Therapeutic Touch, I had a very strong image of Christ, a real compassionate Christ figure, all dressed in white, coming in the room and picking Shawn up, kind of like a *Pieta* and carrying him out of the room.

I continued to work, and when the treatment was over we talked. I told him that as I was doing Therapeutic Touch I could see his body kind of held suspended over the earth by strings.

"You are the only one who knows what those strings are. But they seem to be what's keeping you from letting go."

And he suddenly began to talk in a way he had never been able to, spilling out the happenings inside his psyche and his heart since childhood, the pain and the suffering, the places where he had closed his heart to himself and to the world. I thought of an e.e. cummings quotation that had been important to me when I was Shawn's age:

> To be nobody-but-yourself in a world which is doing its
> best, night and day, to make you everybody else—
> means to fight the hardest battle which any human being can
> fight, and never stop fighting.

Those three hours, Shawn never stopped talking.

He smoked a cigarette, and concluded, "And so I guess I learned to hate myself and when I found out I had AIDS I figured I deserved to die." He said that, now, if he could live, he would be very different—that he does love himself more now but still not completely. Shawn said that he has forgiven all of the people who hurt him in his life, but that he can't forgive himself.

March 12

Shawn is much more at peace, even though lots was opened up yesterday.

"I feel better. Like a burden's off. And I found myself smiling last night."

"Smiling just for no reason."

"No, smiling—really smiling—at people when they came into the room. I just feel better about myself. I guess now I know I just have to forgive myself for not taking more responsibility for my own life along the way. I really want to work with forgiveness."

Shawn put his hands together to feel his own energy and shortly said, "I see a little golden boy standing by the lake looking at the debris washing down the river."

"Walk over to that little golden boy, Shawn, and hold him on your lap and tell him that you love him. Tell him that he is beautiful, and that he is OK just as he is. He doesn't need to be any different than he is. See if you can let that little golden boy cry, and hold him and tell him you love him."

Shawn liked the imagery but said, "I just can't quite love him. But I can kind of feel sorry for him."

March 14

Shawn and I had another really good session. When I came in, he told me to be sure to not let him sleep after Therapeutic Touch, because he wanted to call his mother to get the phone numbers of his friends.

"It's time I told them that I am dying and that I have AIDS. I have to tell them goodbye. I know that I have shut them out, and I don't want to do that anymore."

He also wanted to keep working with forgiveness and loving himself. We continued to work with him contacting the little golden boy. Shawn said he had visualized the two of them in the woods, and they had gotten lost.

"But the little golden boy took my hand, and I knew I could find our way out. And I did."

March 15

Today's was an emotional session but a good one. We were able to say goodbye to each other. He thanked me for my help and for accepting him so that he could accept himself. I thanked him for accepting me and what I had to give and for sharing so much of himself with me.

"It really is kind of a shame that I have to die. It seems like there really ought to be a miracle now and I could walk out of here. I'd be such a different person."

"How would you be different?"

"I'd be so much happier."

March 16

Shawn called two of his friends and told them he had AIDS, and told them to "stop by if they were in the neighborhood." He felt relieved and said that they had "done OK with it."

He wanted to talk to a priest—he wanted to say confession and have last rites.

"Do you remember the priest who came in here when I was first admitted?"

"I certainly do. It caused such an uproar at patient care conference, because for some reason he was given permission to visit you because 'Catholic' was listed on your chart. You quite politely kicked him out."

"Yeah. That's the one. I want to see him. I really want to celebrate Easter. Do you know that Christ was only 27 when he started his ministry?"

He continued to talk about the transformation of self-hatred into self-love and it seems as if he is really beginning to be able to feel it.

"I'm still worried about my body leaving hospice. Do you think it could be here for three days?"

"I don't think so, but we can leave it here the eight hours. If you want, I can come in before you leave and do Therapeutic Touch on your body and surround it with a cocoon of light. And that butterfly can go with you to protect you."

"Yeah, that'd be good," and then he thought about it for a minute, pulled it up and looked at it and said, "but I think I'd like you to take this butterfly. And the crystals."

And then he began to talk about how much he appreciated my involvement and Therapeutic Touch.

"Do you remember the first time we talked?"

"Sure."

"It was so easy to talk. It is kind of like it was meant to be, you know what I mean?"

"It seems that way to me too. It's one of those experiences that will probably change the course of my life and the way in which I work with people and view myself. You've been really important in that, and what I've learned from you I know will be important in working with other people, those with AIDS and those without.

"If that could happen, it would make my dying seem worthwhile. You know that you will really have an ally."

"Yes, I feel like I will. Thank you."

We talked some more about his memorial service, and he asked me if I would be there.

"Of course I'll be there. It will be hard, but I know that it will be your service, and it will be important to me to be there. I want to hear your requiem.

"1:30 the Saturday after I die. Don't forget, OK?"

March 17

Shawn talked a lot about his childhood friend Jeff, who died when he was 19. He had been decapitated in a car accident. I guess the priest is coming in today to give him last rites, and the priest's name is Jeff.

"That seems to be kind of important, that they are both named Jeff. It was real hard for me when Jeff died, but no one ever knew that. I never even cried. But it seemed like after that I didn't care very much any more. I got more into drugs and smoked more. It was the beginning."

There's more fluid in his lungs. It's a quite audible gurgle when he breathes, but he's not expressing discomfort. He talked to one more of his friends about AIDS and his dying and he said that his friends didn't know. He always kind of thought that they did know. His relief was visible that it seemed OK with them, that they still cared for him. Whether they will come and visit, or whether just telling them is enough for Shawn to finally let go is not clear. But it is clear that the sharing with them is a major breakthrough for him.

March 18

Shawn is sleeping more and more and he almost died last night. Apparently his color got real dusky, he had trouble breathing, and he couldn't cough up his sputum. They are working on getting him out of respiratory isolation. I can't stand the idea that he is going to die looking at those blue masks.

He talked about the priest coming and that was important. Yesterday I ran into Father Jeff at the nursing station and he wanted to know what had happened to Shawn—that he was like a totally different person. We wondered whether Shawn would live to celebrate Easter, and Father Jeff said, "I think he's had his Easter."

Shawn was more distant today. He finally said, "What do you want to work on?" and I said, "It's not up to me. What do you want to work on?"

"Nothing."

"You know, Shawn, maybe we're at the end of the emotional work. It's fine if there's nothing to work on. As long as you want to, we can just do Therapeutic Touch for relaxation, and you won't have to work so hard with it. I brought a song I wanted to play for you."

So I played Van Morrison's "Let Go Into the Mystery" because I loved the song and the words really seemed to speak to the transformation Shawn was undergoing. There were ocean sounds on the end of the tape, so I let it continue to play while I finished the Touch session. I saw the ocean and Shawn and his little golden boy there. The little boy was opening his arms to the sun. It was a nice image.

Shawn is real waxy looking; his color is funny. He is still talking about celebrating Easter Mass, so he may live until Easter, but I don't think so.

March 19

I had a good session with Shawn. He was real alert, and he has been asking the nurses to hold the morphine until after we work together, which is new.

"I'm tired of being a zombie during the time. This way, I'll be less groggy. I get so bored. It's like I just don't have anything more to talk about with people."

"You know, Shawn, there is a kind of withdrawal process that people go through as they enter the final stages of life. It's almost like a spiral that gets smaller and smaller. It has always seemed to me that it is part of what people need to do so that they can leave the people they love. Often it's a hard time for families because they see it as rejection. There might be a time that you need to withdraw from me too, and you might not want Therapeutic Touch anymore."

"I might not want Touch?"

"Maybe. I don't know. But if it happens, just tell me, it's OK."

"I just don't think there's anything big left holding me. I just want to die and get it over with. Sometimes I get these nightmare visions of dying. I'm just covered with KS lesions and I can't get up. I want to do something, and I can't move. That is the nightmare. It was scary, the other night, when I almost died. I was afraid I would lose control."

"It seems like you've always had to feel like you were in control of things in order to cope. Is that right?"

"Always. But now I know I just have to trust. I would like to work with that Christ image."

"What image do you see?"

"A long-haired man with tan skin, not like he went to get a tan, but like he's just tan. I can't see the bottom half, just the upper. I would like to see if we can get the little golden boy to float consciously on the lake, trusting."

"Would you like to have that Christ figure holding him up?"

"That's sounds good."

It was a powerful session. Every time now, Shawn has begun doing Touch on his own. Today he had his hands up around his face for a long time. He finally brought them over his heart, and I talked him through bringing healing energy into himself.

Shawn had very clear images of that golden-haired little boy. He said at the end, "I think I just have to let that little boy be carried away."

March 20

Shawn and I didn't talk much today. He always wants to know how I am, and asked me today if I wanted to do Touch.

"Sure, what's up for you?"

"I just want to make sure I love myself. I want to make sure that this big boy loves that little boy."

"Do you feel like it's coming more and more?"

"Definitely, but I just want to make sure."

"Are there any images you want to use?"

"Just the lake and the golden boy."

"Is there anything you want to tell that boy?"

"I want to tell him he's OK just the way he is."

After the session, Shawn thanked me a lot, and was excited.

"I could see that little boy with really beautiful eyes look into my own eyes. I could just notice the love the little boy had for me. It felt so peaceful."

March 21

Shawn was talking a lot today about feeling overwhelmed with too many visitors. The priest came to give him Communion again. He talked again about that withdrawal spiral.

"I feel like I've said goodbye to my family. I don't have anything more to tell them. You know, it's funny, but I've been thinking about how I almost wasn't born. My mother had trouble with the pregnancy and almost miscarried and had to go to bed the last two months.

"Do you wish you hadn't been born?" I wondered as I asked the question what I would say if I were him. I didn't know.

"No, not really." He smiled his wonderful smile, "There's a reason for all this."

As I began doing Therapeutic Touch, after both Shawn and I had centered ourselves, he opened his eyes and said, "You know, this might sound kind of weird, but I think there's a little girl inside of me too."

"It doesn't sound weird at all. We've all got both masculine and feminine in our psyche.

"I want to get in touch with that little girl."

"Is there anything you want to say to her?"

"No, just that I love her."

We worked with the image of the little boy and the little girl at the lake, and at the end of the session, when I was down at Shawn's feet, surrounding him with a cocoon of light, I had a beautiful vision of the three of them—Shawn and his little golden boy and little girl—walking away from the lake, hand in hand. Suddenly the children started to skip and a white horse with wings came out of the woods. They all got on the horse and he just took them away. They soared over the trees.

March 22

For the first time since we have begun to work together, Shawn didn't want Touch—he said things felt OK, and he was listening to a movie. It's funny, but it feels like that image yesterday of the winged horse and the children and Shawn was extremely whole. The horse seemed to symbolize Shawn's power—a power that he had lost but now had back, a power that could take him anywhere he wanted to go. So that really may be the end.

March 23

Shawn wanted to work today, and it was a very gentle, peaceful session. He feels very ready to die.

"I just want to work on keeping feeling good. That's all."

We talked a bit, and suddenly one of Michael's nephews ran by the door, crying.

"What's going on with Michael?"

"He called his family and told them to come in because he is dying. He wanted to tell them goodbye."

"You mean Michael gets to go?"

"I really don't think you have to wait that much longer, Shawn. I don't think you've got much time left. I've never felt that so clearly before."

"I hope not. I am really ready."

"I don't think you are going to have to struggle."

"I don't think so either."

That's good.

March 24

A couple of staff came and talked to me this morning about Shawn. He had kind of moaned all night long and slept really deeply. They had a hard time arousing him. His respirations are low, and they felt this might be it. They wanted me to go see him and help them decide whether to call his parents.

I took a deep breath as I went to open the door. Shawn was no longer just a patient—he hadn't been for a long time. I knew I would be losing a friend, and I kept trying to keep my own grief out of the way of my work with him. I expected to find a semi-comatose figure in the bed, but instead, there was Shawn, watching a movie and eating a donut. I would never understand the roller coaster that was AIDS.

"Hi, how are you doing?"

"Good, I hear you had a rough night."

"I just can't seem to feel very solid. It was really disorienting when they woke me up this morning. I don't really know where I am anymore."

I did Touch more gently than usual, being aware of that raw edge between life and death that Shawn was walking, trying to smooth it out. After the treatment, I sat on the window seat and meditated for awhile as I usually did while he slept. All of a sudden, he woke up and tried to sit up. He looked at me intently.

"Do you know how to get there?"

"Where are we going?"

"Somewhere in Jeff's neighborhood."

It smelled like death in the room today.

March 26

I really thought this was going to be the day that Shawn died. His respirations were way down with big periods of apnea and he could hardly cough he was so weak. I felt emotion with every cough. It was so hard for him to even do that anymore.

I kept telling him to let go and let himself be guided, that he would be safe. Every time I would go through that image, surrounding him in a cocoon of light and imaging the yellow butterfly at the core of his being and imagining the butterfly being released through the top of his head.

It really did seem like Jeff was in the room with us too.

After several hours, he just kind of came out of it, and said, "I think I'm actively dying. Wow. Can I have a cigarette?"

I agreed and then Rosie came into the room and asked Shawn what he was doing.

"I'm dying," he said with a big grin.

Rosie said, "And you've got your favorite people here."

He nodded and said, "It's great."

Then he started to smoke and we talked a bit about what had happened. He was weak and drowsy, but seemed to want to talk.

"It really felt like you were a test pilot, Shawn—like you were doing a trial run or something."

"There were a couple of times I know that I was very very close."

"I know that too. I was having a hard time and got pretty emotional."

"What did you go and do that for?"

"Because I'll miss you."

March 27

Shawn was a little bit withdrawn and very drowsy, kind of apologetically so. When I asked him if there was anything he wanted to work on, he said, "Just leaving. Just leaving and letting go."

March 28

Well, Shawn did it. He finally did it. I got a call at 3:00 this morning. "Bobbie, Shawn's changing very fast and he's calling for you."

I remember racing to hospice. Jan filled me in as we went down the hall. Apparently he had said goodbye to Shona, then Carol. The minister came, with a palm leaf from Palm Sunday. And that night, his two friends came. It made me so happy that they came, and I know that's what he's been waiting for, because an hour after they left, his parents were still there, and he began to get incoherent and kind of agitated. His mother said later that about three times he picked up the butterfly and kissed it.

"Shawn, it's me, Bobbie. I'm here."

And, to my surprise, he came out of the delerium.

"Oh, hi, how are you doing?" Just like he did every day, like it was just a regular day. But he couldn't stay any longer than that, and slipped back into that space between life and death. I began to do Touch, and he seemed to settle down.

Jan said, "Do you know anything about some children? He keeps talking about the children."

I told her yes, and began to talk to Shawn. "You've got them by the hand, Shawn. They are safe and you can help them find their way. Keep looking for the light. You've got them by the hand, the little golden boy and girl. You can take care of them and guide them home."

We decided to call Rosie and his parents, and let them know. His breath came in very deep moans.

He had very few lucid moments, but a couple of times he looked very worried and said, "Shadows. There's shadows."

"Look past the shadows, Shawn. Look for the light. It's there. Keep looking for the light. You're safe."

The moaning continued, but his breathing was stable. It was just Shawn and me for a long long while. I didn't ever sense he was in distress. I just stayed with him, breathing with his breathing and talking him through the releasing. He spoke what were to be his last words, "This is a sad day." And then the moaning stopped, about five minutes before his parents arrived. It was uncanny, but I knew that he had stopped consciously, because he knew they would be upset by the noise.

I looked over toward the door and wondered what it must have taken for them to walk through it. I leaned over close to Shawn's ear and told him, "We're all here now, Shawn—me and Rosie and your parents. Everyone who you wanted with you. It's all right to let go now. We all love you."

Instead, his respirations stabilized, and it really seemed as if he was just kind of curiously watching the interaction between these people he had brought together to be with him. Never in the entire process did I sense that Shawn was not in very conscious control, that his biggest fear had been overcome.

And so he watched while his mom and dad and Rosie and I began to know and trust each other. They were very quiet and hesitant at first. I told them that Shawn could hear them, even if he couldn't respond. His dad said that Shawn had asked them to be there but not to talk, to let Rosie and I talk, and then I remembered that he had been afraid he wouldn't be able to let go if they talked to him. And they honored his request.

I kept talking him toward the light as I told him I would, and used most of the imagery that we had worked with, the clear lake, and how peaceful it was, and the butterfly. We began to share stories of Shawn. His mother kept coming in and out of the room, obviously having a hard time, but I could sense his dad behind me, staying with Shawn.

His dad and I talked a little bit about the crystals, and that they coincidentally had read an article on crystals right before I had given the amethyst to him. He told me how Shawn would just hold on to it and wouldn't let it go, and how he always wanted to make sure the butterfly was straight. I played the Van Morrison song, talking the words to Shawn. It was so much his song—let go into the mystery, open up your arms to the sun, when you open up your heart you get everything you need.

It went on like that for a long time and then suddenly I knew that Shawn was leaving, really leaving this time. I just kept talking to him, having no sense of anything or anyone around me, nothing except for Shawn and his breath. I don't remember what I said exactly, just the letting go and the moving toward the light and the butterfly. But it was amazing because I knew he was right there. He heard what I was saying, and he was doing it, and when he died it was just like a butterfly flying away. You could almost see the little flutter, gentle and soft. It's really like he had been in that cocoon, working to get out, and then he got out. And there was not only peace in that room but it seemed the room became lighter, and I felt the most intense joy fill the room. A very very powerful love/joy/peace all mixed together.

I was so glad because Pat stopped his mother from leaving the room right before he died. She had almost left, but Pat was coming in with the cup of tea that I asked for. His mom said something about struggle and Pat just put her arm around her and said, "No, look at him, he's not struggling. He's so peaceful." And so she stayed.

And his dad for the first time talked to him directly. He said, "Son, you did such a wonderful job." And Rosie and I and his dad just stayed there around Shawn and held hands and cried. We put the passage quilt on him and the crystals and the butterfly. Jan brought a tiny vase of flowers, and candles appeared. And his face: Shawn was smiling, really smiling.

And people began to come in to say goodbye. Shawn's enormous creativity and talent were with him to the end. It was like he was able to take what he needed from each of the players he had cast in his drama during his last days at hospice. From each he got a piece of what he put together to become his unique theater, staged with beauty.

As his parents left, I took the crystals and gave them to his father. I was glad I did that. He grabbed onto them as tightly as Shawn had. And they told me that they wanted me to have the butterfly and offered to take it off. I knew it needed to stay with Shawn until he left hospice, but that offer touched me, because I could only imagine how hard it would have been for them to take that symbol off their son.

I came back to hospice to do Therapeutic Touch on Shawn's body, as I had promised him. As I sat and waited for the mortuary to come for his body I was filled with concern, having heard too many horror stories about attitudes of some mortuaries towards AIDS patients—refusals to handle them, attendants full glove/gown/mask paraphernalia, wrapping bodies in plastic. As I surrounded Shawn with a cocoon of light for the final time, I asked that he be protected and that his body be treated with the dignity it deserved.

The man entered the room, and his attitude immediately allayed my fears. He refused even the gloves that the nurse offered, went over to the bed, and with gentleness and deep compassion, lifted Shawn off the bed, held him in his arms, and carried him over to the gurney. Shawn looked like a crucified Christ. His emaciated body. The way his head hung. And the light that came from him. I thanked the man for his gentleness and respect. We covered Shawn's body with the passage quilt, leaving his head free, as I told him we would, and walked him to the door of hospice. As rain began to hit his face, the man gently asked if he could cover it with the quilt until he was in the car. My tears were tears of sadness to see Shawn leaving, mixed with tears of joy that he could leave with such respect and dignity, carried by a very special soul.

March 29

Shawn died yesterday, but it seems as if the story continues. I woke this morning with a sense of urgency to tell his parents about the man who picked up his body, as I knew it would be important to them, but had missed his dad at home when I called. I hoped I would be able to tell them.

At 11:00, I knew I had to be in my usual place in Shawn's room. As I sat on the window seat and began to meditate, the door opened and it was his father, obviously in a hurry, saying, "I knew you'd be here. I was in a traffic jam, but I kept telling Shawn that I'd get there on time."

We talked for hours. Talked all the way through the dying—the beauty of it—and talked about the changes in Shawn—that he had had to lose everything in order to find out who he really was.

I got a sense of how much he loved Shawn. A very gentle man. And that mixture of joy and sorrow, sorrow for the loss but joy that the softness that was at the heart of Shawn had shone through to so many at the end of his life. I shared the story of the man from the mortuary, and suddenly remembered the vision I had had during one of the later sessions with Shawn, of Christ coming in the room and carrying him out like a *Pieta*. The vision was identical to what the man had done.

He spoke of his determination to talk about AIDS, and to no longer hide. To help others. That who Shawn was needed to live on through us. And his wonder at the beauty of the spring day on which he died—how the sun that day matched Shawn's light and peace.

As he went to take some of Shawn's things to the car, I closed my eyes and could see Shawn's face smiling down. As I watched, I saw him begin to run through a wonderful huge field of yellow daffodils, really running free, hair kind of streaming back, the sun shining. And all of a sudden he had the little golden boy by the hands and began to swing him around. Then he just hugged him, and they were both laughing, still turning in a circle. I shared the image with his dad, and we both felt like Shawn was OK.

April 2

Today was a real celebration of Shawn. Butterflies were everywhere and his memorial was filled with who he was. His parents had put up a notice in the post office that Shawn had died of AIDS, with the time of the memorial, not really knowing what the response of the town would be. People filled the church to overflowing—the Methodist and the Lutheran church women joined together to make all the refreshments. There was sadness there, but you could see and feel the healing that was taking place. Months of silence and suffering could finally be shared.

His dad told Rosie and me of a yellow butterfly that had stopped in front of the lawnmower the day before. Stopped and just stayed there. He said he first wanted to pick it up, but knew that wasn't right. As it flew away, two little baby butterflies just seemed to appear out of nowhere. And his mother was so excited that she had found a present for Rosie and me. Shawn had wanted them to get us something, and she had found butterfly earrings for us.

Shawn was so present, in his music, in the words that Carol spoke, and, I have no doubt, in the flowers. As I looked at those 27 white roses, remembering him telling me that was where he'd be, I saw through them a stained-glass window, and really had trouble believing what I was seeing. There was a very compassionate Christ figure, with his hand on the head of a little blond boy. It was Shawn's little golden boy—the little golden boy who opened him to himself—and let the healing in.

April 3

I keep thinking back over the past months, remembering where I had started. At first, afraid of being around AIDS, not being sure I could do the work, and then being so impacted by its reality and the nature of the people who had it—reading everything I could find, madly searching for a why, or at least some meaning in what seemed senseless. It was as if AIDS challenged on a very deep level my entire spiritual structure, my entire belief system, because its outward manifestations caused such suffering for people. All I could see was the suffering. Shawn let me walk beside him and allowed me to see that amidst even that suffering and that sadness, there had been opportunity, as Shawn said, "to give and receive love."

April 4

Today was the first day that there was another patient in Shawn's room. It was very hard to not be able to go in there and sit at 11:00 and very hard to know that the room had someone other than Shawn in it. I finally went down and sat on the window seat outside of the room and sadness kept coming.

I picked up the blank book that sits there, open for anyone to write their thoughts, and turned to a beautiful letter to Shawn from his father, written the day of his funeral. In the poem that ended the letter I found the words I needed:

A butterfly lights beside us
    like a sunbeam.
And for a brief moment
    its glory and beauty
belong to our world.
But then it flies on again,
    and though we wish
it could have stayed,
    we feel so lucky
to have seen it.

Index